SELECTED LETTERS OF
WILLIAM ALLEN WHITE

SELECTED LETTERS OF

WILLIAM ALLEN WHITE

1899-1943

Edited with an introduction by

WALTER JOHNSON

NEW YORK: HENRY HOLT AND COMPANY

To

ABBY MAY ROLAND

in appreciation of her aid

PREFACE

"MAKE YOUR WORDS DANCE," William Allen White advised young writers. His own editorials, articles, and books sparkled with excellent prose. His letters, too, contain his singular knack of expressing himself in colorful and poignant language. One day I told Mr. White that his best writing was not in his published materials but in his letters. He looked surprised at first, but then a twinkle appeared in his merry blue eyes and he replied, "I think that you are right. The reason is that I write under no restraint in my letters." Furthermore, he went on to add, and his eyes twinkled even more from out of his cherubic, applelike face, "As you probably have decided after reading all of my letters, the angel Gabriel is going to have a hell of a time deciding my case."

This volume of letters contains the cream of the letters in the vast White collection. It was not a case of having too few letters but of having too many to work with. Actually many more volumes of well-written, fascinating White letters could be published. Mr. White retained carbon copies of all the letters that he wrote from 1899 to his death. These letters are a vast treasure house for anyone interested in the growth of American democracy over the past forty or more years. They are comments on the swiftly changing American scene from the pen of a man who became famous as the spokesman of small-town and rural America. I have tried to include letters that would throw light on White as a human being, as an editor, magazine writer, novelist, and biographer, as a prominent liberal Republican, and as a folksy, small-town, middle-class philosopher of democracy.

William Allen White was a careful stylist. He generally proofread his letters, and in purple ink corrected misspellings, slips in grammar, and confusing punctuation that had appeared in his secretary's copy. Many times, however, he did not bother to make the correction on the carbon copy. Since I have seen the Emporia editor take his large red fountain pen and correct letters, I have corrected the errors in grammar, spelling, and punctuation in those carbons where he failed

[vii]

to insert his changes. I, of course, did not alter any colloquial expressions. In some of the carbon copies of early letters, the ink has faded to such a degree that words are sometimes illegible. Whenever this occurs I have inserted the word "[illegible]" or I have reasoned out what the word probably is and added "[?]" after it. Whenever the address of the recipient of a letter adds anything to the meaning of a letter, the address is indicated. All of William Allen White's letters were written in Emporia unless it is otherwise indicated by the inclusion of an address after his name. Whenever any given letter required editorial comment, this is inserted just before the text of the letter. Many letters, however, were complete in themselves and thus required no comment.

Although Mr. White did not preserve carbon copies of the letters that he wrote prior to 1899, I have unearthed a number of the earlier ones. They are not included in this volume, however, since there are not enough of them to lend continuity to the manuscript. I have made valuable use of these early letters in my biography of William Allen White, which will be published by Henry Holt and Company in March, 1947.

I am grateful to Henry Holt and Company and to the Social Science Research Committee of the University of Chicago for financial aid in typing the letters from microfilm. I am greatly indebted to Paul Chandler, formerly of the Emporia *Gazette,* and to Mrs. Johnson for microfilming the White collection for me. Mrs. W. A. White and Mr. and Mrs. W. L. White have been most co-operative and helpful. Jacob Billikopf, Henry Haskell, and Lloyd Lewis were kind enough to read the introduction and offer helpful suggestions. Joseph A. Brandt, John Scoon, and Charlotte Yarborough, of Henry Holt and Company; William Sloane, Phyllis Crawford, and Helen Taylor, formerly of Henry Holt and Company; W. T. Couch, of University of Chicago Press; and Avery Craven, of the Department of History of the University of Chicago, have contributed greatly to this volume of letters.

I am grateful to the Theodore Roosevelt estate for permission to quote from Theodore Roosevelt's letters; to Angelo Scott for permitting me to quote a letter from his father; to Carl Sandburg, Harold Ickes, Ernest Gruening, and the late President Roosevelt for permission to quote from their letters. The Macmillan Company and Farrar & Rinehart were kind enough to allow me to reprint material from books published by them.

WALTER JOHNSON

SELECTED LETTERS OF

WILLIAM ALLEN WHITE

WILLIAM ALLEN WHITE: GRASS-ROOTS AMERICAN

WILLIAM ALLEN WHITE was an American—American in the best and strongest tradition of this country. Indeed, in the last thirty years of his life, he became the symbol of the greatness of small-town America. His editorials and speeches were widely reprinted as examples of the hopes and aspirations of midwestern rural America. Famous as a newspaperman who had refused to desert his small-town paper for large metropolitan dailies, White gained a widespread influence and prestige unlike that of any of his contemporaries in American journalism.

In the span of his life, from February 10, 1868, to January 29, 1944, White saw American life pass through many transitions. The letters in this volume, as well as his editorials, novels, magazine articles, and biographies, describe the swiftly changing American scene. They throw considerable light on the major problems that American democracy has faced since the Civil War. Written from a midwestern prairie town, they portray the struggle of small-town and rural America to adjust itself to the rise of an industrial, urban society and to the development of the United States as a great world power.

White grew to manhood in an era when frontier conditions in Kansas were being replaced by a settled farm society and when industrial capitalism was rising to supremacy in other sections of the nation. About the turn of the twentieth century, he saw this capitalism organize gigantic monopolies and threaten the existence of American democracy. From that time until his death, he worked with other progressively minded individuals, through the Republican party and the short-lived Bull Moose party, to make this capitalism aware of its responsibilities to society.

The Kansas that White grew up in left an indelible stamp on the prairie editor. According to him, Kansas was a state of mind revolving about the word "Puritanism." Kansans like White always believed,

[1]

in spite of historical evidence to the contrary, that their state was founded by Puritan New Englanders, or sons and daughters of Puritan New England, with the supreme desire of destroying injustice and creating a Puritan civilization based on reason and justice. As early as 1904, White was writing that "as a state, Kansas has inherited a Puritan conscience" and twelve years later he further observed that "the glory of Kansas is that she is as a state the sole legatee and custodian of the New England conscience."[1]

The belief of William Allen White's generation that its ancestors had founded Kansas to wipe out wrong had a profound effect on the life of the state. After the abolition of slavery, Kansas turned to the prohibition of liquor, then to political movements like Populism and Progressivism with the same burning ardor. Whenever a wrong was discovered, whether it was the common drinking cup or the wastes resulting from labor disputes, the Kansan launched a crusade to eradicate the evil. White summed up his view of the meaning of Kansas in an editorial in the *Gazette* on April 25, 1922:

> Kansas is a state of the Union, but it is also a state of mind, a neurotic condition, a psychological phase, a symptom, indeed, something undreamt of in your philosophy, an inferiority complex against the tricks and manners of plutocracy—social, political, and economic.
>
> Kansas is the Mother Shipton, the Madam Thebes, the Witch of Endor, and the low barometer of the nation. When anything is going to happen in this country, it happens first in Kansas. Abolition, Prohibition, Populism, the Bull Moose, the exit of the roller towel, the appearance of the bank guarantee, the blue sky law, the adjudication of industrial disputes as distinguished from the arbitration of industrial differences—these things came popping out of Kansas like bats out of hell. Sooner or later other states take up these things, and then Kansas goes on breeding other troubles. Why, no one seems to know.
>
> Kansas, fair, fat, and sixty-one last month, is the nation's tenth muse, the muse of prophecy. There is just one way to stop progress in America; and that is to hire some hungry earthquake to come along and gobble up Kansas. But say, Margot, listen!

[1] "Fifty Years of Kansas," *World's Work*, VIII (June, 1904), p. 4872; "The Glory of the States. Kansas," *American Magazine*, LXXXI (January, 1916), p. 41. Carl Becker, "Kansas," *Essays in American History Dedicated to Frederick Jackson Turner* (New York: Henry Holt and Co., 1910) present a provocative interpretation of the meaning of Kansas to the people of White's generation.

That earthquake would have an awful case of indigestion for two or three epochs afterward.[2]

William Allen White saw Kansas and his town of Emporia rise out of the open prairie, and a civilization take root and flourish. As a result of this experience, his belief in progress and idealism was firmly based on practice and not on theory. His idealism was so eminently practical that it always required some definite object on which to expend itself. With his feet firmly embedded in the reality of the trans-Missouri West, White never lapsed into a feeling of hopeless pessimism or idle contemplation of the unattainable. He was not, however, blind to the injustices and horrors perpetrated by a moneyed plutocracy. Like a real Puritan of old, even though he trusted in God and believed in a benevolent evolution, he kept his powder dry. He was always ready to assist God in marching toward the Holy Commonwealth by observing which way God was going, and, then, helping to remove obstacles from the road.

William Allen White inherited the western sense of being practical along with his reforming Puritan fervor, and the result was that he was willing to compromise and accept what he thought was a slow but steady onward progress to a better society. His intense realism allowed him to accept the achievements of scoundrels, while at the same time denouncing their methods. As he once observed:

> I firmly believe in a benevolent evolution, although I recognize that there are pauses and setbacks which are due to the dual personality in man. This conflict is necessary and wholesome, for it would be a hell of a land if all were angels. In the long run, mankind will slough off these badmen as a tree gradually chops off its rotten branches. Jay Gould was an old Bastard, but people like Theodore Dreiser forget that he left a good railroad system. Many old scoundrels do a good job, while many heroes do a bum job (although, I, of course, do not begrudge them their ideals). Having this belief I escaped the mechanistic pessimism which swept over Henry Adams and Theodore Dreiser. In the long run I can see progress.[3]

In his early days, White was an orthodox conservative. As the world changed he altered his thinking, and during the last forty years of his life he was a middle-class liberal. He was convinced in 1895,

[2] Margot Asquith had made a remark about Kansas and this editorial was White's reply.

[3] To the editor, interview, Sept. 19, 1939.

when he bought the Emporia *Gazette* on a borrowed three thousand dollars, that God had created a perfect society. When the Populist party and William Jennings Bryan preached the doctrine that the government should regulate industrial capitalism in the interest of the people, the young editor denounced such steps as "European, Socialistic, Latin." He felt that the Bryan Democrats and their Populist cohorts in their demands for government control of trusts and monopolies wanted to plant socialism in the nation. White's youthful opposition to the Populist demands was a product of a Republican upbringing by his mother and of conservative influences at the University of Kansas.

While a student at the university, in the class of 1890, he had been taught that the royal road to freedom was through no government regulation of business. Like most young Americans of the time, he had studied the classical economists and their American exponents like Francis Walker, who taught "that this was the best possible world; that the acquisitive faculty was the only talent in the busy world having survival value." Moreover, he absorbed the belief that "poverty was an evidence of sin, or worse, weakness; that those who championed the poor were even worse than the poor themselves, for they would pander to poverty to profit by it. ..."[4] At the university, however, he also studied under James H. Canfield, who did his best to puncture the high tariff arguments and conservatism of his Republican students. Furthermore, he read Edward Bellamy's utopian novel, *Looking Backward*, which attacked the economic structure and the resulting inequalities of American society. These liberalizing influences were quite latent, however, in the conservative editor of 1896.

White left the University of Kansas before graduation to become assistant editor of the El Dorado (Kansas) *Republican*. The editor, Bent Murdock, was a Republican state senator, and White had to run the paper and write the editorials while Murdock was at Topeka attending the legislature. The assistant editor's favorite editorial theme was attacking the Farmers' Alliance (the forerunner of the Populist party) and traveling over Butler County with Republican Charles Curtis fighting such Populist demands as a flexible currency, regulation of the railroads, and the direct primary. Occasionally young Will White wrote short stories for the paper, and one day

4 "What Is the Democratic Process," Commencement Address, Indiana State University, June 5, 1939, printed by the Emporia *Gazette; What It's All About; Being a Reporter's Story of the Early Campaign of 1936* (New York: The Macmillan Co., 1936), p. 4.

there appeared a special feature story entitled, "The Regeneration of Colonel Hucks."[5] This was the tale of a man who had deserted the "Grand Old Republican party" to become a Populist. Then came disillusionment and finally "regeneration" and return to the Republican party. The story was an invitation to all Populists to return to the Republican party and once more partake of the ecstasy of being among the "Chosen People." It glorified the Republican party and satirized the hopelessness and futility of the Populist party. United States Senator Preston B. Plumb had the Republican State Central Committee circulate reprints of the story all over Kansas, and it gave White the same type of recognition in that state that "What's The Matter With Kansas?" was to do in the nation. "The Regeneration of Colonel Hucks" brought the assistant editor of the El Dorado *Republican* offers from both the Kansas City *Star* and the Kansas City *Journal* to write editorials at a considerable advance in salary. He accepted the *Journal's* offer because this was a "respectable" Republican paper, while the *Star*, under William R. Nelson, was an independent Republican paper willing to support a Democrat rather than a Republican if the Democratic candidate was the better man.

While working on the *Journal*, White learned the meaning of a controlled press. The *Journal* was the organ of commerce and business and formulated its editorial policy in accordance with the welfare of "special interests." Its policy was restrained and timid, and finally White left to join the *Star*. From September, 1892, to June, 1895, he was an editorial writer, a short story writer, and a poet for Nelson's *Star*. These three years were decisive ones in White's development and future career. Nelson taught him the importance of devoting a newspaper to public service. The *Star's* continual campaign against special interests seeking monopolistic control of utilities, against loan sharks, shyster lawyers, and landlords who constructed poorly built tenement houses began to open young White's eyes to a more liberal point of view. The editorial page was devoted to advocating the cause of the people in these matters. Colonel Nelson always believed that a successful paper was one which kept close to its readers and made itself indispensable to the community in which it was published. Nelson, also, impressed upon his rotund editorial writer that a newspaperman should not run for political office. The newspaperman who did so would soon lose his influence with his

[5] This story was incorporated in William Allen White's *The Real Issue, A Book of Kansas Stories* (Chicago: Way and Williams, 1896).

[5]

community and, also, his freedom of thought and action. It was while working on the *Star* that White met and married a young schoolteacher, Sallie Lindsay, of Kansas City, Kansas. Mrs. White's insight and suggestions proved to be an active influence and constant guide in the later writings, actions, and decisions made by her husband.

It was in June, 1895, that William Allen White bought the Emporia *Gazette* to have a paper of his own where he could be a real influence in his community. Also, equally important, he wanted the freedom to make his own mistakes and claim his own success. He had for a long time desired fame, and remaining on the *Star* as an anonymous editorial writer was no way toward securing this recognition. The scathing editorial "What's The Matter With Kansas?" which he wrote during the 1896 campaign, lifted him into national prominence. From that time on, playing the role of a country editor, White's opinions were increasingly cited as examples of the common sense, honesty, and sagacity of small-town America. Many times White could have left Emporia for high-salaried positions on city papers, but he was aware that, by remaining as a small-town editor, he had a far better means of attracting attention and influencing his society than if he succumbed to the lure of the city.

"What's The Matter With Kansas?" ridiculed the Populists and Bryan in such bold and picturesque language that Mark Hanna, William McKinley's manager, circulated it as Republican campaign literature. National magazines like *McClure's, Scribner's, Saturday Evening Post,* and *Collier's* now called for short stories and articles. Late in 1896, Way and Williams of Chicago, capitalizing on his newly won fame, published his first volume of short stories, *The Real Issue.*

White retained for a time his views that God was on the side of laissez faire; that for the government to attempt to control the wiles of the rich and powerful corporations was un-American. Then, one day, White was informed that President McKinley was about to appoint him postmaster of Emporia. He hastened to Washington to persuade McKinley that he did not want this position. While in Washington, Charles Curtis introduced the Emporian to Theodore Roosevelt. This meeting with Theodore Roosevelt was a turning point in White's career. Roosevelt had been a subscriber to the *Gazette* ever since the Republican convention of 1896. The two men had exchanged books shortly after this convention and they grew to be friends through their writings and correspondence. Now, after this initial meeting with Roosevelt, White's conservative views began to be altered. In 1934, White described the influence of this meeting in the following manner:

> I had a better opinion of Mark Hanna than of McKinley. Young Roosevelt disillusioned me. He made me see that Hanna and his gay and amiable but ruthless kind were responsible for presidents like McKinley and his kind.
>
> It was a shock. I was a young arrogant protagonist of the divine rule of the plutocracy. I think I called it "brains"! He shattered the foundation of my political ideals. As they crumbled then and there, politically, I put his heel on my neck and I became his man. In the handclasp that followed and the gesture of good-bye he became my life-long liege and I a yeoman in his service.[6]

The editor of the *Gazette* now began to tell his subscribers, with all of his customary fervor, that Theodore Roosevelt would be president some day. The prairie editor had impressed Theodore Roosevelt, too. Roosevelt wrote to Charles G. Dawes, Comptroller of the Currency, on September 10, 1901, that White "is the salt of the earth; and whatever he says can be relied upon absolutely. He is one of the very few men whom I will absolutely guarantee."[7]

During the Roosevelt administration, White blossomed into a publicist for Roosevelt's policy of curbing the "malefactors of great wealth." As the Progressive movement gathered momentum, his editorials and letters reflected an increasing interest in the redistribution of wealth through the income tax, old-age pensions, and unemployment insurance. Now, even regulation of trusts received his active support. The fact that government ownership and regulation of business was on the increase no longer frightened him as being "un-American." The government extension of the police power to restrain cunning and shackle greed and to protect the weak against the strong was considered natural and logical. No longer did he believe the rich to be the chosen people of God. Many wealthy, he felt, had stolen their money. Particularly did wealthy men who exploited six days a week and taught Sunday school the seventh receive the cutting edge of his slashing editorial sword.

[6] Speech before the Roosevelt Memorial Association, Oct. 27, 1934. White Mss.

[7] Roosevelt to Dawes, Sept. 10, 1901. White Mss. That Mr. White had a correspondingly high opinion of Theodore Roosevelt is also true. He opened his speech before the Roosevelt Memorial Association, Oct. 27, 1934, by saying: "A tribute to Theodore Roosevelt from me tonight, would seem superfluous. I have tried to make my life a tribute to him."

[7]

By 1908, or 1909, his views on social and economic questions had changed decisively from the day when he had written "What's The Matter With Kansas?" That he was now advocating many of the Populist demands that he had once ridiculed did not disturb him. He rationalized that these demands were no longer being advocated by "wild-eyed reformers," for under Roosevelt and the Progressives, he declared that "Populism shaved its whiskers, washed its shirt, put on a derby and moved up into the middle of the class—the upper middle class. . . ."[8]

The impression gradually grew in his mind, after the turn of the century, that the benevolent feudalism of money was a myth. The plutocracy was seemingly more the child of Satan than of God. Thereupon, White decided to help God against the ever-present foe. Article after article, incorporating progressive beliefs, was written for nation-wide circulation in the *American Magazine, Collier's Weekly*, the *Saturday Evening Post*, and *McClure's Magazine*. Two novels, breathing the progressive spirit of justice to the common man, came from his pen—*A Certain Rich Man* (1909) and *In the Heart of a Fool* (1918). The former covered the lifetime of John Barclay, a poor boy who rose to be a millionaire, and in so doing lost his soul. Barclay cared little how he exploited the public through his railroads, grain elevators, or adulterated breakfast food. Then, the forces of righteousness led by the Progressives caught up with John Barclay, and he saw the error of his ways and got rid of every "dirty dollar" he had amassed. This novel presupposed the existence of a moral order in the universe, the transgression of which brought its own retribution to the individual or to the nation so transgressing. It was an indictment of malicious greed and revealed the methods of men who used the government and the people for their own selfish ends. This novel, his best-selling work, reached a sale of about 250,000 copies by 1941.

In the Heart of a Fool showed that Mr. White had more of an awareness of the social and economic background of poverty than he did in his first novel. The hero of the book was Grant Adams—a labor leader, who sacrificed himself so that the wages and conditions of laborers might be improved. This, to Adams, was a holy cause, and he spurned love and money to obtain it. During a great strike, a mob led by the employer-businessmen took Adams from a jail and lynched him. The thesis of the book was that Adams did not mind because his

[8] William Allen White, *Masks in a Pageant* (New York: The Macmillan Co., 1929), p. 230.

soul lived on and even the business leaders were moved by his altruism and brought around to a more reasonable point of view.

White's major interest in the Progressive movement from 1901 to 1917 was in the Progressive promise to right the balance between industry and agriculture and to save the farmer from further encroachments by capitalism. To White, the countryside—the great stronghold of the middle class—was the chief source of human virtue. Urban life and industrialism, he implied, killed the great human virtue of neighborly relationships. The Progressive revolt was at its basis, in his estimation, a protest of the small-town middle class against the excesses of a money mad plutocracy.

He always disliked the large industrial city controlled by political machines, which received money from the seekers of special privilege and kept the middle class in line by giving it just enough schools and parks and which fooled the proletariat with benevolences. Until the big cities broke up into small units, he believed that democracy would be a little lame and a little blind. He liked Middletown. There, he believed, existed the Puritan virtues of thrift, reasonable honesty, diligence, and as much tolerance as the times would permit.

This belief in the small town is quite understandable when one remembers that White spent most of his life in small towns. He was born in Emporia (1868) and was raised through his childhood in an even smaller town, El Dorado, Kansas. His father, Dr. Allen White, had the spirit of the true pioneer. His ancestry went back to an old Massachusetts family that had lived around Taunton and Raynham since the 1630's. Then members of the family moved westward to New York, then to Ohio, and finally Dr. Allen White completed the western pilgrimage of this family by settling down in Kansas. When the pioneer town of Emporia began to grow and become too sophisticated, Dr. Allen White, his wife, and their year-old baby, Will, picked up and moved westward to El Dorado, which was a tough town in that early day. With the brief exception of the four years he spent in Kansas City, White lived in towns numbering only a few thousand souls. Although he admitted that large cities had more to offer from the standpoint of music, drama, and art, the small town, he argued, offered contacts with one's neighbors; one's affairs became common; joys were mutual; and even sorrows were shared.

Although White was looked upon as the defender of small-town ways against the inroads of a city society, he actually was more than a simple, provincial, country editor. He was at home, too, in sophisticated city circles. He was widely traveled, and, after the turn of the twentieth century, he and Mrs. White spent long periods of time away from Emporia. Nevertheless, White never forgot that his editorship of the *Gazette* was his by-line to the nation. As editor of this paper, which had a circulation of seven thousand in the last years of his life, he tried to explain Main Street to the rest of America.

William Allen White not only served as a spokesman of the middle class, but he had an active political career both in Kansas and in the nation. Politics, to White, meant support of the Republican party. In his mind, the Republican party represented most adequately the traits of industry, thrift, and honesty—the fundamental traits of his middle class. The Democratic party, he rationalized, was not a constructive party, and it was composed of too many "easygoing" citizens. Furthermore, if you wanted power in Kansas, it was not practical to be a Democrat. Kansas was a Republican state, and White desired to be a political force. From 1901 to 1912, White worked to make the Republican party in Kansas and in the nation follow progressive principles. When Taft was renominated by the Republicans in 1912, White resigned his national committeeman's post and helped organize the Bull Moose party. In 1916, when the Bull Moose party collapsed, the Kansas editor supported Charles Evans Hughes, the Republican nominee.

Now that White was back in the fold of the Republican party, he was to remain there the rest of his life except for his independent campaign for governor in 1924. He felt that his bolt had taught him that he could have more influence by staying in the regular party and working to check reaction from within rather than from the outside. But, although he became a Republican again in 1916, that did not mean he relinquished the right to criticize Republicans and praise deserving Democrats. For instance, his praise of Woodrow Wilson so infuriated Theodore Roosevelt that Roosevelt wrote to White and accused him of having "bats in the belfry" for praising the President, for he considered President Wilson a danger "to the moral fibre of the American people."[9] In 1919, the editor of the *Gazette* assailed the Republicans for obstructing the League of Nations. The Republican party was becoming the "national calamity howler." He warned the leaders that "the constructive minds of

[9] Roosevelt to White, Jan. 1, 1917. White Mss. The last page of this letter has hand-drawn pictures of three bats and one belfry with these words: "unsuccessful effort to draw bats from the belfry of W. A. White."

America, little and big, who heretofore have found in the Republican party the only party which offers a forward-moving program, want progress more than they want a party home. And some party will come along offering men and women of this temperament a place to vote and they will go there."[10]

White started a pre-Republican convention boom for Herbert Hoover in September, 1919. He vigorously opposed another pre-convention move toward Warren Harding, characterizing Harding as a man who had not had an idea in thirty years, and as a man who would out-Taft Taft in reaction. At the convention White voted for Hoover, even on the last ballot that nominated Harding, because he could not "stomach" Harding. Yet a few days after the nomination, he concluded that Harding "will conform to Republican opinion when elected. And every man or woman who calls himself a Republican should vote for Harding. He will be supported by the Emporia Gazette this fall, along with the rest of the Republican ticket. Harding and Coolidge look good to me. . . ."[11]

By September, he felt that there should be no bolt from the Republican ticket. It was not an issue of men, but one of parties. According to White, the Democratic party was the party of the solid South and the venal bosses of the northern cities. Only the leadership of Wilson had kept the party liberal, but Cox was not Wilson and the party under him would slip back into "crass conservatism." Admitting that the Republican party had its failings, he concluded, however, that it was the only party amenable to public sentiment, and he observed somewhat naïvely that "if the Harding administration begins to grow reactionary, or if it is stupid or blind, an enlightened public sentiment can scare it into its senses."[12] Immediately after the election, he tried to bring sentiment to scare Harding into being progressive. He lashed out at Harding's cabinet appointments; he advocated that the President do more to regulate business; and he declared that the government in Washington was not an edifying spectacle made up as it was of ward heelers and state machine bosses. The responsibility for the Teapot Dome scandal he placed squarely on both Harding and Coolidge, stating that only a progressive administration would rid the country of such chicanery.

[10] Emporia *Gazette*, Sept. 13, 1919.
[11] *Ibid.*, June 14, 1920.
[12] *Ibid.*, Sept. 3, 1920. White explained to the writer that he supported Harding in order to hold the party together in Kansas so that he could have influence in the state legislature. Interview, Feb. 12, 1940.

The campaign of 1924 found the Emporia editor running for governor on an independent ticket. Neither of the candidates of the two major parties would come out against the Ku-Klux Klan. White decided to run for governor on a platform calling for the annihilation of the Klan. He had long opposed the Klan or any other similar movement to destroy freedom of speech. He had vigorously denounced the bigotry and reaction of "super patriots" like the Klansmen, and now he decided to launch a drive against the movement in Kansas. He was not elected governor and had not wanted to be. But he did achieve his purpose of exposing the ridiculousness of the Klan.

There was not much time to write editorials in support of Calvin Coolidge, while he was campaigning all over Kansas, but White did urge people to vote for Coolidge. Throughout the decade he supported the Republican party at election time and, then, generally disagreed with most of the laws that Republican administrations passed. During the years of Harding and Coolidge, he deplored the collapse of idealism, and objected to the reactionary forces that had secured control of the Republican party. He devoted a large amount of his time, during the last years of his life, trying to win control of the Republican party away from these reactionary elements. He wanted the party to be essentially a middle-class, sound, and popular party rather than the organ of greed and corporate wealth. One of the tragedies of his life was that he not only failed in this task, but that those forces which he objected to were able to use his support of the straight ticket as a liberal cloak to disguise their own reactionary designs and policies.

When the New Deal came to power in 1933, White felt that Franklin D. Roosevelt was wearing the old mantle of liberalism once worn by Theodore Roosevelt and Woodrow Wilson. In 1934, he felt that all Americans, regardless of party affiliations, should stand by the President. He told a University of Kansas audience: "On the whole and by and large, I am for the New Deal. It is neither Communist nor Fascist. Much of it is necessary. All of it is human. And most of it is long past due."[13] His support of much of the New Deal legislation in this first year was gratefully received by the President.[14]

[13] William Allen White, "Fifty Years Before and After," Commencement Address, June 11, 1934, printed by the University of Kansas, p. 9.

[14] "It gives me a great deal of pleasure to know that you are with us in these strenuous times. . . ." Franklin D. Roosevelt to William Allen White, Jan. 22, 1934. White Mss.

[12]

White was in the Far East in 1935 when the boom for Governor Landon of Kansas was started by the Kansas City *Star* in co-operation with several Kansas editors. When he returned, he aided Landon to the extent of writing a biographical sketch for the *Saturday Evening Post* and the New York *Times Magazine*. In September of 1936, he incorporated them into a campaign book entitled, *What It's All About*. The book was decidedly not partisan. It was remarkably restrained and gave one the impression that White would have felt better if Landon had not been his personal friend. Nowhere in the book did he say, "Vote for Landon." In his editorials, he asked that only Kansans vote for Landon as a gesture to a native son. During the campaign, he did not go to Landon's headquarters at Topeka nor ride on Landon's train. As early as October, he warned Landon that he would not carry even Kansas. On the whole, he felt that the campaign "was a nightmare. It had neither logical sequence in its conception and execution nor any touch of reality."[15]

During the next four years of the New Deal, the relationship between the President and White was friendly and close. White opposed the Supreme Court Bill but supported the administration in general.[16] When there was a vacancy on the Supreme Court in the latter part of 1938, White strongly advocated the appointment of his old friend, Felix Frankfurter. On January 5, 1939, he received a telegram from the President saying, "I have done it." When White had been recuperating from sickness at the Mayo clinic, a year before, Roosevelt wrote that he hoped White got back to writing as soon as he could, "for we all need to jog people into speeding up their 'evolutionary processes of thinking.' "[17] Frequently, the editorials in the *Gazette* especially delighted the President. He wrote to White after one exceptionally good one and asked, "Can't you bribe the New York Times and Herald Tribune to run them occasionally?"[18]

President Roosevelt summed up the relations between White and himself when his special train stopped at Emporia during the 1936 campaign. He told the Emporians that "Bill White is with me three

15 White to T. J. Norton, Feb. 19, 1940. White Mss.

16 When Mr. White wrote to Jim Farley for two tickets to the 1940 Democratic convention, Mr. Farley replied that he would see that the tickets were saved because he (Farley) was glad to be of service "to a deserving democrat." Farley to White, July 9, 1940. White Mss.

17 Roosevelt to White, Jan. 17, 1938. White Mss.

18 *Ibid.*, June 14, 1938.

and a half years out of every four."[19] No statement could have been more appropriate. For three and one half out of every four years, the Emporia editor saw America with amazing clarity. But in the spring of the presidential year, a curious form of amnesia crept over him.[20] Then he ran back to the Republican party and supported it. This was true, however, only six months out of every four years. In the three and one half year periods, he freely criticized his party and·he was always endeavoring to see that the progressive wing had an ascendancy over the conservative members of the party. An endeavor in which he had little success.

In order to understand this paradox one must recall his Kansas heritage. The Republican party had always been associated in the Kansas mind with the party of progress, prohibition, and middle-class virtues. As to the Democratic party, White and many other middle-class Kansans always have felt that along with the sensible Kansas Democrat were "the others, the psychopathic cases, the great unterrified, unregenerate and moronic section of the Democratic party."[21] His father had been an old-line Democrat, but he died while White was a boy. His mother, on the other hand, was a "Black" Republican, a loyal follower of Lincoln ever since the time she had heard him debate with Douglas. Probably more important than these reasons for White's Republicanism was the fact that, he believed, it was not practical to support a ticket without "going down the line." In order to have influence in a state where the Republican party dominated, except when a split occurred between the stand-patters and the progressives, one had to be a Republican. One sacrificed too much power as a local leader by bolting too often. White was practical, and he felt that in the workaday world he could best mold public opinion to work toward what he considered his ideal and purpose in life through the Grand Old Party. He never considered himself to be a scout like Robert M. LaFollette or Eugene V. Debs, away ahead of middle-class opinion. He felt that he was ahead of his neighbors and most politicians, but not way out in front, because this would have cost him his influence.[22]

[19] Hanging on the wall of Mr. White's study is an autographed picture of Franklin Roosevelt in a seersucker suit. It is inscribed: "To William Allen White —from his old friend who is *for* him all 48 months." The letter appended to the picture reads in part, "Dear Bill:—Here is the seersucker picture, duly inscribed by the sucker to the seer!" March 4, 1938.

[20] See Elmer Davis, "Bill White's Emporium," *Saturday Review of Literature,* May 8, 1937.

[21] Emporia *Gazette*, Feb., 23, 1940. [22] To the editor, interview, Feb. 12, 1940.

Throughout White's mature years, American life and politics were closely interwoven with world affairs. He became a national figure in the 1890's, the same decade in which the United States emerged as a great world power. Almost overnight the nation rose from a rural and isolated society into a commanding position in world affairs. The American people, however, were slow to realize America's changed position in world politics. In the last years of his life, as chairman of the Committee to Defend America by Aiding the Allies, White worked to arouse a lethargic America to an awareness of its world position. Actually ever since 1915, he had realized that the United States had to participate in world decisions and be willing to co-operate with other nations to achieve world peace.

When World War I broke out, White was at his cabin in Moraine Park, Colorado, escaping from the heat of a Kansas summer. His reaction to the German invasion of Belgium reflected his abhorrence of war. "War," wrote White, "brings men down to beasts quicker than whiskey, surer than women, and deadlier than the love of money."[23] At first, the editor tried to ignore the war and devote his editorials to progressivism and internal affairs. The sinking of the *Lusitania*, however, aroused him, and he classed Germany as an unrighteous nation, but he felt the sinking was no excuse for the United States "running amuck." To him, the world was mad, and the United States should shut its doors to the contagion. "Americans —South Americans and North Americans—" he editorialized, "hold the ark of the covenant of civilization. In a world war mad, we have the peace that passeth understanding. By God's grace we should keep it."[24] Gradually, his editorials reflected a firmer stand toward Germany and a realization that isolation was impossible. Coming to the conclusion that isolation was no sure road to future world peace, he became a vice-president of the League to Enforce Peace, an organization founded after the outbreak of the war in Europe with the purpose of providing some machinery to replace slaughter as a means of settling future international disputes.

In 1917, although he was too old for military service, he went to Europe as an officer of the Red Cross, in company with Henry J. Allen, his Kansas Bull Moose friend. They were sent by the Red Cross to inspect hospitals and first-aid stations at the front in order to be able to publicize the work of the Red Cross on their return.

[23] Emporia *Gazette*, Aug. 29, 1914.
[24] *Ibid.*, May 10, 1915.

The Martial Adventures of Henry and Me, which he wrote upon his return to the United States, was a humorous book devoted to the task of describing the war to Americans. There were descriptions of the morale of the French and English, and statements that the common people of these countries were earnestly seeking a lasting peace. He felt that out of this war were to come profound social and economic changes with the common man taking away the privileges of the aristocracy. The hope of the Allied peoples, he wrote, was that the war would bring better things for the common man.

With the Armistice, he hoped for a new world but warned that men could only be as free as their hearts were kind. "And unless the great war," he wrote, "has made us all feel the pull of brotherhood in our hearts . . . unless we are willing to submit to some injustices for the larger justice to our neighbors, then we shall soon have the same old world."[25] In December, 1918, he and his son, William L. White, sailed for Europe to report the Peace Conference for a syndicate of American newspapers. From Paris, he soon wrote: "The Americans over here are very radical—all for the President's program, but they feel it is almost hopeless, the way things are lining up. The conservatives of Europe are in the saddle, and they are all Tafts, who know nothing and learn nothing."[26] At the conference, he was on intimate terms with Ray Stannard Baker, who was in charge of publicity for the American Peace Commission, and with Colonel Edward M. House, confidential adviser to the President. After watching the Peace Conference he came to the conclusion that the difference between Kansas politics and world politics was not very great. "You simply play," he wrote, "the same game on the same board with large checkers."[27] He reported that England and France had a low opinion of the League of Nations and the Fourteen Points. Wilson's peace program did not seem to have much of a chance. But he demonstrated his hope in the League of Nations by writing:

> The League of Nations properly policed but representing all the nations in civilization, somewhat in proportion to their degree of civilization and their economic strength, could work out the necessary changes in the map of the world and in the governments of the world to get things going. After that it would have to be a continuous congress . . . the continuous con-

25 Emporia *Gazette*, Nov. 28, 1918.
26 White to Sallie Lindsay White, Jan. 2, 1919. White Mss.
27 *Ibid.*, Jan. 11, 1919.

gress would have much to do to adjust the rights of crowded peoples in an expanding civilization. All cannot be settled, indeed comparatively little may be settled by this peace congress if it holds a year; but if the will to unite in a league based upon mutual help, is manifest genuinely, its political expression does not matter much. Time will work that out.[28]

When the Peace Conference moved to clamp down a rigid censorship on news stories, White was a leading spirit with the other American newspapermen in protesting this action and preventing a complete gag of secrecy.[29] While at the conference, President Wilson asked White to head an Allied delegation to confer with the Soviet Republic at Prinkipo in an attempt to solve outstanding difficulties between the Allies and Russia. He agreed to undertake the task provided full publicity was permitted for the proceedings. The conference, however, never materialized because of French objections. The French felt that their military safety depended on a strong centralized government in Russia which would assume the czarist debt largely held by them.[30]

While White denounced, in his news dispatches, the machinations of the French, Italians, and English in fighting Wilson's desire for a just peace, he, nevertheless, felt that the League of Nations was a possible way of ameliorating the worst features of the treaty. To his American audience, he reiterated that the United States was "part of the world family of nations, and must take her part." She must join the League. The United States could not be isolated. "For to begin with," he wrote, "we are the world's creditor. We have the closest possible relations to the world—we are the world's banker and the world's grocer—and we must hold these jobs for a decade; possibly for a generation. . . . Those are delicate jobs for a nation to hold. They are war breeding jobs. We can have peace with our neighbors only by the establishment of laws—new laws under a League of Nations. . . ."[31]

Before returning to the United States, White spent some time in England visiting friends such as Norman Angell, John Buchan, H. G. Wells, and Frederick Whyte. He also took a trip to Ireland to investigate conditions there, and on his return to London wrote an

[28] Weekly Emporia *Gazette*, Feb. 13, 1919.
[29] White to Sallie Lindsay White, Jan. 18, 1918. White Mss.
[30] *Ibid.*, Feb. 9, 1919; White, "What Happened to Prinkipo," *Metropolitan Magazine*, Dec., 1919.   [31] Weekly Emporia *Gazette*, April 10, 24, 1919.

article for the *New Europe*. He told the English that the French had not been interested in peace; that Germany "smarting under the shame of defeat, must be nursed along into habits of peace, and international tact will be severely strained to keep her out of war; that Japan's aspirations could be more easily realized by war than by peace." The hope for peace in the world depended on co-operation among the English-speaking peoples.

He pointed out to the English that the great obstacle to this co-operation was Ireland. The Republicans in the United States were organizing the Irish vote to defeat Wilson. Their game was to defeat the League by proving to the American people that the League was a British device to rule the world. To prove this, they must show that England was a "grasping oppressor of unwilling captive peoples," and the Irish situation was the example needed. And, he warned England that

> the Americans, thus aroused against England and persuaded that England is backing the League of Nations for British Imperial aims, may lose their heads and permit partisan malice and jealousy to defeat the ratification of the League in the American Senate. If that is done, Wilson and his party are discredited for the 1920 elections, the Republicans will whoop it up against England to justify the slaughter of the League and incidentally to bag the Irish vote and the pro-German vote; and, while the demagogues triumph, humanity will suffer. For, with the League of Nations abandoned, English-speaking peoples will have to spend their energies in wars and preparations for wars. The whole fabric of the plan to check the progress of humanity is based upon the fiction of England as the Cruel Stepmother. Destroy that fiction, prove that England is not oppressing Ireland [by granting her dominion status], and America will ratify the League. . . .[32]

On his return to the United States he gave vigorous support to the League of Nations. He was merciless in his assault on Republicans like Senator Henry Cabot Lodge, who were "jeopardizing the peace of the world." He admitted that it was not a perfect League, but it was "the best of its kind possible, and if it is a shadow of a league it is the shadow of a rising sun." Warning the nation that we must join

[32] William Allen White, "Through American Eyes," in the *New Europe*, XI (June 19, 1919), p. 225; the London *Times*, June 23, 1919, carried excerpts from this article and called it "a striking article."

the League to keep peace in a troubled Europe, he called for the removal of the League question from politics and called for its immediate ratification.[33]

White served on the subcommittee which drew up the Republican platform for 1920. For three days and two nights, this committee wrangled over a declaration on foreign policy. The plank that was finally adopted on the League was a straddle because of the work of Senator Lodge and his friends. The Republicans called for "an international association" and promised to bring about "such agreement with the other nations of the world as shall meet fully the duty of America to civilization and humanity in accordance with American ideals." During the campaign, White stated that a vote for Harding was a vote for the League. The editor of the *Gazette* stood with other leading Republicans like Herbert Hoover, William Howard Taft, Charles Evans Hughes, Elihu Root, and A. Lawrence Lowell, who told the nation that Harding was for the League.

The decade of the 1920's was a nightmare to White. He felt that the people of the world had lost faith in themselves and in their fellow men. "The terror of a vast unbelief is gripping mankind in some sort of spiritual glacial epoch, which threatens chaos," he warned in *Collier's* in 1921.[34] In spite of the smug, complacent attitude that Americans were adopting toward the rest of the world, he warned that the outbreak of war in Europe would inevitably involve the United States. ". . . We cannot keep out of wars if we remain a part of civilization," he declared. "By doing our duty as a neighbor among the nations of the earth we may prevent war."[35]

In August, 1928, White was in Paris at the signing of the Kellogg-Briand Pact to outlaw war. He felt that this was only a gesture, but that it did register the common man's desire for peace. During the 1920's, he advocated the recognition of Russia, although he did not agree with Soviet philosophy. He, also, demanded respect for the rights of Latin America, and served on President Hoover's commission to investigate the American occupation of Haiti. When Presi-

[33] Emporia *Gazette*, Sept. 13, 1919. Eighteen years later, White commented on this editorial in the following manner: "Well, it did not happen that way. But I have a persistent feeling that maybe our entrance into the League with obvious reservations would have made a different world. But also only maybe! History is written in the indicative mood—never in the subjunctive!" Russell H. Fitzgibbon, ed., *Forty Years on Main Street* (New York: Farrar & Rhinehart, Inc., 1937), pp. 179 ff.

[34] "Will They Fool Us Twice?" LXVIII (Oct. 15, 1921), p. 5.

[35] Emporia *Gazette*, May 24, 1921.

dent Franklin D. Roosevelt brought about the recognition of Russia and launched the Good Neighbor policy, White was enthusiastic in his praise of these steps. He, also, hailed Franklin D. Roosevelt's efforts to carry out the Wilsonian ideal of collective security and of the United States assuming its duty in the world.

Japan's aggression in China in 1931 and Italy's march into Ethiopia four years later made White feel that a world conflict might soon develop. If such a conflict came, he was sure that the United States could not stay out of it. We could not keep out of world affairs because, as he wrote, when "even one man's liberty is imperiled, all men's liberties are in danger."[36] White's mind was greatly troubled over the foreign situation in those years. He was torn between two poles—the desire for peace for the United States and the realization that internationalism was necessary for a real peace, although this internationalism meant the danger of a war because of the strife in Europe and Asia. For a time, his desire for peace led his editorials to reflect the isolationist feeling that was sweeping the United States in the middle thirties. He supported the Neutrality legislation (1935–1937), which applied an embargo on the shipment of war goods to belligerents whenever a state of war existed. Although he supported these steps designed to keep America out of war, he was aware that the fascism that was sweeping through Europe would some day threaten democracy in the United States. "During the next decade," he editorialized, "America must face the fascists," and Father Coughlin was the "perfect example of the American fascist."[37]

White's pacifism led him to support the Neutrality Law, but he was clear-sighted enough to realize that this alone would not insure peace for the United States. When the Nazis seized Austria in March, 1938, he feared that England and France might give in to some kind of fascist rule and leave the United States a lone democracy. The United States was threatened with being completely isolated, and he declared:

> We cannot forever be turning the other cheek. It will get bashed in the end and our head will be broken. . . .
> If this country has one supreme duty, it is to call the democracies of the world together and with their power before they crumble, to assemble a world peace conference. There demands of the underprivileged nations may be heard and considered. These underprivileged nations—Germany, Japan, Italy—are nat-

[36] Emporia *Gazette*, Feb. 15, July 20, 1935.
[37] Emporia *Gazette*, Oct. 10, Nov. 9, 1936.

urally motivating their hunger with a lust for war. America must either satisfy them in conference or on the battlefield. The supreme test of the doctrine of Jesus faces the Western world. Are men really Christian sufficiently in their heart of hearts to bring justice to those who are underprivileged? . . .[38]

When war broke out in September, 1939, White became the chairman of the Non-Partisan Committee for Peace through the Revision of the Neutrality Law. The Neutrality Law's embargo on the shipment of arms to belligerents handicapped the democracies in their war against fascism. This committee aided in securing a Congressional revision of the law which permitted the belligerents to buy arms and munitions with cash as long as they transported them in their own ships. In May, 1940, when Hitler smashed through the Low Countries and was threatening the destruction of France, White launched the Committee to Defend America by Aiding the Allies. His committee advocated all legal and possible aid to the Allies. White never denied that such aid might lead to war, but his feeling was that the alternative, isolation, would more surely lead to war because it would mean that England would go down, and then the United States would be left without allies in a hostile world of dictators.

The significant work that the White Committee did in rallying America to an awareness of the menace of an Axis victory was a tremendous contribution to American security.[39] The White Committee helped to show America the need of arming other nations to fight the Axis, while America launched its own defense program. As a result, when war did come, the United States, although by no means completely ready, was better prepared than in 1939, and had allies to assist in the inevitable war against the Axis.

After White resigned as chairman of the Committee to Defend America by Aiding the Allies in January, 1941, he devoted the remaining three years of his life to writing his autobiography, editing the *Gazette*, and mixing in Kansas and Republican party politics. With his passing, on January 29, 1944, America lost a colorful folk hero. "He lived out his span," observed Henry Seidel Canby in the *Saturday Review of Literature*, "and there has been no better and no more rewarding life for friends and country than the career of this editor and man-of-letters and public voice of democracy, who has been for a generation the symbol of the great Middle West."

[38] *Ibid.*, March 3, 1938.
[39] The full story of White's activity in this field is told in the editor's book *The Battle Against Isolation* (University of Chicago Press, 1944).

[21]

White's own struggles to achieve a fuller democratic America are well revealed in the letters in this book. When democracy was endangered from events within or without the borders of the United States, he reached the height of his writing genius. When, for instance, his close friend Henry J. Allen, Governor of Kansas, tried to suppress any expression of sympathy for labor during the railroad strike of 1922, White wrote a Pulitzer prize-winning editorial, entitled, "To an Anxious Friend." It clearly contained his lifelong belief that only under democracy could a better world be achieved:

You tell me that law is above freedom of utterance. And I reply that you can have no wise laws nor free enforcement of wise laws unless there is free expression of the wisdom of the people—and, alas, their folly with it. But if there is freedom, folly will die of its own poison, and the wisdom will survive. That is the history of the race. It is the proof of Man's kinship with God. You say that freedom of utterance is not for time of stress, and I reply with the sad truth that only in time of stress is freedom of utterance in danger. No one questions it in calm days, because it is not needed. And the reverse is true also; only when free utterance is suppressed is it needed and when it is needed, it is most vital to justice. Peace is good. But if you are interested in peace through force and without discussion, that is to say, free utterance decently and in order—your interest in justice is slight. And peace without justice is tyranny, no matter how you may sugar coat it with expediency. This state today is in more danger from suppression than from violence, because, in the end, suppression leads to violence. Violence, indeed, is the child of suppression. Whoever pleads for justice helps to keep the peace; and whoever tramples upon the plea for justice, temperately made in the name of peace, only outrages peace and kills something fine in the heart of man which God put there when we got our manhood. When that is killed, brute meets brute on each side of the line.

So, dear friend, put fear out of your heart. This nation will survive, this state will prosper, the orderly business of life will go forward if only men can speak in whatever way given them to utter what their hearts hold—by voice, by posted card, by letter or by press. Reason never has failed men. Only force and repression have made the wrecks in the world.[40]

[40] Emporia *Gazette*, July 27, 1922.

THE EMPORIA GAZETTE
DAILY AND WEEKLY
W. A. WHITE, EDITOR AND OWNER
W. E. HUGHES, MANAGER
EMPORIA KANSAS

June 8, 1917.

My dear Paine:

I am enclosing herewith the Mark Twain letter
which you desire.

Some place in the biography, I have been told
there is a reference to me. I have never seen the biography, but I know it is a great work-- one of the
greatest biographies any American has ever written if
not the very greatest and I am certainly proud to know
its author.

Truly and sincerely yours,

W A White

Mr. Albert Bigelow Paine,
Bronxville, N. Y.

WAW:FH.

Enclosure.

*Kansas was the first state in the
union to fill her "naval enlistment
quota. Was it the prairie
boys dream of the sea" that
drew him to the navy?*

will

When the following letter was written William Allen White had been editor of the Emporia Gazette *for four years. Now 31 years of age, he was a nationally recognized feature writer for leading magazines, author of* The Real Issue *(1896),* The Court of Boyville *(1899), and a leading figure in the Kansas Republican party. White's promotion of a successful street fair in September, 1899, was an excellent example of the vigor of the young editor. When he bought the* Gazette *in 1895, the Emporia* Republican *was the dominant paper. The* Republican *derided the street fair and ever since White's advent in the town had assailed the new editor. Yet, a year or so after the fair, the* Republican *failed, and White never again was to have really serious competition.*

To JOHN S. PHILLIPS, *McClure's Magazine,* July 3, 1899

MY DEAR JOHN:

I am promoting a street fair and fall carnival for Emporia to occur in September, and I want to get an Automobile to head the flower parade during the carnival. I noticed in the last number of *McClure's* (which by the way was a daisy) your story about the Automobile. What I wish is this: That you would give me an address of some manufacturing company that has a Chicago branch, then I think I can interest him, particularly, if someone around your shop who knows these Automobile people will say a kind word for me, when I address my man. Our flower parade will attract ten thousand people from rich and prosperous sections of Kansas, where they spend thousands of dollars every year on fancy traps, dogcarts and all sorts of red-wheeled rigs. The country hereabouts is perfectly flat and the roads are naturally very good, and I really believe if I could get this Automobile man to send a trap or a dogcart for exhibition here, it would bring him trade. I will arrange for the freight myself, and will pay the traveling expenses and hotel expenses of a man to operate the machine. We will advertise it far and wide, and will run special trains from towns within 100 miles to see the marvel. Somebody around your shop who knows these people can help me. Can you put me onto some man and give me the address of a concern that has a Chicago or St. Louis branch, so that the freight won't cost me so everlasting much?

[23]

The street fair was a great success. People attended it from a radius of a hundred miles around Emporia. White in the Gazette, *October 2, 1899, observed that the fair was an open demonstration that Emporia had changed from a country village to an enterprising town. The following letter to Cyrus Leland, a powerful figure in the Republican party in Kansas, seeking his help in securing Indians, is an excellent demonstration of the hard work and skillful planning that made the street fair a success.*

To Cyrus Leland, Topeka, Kan., August 1, 1899

My Dear Mr. Leland:

. . . Now, I want you to help me. I am promoting a street fair here in Emporia. It is my scheme. I have raised the money by subscription. . . . The man who has charge of the Indians is Tom Ryan. When Tom Ryan was a prospective candidate for his job I roasted the eternal stuffin' out of him. I would not have the slightest weight with him, but I want those Indians, and I want you to get them for me. The date of our fair is September 27th, 28th and 29th. I want them here for one or three days, whichever we can get. I would like to have the Indians from the Potawatomie, but I am not particular where they come from just so they are Indians and can do a "corn dance." I do not know how to go at it; I am as helpless as a child, and I want your help in the matter. . . . It is my particular ambition to have a fine fair here, and beat out Topeka which is going to have some sort of a Soldiers' reunion the same time. We are going to have a Soldiers' reunion ourselves, and I am on the lookout for some good speaker of national reputation. Incidentally, if you can help us there it will be a good thing. . . . We will call that day G.A.R. day and I will undertake to get special trains running into Emporia on the "Katy" and the Sante Fe as far west as Newton. It will be a fine time, and would get the old soldiers in line. . . . So now you know what I want. A lot of Indians to draw the crowd and a big national speaker to interest the soldiers and line them for 1900.

One more thing. *Kill your stenographer:* The next time I get a letter addressed "Hon. Will A. White" I am not going to open it. Address is Hon. Bill White; or Bill White, or W. A. White, or William A. White, or anything in God's beautiful, green world except Will A. White. When a man passes twenty-five and clings to the

[24]

name of "Will" on his correspondence the people get an idea that he is made of mush. I do not want that idea to prevail.

In 1896, the Chicago firm of Way and Williams published White's first book, The Real Issue, *a collection of realistic short stories treating many phases of life in Kansas. Three years later Doubleday & McClure purchased the book from Way and Williams and reissued it with White's new book* The Court of Boyville. *"What's The Matter With Kansas?" written during the 1896 campaign, was to be associated with White's name in the public's mind to the day of his death.*

To DOUBLEDAY & McCLURE, New York City, September 22, 1899

GENTLEMEN:

I have yours of September 18th before me, asking for data and information concerning my dear dead past. Herewith I enclose some such information. Trusting that nothing in the future will come to light that is objectionable, I remain—

P.S. I am very much annoyed to see that in your announcement of the "Real Issue" you have said that the article "What's The Matter With Kansas" would be included in that book. Nothing could displease me more than this announcement, unless it could be possible that you could put in "What's The Matter With Kansas." If I have any rights, title, interest or alimony in that book, allow me once now, for all and forever, to undo any hint or suggestion of using "What's the Matter With Kansas" in it, or even in advertising it. For Heaven's sake let the dead past bury its dead. . . .

The Milwaukee Journal sent a subscription to Editor White for the Gazette. In these early years the editorial page, as the following letter indicates, was not always an important feature of the paper. Whenever the young editor lacked space or had no desire to write an editorial on a given day, the editorial page carried local news. The weekly issue of the Gazette, in this day prior to automobile delivery service and rural free delivery, was designed for the farmers in the surrounding countryside.

To W. R. ANDERSON, Milwaukee *Journal*, October 13, 1899

DEAR SIR:

I fear that you have overestimated the Emporia Gazette. It is simply a little country daily and weekly, devoted entirely to chronicling the important fact that Bill Jones brought in a load of hay today. And Thomas Hughes is recovering from a sprained hip, and that John Smith is putting a new porch on his property on Sylvan Street.

Sometimes I write a little editorial, and sometimes I do not; but when I do I hang it on the hook, and if the local news crowds it out it simply has to go over until the local news gets scarce. Day after day the Gazette appears without a line of editorial in it, and if the local department in chronicling the return of the 20th Kansas crowds out the editorial comment on it, there will not be a line of editorial comment on it, and I do not feel right in taking your subscription. I write enough editorial during the week to fill the first page of the Weekly, and when that is done I quit editorial, and if I do it the first day I do not have any editorial for six days. This may sound a queer program to people used to a metropolitan paper; but it makes money for the Gazette, and that is one of the things the Gazette is running for.

General Funston [General Fred Funston had been a classmate of White's at the University of Kansas and gained fame as a soldier particularly in the occupation of the Philippine Islands during and after the Spanish-American War] is my friend and I shall probably be in Topeka during his reception, and will not have a line of editorial, nine chances to ten, about it. People do not want editorial, they simply want the news.

"What's The Matter With Kansas" was written because I was mad, and I could not do it again, or anything like it.

[26]

I am very grateful for your kind letter, and only wish I was running a paper that I would be glad to send out; but I am not.

White gained national prominence during the 1896 campaign. From that time on leading magazines clamored for his articles. With unusual modesty for a person who enjoyed the national stage, White refused in this letter to write editorials for the Saturday Evening Post. *Shortly after the letter, however, he began writing feature articles for the magazine.*

To The Editor Of The *Saturday Evening Post,* November 11, 1899

Sir:

I have before me your kind letter of November 8th, asking me to write for the editorial page of the *Saturday Evening Post.* I am afraid you have overestimated my ability. I used to be an editorial writer on the Kansas City Star when I was twenty-five years old and full of ideas and ginger and that sort of thing, and could do two men's work; but now I have kind of gotten into a rut here in Emporia running a country daily by day, and writing short stories by night, so that I do not believe that I can think of anything interesting to the readers of the *Post.* However, if I should you may be sure that I shall get it off and send it to you.

I thank you very much for your high estimate of my ability as indicated by your invitation to write for the *Post.*

Doubleday & McClure dissolved shortly after publishing White's short stories, The Court of Boyville. *This friendship with S. S. McClure and the article he wrote for* McClure's Magazine *had been instrumental in his going to Doubleday & McClure as his publisher.*

To F. N. DOUBLEDAY, December 22, 1899

MY DEAR MR. DOUBLEDAY:

I guess I am a champion hoodoo. As soon as the little "Real Issue" got on the way to glory, and I got used to the ways and habits of young Williams [Chauncey L. Williams, White's first publisher and close friend], he went and "busted," and I landed at Doubleday & McClure's because I thought they were young and we could grow old together. Also, because I had a feeling of gratitude for what Mr. McClure had done for me in the Magazine, by printing a couple of stories from the "Real Issue" when the book was unknown, and its author unheard of. And now Doubleday & McClure dissolve partnership. I have just begun to think that I know about all the fellows around the office there, from the printer's devil up to the boss, and could write to the Magazine and to the publishing house in one letter, and cuddle down for the rest of my life and have a good time. Then your letter comes and is the "blow that almost kills father." "I never loved a fair Gazelle to glad me with its dark brown eye"—You know the rest, too sickening to repeat. But I suppose we will have to make the best of it. Of course you have done well with the Boyville book, and I appreciate very sincerely your kindness and shall at the proper time try to put my appreciation in substantial form; but nevertheless, it is an old-fashioned fellow who hates to be yanked up, when he has once got rooted. And one other thing. For Heaven's sake, do not address me at Topeka any more. Both your letters were forwarded from there. The next time I get a letter forwarded from there in your handwriting I am going to wire you "collect" that my address is Emporia.

To F. N. DOUBLEDAY, January 8, 1900

MY DEAR MR. DOUBLEDAY:

Why in the world did you think, because you talked without restraint as a free born American citizen, that you had prejudiced me in any way about anything? Of course your idea along that line is the hallucination of an enfeebled brain. My wife said the day after you left, "Well, I feel a lot more like giving him your books than I did before he came." To which I responded, "Very naturally, that is what he came for." And she said, "Well, I don't care, that is how the matter stands." So you may go ahead and order the paper for the next book I suppose as there is no appeal from the decision of the court.

But seriously, your visit was one of the most pleasant episodes of our four years' stay in Emporia. We only wish that you might come here again and stay longer when the hired girl would be back and we would all have more time to visit. I wish to heaven that I could do something to make Mrs. Doubleday as happy as you made my wife.

Incidentally, the next time that you are sitting at your desk and have nothing to do, go over to the desk of Mr. Thompson and catch his pretty pink ears between your thumb and forefinger and breathe in them the fact that he promised me an autograph copy of the work of Edward Markham, six long weary months ago, and I have not seen the autograph copy of Edward Markham's "Man With the Hoe" since. I would not rub it into Thompson by letter and I desire you to take a currycomb and go over his naked, quivering hide for me along this line.

I hope you met young Williams of Chicago and found him as manly and delightful as I knew him to be.

If you should sell two thousand copies of the Boyville book between now and July I will eat my hat. If you sell a thousand I will be very happy; but I do not think you will sell five hundred, because I think the book is a dead one.

The following incident, wherein White printed an error that appeared in another Kansas paper, is typical of the good-natured ribbing that one country editor gave another over a mistake in that editor's paper. This error gained nation-wide publicity, however, because the Gazette was now widely read by editors outside of Kansas, and they attributed the error to White.

My Dear Mr. Heermans:

I have your favor of January 20th in which you refer to the unfortunate circumstance of the Kipling-David Harum matter. I realize very keenly your situation, and no one deprecates more than I do the publicity that this stupid affair has found. At no time did the Gazette ever say or intimate that Kipling was the author of David Harum. On the editorial page about two or three months ago this item appeared:

> The Gazette is glad to note that culture is pushing westward. The Smith Center Library announced among its new books, "David Harum" by R. Kipling.

I noticed the funny little blunder in the list of the books in the Smith Center Library, as published in the Smith Center paper, and as Kansas towns like to "jolly" each other, I printed the item, supposing, of course, that everybody would know that it was merely a printer's error. Then the item was not printed in small type in an inconspicuous place in the paper, but was printed on the editorial page in the regular editorial type, and I thought no more about it. The Smith Center paper copied it and came back at Emporia with some blunder that we had made as is the manner and custom of Kansas towns made and provided by tradition from time immemorial. But some way or other, the little editorial paragraph got east and people began to write to me calling my attention to the fact that I was wrong in saying that Kipling had written David Harum and telling me positively that it was Mr. Westcott. One man, a librarian in Chicago who seemed to be unusually intelligent, I answered, and wrote a burlesque letter which was so plainly burlesque that I do not see how in the name of heavens he could have mistaken it, and told him he was mistaken, that Kipling did write David Harum, but as far as I was concerned preferred Mr. Kipling's "Fourteen Weeks in Physics" or his "Elementary Trigonometry." The whole letter was equally grotesque, and I supposed of course a man who had sense enough to take care of a library would know that Kipling did not write a "Fourteen Weeks in Physics" or an "Elementary Trigonometry." But the librarian took the letter to the Chicago Post and there it started, with embellishments by Rose Field, a brother to the late Eugene Field, and by the editor of the Post and by anyone else who thought he could have a good time with Mr. Daggett, the librarian.

Telegrams and letters began coming to me, and I have very promptly answered all of them as seriously as I could. About a week ago I ran the enclosed clipping in the Gazette, which I think will thoroughly satisfy the members of the Westcott family, whom I am very sorry to have given the pain which must have come to them with the publicity of this stupid joke. But as you will see, I am not wholly or very largely to blame for the publicity, and I trust that you will correct any impression to the contrary that the Westcotts may hold.

This clipping which I enclose has been given the widest publicity and the one that I send you I clipped from the New York Evening Post. It has appeared in a number of New York evening papers and has been widely circulated, almost as widely I think as the other was.

I trust that this will be satisfactory, and that you will convey to Mr. Westcott's friends and relatives my sincere and heart-felt sympathy in this stupid reopening of old wounds.

Three years after this letter, President Theodore Roosevelt was to gain fame as a trust buster. The concentration of economic power in the hands of a few monopolists had by 1900 become a serious problem for American democracy. H. D. Lloyd in Wealth Against Commonwealth *(1894) first attacked the evil of monopoly and John Moody,* The Truth About the Trusts *(1904), popularized the issue with the public. Governor Roosevelt's message, which prompted the following letter, urged publicity for corporation earnings.*

To Governor Theodore Roosevelt, Albany, N. Y., February 1, 1900

My Dear Governor:

I received and read your message clear through long as it was. I suppose there was a good deal of what Star writers call "local color" in it, but it was all written in good United States English, and you could hear a bell ring on every page, so I enjoyed it. I think you have offered the first sane solution of the trust business. . . .

[31]

I have just completed an office building for the Gazette, and in my own room I want your picture. I have at my house the photograph of Miss Ben Yousef, but I would like a pretty good-sized picture of you taken in your Rough Rider rig, autographed and inscribed across the front to frame and put in my office above my desk, and then when I feel inclined to weaken and say something that I do not think, I will look at my "Joss" and take courage. Can you send me such a picture, autographed across the front, so that I can frame it?

On March 14, 1900, White wrote to S. S. McClure suggesting that McClure syndicate newspaper articles by White on the Democratic National Convention. As the following letter reveals, White would not write for Pulitzer's World *or Hearst's* Journal. *Throughout his lifetime he refused to permit his articles to be syndicated to the Hearst press. Sensational journalism and scare headlines, in White's mind, were destructive of the true ends of newspaper work.*

To JOHN S. PHILLIPS, *McClure's Magazine*, April 9, 1900

MY DEAR JOHN:

You are a good boy, and I like you very, very much but I guess we will have to pass up the convention scheme because I would rather starve to death than to write for the New York World or the New York Journal. Heaven knows I want the money bad enough, but I do not need it that bad. I thought that $10.00 per column could be secured for five or six letters to six or seven newspapers during that week, and that would make the $500.00 that I require. I wanted of course the New York Herald, then I thought a Boston paper, a Chicago paper, a San Francisco paper, and the Kansas City Star or Journal, and a southern paper at Atlanta or at New Orleans, and a Portland Oregon paper, could use the stuff at about $10.00 per column. There will be at least six columns, and the matter could be limited to each paper at $50.00. I could attend to making the copies very easily myself, every night when I filed the stuff by wire. I dislike to offer this stuff to these papers myself, and thought that by getting seven or eight papers at $50.00 McClure's syndicate could carry on the correspondence and make enough to pay them a commission on the business, but I will not write for the World or the Journal. The Herald, or Times, or Sun, or any other morning paper but the World and the Journal in New York would be all right, and if you have gotten so far with the negotiations on the World that you cannot open it up with any other paper, we will just pass the whole scheme up.

I am very grateful to you for the interest you have taken in this matter, and I assure you that I appreciate it, and will show my appreciation in substantial form some time if I ever can. If you still desire to carry the matter on, wire me and I will send the outline that you wanted.

The Bryan article referred to appeared in McClure's Magazine, *July, 1900. White wrote a series of articles on leading political figures during the next year for this magazine. Later some of these appeared in* Masks in a Pageant. *White, along with writers like Lincoln Steffens, Ray Stannard Baker, and Ida M. Tarbell, made* McClure's Magazine *an influential and significant magazine.*

To JOHN S. PHILLIPS, *McClure's Magazine*, May 10, 1900

MY DEAR JOHN:
I suppose you have got the Bryan article by now and have read it over. It has occurred to me that perhaps a series of articles like the Bryan article, including the more interesting figures of public life— Croker, Platt, McKinley, Lodge, Hanna and Roosevelt—written with the absolute candor that I have tried to use in the Bryan business, telling the truth as I see it might be interesting run during the next eighteen months in the Magazine. I wish you would think over the matter, and tell me whether or not you can use it. If you cannot, the Saturday Evening Post of Philadelphia has been after me for some time to think up something I could give them, and I will give them this series if they want it. I could make them shorter than I did the Bryan article, which it seems to me is a trifle long—covering the

[33]

others in three thousand words. Let me know what you think about it.

I am going to have a note due at the bank the 19th of May. If you can persuade the Treasurer to dig up a little in advance of publication it will give me much pleasure and considerable standing with the gentleman who holds my note. As Jacc [August F. Jaccacci, art editor of *McClure's Magazine*] will tell you, I am in a new office building, and just finishing paying for it, and there are lots of little odds and ends that put me rather close to the grindstone. Do the best you can for the poor and the oppressed and the downtrodden and the weak, and believe me, ever—

Just before this letter was written Theodore Roosevelt was nominated for the vice-presidency. On May 9, 1900, White had written Roosevelt that he hoped he would not be nominated for fear that it would end his political career. Son Bill, William L. White, was born on June 18, 1900. Since Mrs. White helped her husband get out the paper, their baby son spent much of his infancy lying in a wastebasket in the Gazette *office. White canceled the proposed European trip mentioned in this letter because of the illness of Mrs. White.*

To THEODORE ROOSEVELT, Oyster Bay, N. Y., June 23, 1900

MY DEAR GOVERNOR ROOSEVELT:

Providence probably knows more than I do about things, and probably Providence has a bigger work for you than I can imagine, and so with an implicit faith in Providence, and a firm belief in Republican victory, I desire to congratulate you upon your place upon the Republican ticket, though I was hoping against hope day after day that you would be permitted to go on with your good work as Governor of New York.

I am going to Europe July 10th, and shall probably leave Emporia July 1st. If I am in the state I want to ride with you from Kansas City to Emporia. We will give you a big "blowout" here. I have arranged for that. I have so many things that I would like to talk to you about that it seems that I would almost forgo my European trip to be with you.

A little son came to our house this week, and that is why I was not at Philadelphia. He is our first born that has lived, and he is a strong little ten-pounder. His name is Bill and anyone who calls him Willie or Will is going to be put out on the first ballot. I guess my duty to little Bill was greater than it was to the Republican party so I did not go to the National Convention. I am going to Europe on business, not on pleasure, or I certainly should stop until you passed through Kansas.

May God bless you, and strengthen and keep you for the great work which I believe He has somehow, somewhere, laid out for you.

The nation as a whole was quite prosperous after the Spanish-American War. White poured his earnings from outside writings into building up the Gazette. The novel mentioned in this letter was not published until 1909. The political story book, Stratagems and Spoils, *was published by Charles Scribner's Sons, 1901, and some of the stories appeared first in* Scribner's Magazine. *The Whites secured the loan from Phillips, bought the house mentioned in this letter, and it soon became a famous midwestern home visited by leading writers and political figures.*

To John S. Phillips, *McClure's Magazine*, May 8, 1901

MY DEAR JOHN:

About a month ago you wrote me a letter in which you made a fatal offer. You offered to let me have some money if I should need it for any business investment out here. This is where you made the mistake of your life. This morning, I have discovered that I can buy the house in which I am now living. This house cost the man who built it, I happen to know, $10,000 in cash besides the lots which cover one hundred and fifty feet. He got into politics, got mixed up with a mortgage and another woman, went to the devil and died, and the house is now in the hands of a Mortgage Company for $6,000. The man who owns the mortgage is a certain Mr. Bowditch who lives in Connecticut. The house is not generally on the market in Emporia, but I have learned authentically that I can get ahold of this house for $6,000, the amount of the mortgage. Now I have not got $6,000. I am paying rent on the house that would amount to the interest on this house at 6%. I can get no money in Emporia, less than 7% on city property. Since I have come to Emporia, I have made and saved $10,000 in the last six years. When I came here, I did not have a cent and borrowed $3,000 at 8% interest and bought the Gazette. I paid that note in 1899. I have put nearly $3,000 in the way of machinery, presses and the like in the Gazette and that is all paid for. I have built a building and paid for that, which I have refused $5,000 for within the last few days. Every cent will be paid off on the Gazette building June 1st, when the last note is due; I will be also out of debt and therefore unhappy. If you will let me have the $6,000, I will give you a mortgage on the residence property which I will buy, and also a chattel mortgage covering the Gazette, and a mortgage on the Gazette building. These last two mortgages I would prefer to have unrecorded for the present, but of course if your banker feels that it is necessary, I will not strongly object. I know the investment is a safe one for me, and I feel that it is an opportunity that I will not have in many years and I am anxious to take it.

During the next fifteen months, I will have my long story, the novel, done. I have always expected to give you the book publication on this though, of course, I have not said so before. There will be, of course, three or four more sketches of American politicians to print in the Magazine before our little book comes out. The book ought to clean at least the interest on this money and perhaps some more for the first year and the above-mentioned sketches ought to reduce the principal one thousand dollars between now and January 1st. I think the Gazette will also pay one thousand dollars on that note between now and January 1st. I, of course, have other sources of income, as I expect to complete the series of politician stories for Mr. Bridges [a member of the Scribner firm] between now and the first of August, and I can see no way honorably or anyway in gratitude to refuse Mr. Bridges his earnest request for this political story book. It, of course, will bring me some more money, at least one thousand dollars, so that at the end of the first year, if everything goes as it should, I can assure you that the first three thousand of the six thousand dollars will be paid. And, if our novel makes any sort of a hit, we can wipe out the remainder of the debt in two years from June 1, 1901. The mortgages should not be dated longer than three years. . . .

Jacc [August F. Jaccacci] knows about the house. It was the house we were in when he visited us last year. It is a three-story, red sandstone and pressed brick affair, finished in hardwood and supplied with all modern plumbing conveniences. If it ever gets on the market in Emporia, and I am afraid it will every day, the price will go considerably above $6,000, as there is a building boom on here and two new railroads actually grading on the townsite, each locating the end of a division and its main shops here. I think I am a pretty conservative fellow when I say the minute I get this house, I can sell it for $9,000. I do not want to sell it, I want to keep it to live in. This is not a real estate speculation at all. I have made this letter too long, but I wanted to explain to you fully the situation so you could decide on the matter intelligently. Do not stand on any ceremony nor be at all afraid of offending me on [?] this proposition. It will make no difference and anything that I have ever intended to do for *McClure's* will be done never-the-less.

Throughout White's career he was assailed by "old-line" Republicans because he frequently wrote critical comments about leading Republicans. The material on McKinley appeared in an article entitled "Hanna," McClure's Magazine, November, 1900. H. S. Lewis, a Kansas Republican, wrote White protesting some of his remarks about President McKinley.

To H. S. Lewis, Hutchinson, Kan., May 20, 1901

My Dear Mr. Lewis:

I am a reasonably good Republican. I suppose that the Gazette has furnished as much copy for Republican exchanges as any paper in the state. During the next twenty years of my active life, if I am

[37]

permitted to live, I will probably keep on being a Republican and furnish copy for Republican papers. Looking over the list of prominent Republican papers in Kansas, I do not now recall one that has not written something which Populist papers have copied with what our old friend Grover Cleveland used to call "ghoulish glee."

The McKinley article which has aroused your ire was garbled; only the unpleasant things were quoted. I took particular pains in that article to say that McKinley is a great, good, wise, efficient president, but that he could not make a speech, and that he was not a scholar, in the sense that college professors are scholars. I also said that he did not read widely. Recently I was a guest of President McKinley's at his home in Canton. He knew that I was there to write him up for a magazine, and he and his private secretary, Mr. Cortelyou, talked with me freely about his range and scope of reading. Mr. Cortelyou said that he prepared for the President lists of current things that would interest him in Forum and the North American Review. Mr. Cortelyou told me expressly and in so many yords, the President is not a wide reader. "He is in no sense a man of books." I replied, "he had a knack of getting men with ideas about him and seemed to rely on their ideas, rather than his own. He does not seem to have any administrative ideas of his own, but rather takes those of men whom his sure, shrewd politician's instinct tells him are to be trusted as men of ideas." Mr. Cortelyou laughed and said, he thought that was about the size of it. I repeated this question to the President verbatim, because it was one that I had prepared in advance for the interview. In answer, the President himself replied, "you are right in part, except that I do not only go to my cabinet for ideas but to the people. I always rely on the people. I am a servant. It is not my place to have ideas, but to express and realize the ideas of others."

Now, my dear Mr. Lewis, that is exactly what I said of President McKinley, adding the fact that he was forcible, wise, conservative, efficient and truly great. Some Republicans that wish to jump on me took out the good things I said of the President, discolored my article, and made me appear in the light of jumping on the President. The "pewee pop papers" in your section of the country copied what I wrote from papers that claim to be Republican papers and did not quote me correctly. I cannot be responsible for caprices of the Populists, nor of the contentions of my enemies. I do not like to have a fat man jump on me and accuse me of something that I did not do; that is why I answer your letter.

[38]

Shortly after Theodore Roosevelt's election as vice-president, White went to work creating sentiment for Roosevelt for president in 1904. Several weeks before the following letter was written White attended a dinner in Colorado with Roosevelt, at which Roosevelt was promised the support of Colorado. White returned home and with renewed vigor did his best to line up both Kansas and Missouri for the Rough Rider.

To THEODORE ROOSEVELT, August 21, 1901

MY DEAR COLONEL:

I went to Topeka and Kansas City, Monday and Tuesday as I promised to. At Topeka I saw and had a long talk with Mr. Leland [Cyrus Leland, powerful Republican boss in Kansas]. He believes that no man in the world can come into Kansas and organize the state against you. Leland (as you probably know) handled Kansas for McKinley, when as he says, there was not half the sentiment for McKinley that there is for you now. Leland did this without taking a dollar of the funds that Hanna had raised, and Kansas is the only state in the Union that went for McKinley without costing McKinley's friends a penny. And it was the first northern state to declare for him. This is why McKinley and Hanna think so well of Leland. If things remain as they are, there will be no doubt in the way of what Kansas will do in the way of a convention in every district and in the state convention. I talked with a number of other people in Topeka, politicians on both sides of the local scrap, and I find that they all believe the sentiment is for you. Fairbanks [Senator Charles W. Fairbanks, who served as vice-president from 1905 to 1909] made no headway here at all. His friends in the state are of the sort that lead me to believe that he is going to spend some money which will do him no good. I talked to Leland rather freely about the situation with Mr. Platt [Senator Thomas Platt, Republican boss of New York]. Leland thinks the best thing Platt can do is to get Quay [Matthew Quay, Republican boss of Pennsylvania] out of the brush in an open declaration for you, if he can do so, as soon as possible, and then to declare himself. In the West, the people think that Mr. Platt is the power in New York politics. A declaration from him would convince a great lot of workers in the West that you were going to have very little trouble, if any, at home. That would make

[39]

them rather more enthusiastic for you than they are now. Leland thinks the Quay business will be a bread and butter proposition, and that you will have no trouble swinging it. But he thinks, and I do too, that if a decent arrangement [can be made] to throw Quay for you early, it will have a great effect for you in the West besides in New York. Leland thinks this of Hanna: That Hanna will see you the strongest candidate before the people, the hardest man to defeat for nomination, and the easiest man to elect in November and that he will line up for you very early if a more perfect square and legitimate arrangement can be agreed upon about the Ohio patronage. I think that when Leland sees Hanna (some time within the next eight or ten months) he will tell Hanna about Kansas and the West. Hanna believes pretty near what Leland says. He at least believes that he is honest and sincere and that he is not a mesmeric fellow. If you think it would help you any, I might bring Leland to Washington very easily and let him talk with Hanna along the lines above suggested. Then it would be time to open negotiations with Hanna about Ohio. Ohio, Pennsylvania and New York can absolutely secure that nomination for you without any question. Ohio and Pennsylvania lined up early for you can put a quiescent that might rise in New York. Leland and I can use our influence with Mr. Hanna in Ohio. This we will be glad to do, and I think that it should be done as early as possible, not later than next March. I think the sooner Senator Platt comes out for you openly the better it will be for your candidacy here in the West, and hence for the western influence in the East. When Senator Platt does come out (if he does so) I would suggest that the news be given to the Washington correspondents of the Kansas City Star and the Kansas City Journal and the Topeka Capital and the Denver papers and the Omaha Bee as soon as possible. They circulate in the territory where you are strongest and where you will want early conventions to be. The only obstacle to early conventions will possibly be the timidity of some of the politicians about the New York situation. An interview from Platt would be important. So much for that phase of the situation. . . .

This seems to be kind of a popular uprising like the crusades. Still I am a great believer in the power of money and the legitimate use of it in a campaign. Kansas and Missouri and probably Colorado will not need any but there will be other states where money can be used legitimately by honest men and square decent fellows. In that effect, I believe the three states just named can contribute something. I would be glad to undertake the job of passing the hat in Kansas.

[40]

I wish you would wire me when you will be in Chicago and I will try and get up, although it may be impossible. At any rate I will be in Washington some time this winter. I will bother you from time to time with letters like these as the occasion seems to demand them.

When Roosevelt received White's letter of August 21, he wrote back that Mark Hanna seemed friendly to his candidacy and that Senator Platt had promised to support him. But Roosevelt added that he did not see how he could seek Matthew Quay's support because there were things that Quay had done that he did not approve.

To THEODORE ROOSEVELT, Chicago, Ill., August 29, 1901

MY DEAR COLONEL:

Your telegram came Tuesday and your letter yesterday. I sent your telegram to Mr. Leland and received from him a very kind and, it seems to me, thoughtful and encouraging reply. I enclose it herewith, having asked Mr. Leland's permission to do so. I believe that the position that he takes is right. I am coming to New York on business about my book next month, then I will see you and talk further with you.

You remember on the lawn one night . . . you said you hadn't asked me if I was for you. I wanted to tell you something then, but I didn't, and if I haven't already told you before it is possible I will write it now. When the war with Spain broke out I wanted to go the worst kind, but my wife was sick and I felt that my first duty was with her. Then when your regiment had such remarkable success and when you came home and were made governor and acquitted yourself so admirably, I formed a great desire to help you to be president of the United States. It has seemed to me that if I could perform some service for you that would land you in the presidency, I would perform as great a service for my country as I could perform upon the battlefield. To that end, I have directed all my political efforts for the last two years. You don't know how eager I am for

[41]

opportunities to help you. I believe honestly and earnestly, that if I could feel in some way that I had been a truly serious factor in making so good and honest a man president of these United States, I would have all the pride a soldier has and you know how much that is. I think the finest part of this feeling is that it has absolutely no sort of selfish self-conscious anticipation. I know you understand this, yet I feel some gratification in writing it in plain, cold words. And now that it is written, you know what I have always known you knew about my motives. So I want to discuss rather freely what you and I shall agree on as the definition of intrigue. No one can abhor more than I, dirty politics. I have tried to make my standard of political honor high. Your career has been my ideal [?] career. So I think, perhaps you have mistaken what I meant in my letter, when I referred to Hanna and to Platt and to Quay. I believe that these men can be made your friends without the sacrifice of the least one of your political ideals or of your personal honor. The things that are strong in you are matched by something that must be strong in them. They have learned the alphabet of political righteousness: to tell the truth. They can spell a few words, you can write a book. Yet I think the language would be just as forceful if it were in one-syllable words, as it would be otherwise. To leave the figure, I say this frankly in the case of Hanna. I know his faults as well as you do. I have gone through him with a lantern and know all the turns of his mental viscera. Probably he can control Ohio. The sentiment of the people may be for you, and if it were undirected by the state machine, it would be for you. Yet I have no doubt but that Hanna can get the Ohio delegation to be for Fairbanks or for Shaw or for you. I don't know anything about the situation now, but I would imagine that Hanna would feel that you are not his friend. He has spoken very kindly to me about you, but nevertheless I believe that Hanna will be against you unless you get him for you. Hanna represents the Republican organization in Ohio. I don't believe it will be intrigue to have your friends bring about a thorough, explicit understanding between you and Senator Hanna to the effect that if the Republican organization in Ohio recommends a square, clean, honest, capable man for any office, and if it is deemed Ohio patronage that the man's candidacy will receive favorable consideration from your hands. I have a notion that Hanna, who doesn't understand the larger words in the code of moral ethics, thinks as deaf men often do, that those who talk what they cannot understand, are plotting against him. Do you see the point? Now, I don't think it's intrigue to try

[42]

to persuade Hanna that all that is good and strong and virile and honest in him is matched in you and if he works for you he will be working for a square man, who, in addition to being honest, is capable of feeling political gratitude.

Take the case of Quay: I hate his intestines. It seems to me that there is no man in American politics that I have such an utter loathing and contempt for as I have for Matthew S. Quay. Now I believe Quay controls Pennsylvania absolutely, and that uncontrolled Pennsylvania will be for you. Yet I would undertake with considerable felicity the task of finding someone who could persuade Senator Quay that in Pennsylvania if a candidate for Republican preferment is clean and straight and honest and capable of the work he aspires to do, the fact that he was urged by the Republican organization would help rather than hinder his candidacy. I do not think I would be intriguing by undertaking this task. I know what Quay would want: he would want you to promise certain definite and specified things—perhaps that you would name certain men in your cabinet—and, of course, I would regard this promise as dishonorable because it would be bartering the public service to private ends. But I think that if the sentiment of the state was for you, Senator Quay could be made to compromise on the lines I have suggested. If he could not, then as your friend I advise you to pass him up.

Now as to the use of money. I want you to understand exactly how I feel about that. I believe that in every campaign for the presidential nomination there is a legitimate, honest, necessary, righteous place for the use of money. That money must come from some source. If the candidate put it up himself he would be buying his office. That would be un-American and unfair. If the money is levied from expectant office seekers or from those who hope for friendly legislation, it is equally un-American and unfair to use it. I believe that in your case a popular fund should be created to defray the expenses of your campaign in states where such expenses would be necessary. Someone has got to pay for the banners; someone has got to pay for buttons; someone has got to pay for marching clubs and bands and that sort of thing that attends every convention. Maybe in your case, the people who march in the marching clubs will pay their own way. I believe they would do it for you more gladly than they would do it for any other human being. Still I believe it would be just as well to have an emergency fund—not too large, but sufficiently large to handle the legitimate expenses of your campaign. In Kansas we could not, by any possibility, use a penny of that sort of money, but yet I believe that your admirers in Kansas would be glad to raise a thousand or so dollars and send it to New York. I feel sure that in the West such a fund could be raised from all sorts and conditions of men, who desire to do their bit just as I would to help along what they believe is a righteous cause, knowing that not one penny would be spent in any way that the men who have it would ever be ashamed of the destination.

Now that I have expressed myself thus frankly, and freely, I want you to tell me with equal frankness what you think. If I can I want to do what you want done in a way that you would have it done. I want to serve you because in serving you in this matter I believe I am serving my country. And if the service is effective, I will feel that I have made up for what I lost in '98. After you are elected president, I want to efface myself from the map. I don't ever want you to think of me except when you need me, and when you want something to play with. Then I will come out of Kansas and help drive dull care away.

McClure's Magazine *carried White's article on Boss Platt of New York in their December, 1901, issue. It was an extremely critical article, and Platt threatened suit for libel. Theodore Roosevelt had arranged White's interview with Platt. Platt and White talked for about half an hour. After the article was printed, Platt tried to persuade President Roosevelt to keep White out of the White House. When the affair had subsided slightly, Roosevelt had Platt come to the White House for an interview at which White was present, but Platt didn't recognize White and didn't pay any attention to Roosevelt's introduction of the* Gazette *editor!*

To August F. Jaccaci, *McClure's Magazine*, October 23, 1901

My Dear Jack:

Here is the Platt piece. We [Mrs. White always worked on her husband's copy] have both worked very hard on it, and I trust it will meet your approval. I have one serious fear for it and that is that it is too scorching. I did not know how to improve that and you can take ahold of it and cut it down as you please. Do not be afraid of offending me. You do the work yourself. Do not let anyone around the office except John [John S. Phillips] help. He and you know what I mean to say. If you think we had better hold it over for a month, I am willing to do so and try and tone it down a little. Let me know at once what you are going to do about it.

Mr. Deford, an acquaintance of White's when he was a student at the University of Kansas, wrote White suggesting that he become a candidate for United States senator.

To WILLIAM A. DEFORD, Ottawa, Kan., November 5, 1901

MY DEAR MR. DEFORD:

. . . You have the audacity to suggest me for senator! Why, man alive, if I would be a candidate there would be a mob in Topeka ten thousand strong, to burn me at the stake.

When I first went into the newspaper business on my own hook, an old banker in El Dorado, Frank Frazier was his name, said to me "My son, during the first five years of your newspaper life, it should be your business to make enemies, get so many people to hating you and hating you hard, that for the rest of your mortal life you will always know that you cannot be elected to any office. Then when some fellow comes along and tries to work you into a candidacy, you will look over the list of your enemies and know that you stand no show, so you will refuse to run for office. And if you can keep from running for office until you are forty years old, you will devote yourself to your business and make money and save it, and then you will be rich and you can put your thumb to your nose and wiggle your fingers at your enemies, for they cannot touch you."

I have devoted myself pretty consistently to following that advice. Generally speaking, I have said what I pleased, when I pleased and about whom I pleased. The Gazette has made money and I have saved it, and I suppose that I have as fine a collection of what might be called staple and fancy enemies, in assorted sizes, as any man in the town of Emporia. However, every fellow has his own particular pride and can always find something to envy in another.

I have a queer association with your name. I never think of you but I think that you married the prettiest girl in West Lawrence and I always think that you must be very happy, even though a Populist!

During his lifetime White was offered many high-salaried positions which would have taken him from Kansas. In a period when young newspapermen were leaving country dailies for big-city journalism, White became unique by remaining in a small town and over the years his small-town background gave him a vantage point of influence that he probably would have lost had he left Emporia.

To CHARLES S. GLEED, New York City, November 16, 1901

MY DEAR MR. GLEED:

I have your letter of November 9th, in which you say that Mr. John Brisbane Walker, editor of the Cosmopolitan, has authorized you to offer me eight thousand dollars a year to work for the Cosmopolitan. I assume that this would take me out of Kansas, and of course I could not go out of Kansas for eight thousand or ten thousand or twice ten thousand. It is not a question of money that keeps me in Kansas. Neither would I go on a regular salary and stay in Kansas. Writing with me is not altogether a matter of money. I really want to do honest work. To do that work, I have to write about the things that interest me. I have never written on orders since I began writing for magazines. I write of the things that have interested me and according to my own way of writing them. I would feel that if I accepted a salary from Mr. Walker, that I would have to do as Mr. Walker says. If he suggested an article on automobiles or anything which pleased him, I would feel in duty bound to write it.

Very soon, I would be doing a grind and nothing else. It is not a question of money at all, it is a question of doing the very best that I can do. I would rather sell Mr. Walker an article for ten dollars, if it represented my honest opinion and my most earnest endeavor, than to work for him at eight thousand dollars a year. I could get all kinds of work, if I cared to work on a salary. It may jar your opinion of my common sense to know that I turned down a salary of three hundred dollars a week to go to Washington and act as correspondent, and this offer was made by a personal friend in New York City, to whom I am under many obligations. The Gazette and Emporia furnish me that recreation and the life that I like. They give me an independence that money could not buy. Incidentally I am making something near the money which Mr. Walker offered me. I may be wrong in this, and of course I appreciate the kindness of Mr. Walker's offer and of your kind interest in the matter. I have tried to make it plain, as I did once to Mr. Walker, how I am situated and how I feel. I want to convey to him my very sincerest thanks for his generous offer.

To John S. Phillips, *McClure's Magazine*, December 17, 1901

Dear John:

...I received a telegram today from the Kansas City World, which says that Platt is going to sue me for libel. It also says that Platt told Roosevelt, "I will get that fellow's scalp if it is the last thing I ever do." However, I shall sleep well tonight and have no fear that if he does get my scalp, LePage's liquid glue, which is advertised in Mc-Clure's Magazine, will stick my scalp on again.

As the following letter indicates, White was a keen student of the value of publicity. His book of political stories, Stratagems and Spoils, *had only recently been published, and he wanted to use the publicity created by Senator Platt to sell the book. Senator Platt never went through with the libel suit.*

To Arthur Scribner, New York City, December 20, 1901

Dear Sir:

In view of the threatened libel suit of Senator Platt against me for the article in McClure's, it occurs to me that we might as well make hay while the sun shines. If you would push the book in the New York papers, also in the Washington papers, I believe that with a line of advertising in the Washington papers, and a hundred books on sale in Brentano's, you could do pretty well. It seems to me that if you could get a window downtown in New York, where old man Platt wouldn't throw rocks at it, we could clean up a thousand or so copies while the scrap is on. I am not, as you observe, a modest wood violet by a mossy stone. I believe in taking advantage of every opportunity to make an honest dollar, and if this man Platt wants to advertise me, I am going to take all the benefit by the advertising. I wish you would push this matter in the New York advertising.

During 1902 White was extremely busy writing articles for McClure's, Saturday Evening Post, Collier's, *and* Cosmopolitan. *He, however, kept his finger in local politics during this election year. Although he was keenly interested in national politics, he never forgot that keeping his own county in the Republican column was of utmost importance. In local politics, White was firmly for the straight ticket all the way down the list of candidates.*

To Dr. D. S. Fisher, Reading, Kan., August 26, 1902

My Dear Dr. Fisher:

I got your letter last week and was glad to hear from you and was glad you came frankly to the point which has been on my mind. Jeff Eastin and Ed Newlin came back from the Reading picnic, and I am told said that you said you did not care for any of the Republican ticket except C. C. Henry and E. N. Evans. This was a surprise and a shock to me and I am glad your straightforward letter placed the

[48]

matter beyond any dispute. We are all of us human, doctor, I as well as the rest of them, and I suppose you are. I am perfectly willing to admit that I have made several "fool breaks" during the last eighteen months. I don't know of any human creature who hasn't during that time. If all of your mistakes of diagnosis and prescriptions were matters as public as my mistakes of editorial, and were scanned by all of your fellow doctors in Lyon County and criticized every day in the week as my editorials are, I suppose I would be standing up for old Doctor Fisher here in Emporia about as much and about as often as old Doctor Fisher is standing up for old Bill White in Reading. There is this difference between writing editorials and writing prescriptions, that in the one case everyone is on to your bad breaks and forgets your good ones, and in the other case you bury your good hits and your bad breaks walk around and advertise you.

Now, Doctor Fisher, a lot of fellows once came down to the Gazette office and threatened to boycott me if I did not withdraw my indorsement for you for postmaster. I stood pat. I took what little boycotting there was lying around loose because I knew if I ever drew on you for value received, I would get it. Now is the time I want value received and I want it bad. . . .

Now, Doctor, as a man of honor in such a case, I ask you, wouldn't you stand by your word? I have made this explanation as a preface to what I am going to ask because I don't want you to do a thing that you think dishonorable, even for me. I have a vital, personal interest in the election of Charles Harris and Jerry Evans. They cannot be elected unless the whole county ticket is elected. To make the fight for them alone would be un-Republican and unsuccessful. I know your strength in Reading Township. I know that you can absolutely bring that township with a normal majority for the whole ticket. It means much more to me than the Reading post office meant to you to have this Republican ticket elected; more I mean in a purely personal way. Now I want you to pull off your coat and go to work for this ticket, tooth and nail [?]. I want you to bring Reading Township in right. If you will do this for me, you may depend upon me to help you in whatever cause I can.

This letter is of course written in confidence from one gentleman to another, yet there is nothing in it that I am ashamed of and which any man may not read who understands the honorable rules governing politics. I shall be out of the county from the tenth of September till the tenth of October. I would come up to Reading and see you, only that you know for some reasons which doubtless you can ex-

[49]

plain a number of Reading people think I have horns and hoofs and a forked tail and breathe fire and brimstone. I cannot help this opinion but I can prevent doing harm to the ticket by keeping as quiet as possible.

During September, 1902, White visited southern Idaho gathering material for articles on the mining region around Thunder Mountain for the Saturday Evening Post. *Four articles were published in the November issues of the* Post. *While in Idaho, White renewed his friendship with W. E. Borah, who had been a fellow student at the University of Kansas. Senator Hanna agreed to the request that White made in this letter.*

To Senator Marcus A. Hanna, Cleveland, Ohio,
November 29, 1902

My Dear Senator:

Your friend ex-Senator Shoup and my friend W. E. Borah of Boise, Idaho, are the two leading candidates for the Senate from Idaho at the coming election. Borah has twenty-five votes tied up good and tight. He needs three more to nominate him. Shoup has five votes and the prestige of his former service.

Now the situation there is this: Our mutual friend Perry Heath down at Salt Lake is for Shoup and has persuaded the politicians out there that you and the Republican committee are particularly interested in Shoup's election. As you are a man with a sense of humor, perhaps you don't realize how much advantage this fact gives a man out here in the West where your judgment is regarded by Republicans as final in matters of policy.

Now I have no doubt that personally, because you are Senator Shoup's old friend, you would be glad to see him come back to the Senate. But on the other hand I feel sure that you would not allow the impression to prevail that you would let the fact of your personal preference and the weight of your place as Republican National

Chairman [weigh] in any man's favor in any contest outside of your home state.

Yet in Idaho, all unknown to you, that is exactly the situation. It seems to me if you could find the opportunity to declare that the National Committee has no interest in the Idaho Senatorial election further than that which comes from the desire to see a Republican win, it would be only fair to all the candidates. Such a note might be addressed to Judge D. W. Stanrod, the National Committeeman from Idaho, who is a decent chap and is also a receptive lightning-rod candidate for the senatorship. Or the note might be addressed to me and I would see that it was published in Idaho without getting it further East.

Now about Borah: he is a young man, was the attorney for the Coeur d'Alene mine operators during their trouble; has the best corporation practice in the state; is shrewd, levelheaded and true. You need not fear him. He admires you as much as I do, and that I believe is the limit. He would be your friend and would listen to you. Of course you have no further interest in his candidacy than to know that he is straight and square. I vouch for him. I realize that to you the election of Senator Shoup would mean the renewal of old ties; yet I am sure that you would not stand in the way of a young man. It is in the interest of fair play that I approach you on this Idaho situation. It seems to me that I am asking nothing that you cannot honorably give. There is of course no hurry about the matter, and you may rest assured that any reply you may make to this letter will be held confidential.

In the early nineties, White was one of the organizers of the Kansas Day Club which met thereafter on January 29 each year to commemorate Kansas' entrance into the Union on January 29, 1861. This was a Republican party affair, and White was politically opposed to Senator Joseph R. Burton and to the Kansas City Journal which backed Burton. Burton was convicted in 1905 of a felony in connection with his official position. White was allied with the other wing of the Kansas Republican party—the Leland wing—in these years. The book that White dedicated to the Kansas City Star—the Journal's implacable

[51]

foe—was Stratagems and Spoils. *The dedication read, in part, "To The Kansas City Star An Honest Newspaper."*

To Willis Gleed, February 2, 1903

My Dear Willis:

The swipe you gave me at the Kansas Day Club is still in my mind. I said "politics is war and war is hell," but I did not say by implication or belief or by even silent intimation that "everything goes in hell." That was added by the Kansas City Journal, a paper of which you may sometimes hear. I wrote after saying that war and politics are hell as follows and to wit: "That means that it is merciless, it is relentless, but that it is nevertheless an honorable estate, and based on the golden rule. The rules of politics are fair. The fair man is he who fights in the open, uses no poisoned bells [?] and gives no quarter till the white flag goes up. Mercy has no place in a political fight nor in a battle till it is ended, but fairness, honesty, and manly courage are always demanded by the rules of every clean game."

Now I submit that this is a lot different from the statement you quoted to me. I think I am particularly scrupulous about what goes in politics. On this mail I am sending back an annual pass from a Kansas railroad attorney; that is one of the things that doesn't go with me. . . . I line up with the Leland crowd because in the main it seems to be decenter than the Burton crowd. But I reserve the right to differ with the Leland crowd and to criticise his actions [?]. The Kansas City Journal, which has been viciously unfair to me ever since I dedicated a book to the Star and has tried to belittle me in every way, is generally supposed by the politicians to be supporting the Burton end of the string. Yet it has never called that gang down . . . as I have called down the Leland gang with which I trot . . . and make no bones of it. . . .

I simply make these remarks in a general way, and in passing, that you may not think I am altogether a moral degenerate. I try to live uprightly in politics. I have no desire to get any office. I do desire to be effective. I desire especially to help Roosevelt. Life is a series of compromises; putting Burton and Leland aside—pairing them, as it were—it seems to me that the Leland crowd is decenter, and as one has to be somewhere to do anything, I line up with Leland, but reserve the right to kick and to draw the line when he goes too far

[52]

and too fast. It seems to me that is the right course. I am doing what I think is right. . . .

Chester I. Long was the newly elected senator from Kansas. White had supported another candidate for the position but now was advocating Republican harmony.

To CHESTER I. LONG, Medicine Lodge, Kan., April 14, 1903

MY DEAR CHESTER:

What the Republican party of Kansas needs just at this particular minute is a Moses, and you are it. Factionalism is running rampant. One side is as uncompromising as the other. A strong man is needed in this situation—a man to say clearly and determinedly that the hell-raising and dog-eating knife-carrying business has got to stop. You are the one man in Kansas who can do this thing. Bailey [Governor W. J. Bailey of Kansas] could have done it at one time, but not now. The reason must be apparent to you, and if you do not grasp the opportunity soon, before this summer is over, it will pass you also.

As you know and everyone who knows me knows, I have but one reason for being in politics and that is to wipe from the name of Kansas the smut-pot of "Burton in the Senate." But this wrangling and rag-chewing and backbiting that is running riot in the party in Kansas now is the best thing for Burton that could happen. When Republicans are hating each other, and calling all men scoundrels, the size of a big scoundrel is not noticed in the crowd and Burton can slip back in.

It behooves you to have a man of your own kind in the Senate, and not one of the other sort. But greater than that need is the need that faces the Republican party to be harmonious and to quit scrapping. Blessed be the peacemakers for they shall inherit the earth, and you are Mr. Goodman with a great big I. The thing for you to do is to tuck your modesty in your hip pocket, there you can get at it handy in case of urgent need, and sail out in the next three months

[53]

preaching peace and harmony. Don't be afraid of people thinking you are presuming. You are the leader of the party. You are the one man to whom the people of this state look now to deliver them from factionalism. You are naturally too shy, but this is the time for you to be bold. Who was it said, "Audacity, and audacity, and again audacity!"?

Perhaps I am foolish in writing this to you, but it seems to me that you can do something that is needed. . . .

Joseph L. Bristow of Kansas, Fourth Assistant Postmaster General, carried out an investigation of the Post Office Department in 1903. He was a relentless foe of fraud and corruption, and his work led to the indictment of a number of individuals including Senator Burton of Kansas. Roosevelt backed up the investigation and prosecutions and gained public esteem and confidence for his willingness to prosecute members of his own party. White, friendly to both Bristow and Roosevelt, was vigorous in his support of Bristow's investigation, and described the affair in "Roosevelt and the Postal Frauds," Mc-Clure's Magazine, September, 1904.

To Senator Henry Cabot Lodge, May 28, 1903

My Dear Senator Lodge:

The whole West is interested in the disclosures in the Post Office Department. Coming as it has come, it has strengthened the President wonderfully. . . . The thing needed now, it seems to me, is to let no guilty man escape.

I am writing you this not because I think you don't know more about it than I know. For I realize you are infinitely better informed. But the time may come when you may be told that the sentiment in the West favors covering this business up for the good of the party. This is not the truth. The good of the party out here demands vigorous prosecution of every man who is guilty of fraud and particularly Machens [August W. Machens, General Superintendent of the

[54]

Free Delivery System]. He has more pull than a policeman. The pull will tell the President that it is bad politics to expose all this scandal. They will say that it may alienate the West. Fellows who are reasonably decent may urge that this matter be postponed till after Congress adjourns, and then till after election. I hope you will be assured that so far as the West goes—and there Roosevelt is strong—sentiment is undividedly in favor of cleaning this business up right now.

I am writing this frankly to you, because I know that you have the President's confidence. And I feel that others whom he may trust (and for every good and proper reason), may tell him to talk cautiously—not to say cat-wise—in this matter. Please do not think I am impertinent in this matter. But his interest is so deeply in my heart that I fear [?] everything that threatens his good fortune. I should write to him directly but I know his mail will be full and I don't care to burden him unnecessarily. And I know that if he needs what I am saying from me, you can tell him, and if he does not need it you may forget all about it.

His trip did him a world of good out here. . . . Five years ahead is a long time to look, but will you permit a suggestion from a friend that you should come West during that time and let the people see something of you. We want to keep the pendulum swinging upward after President Roosevelt drops off.

The vigor with which White went after evidence of Senator Burton's misuse of his high office is indicated in this letter: The Mr. Folk mentioned is Joseph Folk who was gaining wide attention for his prosecution of corrupt politicians and business groups which corrupted the politicians in St. Louis. He was later to be a progressive governor of Missouri. Lincoln Steffens opened his muckraking career with an article on Folk's work in St. Louis in McClure's Magazine, October, 1902.

MY DEAR COLONEL ROOSEVELT:

I am told that the following story is true: Last winter Senator Burton of Kansas met Chief of Inspectors Cochran of the Post Office Department in a hotel and said: "Cochran, I am a poor man and I have an opportunity to make some money. I have some clients in St. Louis whose property was confiscated by your inspectors and this property (consisting of their books and accounts) are to be used as evidence against them in a trial in the state courts. It will mean a good deal of money to me if you can order the books of those people returned by your inspectors." Later Cochran consulted his superior officers, who told him to find out if Burton wanted this done as an attorney or as a United States senator, for it would be an easy matter to refuse an attorney and a proper matter to do as well, but it might be embarrassing to turn down a United States senator. Cochran returned and Burton said he was asking this as the attorney for these people and the request was refused. The Senator's clients were the get-rich-quick people, who are now under indictment by Mr. Folk in St. Louis where Burton also fears indictment for complicity in a swindle.

If this story is true, and if, as I am told, there is a statute against senators practicing before the departments, here is as gross a violation of the law as it is possible to find. If it is true, Mr. Cochran will say so. And if it is a violation of the law, and the District Attorney of Washington hesitates about prosecuting the case, I will not shrink a moment about doing so myself. I have no more in this case than I had in the Post Office scandals. But if this man has violated the law, he should be prosecuted just as Machens and his crowd.

I write you thus because I do not know whom else to address in the matter. The United States District Attorney would think me merely a factionist trying to get even. But as you know Burton is nothing to me. He stands in the way of nothing I desire save a good name for my state. And I write you before making a nasty muss with a United States senator. It is possible that to push this case would embarrass you in larger matters. This of course I don't want to do. I am willing to take any course you may advise, and keep sacredly confidential the nature of that counsel.

Dear Sir:

Replying to your request for a few sickening details of my editorial career, I beg leave to submit the following.

I was born thirty-five years ago in this town, and after growing up in a neighboring town, came here for a few years to go to a little college. I learned a little of the printer's trade during vacations and worked off and on while going to school in the printing offices of this town. Later I took charge of a weekly paper at El Dorado while its editor was in politics and still later worked as editorial writer on the Kansas City Journal and the Kansas City Star. In '93 I married Miss Sallie Lindsay and in '95 bought the Emporia Gazette. It is a small local daily paper of only two thousand circulation, and has practically no subscribers off the townsite of Emporia, though the weekly goes all over Lyon County. It is not a financial success in any large sense. Though it pays its editor and owner three or four thousand dollars every year, which is equal to twice that amount in a city. Its first object is to print the local news. Many papers are issued from the office without a line of editorial of any kind in them. Editorials should be written only when a paper has something to say and not to fill up space. The present editor of the Gazette didn't have any struggle to make the paper go. Though it had but 500 daily subscribers when he took it, he never worked an hour after six o'clock on the paper and he remembers but few Saturday nights when he was particularly worried about the pay-roll. The work on the paper now is easy. It is not a grind and though it is a little town, the news is as interesting as the news in big towns and pretty much of the same nature. Two reporters, a bookkeeper and a copy reader who edits telegraph and does the "society column" are all the help we have in the front room to print and publish and get up a six-column quarto. We print eight columns of local news a day and six columns of telegraphic news, afternoon report, Associated Press, and an average of two-thirds of a column of editorial. That isn't much work for any of us. The paper has grown naturally and if it has any virtue it is that virtue which its esteemed but loathed contemporaries call its "brazen impudence," and which its editor likes to think is its fearlessness.

I have been in the newspaper business nearly twenty years now as printer and as reporter and as proprietor, and it seems to me that the essence of success in a newspaper is wisely directed courage. All the struggles I have had have been due to mistakes I made in temporizing with evil. Whenever the Gazette has been brave and fair it has been easy enough to get money to pay off Saturday night, but when the Gazette has done the "smooth" thing, has played to the gallery, has truckled to its subscribers if they were wrong, when the Gazette has acted the demagogue, it has been hard work to make the paper go. Character is the one essential to running a successful newspaper, whether the success is financial or political. The best epigram ever made about a newspaper was made by the late Secretary of Agriculture Sterling Morton who said: "A newspaper's foes are its assets and its friends its liabilities." It is the man who wants you to keep something out that eats the vitality out of the bank account. This is true on a big paper as well as on a little paper. The same principle makes a good newspaper in a big town that makes it in a little town.

Mr. and Mrs. White spent November and part of December, 1903, in the Grand Canyon where Mr. White recovered from a slight case of pneumonia. When he returned he plunged into writing a series of articles for the Saturday Evening Post. *Roosevelt was up for election to the presidency, and White's support of his candidacy knew no bounds. The following letter refers to White's article "The Dollar in Politics,"* Saturday Evening Post, *July 2, 1904. The spirit of this letter, that men were becoming more honest in politics, was one of the firm beliefs of the progressives who supported Roosevelt.*

To Jefferson Daugherty, Strong City, Kan., July 13, 1904

My Dear Mr. Daugherty:

I was delighted to hear from my father's old friend and I am pleased to know that you liked my article in the Saturday Evening Post. I shall have a series of articles in the Post upon the campaign, which I hope you will do me the honor of following.

You ask me, "Why it is that a man who is honest in business, is

[58]

dishonest in politics?" I have puzzled over that a great deal myself, and have not come to an entirely satisfactory answer. My only theory is this: That when a man does a mean thing in business, he does it to some one particular man or to some small group of men. These men are able to punish him for his meanness and he knows it. It is practically obvious to him that "Honesty is the best policy" when punishment hangs like a cloud over his head. But the mean things a man does in politics are done to a thousand men, and while they make these thousand men angry for a moment, it does not injure these thousand men sufficiently for any one of them to punish the mean man, or for one of them to organize and punish the mean man, whether he is a thief or grafter. So it is not entirely obvious to a man in politics that "Honesty is the best policy," and he lets the devil in him run loose. But I am satisfied that in the long run, honesty in politics is the best policy, and that as the people are becoming more and more intelligent, and more and more interested in the political affairs that they organize against political crooks so swift and so sure that men are becoming more honest in politics than they were formerly.

Oklahoma was the speculative frontier of this western area. Opened to settlers in 1889, by 1904 it was within three years of statehood. Pioneer conditions in many parts of the Oklahoma territory had now given way to a thriving farm economy. White was asked by a group to run a new Oklahoma paper backed by a stock company.

To O. W. MEACHAM, July 14, 1904

MY DEAR OLD FRIEND:

I was glad to have you break the silence of a number of years, and write me the note which came last Wednesday. I have been away from the office all the time since it came, and have been unable to answer it.

I do not want you to be offended that I cannot accept your propo-

[59]

sition at all. I have now reached almost middle life. I am firmly established in Emporia in a paper that is making me three or four thousand dollars a year, and I have built up friends, politically and in a business way, which are my capital in life.

I suppose I could sell the Gazette without very much trouble for fifteen or twenty thousand dollars. I have been approached to sell several times, but I am beholden to no man on earth for my success here. I can say what I please, can do what I please and be what I please, without asking the Republican organization or any other organization or man for permission. While I always expect to run a straight Republican paper, the minute I was tied up to a proposition that I would have to run a straight Republican paper, whether I wanted to or not, there is just Irish enough in me to want to kick over the traces. I wouldn't run a paper for any money that any other human being than myself had a dollar's worth of stock in.

I turned down an offer of $12,000 a year not long ago to go to Chicago for the Chicago Tribune, because I wouldn't take $25,000 a year for my right to be my own boss, and if I went into a stock Company proposition, I would feel that every man that owned one dollar's worth of stock owned an ounce of my blood, and the position would be absolutely intolerable.

I hope you will do well in the Territory. I have great respect for Oklahoma and Indian Territory. I believe it is the field for young men. If I was not tied up as I am, I would certainly go there. . . .

Do not feel that I am trying to be high and mighty in this letter nor taking any lofty position, but I know that I am not cut out for the kind of a job you speak of. I find that as I grow older, I am getting more bullheaded than I used to be, and I know I would make a most miserable failure running a stock Company paper. It was very kind of you to think of me and I appreciate your kindness very much.

The Emporia Gazette *was known in Kansas as White's School of Journalism. Many young newspapermen, trained on the* Gazette, *went into big-city journalism or bought country dailies. The recipient of the following letter was one of White's "boys." White natur-*

ally always took great pride in his "graduates" and followed their careers with keen interest.

To CHARLES M. VERNON, St. Louis, Mo., November 8, 1904

MY DEAR CHARLIE:

There is no special reason why I should write to you. I have no news to tell you or no message to impart, but I have been thinking about you and wondering how you are getting on.

They told me the other day that your Philadelphia girl had gone and got married on you, which I would say was a pretty good thing. Generally speaking, Charlie, a girl who will go and get married on a fellow as she did would make life rather a dreary business.

I knew about that young woman when she was in Emporia, but it was not for me to rise up and knock on her because I had always known when a man knocks on a woman that another man is in love with he usually gets disliked by two people and I wanted to keep myself liked by one.

In this world of sin and sorrow, Charlie, every man has to take a good many hard knocks. One of the hardest knocks to take is a dose which you are passing through. When I was a young man about nineteen years old I had a sufficiency of that sort of delicacy. I used to contemplate murder and suicide as minor misdemeanors, which I would gladly embrace as a way out of my difficulty. Every man who is much of a man has to take once or twice in his life that kind of a horrible jolt. I have a notion that when the Lord gives it to him he gives it as some sort of a test. If the man stands up under it the Lord knows that his shoulders are broad enough to stand greater burdens and greater responsibilities which will bring him a capacity for greater usefulness in life.

This probably does not comfort you just now but the time will come and the longer it's coming and the more you have to honestly suffer in this matter the better it will be for you—I say the time is coming when you will be able to look at the situation with calmness and I trust that with a rather pensive satisfaction.

No man in the world ever gets his back broadened except by some weary sorrow. All you have to do during the next ten years is **to be a man. Keep clean. Do not get sour and keep at work.**

Do not leave St. Louis too soon. Do not leave until you talk it over with me. Do not be afraid to lean pretty hard on me. It is a great pleasure to me and it cannot possibly hurt you.

The following item appeared in the Gazette, *November 18, 1904:* "*Last evening at dusk as the editor of the* Gazette *was starting for home, a few yards from the office door he met Mrs. Delta Meffert, divorced wife of William Meffert, of whom mention was made in these columns recently. She was accompanied by a lady friend, and as the* Gazette *man started to pass, Mrs. Meffert pulled from her cloak a small but effective looking whip. The editor of the paper sidestepped and did what every true gent would do; ran forty yards like a whitehead back to the office by the back door. . . .*" *A number of eastern papers carried the story but stated that White had actually been whipped. He wrote a number of letters like the following to correct this statement.*

To Bliss Perry, Editor of the *Atlantic Monthly*,
November 25, 1904

My Dear Mr. Perry:

There are times when one feels the injustices of life pretty keenly, and I think this is one of the times. I have been making a fight for enforcement of law here at home for two weeks since the election naming specific places where the law was violated, and demanding a grand-jury and furnishing legal evidence to the county attorney. Men had threatened me with violence and I had gone to their places and given them a chance to get me if they wanted to. One evening as I was going home ten days ago a woman, whose divorced husband was violating the law, met me just outside the office, and drew a horsewhip. I was twenty feet away from her. A by-stander held her and I went back into the office—at a pretty lively clip, made what I thought was a flippant local article about the episode and let it go. My little baby was near death, and I forgot everything about it until

I saw in the New York papers most atrociously false stories that I had been horsewhipped and that I was abusing women and got my deserts. I don't know how to run the story down. It was sent out from Topeka, with my trivial local item as a basis, by the newspaper friends of Tom Kelly, an embezzling state treasurer, whose case has received more or less of my attention. There are a score of men in this world whose personal good will I would not lose for anything. I am writing to you as one of them. I hope you will correct the story if you hear it.

Now about your letter of November 18th. I desire to thank you most heartily for what you have done for me and for sending the Atlantic Monthly. I do not write entirely for money. There are some things that I want to say and I would be glad to have them said without receiving money for them just to speak my mind without feeling that I get a dollar for relieving myself.

I have had in mind for the last six months or so an article that does not fit any place else in the world except with you or with the Outlook about the lack of conservatism in the West as is shown by the kind of senators in the U. S. Senate. It seems to me that New England and the conservative East . . . is the leading and dominant force of American politics and is dominant because it is conservative. If you would care to look at the article of that sort I should be delighted to prepare it for you and the matter of the money would not cut any figure with me. I get ten cents a word when I go into the market and bargain but I am not in the market bargaining with the Atlantic Monthly, chiefly because I want very earnestly to say a thing that is in my mind and to say it to the best possible audience.

White objected to the ease with which a congressman could force a competent postmaster out of his position. President Roosevelt wrote to White on January 9, 1905, the following: "I have been telling the post office people all along that they must treat the presumption as being in favor of the man who is in; but that it is impossible to lay down a universal rule as to when this presumption can be treated as overcome, and that I desire each congressman to go on record in writing as to any reasons why he should desire the change of a post-

master. Then we can see whether the reasons are adequate or inade-
quate—I find some Congressmen take this decision one way and some
another. Thus there is one Michigan man who promptly started to
turn out everybody, and who had equally promptly to be hauled up;
while another man, an Indiana man, thanked me most cordially for
the 'rule' on the ground that it relieved him from all pressure to make
changes in his district!"

To THEODORE ROOSEVELT, January 19, 1905

MY DEAR COLONEL ROOSEVELT:

I return here with the correspondence about Congressman Calderhead [W. A. Calderhead, member of Congress from Kansas, 1899–
1911]. It does not seem to me to bear at all on the situation. Calderhead is a man far above the average in moral sense and courage. He
would no more take advantage of an order like the present one in
the postoffice department to remove an enemy from office than he
would commit any other breach of public faith. The man I spoke of
was Congressman —— a person of another sort entirely. He got his
recent congressional nomination by the use of the most flagrant
corruption, and in open scandal he had semi-publicly given it out
that the new order makes it possible to remove his enemies—those
who stood for decency in the district—"Square dealed" as you put
it—*and that they have to go.* On his own unsupported word, your
order allowed him to remove one man *after* the department's inspectors had given the man a *clean bill of health* so far as *his conduct of
the office* went. The only men who are listed to go are those who
objected to [him] for Congress on what seemed to them honest
grounds.

I don't care for ——'s political love affairs. I don't care for the
Michigan man who you say started in to clean out all his enemies in
his district under your order. I don't care seriously about the order
so long as you are president. You have given such an impetus to
decency and are so careful about the actual workings of any order
(good or bad) that little real harm can come in the long run from
any order that you may enforce. What I am complaining about is
this: that if the order stands till the next man comes in—*when conditions begin to snap back a little naturally any way,* the order as it now

[64]

stands will give the Michigan man the opportunity to turn all his enemies out irrespective of their value to the service. *The old system was better than this new system.* Whether you have made an order or whether the postoffice department had construed an order I do not know. But I do know that in the rural districts the fourth class postmasters in districts of crooked congressmen are pretty generally aware of the fact that whereas a year ago they held their places at the will of the postoffice department and *on their records*, now they may be removed on the unsupported word of the congressman who is over them.

And what I am trying to drill into the executive mind, is this: that when any officer of the public service owes his continuation in office not to *a good record* but to the *will of another public servant in quite a different department*, the first public servant is going to serve his real master and not his nominal master. Also that when the master is a congressman (and congressmen manage to befuddle the issue of their real worth enough by their original appointing power, heaven knows) the congressman in question is given the material for a machine which makes his nominations sure. This machine takes the choice of the people in the matter of a congressman out of the Republican party, and makes it necessary to vote for the crooked nominee of the Republican party or vote for a Democrat.

Of course men like Calderhead will treat the order decently. But men like —— and your Michigan man will use the order to corrupt the service, just as soon as you are out of office, and often while you are in office while your back is turned. But it is a very trivial matter compared with the big things on the board. No special harm can come of the order even if —— and the Michigan man and their friend Congressman Legion do have their way for a time. My personal judgment is that it is better to keep the friendship and co-operation of the congressman whose name is Legion than to make them mad on a side issue just now and spoil the whole kettle of fish now frying.

The only thing I have to ask in this matter is this: if by any chance you have confused Congressman Calderhead with Congressman ——, and it has come to Congressman Calderhead's ears that I have been objecting to Calderhead's postal affairs, you will tell Congressman Calderhead that it was a mistake. I have the highest personal and political regard for him. He is absolutely straight. It is immaterial to me, whether or not Congressman —— knows my position. You may use my name with him as you like.

The root of it all is this: that your order introduces into rural

America the same corruption of the party machine that has afflicted our cities by making the country postmaster the political creature of a crooked or uncompetent congressman.

N.B. Kindly note my notation on the Calderhead letter enclosed.

Editor White was always wary of political appointments for himself. He felt that his influence as a newspaperman would be curbed by his acceptance of such an appointment. As this letter reveals, however, he did accept an appointment as a member of the Board of Regents of the University of Kansas, a post which he held until 1913.

To GOVERNOR E. W. HOCH, Topeka, Kan., March 7, 1905

MY DEAR GOVERNOR:

I see by the papers and hear by consulting Mr. McNeal [T. A. McNeal, long-time editor of the Capper publications in Topeka, Kansas] that you have gone and done it. Of course I am grateful. It is the only job in Kansas that I ever wanted, and the only one that I would take. But man alive—Emporia is full of statesmen who really want something and who are just as capable as I am to fill the places they desire, and they think I have legged for this job by neglecting their interests, and I fear that they will not think prettily of either of us.

But that doesn't bother me particularly, but here is something that does bother me. You have hampered my influence for you. I had hoped to be able to help you during the next two years by standing by your administration. I have faith that while in a few things we may disagree, in the main and in the long run, your administration will be the cleanest and ablest Kansas has had for twenty years, not excepting Stanley's for he was not given the opportunity to deal with big vital things that are looming up to make your administration great. But as a member of your administration even in a small capacity,

[66]

I am stopped from saying anything that will carry any real weight with the people. I don't know that anything I might say would carry any weight, but by accepting an office I am dead sure that so far as being able to help you I am powerless. And I had laid great store by what I hoped to do.

Perhaps I can do more good as a regent of the University than I can in the Gazette. Sincerely I hope so. It was kind and generous and thoughtful of you, and from the bottom of my heart I thank you for what you did and the way you did it. I trust my work may be such that you will never be ashamed of your appointment.

Kansas had a sprightly oil boom in 1905. Governor E. W. Hoch and the state, in order to offset a Standard Oil monopoly, established a state refinery as a way of checking Standard's rates and making competition work. White, as the next letter reveals, would not accept Standard Oil advertising in this affair.

To P. C. BOYLE, Topeka, Kan., April 5, 1905

DEAR SIR:

I appreciate deeply the kindly feeling that you and Mr. MacLennen have for me in including me in the list for the Standard Oil advertising. I do not wish to be a Pharisee in this matter, and yet it seems to me that in view of the stand that the state of Kansas as a state has taken in regard to the Standard, it would not be right for me as a citizen to take the other side—even to the extent of printing your copy mark advertising—of the controversy for a fee.

I don't want to be a Miss Nancy, but that is the way it seems to me, and feeling as I do—even though I am wrong, as I may be—I would be more than wrong to violate my conscience. I certainly do not set up my standard of right and wrong for others. I am perfectly willing to confess the logic of those who differ with me. But I simply have this crotchet and cannot yield to it.

[67]

Thanking you again for the good will shown by your courtesy in offering to put your advertising in so small a medium, I remain—

The influence of the railroads in politics was a dynamic issue throughout these years. White in the Gazette, *April 5, 1906, advocated the regulation of the railroads and saw the struggle as a fight between "the people and aggrandized wealth seeking to infringe upon the rights of the people."*

To George T. Nicholson, Sante Fe Railroad, April 5, 1906

My Dear George T. Nicholson:

There are few men in this world to whom I can talk so frankly about the railroad question as to you, for everything in the world I have ever asked of you has been given freely, and with kindness and with no strings. Also in what I want to say about certain objectionable habits of railroad men, there is nothing that can make you wince, or so far as I know any man on the Sante Fe—now. Since your letter came last week, in which you say you will grant the favor I asked, but which I have since found unnecessary, I have been trying to get my ideas in shape to set down some sort of a lucid view of the situation as I see it.

There is obviously considerable agitation in the country over the railroad situation. This agitation sometimes appears in newspapers, and doubtless to thousands of honest men honestly trying to operate railroads fairly as between the interests of stockholders, and the interests of the public, this agitation must appear as a thorn in the side. I do not blame such men for thinking it is demagogic. They themselves have always tried to play the game of life according to the prevailing rules, and they are suddenly pounced upon and called thieves and liars and criminals, and it strikes them as cruel, unfair and desperately mean. And I can see their viewpoint clearly. But the American people are a pretty fair sort, and they don't kick unless

[68]

someone is prodding them. And here is the prod: the so-called railroad attorney. While the traffic department has been going out after business, and the operating department has been handling it, the law department of four American roads out of five has been not trying cases before the courts as hard as it can [?] but playing politics. The political attorneys have created a myth among the other departments of the road that the politicians were holding them up. This justified the use of much mileage, and with their pass-books the attorneys have been playing the game of politics, five-sixths of the time, not to the benefit of the railroad which employs them but for their own personal ends. They have lifted men up and put them down in state politics. They have punished their own enemies, and have made men enemies of the railroads who have no just cause for complaint against the actual operating and traffic departments. These attorneys have sent crooked men to Congress, and to the Senate . . . The Santa Fe has for ten years to my knowledge kept out of Kansas politics, and has made friends by it, but the Missouri Pacific and the Union Pacific and the Rock Island have been in it to their ears . . . No road that is honestly operating has anything to gain in the long run by elevating a crook; sooner or late he is found out, just as he is in business.

Now through long years of this railroad interference in public affairs in many states, these railroad attorneys have brought the honest business of railroading into disrepute that is undeserved. The attorneys have of course covered their tracks; the people today do not see things in their real relations, and the operating and traffic departments get the blame. They are the visible heads. They get the cracks. And what is more they have to do the "fighting back." So there you are . . . So long as the railroads are in politics, they must not object to the people running the railroads. The railroads cannot name senators, pack state conventions, run legislatures and boss politics generally with passes, and then successfully maintain that they are private concerns doing a private business. So long as there are Harrimans and Goulds [E. H. Harriman and Jay Gould, powerful railroad magnates] there will be LaFollettes and Tillmans [Robert M. LaFollette and Ben Tillman, United States senators demanding curbs on the railroads]. One breeds the other . . . I wish with all my heart that the Santa Fe could in some way dissociate itself from the Gould-Harriman power-seeking railroad gang in the minds of the people. If I can help I shall . . . But so long as railroad politicians can bribe their way into politics with passes, the railroad question will be be-

[69]

fore the people. When the railroad politicians get out of politics, the shippers and the real railroad men will settle matters in short order. Do what you please with this long letter, and believe me—

A few days after the following letter was written, White editorially stated that the Republican party bosses who served special interests must be defeated. He observed that "When the party does a worthy thing, the Gazette praises it; when the party sneaks and sells out to the boodlers—the Gazette says so, and is not mealy-mouthed about it. For he is the best partisan who exposes the rogues who try to capture his party, and he is the worst patriot who allows his party's interests to weigh more heavily than his country's."

To Governor E. W. Hoch, May 23, 1906

My Dear Ed Hoch:

. . . I had such high hopes of you as governor. I don't think that I ever asked anything of you that you ever refused me in all of our lives together here as neighbors and friends. I do not remember that you ever printed an unkind word about me, and I remember many kind ones, and yet I feel that if I have any duty in the world it is to criticize honestly things you have done which seem to me against the public policy, or things left undone that would promote the general good. It is hard for me to say right square out and brutally that you have done many things of that sort. I know you have been honest in thinking you are right. I know you have never been influenced by crooked motives, nor by selfish ones. Feeling that perhaps I was wrong in condemning you, and that your course was right, I went to three other men for advice. Two of them are active newspaper men—men who have been Ed Hoch men for twenty years, and have been conspicuous in their friendship for you, and who are now supporting the Republican ticket in their papers. The first man who has a state reputation wrote that he had high hopes of Ed Hoch, he was so clean and seemed so fine and strong when he went into office, but that what he had done was disappointing and made him sad . . . The second editor, who like me is a neighbor and has been for a generation never asked a favor of you—that I ever heard of—and he said: "Will—is it possible we have been overestimating him all along? Is it possible that he has not the wisdom and strength that we gave him credit for?" This man is a good Republican; he is supporting the ticket yet he tells me that never since 1890 has there been such defection from the Republican ticket as there is in his county this year. He says that this defection is not among the irresponsible, but among conservative farmers and business men. The third man of whom I speak is an old man, but a man of culture and refinement. He has no personal grievance but I know he looked forward to great things from your administration. He is so bitter in his disappointment that I cannot tell you what he said. You would be astounded to know the names of these men. But what they said was in confidence, and for my own guidance, and you must trust to the fact that I don't lie except on strong provocation—as the fellow said—to know that I am telling you the truth.

Yet the situation is not hopeless. You still can do something. The people like you; they believe you are honest, but they believe that you lack strength . . . The people feel that you have considered the good of the Republican party first and the good of the state second. What the Republicans of Kansas want to feel is that they have a governor who would gladly send the Republican party straight to hell if the interests of the people of Kansas and the enforcement of the laws of Kansas demand it. You would not be afraid to say that on the stump, yet when it comes down to acting, the fellows get around you and talk you out of acting.

I sit in my office and go on the street and hear these things. The people are mad—not shouting quarrelling mad, but mad clear through, and if you do not do something to convince them that the man at the nominal head of the party in Kansas, is the real head of the party, the people will defeat the party, because they will think that the real head is the Leland, Kelly, Albaugh, Mulvane combine [bosses of the conservative faction of the Republican party], and the people won't stand for it.* Talk won't do. You must act. You must cut loose and be master of the situation. So sure are the people that you are a mere tool that they accept it as foregone that the railroads will make you appoint Curtis [Charles Curtis, former congressman elected to the

* White had now broken with his old friend Cyrus Leland and was helping organize progressive Republicans to secure control of the party.

[71]

United States Senate in 1907] for senator and the people feel that you can be talked into anything by those who have selfish interest to promote. I am trying to tell you the truth as I hear it, though it would be lots easier to flatter you and lie to you. You have been too good to me for that. And the simple truth is that unless you do something to change the situation, the major part of the Republican ticket will go down, and I fear you will go with it. It is up to you. . . .

President Roosevelt was White's ideal statesman. In "Roosevelt: A Force for Righteousness," McClure's Magazine, February, 1907, White published the views mentioned in the early part of this letter.

To THEODORE ROOSEVELT, August 8, 1906

MY DEAR PRESIDENT ROOSEVELT:

. . . There has been something in my crop for a month or so, and I have been about to write to you about it several times, but always you seemed so busy that I disliked to bother you . . . I don't believe a fellow is much of a friend of yours who writes pieces even remotely hinting that you might run in 1908. I have had it in mind to write this kind of an article: Talk of President Roosevelt for a second term in 1908 is unfortunate: first because it assumes him insincere, and second because the country should not have him for president during the next term. He has been president or will have been president in March 1909 seven years and a half. During that time he has led the country in lines of civic righteousness further than any American leader has led it, but also more closely. If we are to get any real benefit from that leadership we should not lean on it. We should begin to try at least to walk alone. Four more years of Roosevelt might make us too dependent upon him, because essentially what every real good he has done must be as a permanent influence upon American political and social life. And if seven years of President Roosevelt can't permanently impress that influence on the people—eleven consecutive years will only make us flabbier and flabbier, for the fault is in the people. I have not written this article, which I should place in the Post (Philadelphia) or McClure's, because I have feared that the fact that you have been kind to me would lend color in certain quarters to the charge that I was merely flattering you, which of course is not my intention. But it seems to me something of that sort should be said. I don't know whether I am the one to say it or not—what do you think?

I see that Secretary Taft [William Howard Taft, secretary of war] is coming West—to Kansas. We shall be glad to have him, and personally I am immensely interested in him. I hope that the opportunity may come to me to meet him where I may become acquainted with him. I note what you say of LaFollette [Robert M. LaFollette, former progressive governor of Wisconsin and now in the Senate] in your recent letter. I never met LaFollette, and have no sort of definite opinion of him. But you speak by the card. I presume he is ambitious. I presume he would like to be president. As I stand now (on the first ballot) I am agin him. Bryan can beat Fairbanks [C. W. Fairbanks, the vice-president] and I fear that he would defeat Mr. Root [Elihu Root, secretary of state]. If Secretary Taft learns the Kansas language as you learned it eight years ago, Kansas will be for him, but he must be mighty "keerful" as there is the devil to pay and no pitch out here this year. Fellow said to the local committeeman in 1899—the Jerry Simpson year [colorful Populist congressman]—"Jim, how is the situation down in Marion county?" And Jim rubbed his chin for a minute and said: "Well, I tell you; I guess it's mostly just situation!"

That's the way it is in Kansas this year. If you care to know about it, I'll lay it out to you, but I have no desire to spoil the fishing at Oyster Bay for a little matter like Kansas politics. But I am very happy, and seem for the first time in my life to be of some use in the world. . . .

The campaign of 1906 found Kansas bubbling over with the new issues of the day. President Roosevelt, Robert M. LaFollette, and many others stirred the people over the menace of corporation control of American politics. The followers of Roosevelt in Kansas—

[73]

*White, Joseph L. Bristow and W. R. Stubbs—tried to wrest control
of the party from the machine politicians who were backing Charles
Curtis for the United States Senate. According to the Topeka Capital,
July 5, 1906, "Old Bill White is taking the fire out of the standpat,
mole-eyed party organs and not batting an eye under their broad-
sides. It is such papers as the Emporia Gazette that make a party
worth its salt as a representative of honest, faithful government."*

To RALPH STOUT, Kansas City *Star*, August 9, 1906

MY DEAR STOUT:

It seems to me that the Star is overlooking an important side bet in
this Kansas situation. Unless I am fooled—and of course I may be
fooled—there is the blamedest explosion fizzing in the fuse out here
that the state has seen since 1890. It is the queerest thing I ever saw,
and not a line of it has got into any paper that I have seen. For instance I do not know a single Republican of my acquaintance who is
going to vote the straight Republican ticket. Yet on the other hand
I do not know a single Republican who can guess what part of the
ticket he will scratch. There is no talking on the street. There is no
temper displayed. Here I have been running a denatured Republican
paper—a kind of wide-open lidless sheet, and not a Republican in the
county has come to the office to abuse me; not a man on the county
ticket has told me that I was hurting his chances. So far as I can find
out not a man of the 4,500 daily and weekly subscribers of the paper
in Lyon county has stopped his paper because of its politics. Ordinarily in a campaign when I get "off" on a candidate or an issue, I
hear from it days and nights and Sundays. . . .

It seems to me that the Star is missing some good stuff by not sending a man out to report this thing. LaFollette came to Kansas and
talked all kinds of hot news stuff—even though it was at Chautauqua,
and not a line was reported adequately in any of the papers. Yet by
word of mouth it has gone all over the state, and the people are
quoting LaFollette. It is a big movement, which may quiet down
before the election, but it is certainly worth handling. And the Star
is the only paper with newspaper sense enough to get it. . . . An organization is forming at Topeka looking to the organization of those
members of the legislature who are against corporate control of affairs. It will really be an anti-Curtis League, and before the Senatorial

[74]

contest ends that league will be pledged to deadlock the Senatorial election rather than vote for Curtis. It is in the air, but it isn't in the Star. There is no doubt but that Bristow, Benson and Stubbs will unite against Curtis, and when the union is made—and it is forming through this Square Deal League right now, there will be the devil to pay. There never was a time when Kansas needed the real God's truth about politics, and when they got so little of it. I am not knocking. I am trying to suggest.

Of course this letter is not for publication. It is nothing to me whether the story is told or not. But it is a corking good story, and someone should record it.

On November 28, 1906, Theodore Roosevelt wrote to White that he had seen the proofs of White's forthcoming article, "Roosevelt: A Force for Righteousness." The President observed that, "there is one thing which I do not like, and that is your even by implication assuming that I or my friends could think of my position as being in any shape or way akin to that of Washington or Lincoln or Franklin—the men of the great crises, the men who I think we can truthfully say are great figures in the history of the world—I am not in the least concerned as to whether I will have any place in history—I want to be a straight and decent man and do good service. . . ."

To THEODORE ROOSEVELT, December 4, 1906

MY DEAR PRESIDENT ROOSEVELT:

. . . Now about your "place in history." All you say about the inconsequence of it I agree with, but for a century or ten times that a good strong man has an influence in making others like himself. That I believe we call greatness. In that you will be great, it seems to me. It is shameful to write this to your face, but so long as the matter is under discussion, we may as well waive your natural shame—as lawyers do that of their witnesses in court. It seemed to me wise to give you all the credit due you—(not to please *you:* I don't care what you think about the article as president, only as you are a friend and a fellow craftsman)—but to influence others toward righteousness, by pointing out the value of decency. I have no more desire to have a place in literature than you have to have a place in history. But I want to count for decency in my trade, just as you do in yours, and I can do it by praising good men moderately and justly, better than by criticizing bad men. When it happens that one of the good men happens to be my friend, and a publisher sends him the advance sheets of my story unbeknownst to me, I want to tell you in confidence that I am just as much abashed as he is!

Trusting this may find you the same I beg to remain— .

The progressive Republicans of Kansas lost their fight to prevent the legislature from electing Charles Curtis to the Senate. They went on, however, in the next few years to elect a number of progressives and secure the passage of a great deal of forward-looking legislation, particularly the direct primary and an anti-pass law.

To Henry J. Allen, Wichita, Kan., January 15, 1907

My Dear Henry:

When they telephoned to the hotel that Curtis's vote was sixty, I reached in behind Ike's grip on the dresser and got my hair brush, grabbed my pajamas from the wardrobe, put them in my valise, shut it with a decisive click, and went out under the eternal stars to think. I wondered how it was that I could feel as cheerful, even as frivolous as I felt. I caught myself whistling, which seemed a shameful thing to do, and I am sincerely glad that you and Joe and Stubbs [Joseph L. Bristow and W. R. Stubbs] did not hear me. I bore up all the way home, and sang a frivolous tune as I shaved the next morning. I had to work up a rage when I wrote my few sensible remarks for the Gazette, for fear my friends in town would think I had come home the slave of the money power. I was tired—bodily and spiritually weary, and was honestly glad that Providence, which seems to have

[76]

some use for Curtis, got it over with so soon. I was—and am, for that matter—sensibly grateful that this thing occurred without any messy sticky scandal, and without any gentleman having his virtue tampered with, as might have been the case if a long-drawn-out contest had ended in the election of Curtis.

These preliminary remarks are written to show you that I am reasonably calm. I am really hoping the best for the injun [Charles Curtis] but my judgment tells me—or is it my prophetic soul?—that he has been lifted up this way for no good end, but only to be used as an object lesson to teach the people their danger and their weakness under the present system of American politics. The people are slow to wrath, but when they are once convinced they move with directness and force. It took thousands of lives to settle the slavery question; should we complain seriously if Kansas has to sacrifice a senator to the cause of industrial evolution? Some way it will all work out for the ultimate good. I have unlimited faith in the justice of things. But my faith does not bind my hands, and I feel it a fearful duty and obligation to keep fighting for the end that seems right.

So it seems to me that it is your duty and that of every man who does not wish to compromise with wrong in this situation to unite to fight for those things which will take power out of the hands of men whose object it is merely to win the game for themselves or their friends, and put it into the hands of the people. I believe that so long as politics is played under the present rules of the present game, Mort and Jim and Dave and Cy [Morton Albaugh, James Simpson, David Mulvane, and Cyrus Leland, bosses of the standpat wing of the Kansas Republican Party] will win. There is no hope for any better condition so long as you have conventions to nominate officers and legislatures to nominate senators. Also there is little hope so long as M. A. Low and Joe Richards [railroad attorneys] have the power to issue passes; for though officers may not be bought to violate their oaths by passes, men *not* in office can be bought by passes to give officials bad advice, and the result is the same. It was men on passes in Topeka nagging at members of the legislature who nominated Curtis.

Now, it seems to me that you should join the hell raisers. By that I don't mean that you should work with Stubbs, but I do mean that every paper which you are interested in and all the weight of your personal influence should be thrown in favor of this direct primary law and for an anti-pass law. It will cost us all some money, but has God been good enough to you and me for us to give something to

[77]

help our state rise above a disgrace like that which has come upon it? You and I both know that if we had our deserts we would be in far different stations from those we occupy today. Then why shouldn't we show our gratitude to the power outside ourselves that has guided us away from the consequences of our own weaknesses and errors to return to that power something that will help the current move onward? Mort and Jim and Dave are good fellows. I hate to offend them. And I know how you feel about them, but we owe more to the great power outside ourselves that has made us all that we are, has given us happy loving families which we don't deserve, than we owe to Mort and Jim Simpson and Grant Hornaday and the fellows. And what is more, as sure as there is a God, which we both believe in, if we forget him now, when we are old, he will forget us. Deathbed repentance may get a man to Heaven, but it won't keep a man from peddling life insurance and harloting around for a clerkship of some miserable commission when he is past sixty. In all the history of Kansas the sort of men who forget their obligations to humanity in their youth and manhood are the scarred-face, bleareyed political strumpets who hang around Topeka in their elder days all but begging for bread. You and I are not smarter than they. We can't beat the game, and clear up our winnings and get out whole after we are sixty, any more than they could. . . .

The political power of the "malefactors of great wealth" was slowly revealed to the public in these progressive days. Lincoln Steffens, Ida Tarbell, and Ray Stannard Baker were describing something of this in their muckraking articles in McClure's. *Upton Sinclair,* The Money Changer (*1908*), *and Thomas Lawson,* Frenzied Finance (*1904*), *also threw light on this problem. The American public was beginning to realize that certain business groups were corrupting politics in order to make sure that politicians granted the favors desired by these vested interests.*

To Theodore Roosevelt, January 26, 1907

My Dear President Roosevelt:

... I am enclosing herewith an editorial from the Gazette on Curtis, which I beg of you to read. There is much in connection with his election, and with numerous other Senatorial elections, of which I would like to talk to you. It seems to me while you are going into the matter of Mr. Harriman's [E. H. Harriman, railroad manipulator]* financial transactions, disclosing his monstrous power in the business world, a correlating examination into his dangerous un-American system of political control, centered in New York City, might also be quietly instituted. It seems to me that the people have the right to know not merely how their senators and representatives vote, but *why* they vote on certain measures the way they do vote. It seems to me that it is as much a national duty to tear the court plaster off the railroad brand on a senator ... as it is a government duty to stockholders to show them how their interests are being jeopardized by unscrupulous manipulators like Harriman. For the impudence of Harriman as a commercial pirate is based largely on his belief that when you are out of the way his political system will leave him undisturbed in his piracy.

You might show the people before you go, just how Harriman's financial system is dependent upon the success of his political system. The records of the political bureau in New York would astound America, as much as the records of the lard syndicate in Chicago would have astounded the people if they might have been exposed in the courts at Chicago.

Fighting Bob LaFollette toured Kansas in 1906 at White's invitation, stirring enthusiasm for progressive fires. Victor Murdock, editor of the Wichita Eagle, *was the most prominent Kansas progressive in Washington. In 1909–10, he was a leader in the fight to check the powers of standpat Speaker Cannon of the House of Representatives.*

* When the government launched an investigation of a railroad monopoly in 1903, Harriman was reported to have said that if he wanted state legislation he could buy it, and that he could buy Congress and the judiciary as well.

*White wrote a similar letter about Murdock to Theodore Roosevelt
on the same day as the LaFollette letter.*

To R. M. LaFollette, February 16, 1907

My Dear Senator Bob:

Help Victor Murdock, congressman, from the Eighth Kansas District—Wichita—where you spoke the last night in Kansas. He has a bill that will cut off five million in stealings from the railroads in the weighing of government mails. Please look him up; talk to him; and if he is crucified in the House, as I fear he will be, please revive his bill in the Senate.

The seed you sowed is bearing fruit in Kansas. Though the railroads elected the Senator we are in a fair way to get our anti-pass laws through. The lower House, which was elected through your efforts, has done great work. The holdover Senate is the only force that is holding us back. But we elect a Senate next year, and the people are aroused. We are thoroughbreds and shall keep up the fight.

In the meantime help Murdock. He is being snubbed and boycotted, and reviled by the machine, but he has a righteous cause.

If after speaking to Murdock you should mention the matter to the President, you need not mention me unless you think it wise.

*In March, 1907, Senator W. E. Borah and a number of the officers
of the Barber Lumber Company were indicted by a Federal Grand
Jury for timber frauds. The leaders of the Republican machine in
Idaho were behind Borah's indictment. Borah wanted a speedy trial,
but he was worried because some of his political enemies were in
charge of the enforcement of federal law in Idaho. Borah asked
White to go to Washington and urge President Roosevelt to send a
special prosecutor for the trial. White went to Roosevelt, and a special prosecutor was sent to Idaho. The trial lasted for ten days. The
jury was out fourteen minutes. Its verdict was "Not guilty." On*

[80]

June 15, 1908, President Roosevelt removed the district attorney and the federal marshal who had been responsible for the "persecution" of Borah. In 1917, White wrote Borah that "I have always felt that the best single day's work I ever did in my life, was that day I put in for you down at Oyster Bay."

To W. E. BORAH, April 17, 1907

MY DEAR BILLY BORAH:

I saw a little twenty line item in the Kansas City Times this morning to the effect that you were going to have your case reviewed by the attorney general and then I hastened to find the Boise Statesman (Saturday morning's) and read all about it. And now I see by a Socialist paper that the Socialists claim credit for the business. I am sending you herewith the Socialist paper. It seems important to me that the President should see that. I know nothing at all of the case nor of the charges, Billy, but you know that I am for you and with you. I want you to feel as free to call on me as I would be to call on you. . . .

Tell Mrs. Borah—God bless her—that Mrs. White and I are with her. You are a big brute of a man, and it really doesn't make so much difference, but she will feel it, and Billy, Billy, it is really for her that Mrs. White and I are anxious today.

The older I get, and the more I am blessed, the more I see that I am not responsible for my good fortune, the more I feel in the core of my heart that there is a God—some great force outside ourselves who moves the checkers, and puts us in the king row or out of it. I believe that in the great crises of our lives if we turn to that force that holds the stars in their courses, it will leave us with it, and I believe that always it protects the innocent and the good. So I believe you will come through and with all my heart I believe it, because your suffering would be her suffering, and the Lord is mindful of his own.

I have no wish to preach in this letter, Billy. I am a member of no church, I do not even go to church, and I am as you know very well, a mighty weak, miserable critter, full of the devil and all that. But I know that the Fate that has been so kind to me will be good to you, and if I can be an instrument in the hands of Fate to help you—you know how I can help. Tell me—direct me. And above all don't feel that any friend in the world has gone back on you, nor any honest man changed his high estimate of you.

MY DEAR PRESIDENT ROOSEVELT:

Enclosed you will find two letters and a newpaper clipping. One letter is important. It is a letter from United States Senator W. E. Borah of Idaho, which is submitted without consulting him, and absolutely without his knowledge, even though in doing so I may be violating a confidence. But I can find no better way to get his matter before you than this. And also, that you may more exactly understand Borah's letter to me, and fully discount my prejudice in his favor, it is but fair that you should have a copy of my letter to Borah which called forth his letter to me.

One word further: I knew Borah in the Kansas State University twenty years ago. We were in many classes together, and surely there he was a clean upright man. In Idaho he has stood for the best things, so far as I know, or ever have heard ... I know that you will give me this friend's privilege, *when I do not seek in any way to impress my view on you.* For you know all the evidence against him, and I know nothing. But I know this about Borah personally. Nearly four years ago through ignorant inadvertence, I got over the legal dead line, and when I found out what I had done, I turned to Borah for advice. Clear as a bell came back the answer, and when I had followed his advice I first dropped the entire matter, and second made a record which would have convicted me before the law, but which would have persuaded any fair-minded man that I was morally blameless. I contend that a lawyer who would advise a lumber company to break the law would have advised me to evade it. Obviously it would be absurd for me to offer you an opinion in this matter. I know nothing of the facts—that is of the evidence and nothing of Borah save what I have just told you. But on the other hand, it has seemed to me that his letter revealed so much of a man that it should be submitted to you entirely to add to what other exhibits you may have, to determine your action or that of Attorney General Bonaparte in passing on Borah's case.

The clipping I am sending you contains a marked article corroboratory of my view of the Borah case, and on the reverse side of the

[82]

sheet you will find a statement from your friend Mr. Debs [Eugene Debs, Socialist leader and critic of Roosevelt], which may give you a pleasant hour in an otherwise cheerless life. You might read the Debs article to the Cabinet and put it to a vote whether you should resign or be hanged. Personally I prefer hanging, but that is on account of my western traditions, and is a mere matter of taste upon which I shall not insist.

Trusting that I have not intruded in this matter, and that Borah's letter may be returned when you have finished with it, I beg to remain—

White devoted a good deal of his time to the problems of the University of Kansas. As the following letter to a fellow member of the Board of Regents reveals, White was troubled by the lack of spiritual and philosophical attitudes in higher education. The crass materialism of America—its emphasis on money as the end of life—was a worry to him throughout his lifetime.

To Scott Hopkins, June 7, 1907

My Dear Scott:

I don't want you to answer this letter until you have thought it over for some time, and have talked it over with Mrs. Hopkins and with anyone else who you think will give you any light on the subject. I have been a long time coming to the point of writing, and you should take your own time to answer.

My trouble is this: I cannot get away from a strong definite unpleasant impression that the University is growing too materialistic—too gross, too worldly, if you will allow the secular use of the phrase. It seems to me—to state the proposition conversely—that the University does not consider its spiritual place in Kansas so much as it considers its bald physical bigness. The talk at the University dinner will illustrate. It was all of buildings, attendance, of appropriations, of influence for more buildings, for more students, for more appropria-

[83]

tions, world without end. It was larger salaries, and God knows what of a carnal spirit that pervaded the atmosphere. To me it was vulgar, cheap and immoral. You know I have always voted for larger salaries. I believe that salaries should be increased to three or four thousand dollars for heads of departments. Also I believe in more buildings, and I would like to see the attendance run into the thousands, but only as a means to an end. To my notion—my earnest conviction, is better—we desire more buildings, better salaries, and more students, that the University may become a powerful agent in the spiritualization of this commonwealth. It is not, according to my notion, important that we turn out two hundred and fifty students graduated from the course. But it is important, it seems to me, that we should turn out two hundred and fifty young men and women who will help to make Kansas a cleaner, decenter, more livable state, more livable in that its citizens see the folly of piling up unnecessary riches, and see the wisdom of neighborly kindness and gentility toward one another. We have come out of the nineteenth century loaded with material things: mines, commerce, invention, and all the clubfooted gods have been at work piling up wealth. But piling it up inequitably. Only institutions like ours can breed a public sentiment that will make men and women wise with kindness and charity, who may attack that pile of wealth, and distribute it fairly among the people of the next generation and the next. But, if our boys and girls hear on state occasions from the head of our State University, nothing but glorification of our crass material progress as a state and as a State University, what in Heaven's name are they to care whether the inheritance of the nineteenth century is spiritualized in equitable laws and customs growing out of gentle Christlike hearts, or whether the devil takes the hindermost. As it stands we are told that money makes a university. Money naturally is important. But the University of Kansas under Marvin and Lippincott [former chancellors of the university] graduated men and women who five and ten years after their graduation amounted to more in Kansas than the newer graduates of the University have amounted to during the decade and a quarter just past.

We are turning out lawyers and doctors and engineers and drug clerks, and what not of butchers, bakers, and candlestick makers, who as such of course are needed in the world, but they are also needed as something more. They are needed as cultured men and women, whose devotion to "reason and the will of God" will be needed to solve honestly and fairly the problems that are growing big on our horizon. If the educated men and women of this country do not contribute their enlightenment and influence to the cause of justice, there will be sad times for all of us.

But how in Heaven's name are they to get any idea of any duty they have to their fellows in society, if all they hear at the State University is that we are so damned fat and big and powerful that we are going to be bigger and fatter and more powerful, so that eventually we will be the fattest, biggest, most powerful school in the West.

I write to you, and to no one else on the Board, because someway I believe you will understand my viewpoint. I do not think the case is at all hopeless. But I do think it needs serious, unfaltering attention. I do not think it is anything that the regents can do as a board; yet I believe that some of us—I can't say just who—should take the matter up, and work on it.

I am perfectly willing to do my part. But I do not feel I should work alone, partly because I fear that nothing would be accomplished, but chiefly because I am not sure that I have a correct view of the situation. You may use this letter as you will, and when you have concluded what is best, command me. I am especially anxious to know how Mrs. Hopkins feels in this matter.

White threw all his power behind the campaign of Joseph L. Bristow for United States senator. The incumbent, Chester Long, was a conservative whereas Bristow was a "righteous" progressive. White wrote articles for the Gazette, *the* Kansas City Star, *and many other Kansas papers to aid Bristow's cause. He also helped organize workers all over the state. The Long-Bristow contest was a fight within the Republican party for control of that party's machinery. The progressive wing emerged triumphant with the election of Bristow as senator and W. R. Stubbs as governor.*

[85]

My Dear Tom Johnston:

I have been trying for ten days to get down to Kansas City to talk to you and the folks about the Kansas Senatorial situation. There is always a "situation" in Kansas, and this particular one seems to need attention. Bristow can win this fight, with the Star back of him. Without it, Long will win. The people do not like Long. The sentiment of the state is overwhelmingly against Long, but for some reason the people have acquired an unreasoning prejudice against Bristow. They do not think he is crooked. They do not believe he is tied up to any interests, but they do believe he is "cold" and that is a worse sin than dishonesty. Given a good warm campaign for Bristow by the Star, and he can win. The people in the country are for him, and all he needs is a little newspaper ginger. He is out making speeches all the time, and is really making headway. But he lacks steam, and there you are.

I would like to write a series of "pieces" about Bristow for the Gazette and the Star, and would like to begin with a kind of two-column character sketch some Sunday, say next Sunday. I could have the copy in a day before if you cared for it. I am perfectly willing to do anything I can and what the Star desires for Bristow. I have no other interest whatever, but I do want to help.

Think it over, and talk it over with the folks and let me hear from you.

To Congressman Victor Murdock, Washington, D. C.,
April 29, 1908

My Dear Victor:

Life is a gorgeously beautiful thing. The kaleidoscope of events is forever turning men upside down, and topside under into such interesting heaps and such grotesque piles that it is one of God's great blessings to look at them through interested and withal loving eyes.

These philosophical reflections came to me after your letter came, a week after two wounded doe letters from Scott and Dan Anthony [Charles Scott and Dan Anthony, two conservative Kansas congressmen whom White was opposing for re-election]. For Dan I am sorry. I wouldn't hurt him for the world. I like him and believe that he will come "to" after a while and be one of the folks. As for Scott, he has become completely blinded to real conditions in Kansas, and seems to have lost whatever vision he once had, and will have to come back and live with the people a while to get his eyesight back. What a remarkable fable that was about Nebuchadnezzar going out to grass for nine years. Gosh—Victor—every king, potentate, princeling and power has to get to grass every so often or he loses his efficiency. The American Congress as it is now constituted needs to go to grass terribly bad. . . .

Always with Joseph L. Bristow, White was devastatingly frank. During Bristow's six-year term in the Senate, White frequently told him that he was too "cold" and did not know how to advertise himself. While in the Senate, Bristow was an able, conscientous progressive, but he never obtained the nation-wide popularity of men like Robert M. LaFollette and Albert J. Beveridge. White skillfully built the "cold" Bristow up in the 1908 campaign as being "against sin." As part of this procedure, White brought Fighting Bob LaFollette and Ida M. Tarbell to Kansas to speak in Bristow's behalf.

To Joseph L. Bristow, May 4, 1908

My Dear Joe:

I am convinced that you are wrong, dead wrong on your proposition not to have a joint debate with Long. While it is true that you are doing some good up in the Sixth District and down in the Seventh, and in spots here in the Fourth, also in the Fifth, still as a state proposition you are not getting anywhere. You are simply not in the fight before anything but the limited audiences to which you speak. I have cast my fortunes with you. I believe that you will make an ideal senator, but you don't seem to consider my advice at all.

I wrote to the Star last week—to Tommy Johnston—and told him that with the Star you could win this fight, and asked him to begin as soon as possible. He replied that after talking with Colonel Nelson

[W. R. Nelson, the publisher of the *Star*] he did not believe you were in the fight, and that the Star did not want to do anything to antagonize Long. There you are. You will find that all over the Third District and all over the River counties they think that you are Long's stool pigeon. The Senatorial race is dead. You make a loud noise and the roaring in your head makes you think there is something doing, but there isn't.

You have got to appeal to the state. You don't appeal to the state for a minute. You are appealing only to the districts where you go, and after you leave it all dies down.

The story is generally circulated and firmly believed by men who hate Long that you and Long have an agreement by which he is to go into the cabinet at your suggestion if you win, and if he wins you are to be made postmaster general. This story of course circulates because you have done no single thing to attract the attention of the whole state to the fact that you are in earnest in your race against Long. It seems to me that it is absolutely necessary for you to win, first to challenge Long to debate; second to dent that story explicitly and in terms, declaring that if defeated you will accept nothing at Long's hands, and that if the people of Kansas retire him you will not recommend him for any public office; third to print his record in pamphlet form, and circulate it.

Now as regards what the Star will do. They have said that they will print anything I write about you with the understanding that whatever is written about Long will have an equal show, and I am going to get up a "character sketch" of you for next Sunday's paper. It will be three columns of my very best stuff, and I am going to manifold it and ask the Eagle [Wichita *Eagle*] and the Topeka Capital to take it also.

Also I have taken up through Miss Tarbell the matter of borrowing [illegible] thousand dollars from a wealthy philanthropist named Crane [Charles R. Crane] of Chicago, and have asked him to come out here and investigate the situation. The matter is still in the air. I have not pushed the matter with Morrill [E. N. Morrill, former governor of Kansas] and shall not until I hear from Crane. Then I shall go after something nearer home.

But in the meantime, Joe, I do wish you would not be so blamed sure of yourself. I wish you would realize that Henry Allen and I have a view of this matter that you do not have. And also I wish you would show some evidence of the fact that you think that Henry and I are worthy of some consideration.

[88]

The following is an excellent example of the delightful type of reminiscing letter that White occasionally wrote to his old friends. It is also a splendid example of his admirable style and fundamental human quality.

To DALE MESSMAN, June 1, 1908

MY DEAR DALE:

I have been very busy since your letter came and you don't know how often it has been on my mind. It has brought back a thousand pleasant memories of our childhood that have not seen the light of recollection for a good many years. Your letter brought back the old days along the river when we used to go fishing north of the old North Bridge and under the middle bridge, fishing for Sunnies and Silver Sides with pin hooks and thread lines and pawpaw poles. I remember that we used to go fishing up north of the old bridge on what was after called the Flat Bottom swimming hole. I remember your Aunt used to go with us and I can see her yet holding her pole and flopping her hook in the water in her awkward way.

I remember your grandmother too who lived across the middle bridge; I remember we used to play among the grapevines in the old timber before the brush was cut out. And I remember the pokeberry patch in the corner of the fence where we used to get berries and make red ink. Lord! how it used to smell. I can smell it yet. And I can remember the stick horse livery stable we used to keep. I wonder if you can remember all those things. That was thirty-five years ago more or less and here we have been wandering over the earth apart and now all those things seem as vivid as if they were yesterday.

I am sending you my paper free. Your money is no good. Write to me sometimes, and if you want to please me vote in the August primary for Bristow and Stubbs. Write to me sometimes. I remain very sincerely—

About that paper of mine: I am only sending it to you to get even on an old debt. You gave me the measles when we were boys. I am sending you the Gazette to pay for it!

[89]

White reported the Republican convention at Chicago, which nom-
inated William Howard Taft for the presidency. The principles of
Roosevelt—The Square Deal—seemed to dominate the Republican
party, and yet within two years the party was split asunder between
the progressives and the standpatters. Roosevelt replied to White's
letter that "I enjoyed your letter so much, and was so pleased with
it, and laughed over it so much, that I sent it on to my sister, after first
submitting it to Mrs. Roosevelt. . . ."

To THEODORE ROOSEVELT, June 23, 1908

MY DEAR PRESIDENT ROOSEVELT:

I have just returned from Chicago where I had a string of thirty papers . . . and did what I could for the good of the order. I am sending you herewith enclosed an editorial which is having some vogue out here . . . I took some joy in writing it in the hope that you would find some comfort in reading it.

For I really owe you a great deal. First I owe you a debt of gratitude for being a great and good president, but that is mere detail. They are common enough. Taft will be one after you are gone. So we will let that pass, but the especial thing for which I desire to thank you is for being brother to so fine an American woman as Mrs. Robinson, beside whom the good Lord or Harry New [chairman of the Republican National Committee] sat me at the Chicago convention, and made my otherwise lonely watch in Chicago without Mrs. White, a real comfort, approaching as nearly joy as any man should approach, six hundred miles from Sallie and Bill and Mary. I have been given to understand by kind and loving friends that we do not agree on all the points of the compass, and while you may not wish to subscribe to my belief that you are the greatest man in the world, and I may not care to go with you into your mad blind unreasonable infatuation for Uncle Joe [Joseph Cannon, speaker of the House],* we will still stand together on the platform that Mrs. Douglas Robinson is a credit to her sex, and on that platform go before a disrupted party and a radical nation, and defy either Burrows [Julius Caesar Burrows, conservative Republican senator from Michigan]

* White was obviously jesting with Roosevelt for working with the reactionary speaker.

[90]

or LaFollette to disprove it. Personally since I have had a White House meal ticket, the presidential job has not looked alluring to me. But I never had a sister, and if it was put up to me to say what was the most distinguished act of your useful life, I should say that being born brother to your two sisters was the finest, longest-headed piece of work you ever did, except to marry Mrs. Roosevelt and that of course was probably sheer luck, for which you deserve no credit, as you do for choosing your sisters.

There is to be no politics in this letter. This is my moulting season politically, and I don't look pretty. Anyway I had some feathers picked out of my neck by one of our mutual friends and you wouldn't care to see me. But I do hope you are happy and that you realize fully just how many days it will be until March Fourth when the sun will shine for the big man! We may be happy yet, perhaps!

What a fine speech was that of Senator Lodge at the convention!* It was one of the big speeches in American history and it marks an epoch in the advance of American political thought. Not so much by what he said, for it had been said before many times, but by the way he said it, by the place where it was said and by the way it was received. What a privilege it is to live in a country that almost to a man endorses that kind of gospel. While I believe that in the end LaFollette will lick Burrows, using the men as types, yet it does not matter so much after all, so long as both agree fundamentally with Lodge, using him also as a type. This is my cheerful morning, and I am trying to pass it on, as the boy said when he pinched the fellow next to him.

To Theodore Roosevelt, August 15, 1908

My Dear President Roosevelt:

In your good letter of August 11, you ask is Kansas safe for Taft. My judgment is that Kansas is safe for Taft as the matter now stands. There is no Bryan enthusiasm in Kansas. The Democrats have no ginger in their fight. Their state ticket is impossible and their Congressional ticket is absurd. Moreover our state and Congressional tickets are strong and we have just passed through a vigorous primary contest, and we are in fighting trim. Stubbs, the gubernatorial candidate,

* Henry Cabot Lodge made an address, as permanent chairman, praising the accomplishments of Roosevelt, which received a long ovation.

[91]

and Bristow are advocating your policies out of both sides of their mouths. The trouble with Long was that he talked Roosevelt policies out of one side of his mouth, and every time there was a Senate line-up by your enemies ... he voted and acted with Aldrich [Senator Nelson Aldrich of Rhode Island, who was the leader of the reactionary group in the Senate].* During the whole of last year, Long's record shows that he didn't vote away from Aldrich on a single important matter. Now this is not diverting matters from Taft, as you will see, but it leads up to the Taft situation in Kansas. Stubbs and Bristow, who talked your policies, and had no Aldrich records to make mockery of them, were nominated. Long was defeated, but his campaign, which was the strongest ever made in Kansas, gave the people an idea that Taft is with Long, that he is a conservative of the Aldrich type when it comes to actual votes and deeds. . . .

Long used every letter and every scrap of correspondence he had with Taft to show that Taft was for him, and as the people of Kansas are against Long they will have to get over the notion that Taft and Long stand for the same things, before Taft will be as strong as Stubbs and Bristow in Kansas. Stubbs and Bristow made no reference to Taft or to you in their campaign. They simply talked of the principles you stand for, and discussed them as issues on their merits, not as your policies or Taft's or anyone's but as fundamental truths, and so it happened that Stubbs and Bristow won without claiming any personal connection whatever with you or with Taft, and Long lost, claiming personal connection with you and Taft, but with a record against the issues which you have stood for. And in losing Long has hurt Taft, and there is no question about it. Long's recorded votes, always with Aldrich, when other Republican senators from the West were voting as they pleased, gave the people a bad impression when he claimed close political intimacy with Taft. Of course the claim was spurious. But for the moment the impression holds, and while I do not think it is deep or at all permanent, if there should be the least Bryan enthusiasm, it would make Kansas fightable ground. At present Kansas is for Taft.

I cannot see how any Bryan enthusiasm can come up. I cannot see how any turn may be taken which will make Kansas Democratic. Yet these are the facts, and you are entitled to know them. The Kansas situation is duplicated in Iowa, and in Nebraska, and in the Da-

* During the Long-Bristow primary, Norman Hapgood, editor of *Collier's*, charged that Long was attempting "to make Kansas a great conservative stronghold—a sort of western Rhode Island."

kotas. A situation much like it is found in Missouri and, the fellows say, it is duplicated in Illinois. Which means that the people are convinced that the Roosevelt policies are right, and that the people desire representatives who will put those policies into law, in good faith, and not representatives who are for Roosevelt out West and for Aldrich back in Washington.

So what is true of Kansas is true of this whole Middle West. It is for Taft as matters stand, and so far as I can see there is no likelihood of change. But the people who spend money in politics are trying to discourage progressive Republicanism out West, and would rather have Bryan and a Democratic Senatorial representative (which would merely bark and not bite), than Taft and a Republican Senatorial representation.

The Kansas City Journal, owned by the Santa Fe railroad, is an apt example of that tendency of the rich lawbreakers. Just now it is bolting Bristow, on the ground that Bristow is not with Taft. This bolt of course the Journal knows will not hurt Bristow, but it will hurt Taft whom the Journal praises for his reactionary virtues. This of course is futile now. It will not hurt anything. It merely shows the tendency of the men who are against the progress of good government. But if there should be a Bryan wave in October, this tendency all over the West might become dangerous. And if money can make a Bryan wave, there will be plenty of money on hand. For out here at least, the railroads are for Bryan, who will make a horrible example of reform, as against Taft, who will round out the work now begun. And particularly the moneyed interests are against the kind of Republicans who under the primary are becoming dominant out in the Mississippi valley. Pardon this long letter, and believe me—

Probably the most adequate expression of Roosevelt's philosophy, which White urged in this letter, is to be found in the speeches he delivered in 1912 while seeking the Republican nomination for the presidency. These have been collected in A Charter for Democracy.

My Dear President Roosevelt:

I see by the papers that you are working on your annual message. You will probably get a carload of letters about it, but I have had it in mind for a long time to write to you with a suggestion that is troubling me and will trouble me until it is out of my system. It is this: of course you have to include the usual routine business in your message, but it seems to me some place either in that message or in a special message you should make a sort of parting review, résumé, or what not of the political creed that has dominated you. The time has come in the history of this country when our public records should have for future historians a simple direct statement of the creed of the millions of Americans who are behind you (consciously or unconsciously) in the struggle to make this government more democratic, and less plutocratic.

Your message of January last*—I mean the stem-winder—barely escaped being a classic, but with all its strength it did escape because it was, unavoidably, cluttered with details, evidence, correspondence and what not of corroborative facts needed at the time but which broke the force of the message as an universal appeal.

It seems to me that before you go some such ideal message should be left behind, something that would go into literature and have a wider reading and therefore a more general influence than an ordinary public document. I realize that those things may not be made out of hand. There is, of course, the element of the man, the subject and the occasion, as there is in "true oratory." And yet it seems to me without making too obviously a farewell address, you should leave some one particular state paper embodying your confession of faith. It should not be over 3,000 words and would be better if it were 2,000 words long. But it should briefly sketch things as they were in the middle nineties, then outline simply the progress that has been made, and rise to some power in the expression of the hope of what in reason and in justice may be expected within the lives of those who are now in this fight.

Such a paper, without the clutter of unnecessary encyclopedic matter, might be properly a statement of the substance of things hoped for, and the evidence of things not seen. It might be issued

* Message to Congress on Jan. 31, 1908, in which Roosevelt demanded "the moral regeneration of business," urged private employers to adopt workmen's compensation, and criticized the abuses of the injunction in labor disputes.

in support of any particular measure which appealed to you—the income tax, child labor, postal savings banks, restricted capitalization of interstate commerce corporations, or any subject of that sort which seemed at the moment to need a boost. Or the document might preface your message to Congress of December 1st, though it seems to me that its entity might be lost in the big message. But in some place somehow, in some form, it seems to me that you should leave as a text for those of us who are to stay in the fight, your reason for being. You are the first president who has been on the job since Lincoln who had the gift of expression and it seems to me that you should not hide your talent in a napkin. . . .

If there is anything in the world that I can do to help let me know. I feel that Bryan is whipped, thoroughly whipped; and now it seems to me that it is the first duty of Republican friends of Judge Taft to bring to his support the moral backing of those men who blindly followed Bryan, without thinking of his stupendous folly, but who saw only that he was going ahead, and not pulling back. The danger that Judge Taft faces is that the course he may have to take will be too technically correct to appeal to the masses, and that his personality will not dramatize itself to the public so that they will make his cause theirs, in the conviction that he has made their cause his. The questions to be settled are so entirely technical, so nice in their adjustment, that it will strain democracy to its utmost to furnish public wisdom to see the truth and keep the demagogue's foot off the scales. You and Taft together might get the work done. But the best you can do for him is to leave for him in the minds of the people a direct, understandable statement of the case as it now stands and then—"with God be the rest."

Pardon this long letter, and believe me—

Politically White was elated over the election returns. Taft, Stubbs, and Bristow were successful. His satisfaction bubbles over in this letter to the President who was planning a safari to Africa after he left office. The conservatism of the courts, however, disturbed him amidst the otherwise seemingly progressive nature of the country. Roosevelt answered this letter by observing: "I had originally written what I had to say about the judges in far stronger form—There is altogether too much power in the bench."

[95]

MY DEAR PRESIDENT:

Thanksgiving day I read the advance copy of your message [Message to Congress on Dec. 8, 1908, in which Roosevelt criticized the courts for their conservative leanings] sent to the AP and it was like a letter from a long lost brother. The strawberry mark on the left arm that gave that fine electrical jolt to the reactionary courts was visible to the naked eye, and I was glad to know that your Heart is Still True! I shall sit up all night December 7th [?] to hear how the New York Sun "takes" it. I wish I had a million dollars. I would hire a ballet, and have those few brief sensible guarded remarks set to music and yipped and kiyoodled and yodled into the pretty pink ear of Brewer [Associate Justice Brewer, who opposed progressive regulation of business], and all his kith and kind. Lord, Lord, how we do need to make the courts serve our democracy. The only thing I would like to have political power for would be to name some judge who would hand down an opinion declaring that courts had only judicial and not political powers. And that the attempt to make them a part of the legislative system, giving them veto power over all state and national legislatures, is without warrant of authority in the constitution, and is the result of a gradual encroachment of power that in some day when the radicals sweep the country will be the only serious menace to our institutions. For God knows what would become of this country if it ever ran amuck and had all that power in the hands of the court, named by a man like Bryan. It is not that today the reactionaries use that power stupidly (for the people are learning the grace of patience that they need under the reactionary control); the danger to free government is of having that much unrestrained power in any branch of the government. They make laws by interpretation, and execute them by injunctions, while the executive and legislative branches of the government are powerless to protest, without being called to account for contempt of court.

Excuse this barbaric yelp! . . .

Here's wishing you a merry Christmas and a happy New Year and a glorious time [?] in the Jungle. I see they are afraid the boa constrictors will get you. If one tackles you, pull him apart! A man who has wintered with . . . Hale and Foraker and Cannon [Senator Eugene Hale of Maine, Senator J. B. Foraker of Ohio, and Speaker of the House Joseph Cannon] and the ladies of the war and navy departments has little to fear and nothing to learn about the ferocity or the duplicity of anything that walks.

Again thanking you for your message believe me—

White had been with Roosevelt in Washington, in September, 1901, shortly after McKinley's death occurred. White spent one of the first evenings of Roosevelt's presidency with the new president, who discussed his hopes and fears for the future.

To THEODORE ROOSEVELT, Oyster Bay, March, 1909

MY DEAR FRIEND:

I have been reading in the Associated Press reports today—yellow sheets typewritten that come across my desk—about the closing days of your administration, and my memory goes back to that first night in Washington at Captain Cowles's [Theodore Roosevelt's brother-in-law, at whose house Roosevelt stayed until Mrs. McKinley vacated the White House].

How much water has gone under the bridge since then! How well you have kept the faith. How true you have been to all you hoped and believed in that night. Of all the things you have done—and you have done so many—the best, it seems to me, is that you have lived so clean and so decently through it all that you have come out with the illusion of youth and of strength and of a righteous faith.

I wondered that night seven years ago after the evening at Captain Cowles's what the press of the years in the White House would do to you. I felt sad, I know, at the thought that perhaps you might come out broken in faith and disillusioned. But it seems to me your faith has deepened as the people have trusted you, and your ideals are set higher now than they were then. All of which is good. It is the best of all to me. I don't care much more than you do that your name and fame are secure. But it is a fine thing to have been nearly eight years in the most powerful place in the world and come out so clean that your faith in men and God is unshattered. For I think our ideals are measured by our conduct. The cynic is one who knows he has failed to keep the faith. The optimist has done his own level best.

[97]

All this is written to greet you at home, where you are happiest and where I trust the affection of millions of fellow citizens who are grateful to you for what you are (as well as for what you have done) always will abide with you.

I wish I might have helped you more during the years past, but I am glad that you did not need my help at all.

Following the 1908 campaign, White put the finishing touches on his novel A Certain Rich Man. *In March, 1909, the Whites left for a European trip, and the novel was published while they were abroad. It caught on immediately and became a best seller. The New York* Times *hailed the novel as holding "the mirror up to more that is truly native and characteristic in American life than has been reflected by any other story teller who has essayed the task."*

SOMEWHERE IN EUROPE, TO THE *Gazette* STAFF, April 30, 1909

MY DEAR GOOD FRIENDS:

For 2 weeks now we have been getting the Gazette regularly, and it has been a joy. It is two weeks old but it seems like a dream come true. You never made so good a paper, lots of little short stuff and lots of good stories. There has been nothing to criticize and everyone to praise. The editorial has been especially good and strong and interesting. And the advertising is a sight for sore eyes.

I am sending a letter and will have two or three more in a few days. It has been hard to write since I landed, but we are all well and exceedingly happy. Send mail to Florence, care of the American Express Co. We will be there 2 weeks and hope the letters may come more regularly after this about one a week.

Please have the following letter written in typewriter—*not* printed —to the addresses enclosed with the first lines as I have indicated them. Address envelopes for each one, but don't enclose the letters. Have them written on the thinnest paper you have but have Mr. Goodwin print the line—The Emporia Gazette—in the very plainest thickest type right in the middle of the top of a sheet (folded) about the size of this paper. Then do the whole business, letters, envelopes and all in one package and send it to me just as quick as you can to Florence c/o American Express Co. Get Miss Liggett to type the letters. The letter should be as fussy a job as can be done. Here is the copy:

(typewritten)   June 10th   Paris
THE EMPORIA GAZETTE
My dear Mr. Howells:

I have asked the Macmillan Company of New York to send you a copy of my novel "A Certain Rich Man." Also, I sent an autographed flyleaf to be bound in the book. You should get it sometime between now and July 1st. If not, kindly notify me at Emporia, and the letter will be forwarded and I'll see to it that the book goes out. I shall be in Europe, probably until September 1st. I hope you will like the book.*

Wm. Dean Howells
130 West 51st Street
New York

. . . You cannot know how happy I am at the fine way things are going. . . .

Mr. and Mrs. T. W. Johnston had been good friends of the Whites ever since White had worked on the Kansas City Star, with Mr. Johnston.

* White, with a keen sense of publicity, always sent copies of his books to leading literary and newspaper people.

Dear Mrs. T. W.:

Now that the journey is over—at least the foreign part of it—more and more our thoughts return to your good ship-letter that reached us late in June at Lucerne. It was a beautiful letter and we read it over and over. But to have answered it then with impressions piling in upon us would have been absurd, for you would have had no sort of idea of our beautiful summer from such a letter as a letter from Lucerne must have been. I am using the word summer purposely. For we found the lilacs at Madeira in April, followed them into Italy, through Switzerland and into Germany in June and saw the very ragged last of them in France. We had three weeks in Paris and five weeks of England and ten days in Ireland. We carried few letters of introduction. Mr. Howells [William Dean Howells] gave us a letter to his brother-in-law Larkin G. Mead, a dear old expatriated American sculptor with the slang of the sixties still in his mouth; and also Mr. Howells gave us a letter to Henry James. These two were the only social letters we presented. And we did not use some credentials that President Taft was kind enough to send. We had a business letter to the English Macmillans—the publishers and through them I met Mr. Thos. Hardy. Mr. Hardy and Mr. James were the only people in the writing way we met. I went on a pilgrimage to James's home at his invitation. He lives at Rye in Sussex, most charmingly in an old though modest house with a little walled garden back of it. The garden and the house and Henry James are all one. We had a luncheon and a long talk under a great spreading tree in the garden and then a walk and a visit to an old church, a pitch down a steep cobblestone street past antique shops and old old people to a modern station where we waited stuffily for a never coming train. Personally, Mr. James impresses one as being as kind as Mr. Howells but braver and therefore more likely to be just. He is of a middle height, high-domed, stocky though not chubby, and he has lived alone so much and written so much that he fumbles through the whole basket of his conversational vocabulary for the exact word to use in most ordinary matters. So he creaks when he talks. But he talks well and is altogether a joy.

As for Mr. Thomas Hardy, he is a modest soft-voiced self-deprecatory man, thinned and more serious than Noble Prentis [long-time editorial writer for the Kansas City *Star*], but no more assertive. He wears his clothes as an afterthought, and has a scrubby wayward little mustache of blond gray that has had its own way too long to be taken in hand now. He attended the operatic performance of "Tess" last month in London the first night, and sat by and clapped his hands for the composer to come out and the singer and all the people, but no one called for him and it did not occur to him probably that anyone should call for him. He is a dear.

Presumably T. W. J. has brought home "A Certain Rich Man" and you may have waded through the first part and found some compensation in the last part. At least I hope you will. Mrs. White and I are so anxious to see you and T.W.J. Why don't you come down some Sunday this fall? Please do and we can talk it all out. In the meantime remember us both affectionately to the big handsome man and believe me.

By the autumn of 1909, a full-fledged progressive Republican revolt against Taft was under way. The precipitating issue in this fight was the Payne-Aldrich Tariff of 1909. The Republican platform had called for downward revision of the tariff, but the bill that emerged from Congress was a high protective measure. Progressive senators like LaFollette, Bristow, Beveridge, Cummins, and Dolliver of Iowa attacked the high rates and demonstrated to the country the connection between tariffs and monopolists. Taft not only signed the bill, but in a speech at Winona, Minn., he pronounced it "the best tariff bill that the Republican party ever passed." This was treason in progressive eyes.

To W. R. NELSON, Kansas City *Star*, September 23, 1909

DEAR COLONEL NELSON:

I was out of the country when your letter of August 17 came and I have waited a month before replying; chiefly because I wanted to look around and see what was doing. If I have any notion of public sentiment in Kansas and I have been in five of the eight districts since

I came home and have had letters from people all over the state, you may rest assured that Taft has not even made a dent in the sentiment of Kansas. The fellows who were insurgent are still insurgent, only more so. I do not know of a man who has been led to even flicker on account of the President's attitude. He has lost and the insurgents have gained, for they are now in the attitude of being persecuted by those in high authority. I think the Star's attitude of restraint is very admirable. I also believe that the western insurgents have acted very decently. This is not their time to talk and it is not necessary for them to act. Unless sentiment changes, I do not think it would be possible to get a Taft delegation from any prairie state, providing some grave mistake is not made by the insurgents themselves. . . .

Harry Kemp, known as "the tramp poet of Kansas," worked his way around the world as a youth and then decided to study at the University of Kansas. White was extremely interested in Kemp's talents, lent him money and secured grants from wealthy men to make it possible for Kemp to live while writing his poetry. Century, American, Everybody's, *and* Munsey's *were some of magazines that published Kemp's work.*

To HARRY KEMP, Lawrence, Kan., September 25, 1909

MY DEAR HARRY KEMP:

I was glad to hear from you, because Mrs. White and I have been thinking of you, and talking of you a great deal of late. You will smile probably, but when you were with us most was in Rome, for it was in Rome that we were much with Keats, and to us you seem a kindred spirit. We visited the Keats memorial and saw the little room where he died a most miserable death, railing at the materialism of a cold world that afterward took him to its heart. You are impressed in the room, by the struggle the poor fellow made. It is all fixed up now, but when he died there it must have been a dingy little cubbyhole, and his misery, alone with Severn, must have been grinding and real.

Then we went to the cemetery where he lies buried. It is in an old part of the cemetery, fenced off by a high wall. The graves in that part of the cemetery, an area perhaps 200 x 200 feet square, are covered with long dry blue grass. Here and there is a tree. Shafts of shade fall across the place, and among the tangled grass and half-wild flowers, little mounds are made, as though the sleepers had half turned over in their sleep. A path, straight across the other mounds, is marked in the long grass to Keats' grave. We followed it and came to this grave with that of his friend beside it, and the little child of his friend near it. The famous inscription "Here lies one whose name is writ in Water" is prefaced with some bitter phrases that bring all the suffering and heart sobs of Keats' last days back to one. And then the loneliness of the abandoned graveyard, its unkempt graves and tangled grass all give one the idea of a solitary spirit. So we picked some clover blossoms, and some blue flowers growing in the grass, and put them on the grave and sighed and went away.

In the main part of the cemetery, through the gate across the high wall, it is entirely different from the lonesomeness of the place where Keats lies. Here in the main part Shelley's heart lies buried. It is indeed a peaceful beautiful spot. It seems full of the joy of death. I have never in my life seen a more beautiful spot, and always we longed for you. We thought how you would enjoy it, how it would inspire and encourage you. It is well kept, like a picture. Scores of trimmed graves covered with beautiful memorial marble are there. Great plumy poplars and spreading deodars shade and adorn the place. It is so exquisite a refinement of landscape beauty that one can hardly believe that it is real. If you could only see it!

In England we visited Stoke Poges—or something like that; the church where Gray sleeps and wherein he wrote his elegy. It is a peaceful sleeping place, and such a spot as one would choose if he wished only to rest. Shakespeare's grave in Stratford is like being buried on Massachusetts Street. We did not fancy it.

But this letter is too long as it is. Come down sometime. Let me know beforehand, and we will be glad to see you, and Mrs. White will tell you all about it.

The progressive movement basically was founded on the idea of Christian fellowship and service to one's community. The political leaders of progressivism were very close to a number of militant preachers who were putting forth the social gospel of Christianity from their pulpits. White, for instance, was a good friend of that socially minded preacher, Washington Gladden.

To The Rev. William E. Barton, Oak Park, Ill.,
December 20, 1909

Dear Sir:

I was very glad to get your letter of December 15. I note that you ask: "Is the spirit of Jesus more dominant in politics and business and international affairs than when you entered active life?" and "Is it an advantage or a disadvantage for a public man today to be known as a professing Christian?" I feel entirely sure that there never has been a time in the history of the world when the Christian message was more deeply embedded in the life of the people than it is today. More and more are our institutions reflections of the spirit of Christ. More and more are the relations of the people to one another honest and kind and simple. I think there never has been a time in the world when all men had so much good will toward one another nor when this good will was so much a part of human institutions, political and commercial and religious.

It seems to me that the time is passed when the Sunday-school politician or business man may be sneered at. It was a fashion twenty years ago to sneer at Sunday-school men, but today more and more the bad man is getting out of politics and the good man is taking his place and generally speaking the good man is anchored to some church or creed which he is not at all ashamed to proclaim and testify to.

The insurgent movement of the progressives within the Republican party was in full swing during 1910. White was the mainspring be-

*hind the fight in Kansas. He aided progressives outside of Kansas, too,
with editorials and articles.*

To President William Howard Taft, February 3, 1910

My Dear Mr. President:

. . . I have wished for five months, ever since I returned from
Europe, to find some decent opportunity to tell you that if you will
just let the insurgents alone they will come home like little Bo-peep's
sheep. They are not against your administration. For the most part
they favor your legislative program. They are not mixed up in any
return from Elba conspiracy, even if Colonel Roosevelt could be
base enough to permit such a shameful thing. The insurgents so far
as I know them would rather see you successful for two terms than
not.

But they will not work with Senator Aldrich and Mr. Cannon.
Moreover they are openly contesting inside of the Republican party
the leadership of these men. That is their Republican right. For instance in every Kansas Congressional district except Murdock's and
Madison's [Victor Murdock and E. H. Madison, Kansas congress-
men] we have opponents of the Kansas congressmen who are allied
with Cannon. What is still more when you bid those Kansas congressmen good-bye next spring do a good job, for it will be for the last
time.

My point in giving myself to this movement is that only by defeat
of these congressmen at the primaries may Kansas be saved for a Republican Congressional delegation in November. It's useless to argue
with the people. . . .

They will not stand for the Cannon-Aldrich leadership. Incidentally they think more of Cannon than of Aldrich. The Senatorial elections will prove that. The movement distinctly is not against you; it
is not against your program. But it is against the leadership you are
compelled to recognize.

We propose to try to change that leadership by sending men back
to Congress who will not submit to it, hence insurgents. This leadership, through its political ganglia, is trying to convince you of the
treachery to you and to the party, of the insurgents. So an unhappy
situation has arisen. The people have begun to confuse you with the
leadership. So they don't understand you, and perhaps you do not

[105]

understand the people. When you discipline a man like Bristow who has the people behind him, you are merely disciplining the people.* They don't care who has the offices. It is a foolish question, that of patronage. It is the least of the worries of a man like Bristow. But it annoys the folks to see their senator snubbed. So the breach widens. It is not your fault, not fundamentally. You have to take things as they are. The leadership of the party remains under the present status with Senator Aldrich and Mr. Cannon. You are more or less bound to take their advice, and of course their advice is for discipline. But it will be hard on majorities next November. I don't know what to do. I wish your administration to succeed. I wish you well in every possible way. My paper has said nothing unkind of you. I believe in your program. But I am supposed to be against you because I am putting up a Congressional delegation that will put skids under five out of the seven Kansas congressmen, and replace them with men who are like Murdock and Madison and Bristow.

It is a puzzle. There is nothing for you to answer in this letter. I do not expect an answer. What will happen, I can answer as you answered to the socialist in Cooper Union, "God knows."

In the meantime here's hopin'—

The recipient of the following letter wrote to White objecting to such reforms as the direct primary since they gave too much power to poorly educated people. White, in his answer, reveals his fundamental acceptance of the Jeffersonian principle that democracy to survive must have an intelligent, educated people.

To M. C. POLLEY, Manhattan, Kan., February 14, 1910

MY DEAR MR. POLLEY:

I have been very busy since your good letter of January 31 came, and I know you will pardon me for leaving it unanswered so long.

* President Taft refused patronage to Senator Bristow because of his insurgent attitude.

I was greatly interested in your letter and in the proposition which you set forth. If we concede that there is to be no progress, that our common schools are not to take the average of public intelligence beyond the sixth grade, then there is no question but that the primary system is a mistake. If, however, the schools and the newspapers may be depended upon as I believe they may be, to take the average intelligence of men past that grade, then popular government will succeed. If I did not have faith in the public schools, I should not believe in the extension of the rights of self-government to the masses. It seems to me that in Kansas, Nebraska, Iowa, Wisconsin and the Dakotas and in Oregon, where the people have tried somewhat more extensive self-government than they have had heretofore, the experiment on the whole has been successful. For though it may be admitted that they have not always chosen wisely, the added responsibility has deepened public interest in public questions, and I believe that the American when he gives his government something more than casual attention will give it a pretty sound, sane, true Yankee verdict on every question. So that I look forward to the extension of the primary to the remaining third of the American states without any alarm. Moreover I see the progress of the recall which has extended to something like two million people dwelling in cities within the last eighteen months without any qualms. It is remarkable to know that thirty-one states now have the primary whereas when Roosevelt came to the White House the primary was practically unknown in our politics. Today eight or nine states have state-wide initiative and referendum and fifty-six cities from Boston to Los Angeles in twenty-five states have the initiative, referendum, the recall and the non-partisan primary. In all I believe it is said that five million people are living today under these newfangled contraptions. Yet the idea is scarcely half a decade old. If it grows during the next ten years as it has grown during the last five years, we may expect a working minority of the urban population of the United States to be living under the initiative, referendum and recall.

If the public schools do not do their duty, if we do not educate the masses beyond the sixth grade, if we have long hours for working men, poor pay and little time for sane reflection, if we are, in short, to have an ignorant population to pass upon momentous questions, the prospect is appalling. But I do not fear because I believe the American people will have sense enough to extend their defenses along the line of the public schools and that we may escape from any of the perils that ignorance would bring to us. I thank you most sincerely for your good letter and wish you to know that I appreciate its sentiment and while I may differ with its conclusions, I respect the patriotism that inspires it.

Congressman Charles F. Scott, editor of the Iola (Kansas) Register was a personal friend of White's, but politically was a standpat Republican. White broke with him politically in these years, but, in 1924, when White ran for governor on an anti-Ku-Klux-Klan program, Scott was one of his ardent supporters.

To CHARLES SCOTT, Washington, D.C., March 11, 1910

MY DEAR SCOTT:

Your letter of February 16 reached me just before I was starting east and I did not take time to answer it. I desired to give you time to reflect and to get over your tantrum.* I know that by now you have regained your poise and that you know, of course, that no man in his senses deliberately misrepresents another man, and if there are any misstatements of fact in my article concerning you, I shall be glad to know what they are. As for my opposition to you, of course it is entirely political. I would have opposed Victor Murdock or my own brother or my own father as quickly as I would you. One's friendship must not prevent him from doing his duty in a matter like this. I think your record was the result of mistaken judgment, but it is made and I have not heard that you have repented or recanted. The difference between the insurgents and the Cannon Republicans is fundamental. They believe in the growing rights of men, you believe in the growing rights of property. The thing has got to be fought out in the Republican party, and we will see who owns the party, the people or the corporations. I have absolutely no personal feeling in this matter except one of exceeding sadness that I am compelled to

* Scott had objected to a critical *Gazette* editorial. After receiving this letter, Scott replied to White on March 14, that, "A soft answer turneth away wrath. Your letter of the 11th makes me feel a good deal ashamed of myself for the bitterness of the protest which called it forth. . . ."

line up against a friend, but I do it without a quiver as I should expect my friends to line up against me when we differ in matters of fundamental principle.

While a member of the Board of Regents at the University of Kansas, White was opposed to college football. He felt that, as it was then played, it was dangerous to the participants, and that the sporting public turned the game into an affair uncomplimentary to an educational institution.

To Chancellor F. H. Strong, University of Kansas,
April 14, 1910

My Dear Chancellor:

I was delighted to get your letter about the football situation. I want to say before answering it that I have watched very carefully the way you have handled the local situation, and I must tell you that I have never seen a situation so tactfully and wisely and kindly and bravely handled before in a similar crisis, and I should be inclined to follow your judgment a long way. Until I can talk the matter over with you and the other members of the Board, it does not seem to me that I am competent to state where I stand in the matter. I realize that we have got without a struggle a great gain in this football situation. And I realize that there is a certain danger in going further than we can carry University sentiment with us, and yet I feel, naturally, I desire to gain every inch that we can and do not wish to stop until I am sure that we have reached the end of the rope. But you may rest assured that your judgment in the matter will be my leading guide.

How would this do as a little further compromise: to reserve the right to stop the progress of the game any time during the coming season when it may seem wise to the Board to do so. That means this: that if under the new rules accidents and death continue during the first part of the season in other colleges, we may assume that the risk is too great to permit the game to continue in the University. It seems to me that this is a fair question of rights to the Board in the matter. What do you think of it?

To Theodore Roosevelt
[no date—but written to reach him as he landed
from Africa and Europe, June, 1910]

My Dear Colonel:

It seems good to have you with us again. We need you in our business. The American people are terribly sentimental. It seems to me they are the most sentimental people in the world; that is, they will do more for what seems the larger good, for the intelligently unselfish end, than any other people. And they have had a year or so without an appeal to that side of their natures from those in high places. That is the whole trouble with President Taft. His appeal has been to the heads, not to the hearts of the people. You know when I saw you last we thought he would be the most beloved of our presidents. It is not impossible that he will be the most respected of our presidents. No one dislikes President Taft; there is no anger at him. But no one feels any affection for him. His appeal has been that of a lawyer to a court, and after all we are the jury. He has aroused no enthusiasm of high purpose, and his cabinet has made the people distrustful of the whole administration. The corporation in essence is selfish; it is the only entirely selfish organism in society, and with great propriety. It is society's centripetal force. But men who have devoted their activities to corporations for years, as agents or attorneys, become like what they serve. They lose balance on the wrong side. They cannot understand how much altruism is in life. They cannot appreciate high motives. To these men a consecrated life like your life seems insane. Taft has needed much of the other kind of influence. It has been wanting, and his administration has suffered. Hence, to return to my first proposition, we need you in our business.

But—and this is the second proposition—we do not need you for president. I am against that movement. I have said nothing unkind of President Taft and have not criticized his administration. Yet I may not be classed as an ardent supporter of it. Its intense materialism has saddened me, and I have been unhappy many times at the way things have gone. But I believe sincerely that the country would be better off with Taft until 1916, than with you in the next presidential term. Not that the country would not be further along in 1916 with you in office; you would take us a long way ahead. But on the other hand as matters stand the people are not looking to the presidential office for leadership now. They are beginning to walk alone. They are going ahead themselves in their own way. There is a distinctly growing automatically organizing public opinion in America today that is the same in every section and corner of the Republic. It knows no class or occupation. It is National. And it will triumph over any president or congress or court that can be formed. It is the outgrowth of necessity. With you in the White House the people feel secure. So the necessity of a self-guarding public sentiment is removed, and if you were in office in 1916 we would undoubtedly have better laws, and a cleaner administration than we may have with you out, but [without you in office] what we have would be our own net gain, and we would be in a position to fight whatever devils were sent against us in the future with greater success than if we did the ornamental standing around for four years while you did the real work.

Now along with the wonderful economic changes that are coming into American life, are coming—and this is the third proposition—radical changes in our political forms. A new form is coming inevitably that is distinctly new. Hamilton would not enjoy it, and Jefferson would not understand it. Two thirds of the American people are now living under the operation of the direct primary. One fifth of the people are now enjoying direct legislation in municipal affairs, and the list of cities adopting the new rule is growing rapidly. The initiative and referendum is now a state-wide law in eight states, and is an issue endorsed by the dominant party in five other states. More people are living under the recall than were under the direct primary when you came to the White House. The people are hungry for direct political responsibility. And they are taking it away from the politicians. Moreover under the new responsibility the people are growing worthy of it.

But there is one serious danger in the situation, and that is—the fourth proposition—selfish or ignorant leadership. The Nation must not become an exalted Oklahoma. Oregon has done marvelously well. But Oregon, with all her crooks, has had much unselfish and well-directed leadership. And so we need you in our business. We need your voice sounded in such a way that no one will suspect that ambition is moving you. We need your influence as an unselfish leader working with the people as one of them, not as their ruler. We need a brother and not a master nor a servant.

And now finally for the practical work at hand. I believe it is the revivifying of the Republican party. We must change leadership. Cannon is gone,* but all that he stands for is very much alive in the party. The alliance between politics and wealth that would merely aggrandize itself with no thought of its social obligation must be everlastingly smashed. There should be no compromise, no conciliation, no monkey business about that contest. It is fundamental. The people must control or be controlled. They can't go halvers with the Interests. The people are fair. But they must be trusted. They must have the power in their own hands to be fair or unfair. It is their government, and they will suffer from their unfairness more than those whom they seek to injure. So they will learn wisdom . . . and the sooner they learn—even in folly—the more secure will property rights be in this country. And it seems to me that your job is to go with them into this fight—as a Republican wherever you can and as far as you can—but as a friend and brother and equal of them all. They need you. They have a right to expect you to serve them, in this higher service, this more unselfish and more practical service without reward and without official honor.

Of course you may depend upon me. In any event in any program I am for you, and shall be with you. And I assume that you desire my views. Probably you are overwhelmed with views. But there they are. Take them for what they are worth. Discount them, do what you please with them. I make no claim to omniscience. There is the other side. Only know this: that I wish most sincerely to be your friend. I wish to help. I wish to be with you, and I have no favors to ask, no ends to further.

If there is any specific suggestion I should make it is to take no sides in the Republican contest until after the primaries in August and September, and then in so far as it deserves support, support the party. You can make it plain enough that party support does not mean allegiance to Cannon and Aldrich and Ballinger [Secretary of the Interior Ballinger, major actor in the Ballinger-Pinchot controversy over the handling of public lands].† I shall not be in New York probably until you come west. But of course I shall see you then.

* This refers to the progressive victory in stripping Speaker Cannon of some of his dictatorial powers.

† The progressives maintained that Ballinger was guilty of using public land for the benefit of special interests.

Theodore Roosevelt's desire for reform had not been dulled by his African hunting trip. Speaking on August 31, 1910, at Osawatomie, Kansas, the scene of John Brown's massacre in the days of Bleeding Kansas, Roosevelt announced that "We must drive special interests out of politics" and proclaimed that "I stand for the square deal . . . I mean not merely that I stand for fair play under the present rules of the game, but that I stand for having those rules changed so as to work for a more substantial equality of opportunity and of reward for equally good service."

To THEODORE ROOSEVELT, Oyster Bay, June 2, 1910

MY DEAR COLONEL ROOSEVELT:

There is no advice in this letter. I was never an ex-president, and I don't know how one should act: perhaps they have human intelligence these ex-presidents; perhaps they reason as we do; perhaps habit has developed the thing we call instinct in them; perhaps that instinct may mount nearly to heaven at times—I do not know. Only this I feel that the poor dumb critters should have our sympathy.

I shall not be in the East until fall. You will be coming West in August. Of course I shall see you. I hope to see much of you, not that I desire to take you on my knee and tell you stories of "the situation," but there are many things which we have in common.

I note you are to talk about John Brown. I observe a lot of fellows unfold their ample jaws and yip and kyoodle about old John and the Cause of freedom who, when the Big Fight is on today, hide under the bed, pull down the blinds, fasten the doors and chatter about the danger to American institutions that lurks in a good squared-toe combat for American Manhood against the never-sweats on Wall Street and their brothers in idleness at the water tank down by the railroad. But this is all beside the point. The object of this letter is to ask how can I see you? Won't you come to Emporia for a day?—no speeches, no reception, no brass band, no reporters. Just a ride under the elm trees, and, if you want it, a walk over the hills and in the valleys at sunset. The prairies are beautiful now. Come and hear the meadow lark at twilight and perhaps the gods of other [?] days will come back and commune with you. I'll guarantee that you shall not be bothered with statesmen nor naturalists nor reformers.

I see by the papers that you are still keeping hotel at Oyster Bay.

[113]

My compliments to the landlady and tell her that if hired girls are as hard to get in Oyster Bay as in Emporia she has our sympathy.

Mrs. White sends affectionate greetings.

Although busy with his writing and political careers, White did not neglect a close human relationship with his employees, as the following letter to an Emporia neighbor reveals.

[no date, but sometime in June, 1910]

MY DEAR LOUIE:

Humphrey ——, who I believe is a relative of yours and a very nice young man, has been carrying papers for the Gazette for some time but, like many boys, needs the watchful care of a man over his affairs. Humphrey has gradually got behind in his bills until he owes $90, and he has left town. A few weeks before leaving town we called his attention to this matter, and he was very penitent and came in and made some beautiful promises and seemed to be all right.

Now I think Humphrey is all right at bottom, but he likes to dress and go to the dances and live a little beyond his means. I cannot talk to him, but I believe you can. Some man ought to talk to him, because a boy needs a man at that age. The $90 is not worrying me, I should give it and more to see Humphrey get into different ways, into a more manly method of handling his little affair. I am wondering if you, or some of your relatives, could not talk plainly to Humphrey and tell him that he must not begin life by muddling things, for that it will last him all his days and that the habit of exact truth telling now will grow on him just as the opposite habit will. He is a particularly good boy and I like him and I would make a considerable sacrifice to see him started right. I am coming to you with this because I believe he likes and respects you and a word from you would mean a good deal to him.

[114]

MY DEAR HASKELL:

I have yours of June 4 acknowledging receipt of my book [*The Old Order Changeth* (1910), a description of the working of progressive legislation in the states]. Of course I am glad you like it. Mrs. White and I had a beautiful time in Chicago, New York and Washington. I had luncheon with Ambassador Bryce, also with the President, to which I shall return later, dined with Henry Watterson, Mr. and Mrs. Charles Dana Gibson, spent the week-end with the Morgans, that is to say, Miss Anne and her mother, up on the Hudson [James Bryce, British ambassador; Henry Watterson, editor of the Louisville *Courier-Journal*; Charles Dana Gibson, creator of the Gibson Girl; Mrs. J. P. Morgan and her daughter Anne] . . . then we played with the fellows down at the American office and had a good time generally. I went to a dinner one night where Judge Gary, of the steel trust, Mr. Lovett of the Union Pacific, Joseph Choate, Charles R. Alexander, the big trust-defending attorney and about a dozen other men of that kind and caliber were present, and as nearly as I can make it out, they feel exactly as we do. There is a unanimous opinion in all classes in all parts of the United States about Taft. The luncheon at the White House at which I was the only guest was most interesting. We talked for one hour perhaps longer about a number of things. First politics was not mentioned. We talked of . . . art, about European movements, about architecture . . . about everything under the sun but politics. So long as it was at his house, I did not think it was necessary for me to turn the conversation that way. It was all very queer and very amusing. If Colonel Nelson is in town, tell him about this luncheon. It was a grand day. The situation in Kansas looks particularly hopeful. I believe we shall win in four of the six Congressional districts and get Stubbs without any trouble.

The Republican primary in Kansas brought the defeat of four of the six Congressional followers of Speaker Cannon. The progressives re-

[115]

lied heavily on the support of organized labor and special circulars were distributed to the workers by the progressive Republicans.

To SAMUEL GOMPERS, American Federation of Labor,
August 8, 1910

MY DEAR MR. GOMPERS:

. . . As you know we cleaned up four out of the six congressmen who were running on the Cannon issue. If at any time I can help you, or the Emporia Gazette can help you, in the struggle to have labor recognized in its struggle for collective bargaining, in its demand for a living wage, in its struggle for the right of a man to his job upon an equality of capital . . . or for any of the fundamental things that organized labor is struggling for in legislatures and out, I shall be pleased to help you. It seems to me that, as we are widening our democratic control of America by instituting the initiative and referendum, the primary and the recall on our political life, only one thing will save our democracy from ruin. That is an intelligent voting majority which only may be had as labor gets shorter hours, better wages and a higher social and economic status and a royal American privilege to look every man, class or profession squarely in the eye and tell it to go straight up.

White's editorial style, as well as his creative writing in articles and books, was so lucid and distinctive that he frequently received inquiries, from people he did not know, as to his writing methods. The following letter is illustrative of the care that went into his work.

Dear Mr. Brown:

I shall be glad to reply to your questions as well as I may. Question no. 1: The only conscious effort I ever made to learn to write well was during my apprenticeship as a reporter and as an editorial writer on newspapers, when I tried to get the largest possible meaning in the shortest possible space. Question 2: I never carried notebooks to catch stray thoughts. I rarely use a written outline. The only time I ever used it was in writing a "A Certain Rich Man," wherein I outlined each chapter the day before I began writing it. Question 4: I did not utilize notes. Generally speaking I am more or less moody, but when I get into a subject I find few days that are not productive. I generally revise every serious thing I write two or three times. Everything I put in book covers is revised five or six times. "A Certain Rich Man" was written four times completely.

The following letter was written to a person who knew White when he was growing up in El Dorado. His own daughter, Mary, was now seven years old.

To Mrs. E. J. Wheeler, Milwaukee, Wis., March 22, 1911

Dear Mrs. Wheeler:

You do not know the pleasure I got from the few moments' visit with your daughter. What a fine, clear-eyed, beautiful child she is and how serenely and hopefully she is looking at life. It was so good to see her. I think she has the best of both her father and her mother in her—sweet, strong, wholesome and beautiful. What other flower in the world is so beautiful as a young girl in her teens? I can think of nothing else in this created universe so fine. To be the mother or father of such a girl is to have created greater than Michelangelo or the Grecian sculptors for your creation is for eternity, theirs is for time.

Life has brought me many beautiful things and some opportunity for usefulness, which is better even than the beautiful experiences. But I hold best of all the fact that in spite of my shortcomings, which are many and which I know better than anyone else, I have in some measure the respect and confidence of people like you, who knew me in the old days when I was working my way out of the gawkiness and stupidity of boyhood into some of the visions of youth. You were all so kind to me and so good to me that I shall always remember you with gratitude.

Please remember me especially to your husband. Helen [the Wheeler daughter] said that he saw her to the train, and I was of course glad to know that. She is like him in so many ways and yet she is immensely like her mother and her aunts. How wonderfully the blend of heredity is manifesting in a child. Pardon this long letter and believe me—

To W. H. CARRUTH, University of Kansas, April 18, 1911

MY DEAR WILL:

I have got two grudges against you. The first one is that you addressed me Honorable. Nothing makes me so mad as to be addressed Honorable, unless it is to be called Hon.—H O N. That is grudge No. 1. Grudge No. 2 is this: you assume in your letter that the Committee on Efficiency is going to put everybody in the State University on an exact hours-of-service basis.* That Committee is composed of Sheffield Ingalls, a graduate of your institution, A. L. Sponsler, a graduate of Knox College, and the undersigned. I think, excepting myself, each of them has been around a college long enough to know that a college professor cannot be hired and paid with a time-clock key. It is to be assumed that certain members of the faculty of all the schools must be giving high-grade service without teaching fourteen hours a day. It was repeatedly said in the meeting of the Committee in the Governor's office recently that it was simply to justify the state institutions before the tax payers and that no serious faults would be found. I am satisfied that so far as the University is concerned there is not a man on there who is not earning his salary. Otherwise I should have complained about it years ago. I have said in Regents' meetings and I have said in public that I did not think

* Governor W. R. Stubbs appointed White on this committee.

that the advertising agent of the athletic association is a necessary adjunct to the State University and, if one vote would knock him out, my vote would do it. Personally I do not think that the relations between the Alumni Association and the faculty should be so close that an editorial in the Alumni Magazine could have any possible official significance in relation to the institution any more than the Kansan [the student paper]. If I could stop that, I should, but to indicate or even hint that your services as vice-chancellor are not appreciated would be perfectly absurd and I have got a grudge be-caused your letter seemed to indicate that I did not appreciate it.

This letter to his old newspaper friend, Arthur Capper, contains White's lifelong doubt as to the advisability of newspaper editors running for political office. Capper, however, served as governor and was, then, elected to the United States Senate.

To Arthur Capper, Topeka *Capital*, April 19, 1911

My Dear Arthur:

I have been ranting around more or less to Bristow and Madison and Murdock [Joseph L. Bristow, E. H. Madison, and Victor Murdock] and others of our friends about your candidacy for governor. You are absolutely sure of the support of every man in the so-called square-deal camp, if you decide to run. As you know I have never urged you in this matter because I have believed that it was too serious a question to decide in a moment. It has seemed to me something like this: the Capital is as permanent as an institution in this state. It has done more than any other one force in this state to bring us up to our present progressive standard and during the next four years, it seems to me, we cannot well afford to have the influence of the Capital crippled, as necessarily it must be crippled if you run for governor. While you might feel that the Capital should be as active in public affairs as it always has been under your management, still its activity would be discredited by the fact of your candidacy. I have felt exactly the same handicap when I have been urged by our friends to run for an office. I have felt that it would in a measure reduce what small usefulness I have, and I fear greatly the same effect upon the Capital of your candidacy. I know that Governor Stubbs is sincerely and heartily for you, but I feel that he is letting an impulse rather than his judgment govern him, because if Curtis [Senator Charles Curtis, up for re-election in 1912] supports you, and I assume of course that he would not be foolish enough actively to oppose you, he could then very plausibly claim to be a square-dealer, or an insurgent, or a progressive, so long as he was supporting you, and Stubbs will need every vote that he can get. I do not much fear Stubbs' ability to beat Curtis in the primary, but I think it is going to be a mighty close shave in the election. No man ever has been elected senator after a four-year term as governor in this state. Stubbs will be weaker in many ways at the end of his second term than he was at the end of his first term. For I assume that he got a few thousand votes from men who had a lively anticipation of favors to come and he would not have even that small strength if he was to be made senator because it would be known that he was going to Washington with about the same patronage status as Bristow. Therefore, from Stubbs' standpoint, it seems to me that his enthusiasm for your candidacy is a better testimonial to his loyalty and personal impulses than to his judgment in politics.

I am not writing this letter to discourage you, but to let you see things at an angle that I see them. You need have no fear that if you actually launch your boom and become a candidate, you will have the solid support of Stubbs, Bristow and the progressive congressmen in this state. . . .

Please, above everything, do not take this as a bucket of cold water on your boom. It is simply the misgivings of a friend who wants to point out every discouragement before it is too late, so that you can have the whole ground before you when you act and when you do act you may depend upon me to do all that I can to help you.

Walt Mason was an outstanding midwestern newspaperman and poet. For twenty years, through an addiction to alcohol, he could never hold a job very long. In 1907, while White was in Colorado, Mason wrote and asked for a job on the Gazette. *In the* Gazette *atmosphere Mason gave up alcohol and became a valuable member of the staff writing local copy ánd editorials. One day he started writing prose verses, which quickly attracted attention. White sent some of these to the George Matthew Adams syndicate and before long some two hundred papers were carrying Mason's rhymes. Following this letter of White's, Mason did only editorial writing and spent the rest of his time on his verses.*

To WALT MASON, Emporia, May 5, 1911

MY DEAR WALT:

As I do not see you when you are downtown, and as I can't talk conveniently over the telephone, I want to write you a little note. We miss you in the office more than you can know. I feel lonesome without you around. I was out of town yesterday, and they were all anxious to know about you in Topeka. It has seemed to me for a year that you were wasting a lot of your valuable time fooling around the office cutting out reprint and editing telegraph, and I have been wondering why you did it. This morning Walt Hughes [business manager of the *Gazette* until 1932] came to me with a suggestion, which he said he had mentioned to you, but did not say what you had thought of it. Walter's idea is for you to come down and work two or three hours in the morning, get up enough editorial to fill the first column and turn the second, in all say twenty-five inches or so every day, and then feel that your day's work is done. You would not be responsible for any clippings or for any telegraph, and you could have the run of the paper and have the office for your own convenience either the rest of the day or as much of the day as you please. If any day you do not feel like writing so much, you need be under no compulsion to do so, and if, on the other hand, you wanted to exceed a column and a fourth or a column and a half, you might always be free to do so. Anything from half a column to two columns would be acceptable and you need feel bound to do no special amount. The rest of the day would be yours to devote to your best work. I feel that the next ten years must be your harvest time. I feel that it is the height of folly to spend your good time and energy and strength on the grind that you have been tramping.

[121]

What do you think this editorial anywhere from half a column to a column and a half would be worth? I am willing to let you set the price on it, and I shall make other arrangements for the other work you have been doing. This arrangement would please me from two standpoints: I should not feel that I was imposing on the best years of your life, and I should then have an opportunity to make some other changes in the office that have been needed for some time in other departments than yours.

Fortunately for the newpaper world and the reading public, White never carried through the idea of selling the Gazette. *Instead he went on writing editorials, popular articles, another long novel, and a series of nonfiction books. His interest in politics, too, did not slacken, as it might have, had he retired from active newspaperwork.*

To FRED C. TRIGG, Kansas City *Star*, May 29, 1911

MY DEAR TRIGG:

Here is something that has been on my mind for some time. I have been a year coming to this conclusion, and it is definitely set in my consciousness, yet Henry Allen [editor of the Wichita *Beacon*] is the only other person in whom I have confided. This is my case.

I am forty-three years old. I have a talent for writing. I can write a novel; I have written one and have another just as good in my head. It has been growing for over a year. I am at this moment, and have been for two months, preparing to go to Colorado to write this novel, and the preparations are as serious as though I were going to die. For it is hard to leave the Gazette. It has a circulation of 3,700 or a little more or less as the days go, and it has a good job and bindery business, and in all a payroll of $250 a week, sometimes as in rush seasons like the present $350 a week. It is making money—say from $6,500 to $8,000 a year. But when I take my hand off the wheel, it goes wrong. At the rate of $300 a week things can go wrong awfully fast. That is the trouble. So long as it was a little paper with 2,000 subscribers and a payroll of $150 a week, it couldn't go wrong badly, and when I wanted to leave it for a week or a month or a season, I could do so and write an article or two and bring it up to level again.

But the trouble with the thing is that it needs me and that it is growing. I can get 500 more circulation and boost the rate accordingly. The merchants here seem to want one paper and have never kicked on the rate. But to do these things requires all of my time.

I must either be an editor or an author. I am going to be an author. I feel that I must soon sell the Gazette. Soon doesn't mean within a month or even a year. But I have come to the parting of the ways. I have a little property, perhaps forty thousand, without the Gazette, and by selling it and investing the money I could have enough to live on, and not be pushed. But I don't think I am lazy, and I know that with the Gazette off my shoulders I could write two or three good novels. I have my vanity of course. I believe those novels would do more permanent good than my work in the newspaper. Also I can get up other books than novels. I have only twenty years more of kick in me, and I feel that the best will not be forthcoming from the newspaper business. For even if the Gazette didn't need me all the time, to be editor of the Gazette would keep me more in politics, and politics is taking too much of my time. I am going to stay by Stubbs through the Senatorial fight. I believe he is straight and clean and intelligent and strong. I believe he will make a great United States senator. Also I am going to stay with the fight for the initiative and referendum and recall, even though I get out of the Gazette. For these causes I'll be enlisted for thirty days or for the war. But after Stubbs is in the Senate, and Kansas gets the initiative and referendum, I want to kind of back out of the game and let the sovereign squats do their own squatting. There are plenty of men who can do that work. And I seem to have my own peculiar job. I someway feel I am wrapping my one little old talent in a napkin. Instead of which I wish to hang my banner on the outer wall.

Now then—why don't you buy the Gazette? You haven't any money, I presume. I didn't have a dollar when I bought it. Yet I paid Bill Morgan [W. Y. Morgan, editor of the Hutchinson *News* after he sold the *Gazette*] cash for it. The Gazette is the apple of my eye. I want to see it fall into kind and worthy hands. I turn naturally to you. The only thing I want it to be is to be progressive. I realize that in a few years party lines will change, and will amount to something entirely different from what they mean now. So that doesn't interest me. But to have it with its face forward does interest me. That is why

[123]

I turn to you. Probably the town would subscribe $10,000 in stock without any strings on you. It is likely that our political friends in Topeka would subscribe something, giving you the privilege of buying them out from time to time as you could. You would need a business manager, and he might raise something. Henry Allen thinks the paper with its job office and bindery is worth about $50,000. So do I. And that is what I must sell for.

There is no hurry about this thing. I am going to take my time. I am not going to peddle it around. And I don't want you to tell folks my feeling in the matter, except as it is necessary in business. I am coming to you first because I suppose you and I feel more nearly alike upon all questions that concern a newspaper than anyone else.

From June to October, 1911, the Whites were at Moraine Park, Colorado, where White started to write his novel, In the Heart of a Fool. *This manuscript went through many revisions and was not published until 1918. It was a book breathing the progressive spirit, but by the time it was published the nation had turned away from domestic reform and was concentrating on World War I.*

To THEODORE ROOSEVELT, October 18, 1911

MY DEAR COLONEL ROOSEVELT:

Herein enclosed you will find a sheet of paper upon which I wish you would write some sort of an inscription to go in your African Trails book that I have given to my boy Bill. William Lindsay White is Bill's name, though I do not suppose he knows himself, being mostly known as Bill. There is no particular hurry about this, ten days or two weeks will be soon enough. When it comes, I shall have it bound in the book at our bindery, so that he may always feel the personal element with him in reading the book. I have been in Colorado all summer working on a novel. I believe it is a pretty good novel and I hope you will like it, but it is going to take a year to revise it. I write in haste and revise at leisure. The book is written chiefly, I think, to prove that there are not necessarily spiritual rewards for material service in this world, nor are there material punishments for material transgressions, but that whatever rewards or punishments the scheme of things holds, there really are spiritual rewards for spiritual service and spiritual punishments for spiritual transgressions. It is rather a hard thesis to work out and demonstrate, but I believe I have done it fairly well. I have turned the dramatics upon the evils of unnecessary divorce and the need of a workingman's compensation, two subjects which seem at first sight rather incongruous, but all subjects are rather related, I suppose, if we can find the string to string them on.

I did not go to the Chicago Progressive Conference [a meeting to boom the candidacy of Senator LaFollette for the Republican presidential nomination] because I rather felt it was a battle of wooden guns. Sham battle never interested me. I have no special desire for tin swords and rooster feathers and some way or other I did not warm up to the Chicago conference. I am persuaded that Taft never could be elected under any possible circumstances and my wholesome respect for the acumen of the American politician leads me to believe that in the end the Republican politicians will dump Mr. Taft. For after all, the strongest purely political influence in America is the county ticket. You persuade the fellows at the courthouse that they are going to have a load on their necks with a presidential candidate, get it thoroughly in their noggins that any leader is a deadweight, and unless that leader happens to represent a mighty righteous cause, they will dump that leader. On the other hand, when the American politician, that is to say the little fellow down in the county courthouse, gets it into his head that he can win with a certain leader and that leader will make votes for the candidates for county attorney, treasurer, sheriff and register of deeds, that little politician is going to line up behind that leader no matter whether the little fellow agrees with the big fellow or not. It was that feeling that nominated you in 1904. I should say on the whole the politicians around the courthouse had not very much use for you in 1904. They were for the man of the Hanna type at that time, but they saw that you made votes and they stood for you. To me it is utterly unbelievable to imagine the courthouse bunch filling a national convention with delegates for Taft, when they know that Taft stands to lose them from two hundred to two thousand votes in every county in the United States on the county ticket. This large illuminated fact is before their eyes now every moment of the day. The courthouse bunch is getting it thoroughly in mind that Taft means trouble, and I think the courthouse

[125]

bunch will dump Taft. I do not know just how they are going to do it. Of course it will first appear crystallized in some movement higher up for some new candidate like Seth Low or Theo. Burton [Mayor Seth Low of New York City and Senator T. E. Burton of Ohio] or some highly respectable person without teeth or claws, and then the fellows down in Wall Street will begin stealing the South away from Taft. They won't expect to win with their eminently respectable person, but I believe the game is this: they hope to tie up the convention for a ballot or two between LaFollette and Taft and Eminently Respectable Party and then let off the fireworks and stampede her to you. I think you might just as well prepare for the fireworks because it is coming. You can't stave it off, and while up to the present time I have been very excitedly against your being a standing candidate for 1912 and have believed that it would be a calamity to submit your name formally to any state convention, yet I am not altogether sure that it will not be about the best we can do to let the fireworks do their work, and that was one reason why I did not go to the Chicago conference. I have the utmost respect for Senator LaFollette's sincerity and for his fighting capacity. I have always said that I thought the country was not quite ready for him. I think he is due in 1916, and while, of course, if there is no other way out I am going to be for LaFollette bigger than a wolf, yet I did not want to get complicated in the situation by being a LaFollette boomer when I sincerely believe there is no immediate prospect of LaFollette's nomination.

I am writing to you so that you may have at least one evidence of sentiment in the West. I have been, as I believe I told you above, in Colorado. I was the moving spirit at a state meeting of progressives in Colorado where we organized by precincts and counties to send a progressive delegation to the National Republican Convention and help to initiate certain measures, the anti-pass law, workingman's compensation law, the eight-hour law for women, and a better primary law than they were able to get out of the legislature. The meeting was large and full of enthusiasm and I feel sure that, if Colorado could have a direct vote on presidential nominees, Taft would not stand any more show than a rabbit of getting the Colorado delegation. So far as I can see, it is so every place. I tried out the names of Taft, Roosevelt and LaFollette and Taft did not get a "hand" and they lifted the roof for you and LaFollette. The audiences that Taft is getting are charitably well described as "orderly and well behaved," but never is there any enthusiasm. His sun is set politically and I think will never rise again, though I am persuaded that he always will have the respect and perhaps the affection of the people, but never their confidence. You need not bother to answer this letter. It was not to draw out any answer from you, but I do not want you to forget to write in the flyleaf for the book, for Bill.

William Dean Howells was a source of inspiration for many young writers. As the editor of the Atlantic Monthly, *he launched many a young writer's career. In 1901, Howells had written that one of White's short stories "had seemed to me so perfect in its way that I should not have known how to better it."*

To WILLIAM DEAN HOWELLS, November 10, 1911

MY DEAR MR. HOWELLS:

I bought this morning the first six volumes of your complete works. They have certainly put you up in a most quiet magnificence, and I have enjoyed the books as books exceedingly. I have ordered the complete set. It is a great joy to me to have these books in this form. I am sending you herewith two dozen blank flyleaves. I should be pleased indeed if you would autograph these leaves and send them to me, and I shall have our bindery insert them in the books as they come out. It would give me great joy also if you would send me an autograph photograph, or a print of any kind, with your name on it. You will never know what I have got from reading your works. Probably my work is of so poor a character that it does not show it, but it would have been much poorer if it had not been for you and your set. Mrs. White and I have been talking of you and still hold the hope that you will come and visit us in a quiet way without having to catch trains or do anything but sit on the porch or in your room and ride out behind an old family horse in a two-seated family surrey. We have most beautiful autumns and delightful Mays. I wish that you and your daughter might find it possible to saunter out here sometime and see us. You may be interested in knowing that I have about completed another novel of something like two hundred thousand words. When

I say completed I mean that I have written the first draft. It will take six months or a year to revise it. I seem to write in haste and revise at leisure. Mrs. White and I particularly wish to be remembered to Miss Howells and of course Mrs. White joins me in the invitation above.

The advertising carried by the Gazette *varied widely from that of some country dailies. Frequently, individuals like the recipient of the following letter, wrote White and asked what his advertising policy was.*

To ERNEST H. CHERRINGTON, November 29, 1911

DEAR MR. CHERRINGTON:

We do not run liquor advertisements of any kind, not even Peruna or lemon extract. We do not accept even Hostetter's Bitters or Pabst Malt. We used to take Pabst Malt and Hostetter's, but when we found they were largely booze, we cut them out as we did Peruna. We do not accept cigarette advertisements nor advertising for the "making's." We find on the whole that it pays us to make this elimination.

Progressive Republicans in Congress organized a Progressive League in 1911 which stirred sentiment for Robert M. LaFollette as the Republican nominee for president in 1912. Although White was sympathetic to this boom, by late 1911 he realized that popular feeling seemed to be for Theodore Roosevelt.

My Dear Joe:

I am enclosing you herewith the copy of a letter that I just received from Judge Burnette [Judge J. A. Burnette of Winfield, Kansas]. I have just returned from a business trip to Butler County. Also I have received a lot of letters, business and personal, and in those letters the subject of politics is generally touched upon and in almost every instance I find the writers mentioning Roosevelt in about the same strain that Judge Burnette mentions him. I think there is absolutely no doubt at all but that Kansas would be for Roosevelt overwhelmingly against either LaFollette or Taft or against both LaFollette and Taft, and I think you will find that the sentiment of Kansas is the sentiment of the nation. I have expressed to you privately, and have written publicly many times, my clear conviction as to the worth and character of Senator LaFollette and as to my choice between them. I know of course that with LaFollette as president we should go further, much further, so far as the executive department of the government is concerned than with Mr. Roosevelt or with anyone else. I know perfectly well, and have so set forth in the Gazette and in the American Magazine, that Roosevelt has a weakness for compromise. He believes it is his strength, but men like you and I believe it is his weakness. But it is just that weakness that makes him strong in this crisis. We can and will nominate Roosevelt. And while I believe it is all right for Senator LaFollette to keep up the fight, and so long as he is in the fight I shall support him, yet I believe his chances for nomination are so remote as to be negligible, and I think you ought to know the truth. Moreover, assuming that we should get a delegation for Roosevelt from Kansas, no one who is possible as a convention delegate from Kansas for Roosevelt would fail to land for LaFollette quicker than a wink, if there was any chance to nominate LaFollette. So that I do not regard the growing Roosevelt sentiment, which I have not fostered by the way, with any degree of alarm to the progressive cause. But we must remember this about Roosevelt, that when he was in the White House before, he was confronted with a reactionary Congress. There was no considerable organized progressive minority in Congress. If he should go to the White House now, he would be confronted with an active, militant, effectively organized progressive group in both Houses and in both parties, and I cannot imagine Roosevelt allowing anyone to be more progressive than he. Therefore I do not consider with any trepidation the rise

[129]

of the Roosevelt wave, which I am sure is strong and permanent and will be overwhelming. . . .

Ex-President Roosevelt, at this point, was an associate editor of Outlook, *and this post afforded him an organ to help keep his views before the public.*

To Theodore Roosevelt, January 16, 1912

My Dear Colonel Roosevelt:

Best of all the things you do I like your interpretations of books. It seems to me that you get a larger appeal to the intellectual leadership of America through those than through any other medium that you have. I am wondering if you have read a book called "Mother" by Kathleen Norris, published by Doubleday, Page and Co. If you have not, I believe you should get it. It comes nearer interpreting in terms of fiction the best aspirations of life as we Americans know it than any other book of its kind I know. If I were sure you did not have it, I should send you a copy because I do not know of a book I should rather give to you than that book, not necessarily for review, but simply to read. I have just finished reading a book called "The Call of the Carpenter" [written by Bouck White]. It seems to me that it should have a wide reading, but it should be introduced by someone who can tell the average reader that he must accept the book with large reservations and allowances for the overstatement that a propagandist of necessity has to make. We need a new interpretation of Christ. I think this age and generation has to find its own Christ. I like Dr. Abbott's [Dr. Lyman Abbott, pastor of the Brooklyn Plymouth Congregational Church and editor of the *Outlook*] Christ immensely and I think there is something in this book "The Call of the Carpenter," after allowing for its propagandist character, that should be generally read by the people. I do not like the idea of the pale, feminine, wishy-washy, otherworldly Christ that has grown out of the monkish idea of religion. I have always thought that

[130]

Paul was an old standpatter who came in and captured the Christian caucus and ran it into the organization. I wish you would read the book and tell me what you think of it. I know nothing about the authors of these two books. I have never seen them or heard from them, and I may be wrong about the publishers as they are not before me while I am writing, but it seems to me that they are mighty fine expressions of something that badly needs expression, though I wish that the "Call of the Carpenter" had been written more in the spirit of Tolstoy . . . but even as it stands it is well worth reading.

I won't fuss with you for a minute about your presidential boom, but I want to quarrel with you about the style of writing you are dropping into. You remember years ago how we used to fuss about McKinley's long, involved sentences that didn't get anywhere. They had a tendency to fatigue the reader. I am afraid you are going to fall into that habit yourself. I have taken your article in this week's Outlook and have marked up a lot of the sentences to show you what I mean. It seems to me that you are developing a nervous rather than a lucid style. You seem to be in a hurry to get it said and out of your way. You put in too many parenthetical explanations. If I were you, I should make it a point to break up my sentences. I have gone over your last article, and I find you have a lot of sentences running from seven to twenty lines. A man is entitled in a two thousand word article to have three sentences that long, but you had a lot of them that long. Your famous message of January 13, 1908 [probably refers to Roosevelt's message to Congress on Jan. 31, 1908, denouncing business corruption], I think it was, was a great message, but it also had a lot of those long sentences. It is the sort of writing that a lawyer does, and not the sort of writing that a craftsman does, and I wish you would quit it. Speaking of the famous message, it would have been forty per cent better if you could have trimmed down those sentences and put it more into Lincoln's style. Lincoln was one of the few lawyer-writers whose style did not read like a publication notice or a sheriff's sale. I love to read him. You have an immense fund of ideas, and they come crowding in on you, but what you want to do is to take a club and bat them off. End your sentence and then reach out and get another idea and put it down in another sentence. Take this to Mrs. Roosevelt and ask her if what I say is not true.

P.S. Since reading the above to Sallie she says you have read and written about "Mother." If you have I'm glad.

On February 21, 1912, Theodore Roosevelt openly announced that his hat was in the ring for the Republican nomination. White helped secure a Roosevelt delegation from Kansas and in the process was himself elected Republican national committeeman from Kansas. He had high hopes that Roosevelt could capture the national convention.

To C. A. MILLS, Topeka, Kan., May 10, 1912

MY DEAR MR. MILLS:

Certainly I appreciate to the full the fine spirit that was upon you when you obeyed the impulse to write your kind letter to me congratulating me upon my selection for national committeeman. It is always a good thing to obey a fine impulse, and I thank you for it. Naturally, I have no illusions in the matter of this National Committee job. I do not think it will add particularly to my prestige and all that it will add to my power will come at the expense of considerable time that might otherwise be employed with profit. However, I sought the job with my eyes open and with a distinct purpose in view. I wish to be on that National Committee four years from now when we will probably have the problem of reorganizing the Republican party. It will be the biggest problem before the country. I believe the storm will break in the National Committee. I believe it will break upon the question of the apportionment of delegates. I believe that our party must be definitely either liberal or else definitely reactionary. I believe that it cannot be liberal unless it is prepared to go into the last ditch and fight for principle time and again, putting up platforms and candidates with only secondary regard for temporary victories. I do not believe a national party can be organized along those high lines until it has eliminated all the mercenary elements in it. I believe for instance that the present apportionment of delegates upon the basis of Congressional districts rather than upon the basis of votes puts our party in the attitude of hiring Hessians for the fight and Hessians are not last-ditch fighters. We must discharge the Hessians. We must recruit the army from volunteers who believe in the cause as a cause and not as a meal ticket. With that definite end in view, I acquired and promoted a ravening ambition to be national committeeman. I may not have large influence, but I am at least going to do my best and I believe my time will come three or four years from now. My only hope is that I may have wisdom and courage and kindness sufficient to be of some account in the large fight. I thank you again for your good letter.

Fighting Bob LaFollette stayed in the race for the Republican nomination to the end. He was extremely bitter toward the Roosevelt candidacy. After Taft was renominated, and Roosevelt withdrew to form the Bull Moose party, LaFollette remained within the Republican party fold. His strategy was to let the Old Guard lead the party to defeat and wait for 1916, when he hoped that the progressives could gain control.

To President Charles Van Hise, University of Wisconsin,
May 24, 1912

My Dear Mr. Van Hise:

I hope that our mutual friendship for Senator LaFollette will be sufficient excuse for writing this letter to you. I am deeply pained and in great anxiety at the conduct of Senator LaFollette in the campaign at this time. I feel that he is acting under a sad misapprehension of the facts. I feel that he is exhibiting animus against Colonel Roosevelt which, even if based upon the facts that LaFollette presupposed, would be unmanly, undignified and politically suicidal to him, and absolutely disastrous to the cause for which we are all working. I see by the papers that in Ohio Senator LaFollette devoted most of his time to abusing Colonel Roosevelt. Colonel Roosevelt is a very human person. He has done a number of things which I cannot agree with. I feel very strongly about some of his faults. But, on the other hand, I believe that his faults are entirely secondary faults, temperamental rather than fundamental. I think he has done great service to the progressive cause as a preacher. I have not regarded him as a great constructive statesman, and I think in the past he has been prone to compromise in things that I have regarded as vital. But he has learned in the bitter school of experience much in the last four years that will make him a sounder, safer man and more aggressive president than he ever was. He knows whom to appoint for federal judge, he understands the state boss system, he would never tie up with a Payne or a Spooner [Congressman S. E. Payne, coauthor of the Payne-Aldrich Tariff, and conservative Senator Spooner of Wisconsin], he knows how the railroads and insurance companies and brewers form an autocracy in state government. He knows it because that autocracy has opposed him in this fight in every American state. He does not know it as LaFollette knew it, as a lifelong struggle, but nevertheless Roosevelt has got the idea of what the autocracy of politics means thoroughly into his head.

Moreover, he did not crowd LaFollette out of the race. I thought in November and December that LaFollette could win against Taft. I became thoroughly convinced in January and February that La-Follette could not carry Kansas, and if he could not carry Kansas he could not make a very strong race. I went over our community thoroughly when I found that LaFollette was not holding his own. I studied the men from one end of our town and county to the other carefully. I did not want Roosevelt to run. The files of my letter-book will show that I wrote letter after letter telling him that I thought his candidacy would be a mistake. When he got in, it was all one way in Kansas. In the counties wherein we put LaFollette's name on the ballot, LaFollette did not receive to exceed thirty or forty votes to a county. It has been the same all over the United States. If LaFollette had been pitted against Taft, Taft would have won. It was not that LaFollette is not in many ways better equipped than Roosevelt. The whole thing lies in the fact that the prestige of the ex-presidency was a powerful weapon in this contest.

I am writing to you in the hope that you may say some word or will have some influence upon Senator LaFollette that will make him see things as they are. It would be a serious mistake for him to tie up with the Taft forces in the organs of the National Convention. Moreover, it would be a calamity if he should vote alone and allow the Taft forces to organize that convention. If he would tie up the nomination, that is his fair play, but to tie up the organization of the convention, to give the reactionary forces in that convention the immense advantages of organization, so that by force and violence and cheating they might force the progressive delegates into a bolt and leave the reactionary forces in control of the party organization for the next ten years, would put an immense machinery and weapon for righteousness into their hands, and I hope he may not do that. I am not writing this letter at the suggestion, direct or indirect, of Colonel

Roosevelt or any friend of Colonel Roosevelt's. I have talked only to Mrs. White. But it does seem to me if you have any influence with Senator LaFollette, as a patriot and as a friend, it is your opportunity to use it for good. I have been accused of deserting Senator LaFollette. I did not desert him at all. In forming our "Roosevelt for President" league in Kansas, I made part of the platform declaration a message of congratulation to Senator LaFollette for his North Dakota victory and a specific declaration of him as a pioneer leader in the progressive movement. In our Republican state platform, which I largely wrote, I inserted an endorsement of Senator LaFollette and a specific instruction for our delegates to vote with his delegates upon the organization of the convention. Moreover, so far as it was within my power, I saw to it that no man was named by the Kansas progressives for delegate to Chicago who would not, if it ever became wise or expedient, vote for LaFollette for president. This last I did under a definite promise from Mr. McKenzie at the LaFollette headquarters in Washington last March that I would do so. So that whatever suspicion lurks in LaFollette's mind that I have deserted him is without warrant or foundation. If I had put the name of Senator LaFollette on the ballot in Kansas, it would have resulted in a defeat for him and possibly a victory for Taft. I set these things down to let you know my attitude toward the Senator and to make it plain why I turn to you rather than to him personally at this time. If you know of anybody in Wisconsin to whom this letter may be turned over in confidence, you have my permission to use it as you will, except that I do not want it made a public document or printed in any newspaper at this time.

Kindly remember me to Mrs. Van Hise and your family and to my acquaintances about the University.

Thirteen states chose their delegates to the Republican convention by primaries and in these states Theodore Roosevelt swept the field. The bosses, however, were for Taft and where delegates were chosen by state conventions, Taft was overwhelmingly successful. At the convention, the credentials of two hundred delegates were in dispute. When these seats were awarded to Taft men, Roosevelt and his fol-

lowers withdrew and amid scenes of ardent enthusiasm launched the Progressive (Bull Moose) party. White resigned his post as Republican national committeeman and accepted a similar post in the new party. He helped to write the party platform, and he ran the Roosevelt campaign in Kansas.

To John S. Phillips, *American Magazine*, August 20, 1912

My Dear John:

... Mrs. White and the children will be in Colorado until school begins so that they can come home fresh and happy. I was called back by politics and have charge of the Kansas campaign and will be here from now until November. I think you fellows overemphasize Roosevelt. He is a mere incident to this new party. If you had been with me, John, through the four or five days' session of the subcommittee on platform and through the all-night session of the General Committee, and, if you had seen the crowd and understood the spirit of the session of the Progressive party, you would understand that Roosevelt is not the Progressive party, but that the fighting men in the progressive ranks of both parties are in this thing and mean business and no man on earth can divert them. The Progressive party is here to stay as the definitely radical party of this Nation, and, if any man tries to divert it to his personal ends, so much the worse for that man.* The Progressive party is here to stay, and I am satisfied it is going to have a place, perhaps not a winning place, but a definite place in American politics for the next thirty years as [?] a great stirring movement in our country, a movement to change the environment of poverty so that whatever of poverty is due to environment may be removed. That is the meaning and core of the whole Progressive movement. Change the environment of men in these conditions so that environment may not react and cause chronic poverty, that is an idea bigger than Theodore Roosevelt, bigger than the tariff and bigger than any little two-by-four scheme of reform that ever has struck any party. This Progressive movement is a great humanitarian movement, and that is why it is guided by the passion for humanity as evidenced in all of its writings and all of its work.

* In spite of White's optimism that the Bull Moose party was not a vehicle for Roosevelt, the party collapsed when Roosevelt refused to be its candidate in 1916.

Throughout his lifetime, White was an ardent exponent of civil liberties and equal rights for all, regardless of race, creed, or color. His most notable struggle against religious and racial hatred came with his attacks on the Ku-Klux Klan in the early 1920's. The following letter was written to a colored student at the University of Kansas who had written him protesting racial discriminaion in the University gymnasium.

To Hazel McDaniel, Lawrence, Kan. September 28, 1912

My Dear Miss McDaniel:

I have your letter of September 26. Your letter was the first information I had as to the situation of which you speak. I was born and grew up in Kansas and had for my playmates, and have retained through life, the friendship of members of your race. Personally, I have never known the curious psychical mania known as race prejudice, yet I know that it does exist and brings a great deal of sorrow and injustice into the world. Your story of the discrimination against the colored people at the State University in the gymnasium interests me. I do not know what if any power the Regents have in the matter. I feel, however, that if there is anything we can do, I for one should be glad to do anything I could to ameliorate the situation as you describe it. The Board will meet October 22, I believe. You may find the exact date from the Chancellor. At that time I shall be glad, and I feel that the whole Board would be glad, to talk to an authorized committee of your people.

You doubtless know that the problem that you present is full of difficulties and embarrassments on both sides. It is only a phase of one of our greatest national problems. We must meet it squarely and with kind hearts and common sense on both sides, your race and my race. It seems to me that the great danger in the big problem, and in our particular little problem, is from a lack of kind hearts and common sense upon both sides. And I know that it is particularly hard to be sensible and gentle while suffering under injustice, and yet unless both sides do use common sense and kindness, no solution is possible.

I should suggest that you go to Chancellor Strong with your case. Present it to him as dispassionately as possible while waiting for the Board of Regents to meet. Chancellor Strong is a broad-minded, conscientious man. I believe that he, on the ground, knowing the conditions, will be able to frame up some kind of a working plan that will be satisfactory to you and your friends, that the Board will approve.

I thank you most sincerely for giving me the opportunity you have given me to express my deep sympathy with the heroic struggle your people are making to get into an intellectual and social stratum wherein you may know something of the more abundant life which our civilization holds and to attain which is the greatest of human aspirations.

In the presidential campaign, Taft and the Republicans definitely represented the forces of conservatism while Roosevelt and Wilson were in the liberal tradition. Wilson polled only 42 per cent of the popular vote, but won an overwhelming victory in the electoral college. Roosevelt won 27 per cent of the popular vote and carried six states. Taft with 23 per cent of the vote carried only Utah and Vermont. Wilson carried Kansas by 15,000 votes. W. R. Stubbs was defeated for the Senate by the Democratic candidate, and Arthur Capper just barely lost the governorship.

To Theodore Roosevelt, November 14, 1912

My Dear Colonel:

I have not written to you before because I supposed everybody else was writing to you and letters would clutter up your desk. We lost, but on the whole I am entirely satisfied. Stubbs was defeated, which was too bad, but it is the fortunes of politics and he must take it. The fact that the prohibition law has to be enforced in a state like this makes it impossible for a man to live long in politics. Of course all the reactionaries were against him, and the wet vote, which is generally Progressive, but never Progressive before it is wet, made the result inevitable. Stubbs, however, is a thoroughbred and will be of more value outside the Senate than in it. For he is going to devote himself to the cause in Kansas, during the next few years, as an organizer. And we will have more of him at home, and less of him at Washington, than we would have had otherwise. I think he is more enthusiastic than ever for the Progressive party.

[138]

As you know we did not have a party organization in this state because the election law prevents a party from going on the ballot that has not been organized six months. We lost everything in the state except Murdock [Victor Murdock] who came through with a good majority and whose district was the only district in the state that was for you. Do not forget that in sizing up Murdock. We spent $11,000 in the campaigns, the one before the primary and the one after the Progressive National Convention. We had $400 in the bank the morning after the election and we had $400 additional ready to send to the National Committee. I asked Mr. Perkins [George W. Perkins, chairman of the Executive Committee of the Bull Moose Party] if we could use this money to put our state organization on its feet, and he gave me permission to do so. So we have $800 and are starting out to organize the state for the new party from the township up. Eighty of the one hundred and five county Republican committeemen have been working with us for the last four months, and we expect all of them to go into the new party. I am now testing them out by letter and asking them to fill out such of their committeemen as will not come with us, and we will put county organizations in the other counties. By January 29 we expect to have a big state-wide meeting and hold a banquet in honor of the fifty-second anniversary of the admission of Kansas to the Union and formally make our state organization, organize the State Central Committee, electing state chairman and putting ourselves where we can get on the ballot for the 1914 election. I have no doubt that we shall be able to carry the state two years from now. And at that time Senator Bristow will run for re-election, and I feel sure that he will run as a Progressive on the Progressive ticket. Murdock of course will be with us. Capper, Republican nominee for governor in the recent election, who seems to be elected by twenty-six majority—a bare squeak—I feel also will be with us in 1914 as he supported you in this campaign.

Mrs. White has not been well since you left Emporia.* She has hardly been able to be out of her room. I never was so well in my life and never had a more beautiful time than the last six or eight months I have put in working for the Progressive cause. I hope now to get a year in which I may work on a new novel, which I have not even looked at since we began the hike for Armageddon. If the Lord and the Progressives will let me have a year to myself, I believe I can turn out a real story. I have written the thing through, but revision is always the greater part of my work.

* During the campaign, Roosevelt spent a Sunday with White in Emporia.

The publishers of James Whitcomb Riley's poetry, the Bobbs-Merrill Company, wrote to Editor White objecting to his printing of a Riley poem without copyright permission.

To the BOBBS-MERRILL COMPANY, Indianapolis, Ind.,
November 21, 1912

GENTLEMEN:

I received your courteous note of November 12 calling my attention to the fact that the Emporia Gazette on November 4 published a poem, "When the Frost is on the Pumpkin," by Mr. James Whitcomb Riley. I note you desire to know by what authority we are publishing Mr. Riley's poems without credit. Replying I take pleasure in saying that during the first few days of every November for the past seventeen years I have printed "When the Frost is on the Pumpkin" and during the first few days of every April for the past seventeen years I have printed "When the Green Gets Back in the Trees." These are the only two poems excepting Walt Mason's rhymes which the Gazette prints. The habit is confirmed. Hereafter we shall try to give credit to the Bobbs-Merrill Co. If you desire to sue us, I am perfectly willing to go to jail and rot there for the privilege of giving my readers the benefit of these two poems. Kindly take this up with my friend Billy Bobbs [president of the company], and ask him if I shall prepare to have my meals served in jail. If so, I shall take more interest in the candidate for sheriff and less interest in the candidate for president than I have heretofore. With great respect I am—

The Whites spent the winter and spring of 1913 at La Jolla, California, where White worked on the revision of In the Heart of a Fool. *On White's birthday, February 10, the* Gazette *force sent him a telegram signed by the entire staff. The next mail from California brought this reply.*

DEAR FRIENDS:

Your telegram on my birthday was the finest thing outside of the love of my family that came to me. God has been good to me, exceedingly good. Without anything like adequate return or service from me, he has given me freely everything in this world that wise men wish: opportunity for usefulness, health, comfort, the love of those near to me. And among all the good things I know, your love and loyalty stands deep and precious in my grateful heart. I hope I may be worthy of it.

Progressive party affairs occupied a considerable share of White's time until the death of the party in 1916. George Perkins, the recipient of this letter, was chairman of the Executive Committee of the party. The western Progressives, in general, came to have an acute distaste for Perkins, largely because of his close connection with Wall Street.

To GEORGE PERKINS, New York City, June 24, 1913

MY DEAR MR. PERKINS:

I received today by express a package containing one hundred copies of the Progressive platform from the National headquarters, for which I am much obliged. The express on the package was 75¢. I took it to the postoffice and found that the package could have been sent third class mail for 40¢, thus saving 35¢. Of course, this is not a large matter, but it is a considerable matter when it runs into thousands of packages as it did last fall. The mailing department of the Progressives at the National headquarters during the last campaign was run without the slightest manifestation of human intelligence. Thousands of dollars worth of stuff was sent out by express, which might just as well have been sent out in carload lots by freight and distributed from Chicago, Denver and San Francisco. This little package which cost 40% more than was necessary is but a continuation of that policy. A good, intelligent sixteen-year-old office boy could beat it. If our party means anything, it means efficient management of large affairs, and to exhibit such crass, unjustifiable inefficiency in the very first movement toward free government shakes one's faith in the whole Progressive proposition. I have talked with committeemen from a number of our western states, and we all have exactly the same feelings that either we must have a new office boy in New York or a new party.

On many occasions during his lifetime White helped raise money for the families of dead newspaper friends or the families of old childhood friends. He also aided a number of young people to acquire a college education. When Lew Smucker, old El Dorado chum, died, White pitched in to aid the widow and children.

To CHARLES W. SMITH, Kingfisher, Okla., June 25, 1913

MY DEAR MR. SMITH:

You probably do not remember me as a little boy running around El Dorado with Lew Smucker thirty years ago. I used to carry notes for you up to Smuckers' when you and Frank Ramond and the other young blades of El Dorado had intentions on the pretty Smucker girls. I asked Carrie Smucker to come up and visit us for two days, and I have gone over her situation very carefully. I need not outline it to you, as you know it as well as I. I feel a deep sense of duty to help Carrie in her problem. Mrs. White and I feel that, if she could come to Emporia and rent a small modern cottage such as she could get for $12 or $15, by renting one or two rooms to girl students, she might split her rent to $6 or $8, and then if she had a steady income of about $40 or $45 a month, she could live without going out to work and neglecting her little brood. I once met Charles Smucker in Emporia and I have taken the liberty that a lifelong friendship with Lew might permit of writing to him asking if he can appropriate something toward that income. Naturally, I expect to put in my share, and

Mrs. White and I expect by daily watchfulness and care to do what can be done, and in that way make life easier for Carrie and the children. I know you will not think I am intruding into the private affairs of your family in taking this deep interest in Carrie, and I know you will understand the spirit that prompts me to hope that you may be so circumstanced that you can give us some help in this problem. I should be pleased to hear from you at length, and wish you would remember me most kindly to your wife, whom I have not seen in years. I remember your children as little girls hardly in their teens it seems to me, playing about the Smucker home and now they say they are young women married and settled in life. This seems most marvelous to me. I remember well when you and Kitty Smucker, as a bridal pair, boarded at our house, and I was only fifteen years old, yet it was thirty years ago. Time certainly does pull out the throttle and let her go. Hoping you will pardon me for this intrusion and let my affection for Lew be my excuse, I remain—

Increasingly over the years, White received a large number of letters from people he did not know, asking his advice on a wide variety of problems. He followed the practice of answering all these letters.

To Miss Elizabeth Roberts, Park College, Parkville, Mo.,
September 11, 1913

Dear Miss Roberts:

Replying to your letter of September 8, inquiring about the fundamental problems that arise in my business and the qualities required to meet them, I will say that the thing that causes me most trouble is a lack of intelligence and courage, and the things that I need most to overcome my troubles are intelligence and courage. After that, pretty nearly everything else will follow because, when one is intelligent and brave, he is generally kind. It is only ignorant people who are cruel, and kindness, wisdom and courage are the three things in this world that are the fundamental virtues, as I see it.

[143]

In the fall of 1913, Theodore Roosevelt was to leave on an expedition up the Amazon River. White had spent the summer in Colorado and had returned to Emporia in late September when this letter was written. White's analysis of the forces that made up the Progressive party has considerable insight and importance.

To THEODORE ROOSEVELT, September 24, 1913

MY DEAR COLONEL:

I have been figuring for three weeks, ever since I got home from Colorado, that I ought to write to you at last before you went to South America. While in Colorado, I had an opportunity to see considerable of the Progressives, and I was a guest of honor at a Progressive banquet in Denver, a most enthusiastic banquet, about three weeks ago. The spirit there was splendid and I never addressed a more encouraging meeting. I find the same thing in Arizona and in California, as I believe I may have written you during the summer.

For all these outward manifestations of unflagging interest, it seems to me we are in a rather curious psychological condition as a party. Coming home, I find that our state organization is intact, that not a man who had left the Republican party and joined our organization has gone back. Our county organizations, as nearly as I can tell, are perfect. The state chairman writes me that there have been no breaks in any of our organization people, and yet I have a curious, indefinable feeling—the feeling I had two years ago when I wrote you along in October that you would have to run for president, although I was for LaFollette at the time—I say I have this curious feeling that there has been an immense slump of what might be called the "sheep vote." As nearly as I can figure it out, we have attracted to ourselves thousands of men of the college professor, country lawyer, country doctor and country merchant type, men of considerable education and much more than the average intelligence of their fellows. These men, in the aggregate, number a million votes. They are the leaders of thought in the community, and they have not been fazed. I think they are as strong, if not stronger, than they were last year in the faith, but their clerks and the small farmer and the unskilled laboring man have minds that are moved largely by two things—tradition and noise. Our noise has subsided and party tradition is pulling them. Whether or not our noise will attract them again, I cannot say . . . There was, in addition

[144]

to the sheep votes, in our four million total, I should think, a million, perhaps not quite so many, Teddy votes—votes of men who had confidence in you personally without having any particular intelligent reason to give why; except that you were a masculine sort of a person with extremely masculine virtues and palpably masculine faults, for which they loved you, but who voted with the Progressives, without caring a cent for the minimum wage or the initiative and referendum, or the mother's pension, merely because they wanted to vote for you. We are going to lose the sheep votes and the Teddy votes, though we will probably get them from time to time, but it will be many years before we can hold the sheep votes. By all the chains of tradition, they are bound to the Republican party and unless you are the candidate, we will not get the Teddy votes, and certainly will not get them in our Congressional and state elections. There are, it seems to me, a fairly good two million votes in the box that will not be shaken by defeat and that may be counted on to run along for four years, maybe six, possibly eight. . . .

Now the question that we must all settle is, what are we going to do about it? Personally, I would favor going ahead, holding our own, trusting to events to show the country the futility of having a so-called Progressive faction in either of the old parties, and hoping that either in three or five years we may accumulate enough from the Democrats and from the sheep votes of the Republicans to carry a national election and dominate Congress.

Until recently I have not thought you should run in 1916. I have thought that it would be better to demonstrate that we were not a one-man party, that our platform was more important than our candidates.

I have changed my mind definitely. I believe that, if we hold together as a party organization, you must run in 1916, and that if you are not prepared to make the sacrifice, it would be rather unwise to maintain a party organization. I know this will strike you as being rather a radical position for me to take, but I believe that your popularity is a political fact that we cannot ignore, and that you will dramatize our platform better than any other man in the United States now can do it. Naturally, it is not time for you to say that you will be a candidate in 1916. It would be a tragical mistake for you to do so but, nevertheless, you must get it into your head and keep it there and govern yourself accordingly. . . .

I do not want you to trouble to answer this in the hurry of your preparations for going away, but when you are out at sea or in the wilderness, or are any place where you feel that you would like to tell your troubles to a policeman, you can write me what you think about things in general. I wish from time to time you would send me some sort of an itinerary, so I will know where a letter could reach you. I think I know the political situation in this part of the country fairly well, and I think you should know it from a confidential standpoint, and if you care for it blood raw, without any seasoning, I will give it to you. . . .

Woodrow Wilson's success in enacting a remarkable number of progressive laws led White to write editorials praising the Democratic administration. A number of people, thereupon, wrote White asking why he didn't join the Democratic party.

To Mr. Carl W. Moore, Kinsley, Kan., November 25, 1913

My Dear Mr. Moore:

I find your letter of the 21st on my desk when I returned from Kansas City where I have been with Mrs. White, who is under medical treatment, and only my absence from my desk has delayed my answering your letter.

I appreciate very much your kindness in going into this matter so thoroughly. You are, however, under one very serious misapprehension. I do not regard the Democratic party as progressive. It can never be progressive. It must be historically and constitutionally the conservative party of this nation. Just now, it is under a temporary aberration in having two progressive leaders, Bryan and Wilson, the one being a sincere but rather second-rate man mentally, and the other being a highly intellectual man without very much but intellect to commend him. But the Democratic party, it seems to me, and I have always said, is the inevitable residuary legatee of all conservatism in this country. I would sooner think of being a third-party Prohibitionist or a Socialist than of being a Democrat as the party is now constituted, so long as it is fettered by the ideas of state rights and free trade. These two ideas make it inexorably conservative. I have never at any time said that I thought the Democratic party was a progressive party, and if the Progressive party is to break up, I, for one, would advise every sincere Progressive to beware of Democratic promises under any consideration, no matter how fair they might temporarily sound. What I have said is this: that so long as the Democratic party is under its present progressive leadership, it will be hard sledding for the Progressives. I have a hope that we can make the Progressive party a party definitely and consistently progressive without having to spend any of the time we would have to spend in the Republican party converting our fellow partisans. Then, when we win a victory, which may be some time off, the victory will mean something definite and will not mean a compromise with those in the party who believe something else. I realize that you do not think this way and, of course, I cannot convince you, but I at least wish you would give me credit for having such rudiments of common sense as would see that the Democratic party is not and never can be a progressive party. I admire Mr. Wilson very much. I respect the sincerity and courage of Mr. Bryan, though I do not have much belief in his intellectual clarity, and I think they are doing a pretty fair job of redeeming the Democratic promises, but I have a low opinion of the Democratic promises which they are redeeming.

In discussing these matters, it seems to me that it is only fair that we should each admit that the other is reasonably honest in his position. There is no absolute black nor absolute white, nor right and wrong in this situation. There is a large gray area in which perfectly honest men may stand and entirely disagree with one another. . . .

To ROBERT BRIDGES, Charles Scribner's Sons, December 29, 1913

DEAR MR. BRIDGES:

. . . It may interest you in passing to know that I am still carrying the Progressive banner out here in the wilderness and am very happy in the job, though the whole trouble with the Progressive proposition is that your man Wilson has rather oversold the Progressive territory, and it makes it hard to take orders. What a fine, levelheaded president he is making! Really, the Progressives do not care who gets the progressive things done just so they are done, and President Wilson certainly is doing a fine job of getting many progressive things done.

To WILLIAM DEAN HOWELLS, New York City, January 29, 1914

DEAR MR. HOWELLS:

Mrs. White has been sick for the last month in Kansas City, and I have been going up to see her every week. Last week she gave me "The Quality of Mercy" to read. It had cheered her lonely hours for a day or two, and I have had it with me for four or five days, and have most finished it. It has been twenty years or more since I read it in the newspapers when Sam McClure [S. S. McClure, the first man to capitalize on syndicating material to newspapers] was syndicating it around, as I recollect it. I was not old enough to appreciate it to the full then, and I hope that the next twenty years may give me as much as the last twenty years has brought me, so that I may read it again and have the joy in it that I have just received. It is a wonderfully fine book. I have always thought that "Bartley Hubbard," "Silas Lapham" and "Fulkerson" were your great achievements, but I guess "Northwick" will have to stand with them. What a great pleasure it must be to you to know that all the time in the world somebody is reading the beautiful things you have done, and is being led to better and stronger living by what you have done. I only wish that you would get out that set of your complete works. It ought to be done, and you ought to do it yourself. I most earnestly hope that within the next year you will have that job finished.

Give my sincerest regards to Miss Howells and to your son and his wife and the dear little baby whom I saw two years ago.

Is not Wilson doing fine and splendid things? The appointment of Brand Whitlock [reform mayor of Toledo, Ohio, appointed minister to Belgium] gave me great joy.

The Gazette *printed letters from its readers in a column entitled "The Wailing Place." Editor White, however, would not print anonymous letters nor letters designed to stir racial and religious hatreds.*

To F. W. Ives, Emporia, Kan., February 3, 1914

Dear Mr. Ives:

I regret exceedingly that I cannot publish your article attacking the Catholic Church. The Catholic Church in Emporia I do not regard as a serious menace and, after all, the Gazette has to be more or less local in its sphere. I know a good many things about the Methodist Church that I do not like, and some things about the Congregational Church that are highly disagreeable to me, although I pay toward its support. I do not believe in stirring up religious feeling in an otherwise quiet community, when the community life does not seem to justify it.

If there is ever a serious attempt to shut off the free press, and if that attempt very seriously threatens, I shall be glad to stand for a free press . . . It is not seriously threatened, and I regard the agitation as largely for political purposes.

I trust this is a satisfactory reason for declining to print your communication, and you may so communicate it to your Lodge.

To George Perkins, Progressive Party Headquarters,
February 20, 1914

My Dear Mr. Perkins:

I have your letter and note that you say there is considerable demand for Col. Roosevelt running for governor of New York. I think it would be a mistake. I am not even sure that it is wise for him to run for the presidency in 1916, though I did think so last October, but it begins to look as though it would not be wise to risk him for 1916 when we can make dead sure winning in 1920.

I do not figure it out that the Progressive party is dead by a long shot. I think we are more alive than we have been since the start, not that we have more votes, but we have more intelligent, coherent sentiment for a party as a party and not a big noise around the Colonel's name. I think the Colonel should get into the campaign in 1916, and I think he should be more or less active in 1914, making speeches in those states where there is a chance for us to win something or where there is a chance for us to make a real killing, as in Pennsylvania, Ohio, Illinois, Kansas, California, and a few states like that. In a state like Connecticut, where there is no show, I do not believe it is sensible for the Colonel to talk. I believe there is a chance in Massachusetts. It looks good in Maine, and probably Vermont is better than New Hampshire, though why it should be Heaven only knows. But, nevertheless, I do not believe that it is wise for the Colonel to throw away his prestige by going to states where there is no show either in 1914 or 1916. And if he were beaten in New York in 1914, he would not be worth so much for us in 1916.

This, however, is all the opinion of a man who looks at the situation fifteen hundred miles from the center of it, and is subject to amendment and debate.

The following letter is an excellent analysis of the main problem that has beset both Republican and Democratic parties for the past fifty years. Both parties have contained conservatives as well as progressives. White felt, in 1914, that little progress could develop from such a situation. A new party containing all liberal-minded people was his solution. The 1914 situation in Kansas was delicate because Senator Bristow insisted on running in the Republican primary, as did Arthur Capper, for the post of governor. In order to hold the Progressive party intact, the Progressive party ran Victor Murdock for the Senate and Henry J. Allen for governor.

To Judge J. A. Burnette, Topeka, Kan., March 7, 1914

My Dear Judge:

Your letter was frank, and I liked it. I had a lot rather have a letter like that than a pollyfoxing letter, because your letter was all man, and while it gave me a bad morning, I am glad it came, and I think more of you for writing it than if you had ducked or sidestepped. The reason why you gave me a bad morning is that I got a look at myself through friendly eyes, and yet eyes that I know must be essentially kind toward me. I have had an idea that I was treating Bristow and Capper with the utmost fairness and consideration. I had no sort of an idea that I was abusing them. I do not remember that I have ever called Bristow a traitor, and I do not remember that I have ever called him a coward. I do think he did a dishonest thing to become a Republican merely to secure the traditional party vote. I think Capper is a little rabbity, but that is his nature and not the result of any particular combination of circumstances. He has caution developed where I have not and probably it would be better for me if I did have.

I have tried to make my position clear in this situation—that it is not for anybody's election, either to the Senate or as governor that I am striving. Personally, I have a high opinion of all the men running for governor, though I think Hodges [incumbent Democratic governor] has disappointed me by his petty partisan view of things, and yet I believe that even Hodges is honest and that Capper and Bristow and Allen and Murdock are square men. It is not a question of men with me. It is not even a question of the success or election of these men to any office . . . If one believes that it is most important to elect a thoroughly competent, entirely honest, and unusually wise man United States senator from Kansas this year, there can be no question but that my course is wrong and that your course is right.

I do not believe, however, that the most important thing in politics right now is to elect anyone in particular. The most important thing I see in politics right now is to establish in this nation a party—even a minority party—having a common belief in political, economic and social advancement. A party that shall believe the same thing in Kansas, Oregon, Florida or Maine. There is no such party now. Under the old parties, there can be no such party. For they are factional and sectional. It is not a question of bad men or good men. There are just as many Progressives who mistreat their wives and tap tills as there are Republicans or Democrats. . . .

I have been fighting in a factional party for ten years, and so long

[151]

as there is a . . . hope of organizing a non-factional, non-sectional party, as the Republican party was before it faced these new issues, I am going to make the fight for that party the chief consideration of my political activity. With me, it is not important that Bristow should be elected senator nor Murdock nor anyone else. Call it partisanship if you care to, call it party prejudice or party pride if you care to (and there is justice in the charge), but the fact remains that as I see the right I must follow it without compromise and without variableness or shadow of turning.

The end is, however, reasonably certain. Either this course on the part of the progressives all over the country will result in putting life into the Progressive party and making it a genuine vital force among the parties, or it will repeat defeat for the Republican party until the reactionaries in that party will grow discouraged and quit it, when it will be a progressive party. But one thing is sure. Real progress in American politics will never come with the party divisions as they are. With each of the old parties half free and half controlled by reactionaries, there is too much lost motion. By the time the advocates of a proposition have won a primary, have nominated candidates and have stated the proposition in a party platform, they are worn out. Then, in the legislature or Congress they have to meet a lot of men who are of their own party who disbelieve in the proposition, and there the fight begins anew. As a result, the desired law when it finally comes often is a compromise. As a result, America is behind the civilized world in social and industrial legislation. Our political forms are more reactionary and less responsive to public opinion than they are in many a monarchy, and with all our boast of being the land of the free, we are behind civilization in too many things. It will be so just as long as the party system is what it is today, and to change that system, to smash it, many men will have to be sacrificed. I believe Kansas, for instance, is progressive. If Bristow had run as a Progressive, he would have had with him all the Progressives and all of the progressive Republicans, for Curtis [Charles Curtis, Bristow's opponent in the Republican primary] would have had the Republican nomination and the Republican party in Kansas would have been negligible. I told Bristow by letter, by wire and by word of mouth that Murdock was going to run, if Bristow did not run, and that I would support Murdock and not Bristow. So there was no deception. He knew just exactly where he was going. But he said to me: "Will, there are fifty thousand Republican voters who will vote for me on the Republican ticket, who will vote for Curtis, or for anyone else, and we need those votes to win." That I admit, if winning is the only thing you want. But I said: "In getting these fifty thousand voters who can't think, you will lose fifty thousand who do think—so there you are." He answered: "I'll not lose 'em." It is evident now that he will lose them.

But the whole difference between us hinges on these "fifty thousand voters who will vote for anyone on the Republican ticket." That is the drag on progress. They will sustain a reactionary in his stand; they will sustain a progressive in his stand. But they will not sustain a progressive in his stand against party organization. They are the people in each party, who keep both parties half free and half conservative. This undigested, meaningless vote, must be broken up; must be made to think; must be made to take a stand on its own judgment. For when a progressive Republican finds that it is either his country or his party, these men who are governed "by habit, tradition and inheritance" may stand by the party. They are the slow boats that break the speed of the fleet. And my theme in glory is to blast the rock. If they stay in the Republican party, they must be jolted into knowing what they are there for, if the Progressives go back. And today these fifty thousand unthinking voters do not know anything about the issues.

The fifty thousand Kansas Progressives do know about the issues. Every vote there will back a man up in going the distance. Every Progressive voter knows why he is a Progressive. The Progressive will appeal to the independent voter and will get a lot of them in Kansas—and a few Democrats; not as many as the fellows think, but a few. They will be the second party, and it is not impossible that they may land a few prizes. But that is unimportant, considering matters as I consider them, and as all the Progressive leaders I know consider things. We don't care what happens next autumn. We don't care what happens two years from now. We don't even care whether we finally get into the St. John [former governor of Kansas and for many years the regular presidential candidate of the Prohibition party] class, for our work will be accomplished. Others shall reap where we have sown, which is all right. We don't care to reap, but we do care that there shall be a harvest. We are now chiefly interested in planting the seed.

I have said all along—if you have read the Gazette as a penance for your sins, you may remember—that the Progressive party is no place for the fellows who want jobs.

The Progressives should enlist those who are willing to take long marches with hard bivouacs, and in the end only leave their unidentified political bones to mark the forward trail. We may become a great party. It is more than likely, but the problems which we have set forth will not be solved until either our party or some other party (and whatever comes it will not be the Democratic party, for Democracy is made irrevocably reactionary by the Negro question in the South) —until our party or some other party entirely reconstructed, entirely free of the unthinking votes and the reactionary faction, rises in the country, wholly consecrated to our ideals. I am fairly intimate with the Progressive leaders in this state and this nation. I talk with the Kansas leaders over the phone every day or two. I hear from the national leaders frequently. And I know they are not fooling me. I know that I share the common feeling as to our party, its aims and its destiny.

White was always a great admirer of James Whitcomb Riley's home-spun verse. In the early nineties, White wrote poetry modeled after Riley's and published it, with some of Albert Bigelow Paine's, in a book entitled Rhymes by Two Friends *(1893).*

To JAMES WHITCOMB RILEY, Indianapolis, Ind. April 25, 1914

MY DEAR OLD ARMY FRIEND:

I have been reading your complete works in the last few weeks and have read them through from "kiver to kiver." I do not know when I have had such a pleasant time. You have done a great and beautiful life's work. What a marvelous thing you did to pioneer along the line of homespun sentiment, in homespun language, for homespun folks. . . .

White regularly bestowed editorial praise on Wilson's "extraor-dinary" administration. During the summer of 1914, when World War I broke out, the Whites were in Colorado. Immediately, as this letter indicates, the attention of the public turned away from domestic reform to watch the course of the war. The war, plus the liberalism of Wilson, were two factors that greatly weakened the continuation of the Progressive party.

To JOSEPH TUMULTY, White House, Washington, D.C.,
September 4, 1914

MY DEAR MR. TUMULTY:

Just before I left on my vacation last summer, I received a beautiful letter from the President about a little editorial, which appeared in the Gazette, concerning his administration. I did not acknowledge the letter because I know that the White House mail is clogged every day by unimportant letters. Yet, I cannot help feeling that I should like to have the President know how deeply touched I was by his letter. If the opportunity ever comes, would you be kind enough to tell him for me that I appreciate his goodness in writing to me? It has been my pleasurable duty as I see it, to speak nothing but the kindest words of his administration, though I am a Progressive and a member of the executive committee of the national organization. I certainly feel that the President has gone further than any other Democrat could have gone along the road toward real progress in this country. How sad it is that the war is taking the national attention away from justice.

. . . The President has done great things and nothing can detract from them.

This letter is not for his eyes, except that I wish you would tell him how deeply I appreciate his writing to me.

The Kansas Progressive party went down to defeat at the polls in November, 1914. Capper, the Republican, won the governorship, and Republican Charles Curtis was elected to the Senate. Victor Murdock, defeated for the senatorship, did not run for office again, but Henry J. Allen, after the Progressives had returned to the Republican fold, was elected governor in 1918.

To ARTHUR CAPPER, TOPEKA, Kan., November 6, 1914

MY DEAR ARTHUR:

I was indeed pleased to get your letter. I presume sometimes in throwing the loose portions of the landscape around during the campaign, a fellow may inadvertently grab ahold of something and let drive things that should not be thrown. But I tried to be as careful as a man can be when he is in a hurry. Henry never, at any time, wanted to win. He did not care to be governor, and only in the last ten days or two weeks did he think he had a chance. I believe he would have been glad to take second place. Vic, of course, was disappointed, although I have not talked with him. He is sick in bed and was in the hospital, I believe, for an operation, on election day. But I think it will be better for him to be defeated than not, for he can get back on the Eagle [the Wichita *Eagle*] and make it a real newspaper.

Because you seemed to want the job, I am glad you got it, but I cannot see why in the world you did want it, or what in the world there is in it to attract you. However, you got hold of the tail of the bear and cannot let loose for two years at least.

I do not suppose there is very much I can do to help you. I am cast in outer darkness politically. I have not thought forward very much what I am going to do politically, but generally speaking, I should say that I would stay by the crowd, stack up the Bull Moose votes this year. I judge there was somewhere around 75,000 of them in the state.

My letters since the election are just as gingery as before the election. I have no desire to be obdurate, and I have no desire to cave in. I am going to watch events shape themselves for the next few months, and we will see what we will see. In the meantime, the Gazette is going to back you up in every good thing, and I cannot imagine you doing any other kind of thing. . . .

The 1914 campaign was the last election for the Progressive party.
The following letter affords an excellent insight into one grave weak-
ness of the party—its lack of support by the average American.

To THEODORE ROOSEVELT, December 15, 1914

DEAR COLONEL ROOSEVELT:

The long letter you were good enough to send me last month was
one of the most illuminating human documents I ever received; certainly the most revealing I ever received. It was so honest, so strong,
so deeply human and so simple and direct in its humanness that I
shall remember it always. If I have no other rewards or satisfaction
for the time I have put into this Progressive movement (and I have
had scores of deep satisfactions), that letter would more than pay me.

Now, the first thing I should do in answering your letter is to tell
you what I saw at the Chicago conference [a meeting of Progressives shortly after the 1914 elections]; not that the others have
not told you what they saw, but perhaps it will take the composite
stories of all of us to give you an idea of what happened there. First
of all, I was struck by the big fact that everyone was spirtually weary.
We were sapped dry. We could reach down in the well and bring up
courage, more or less of it. We could bring up enthusiasm, or a good
counterfeit of enthusiasm. We could even laugh, and that was genuine.
But we were all dead tired. For two or three, and in some cases for
four years—since 1910—we have been living upon our emotions. We
have been putting spirit into others. We have been spurring literally
thousands at first hand, and holding ten thousands almost at first hand,
in fighting trim. And the thing I saw was that we went through the
motions—all the wonted motions of real crusading soldiers—but the
whole thing was automatic. The spiritual well from which we dipped
was *physically* low. We need emotional rest. We need complete
change. Give that crowd a year or eighteen months to restore itself,
and it can whip the world.

For it has lost no faith. It is not discouraged. It is merely drained of
its spirit. It is kind of bagging at the knees.

Now, what I found at Chicago, I find among the leaders—the district
and county leaders here in Kansas. I have yet to learn of a man of them
who wants to go back to the Republican party or over to the Democratic party. And I get the finest kind of letters of joyful satisfaction

[157]

about the fight we have fought. But I don't know one who could last through another campaign, if it came next year. Fortunately, we have no election next year in Kansas. We polled around 100,000 votes—Allen 84,000, Murdock 116,000. Our vote was a town vote, an upper middle-class vote, so far as Kansas may be said to have any upper middle-class vote. By this I mean the professional man, the college professor—who is of the legion family in Kansas, as the state is full of little colleges—the young doctor, the lawyer, the railway engineer, the conductor, the banker and successful merchant. We didn't get the clerk. We didn't get the real estate dealer. We didn't get the tenant farmer, nor the small farmer. But we did get the old codger who used to bring in his township to the county convention in the old days of the convention, and who still keeps the run of politics in his head, and remembers for instance how you were nominated in 1904 and what defeated Fairbanks in 1908. He was with us. But the average farmer was not with us. He was getting splendid prices for a big crop. It wasn't the belly issue with him. It was party tradition. We did not get our issues across the footlights with him. He bolted two years ago, because he saw the issue; but he had forgotten it, and we couldn't revive his memory, and any way it wasn't worth while to keep pumping indignation into him. Until we can dramatize, or better, until the times dramatize our issues effectively, there's no use trying to put the bellows to the ashes of 1912.

What is true of the farmer is equally true of labor. We haven't a large industrial vote in Kansas. Labor sent representatives to all the party conventions making platforms last summer. The Democrats tried to fool them, and the Republicans flatly turned the labor representatives down. We invited them into the platform committee's room, and showed them that we had already put all their just demands into our platform. The men whom we conferred with were sincerely for us. They were engineers and conductors, the plutocracy of labor. But they couldn't interest the man at the forge or in the switch-shanty. In Kansas the railroads, for the first time in years, kept hands off. I think they may have done this generally. Indeed I am sure that the former railroad bosses were as surprised at the results—at for instance, Curtis's election—as we were. For no one believed he had the ghost of a show. His meetings were often abandoned for want of attendance. He was a joke in the campaign. Yet thousands of colorless people, who only remember vaguely the events upon which the campaign of 1912 hinged, and have no notion at all of 1910, perfectly honest people . . . voted for him, because he was the Republican nominee and they were assured that the Republican party had amended its convention rules and was ninety per cent progressive.

Now these people are the fundamental strength of the Republican party, and at the same time its weakness, for they won't stand for the evil they endorse after it works itself out. But they cannot now be aroused to revolt by oratory. They are story minded, picture minded. We have no story to tell, nor razors to grind, so it seems to me wise, everything considered, to fade. In Kansas, we shall maintain our organization, keep in touch with our leadership, write letters from time to time to those who need letters, but not try to stir up the people, not in 1915, unless some unexpected event occurs. The Republicans and the Democrats will make blunders and will call attention to one another's blunders. But someway I feel that the more we try to call attention to their blunders, the more our motives will be questioned, and the less will the blunders be punished. The family row is at that stage where outside interference between the parties will only hurt the intruder. Later events will shape themselves so that it will be obvious that someone must step in. To me it seems wise to wait. This is an opportunist position. Yet it seems to be the only alternative. To blow up the boat and enlist elsewhere just now seems to me premature. But to tie up the boat and wait for the tide seems about the best we can do.

In the meantime I shall devote myself to the frivolous pursuit of literature, to certain benevolences and charities, to the newspaper business and to insolent hooting comment upon the passing show. I shall not get excited about politics no matter what happens for a year. I shall not even say I told you so. I think it would be wise for all of us to take something of such an attitude. Our own people don't need exhortation. Others won't take it. So what's the use? . . .

Mrs. White, who has just come into the room, is jeering at the length of this letter. She asks if this is an endurance contest in letter writing that we are promoting. And then she insists that I lengthen the letter by insisting that you and Mrs. Roosevelt come out to Colorado with us next summer. We have a camp there, two cabins and some sleeping houses. We are nearly 9,000 feet in the air, about 40 miles from the railroad, within a few hours' walk of snow, and fairly out of the heavy tourist traffic. You and Mrs. Roosevelt could have a log cabin with a fireplace, and a tin bathtub, and a fourposter bed made of lodgepole pines. You could write, and we could tramp two or three days a week among the high Rockies. Longs Peak is but a day's walk from the cabin, and the motoring is splendid in the little parks and valleys that lie under the shoulder of the Peak. Enos Mills is only three hours away, by trail, and the Front Range lies looming six hours away on our west. Of course, there's no shooting, but its wild enough among the high Rockies all around us, and plenty of sheep and bear and deer may be seen any fine day by one who cares to go after them. Fishing is excellent. Young Bill does the family fishing, and keeps us in trout. It is always cool and fresh and fine and stimulating there in the summer; no malaria, lots of huckleberries and red raspberries and no reporters. The trails are good enough to keep you guessing more or less about where you're going, and the pinto and cayuse plugs of the country are gingery enough to add zest to life, if you lack it otherwise. Personally I don't use the horses, having in general a low opinion of a horse as a method of communication or transportation. I prefer to walk. But the horses are there or, if you prefer to go in state and style, we might scare up an auto that would take us on the lower levels.

At all events, it's the place for you to come to renew yourself. Our place is in Moraine Park, a spur of Estes Park and rather out of the way. We have five acres, and you need see no one you don't care to see and in an hour's ride we could be among the rich and the great down in the village. I shall be working more or less of the time on the Great American Novel, and would not bother you, but would be ready to tote you around whenever you cared to go. We have two burros that pack and there are many packing trips of two days or a week, and we love to camp. "So come with me and be my love."

The sinking of the passenger liner Lusitania *on May 7, 1915, by a German U-boat resulted in the loss of over eleven hundred lives, including 128 American citizens. The American public was horrified. Theodore Roosevelt and some newspapers clamored for war. Wilson, however, refused to rush into such an act and dispatched two notes to Germany demanding the cessation of unrestricted submarine warfare. White and the Middle West were less conscious than the East of the significance of the Allied war against Germany.*

To President Woodrow Wilson (telegram)
[sometime in May, 1915]

As citizen, I feel it my duty to let you know that the feeling of people in this vicinity is very strongly against using German barbarities as justification for entering the world war. Properly, we should make known our horror at the ruthless savage cruelty of these acts, but it seems to me in this time of world madness we should retain our sanity. Running amuck with the rest of the world will accomplish nothing for humanity's ultimate gain.

As the Progressive party began to disintegrate, White received many queries as to when he was going to re-enter the Republican fold.

To J. H. Stewart, Wichita, Kan., September 25, 1915

My Dear Senator:

I have your kind note of the 24th and am glad to note that you think I am an altruist. If you had to rustle a three or four hundred dollar payroll every week as I do, and dig up $1,500 worth of taxes every twenty minutes (as it seems to me), you would get the notion out of your head that I am an altruist, but I am mighty glad to know that you think I am worthy to come into the Republican fold. It may be that I shall round up there later, but in my present mood I am inclined to regard the Republican party as the drunken man regards his home, "a good place to go after everything else is closed." . . .

I note what you say about me running a benevolent despotism.* That looks good from the outside, but I tried it during the Stubbs administration and somehow it was not all it was cracked up to be.

Anyway I am glad for your letter and appreciate your goodness in thinking of me.

* The charge was frequently made that White was a domineering political boss.

[161]

Columnist Franklin P. Adams and White had been friends for many years. Very frequently Adams quoted Gazette editorials in his column. The Whites were in the East in the fall of 1915, and when they left, Adams asked Mr. White to write his impressions of visiting New York City.

To Franklin P. Adams, New York *Tribune*, November 30, 1915

My Dear Frank:

... Now about your visitor's story. When Sallie and I were pulling out of Washington on the last leg of the journey, I squared round to her and said, "Now, next to the children, what would you rather have than anything else, when you get home?" "Well," she says, "you say first." "Veal stew and dumplings," and she said, "Neck of mutton with curry." We were tired of rich food. We wanted to get down to 15 cent shoulder cuts, boiled with carrots and rice and peppers, and the short and simple groceries of the poor, and I think every visitor who starts in stuffing himself with high-priced food covered with white French sauces, comes to a time when he desires brown gravy and lots of it, when he wants bacon and eggs for breakfast.

We had the finest assortment of grub ever laid out before two people in the world, and at the end of it we longed for the cheap grub of home. . . .

Also we wanted to get home where the newspapers printed something. We could not get any news out of the New York papers as we could get it out of the Star and the Gazette. The love stories of the great papers, running in connection with their crime department, didn't get us. We couldn't find things in the New York papers the way we can find them in the Star and the Gazette, and when we found a Kansas City Star on the road home, we read it from cover to cover.

Another thing, why not make something of the relation between the way one's feet get tired seeing things? I do four times as much walking in Emporia as I do in New York, but because I am looking at new things in New York my feet begin to get tired and hurt. There is some psychological relation in this that I wish you would work out. Perhaps tomorrow, after I talk with Sallie, I may get some more ideas and will write you again. In the meantime, give our affectionate regards to Minna. If you see the divine Edna, tell her we are thinking of her. [Minna was Mrs. Adams and "the divine Edna" refers to Edna Ferber.]

White was asked by the National Education Association for his opinion of what should be the basis for peace terms to Germany. His idealism and fundamental belief in a free democracy are well revealed in this letter.

To The National Education Association, January 8, 1916

The terms of peace in Europe should not hinge upon things geographical. They should hinge upon things spiritual. It makes no vast amount of difference what territory at the end of the war belongs in what hands, but it makes a vast amount of difference what the spirit directing the conquering hands shall be. Until Germany has realized that there is something in the world besides materialism, that there is a God in Israel, and that might does not make right, the peace of Europe should not be declared upon any terms.

The German system of order and obedience has produced great talent, but order and obedience does not produce genius, and genius after all, directs the world, moves it forward, releases those new springs of life that move men forward. Talent does not move men forward. Talent merely keeps men in a groove. Talent provides for efficiency, but not for forward-moving changes, and until the everlasting daylights are knocked out of order and obedience, and a more democratic system established, a system that will give men elbow room for growth and for those sudden expansions of men into genius that move the world forward, I for one, hope for no peace. And, when that is done, then democracy shall triumph. I do not care how much thinking Germany has or how little. It is the idea and not the kaiser, nor the king, nor the emperor that must win the peace of Europe.

The continuance of unrestricted submarine warfare by Germany, threatening the American belief in freedom of the seas, brought the United States closer and closer to war. In 1916, President Wilson launched a preparedness program that increased the size of the army and navy. Early in 1916, after raids on American soil by the bandit Pancho Villa, an American expeditionary force under General Pershing was sent into Mexico in pursuit of Villa.

To FRANK DALE, Chicago, March 13, 1916

DEAR MR. DALE:

. . . My feeling would be that we had better go forward with our diplomatic relations and establish our right to the sea first. Then, pass our warning resolutions, which would not in any way seem to be backing down on our rights in the matter. I would not have held this position six months ago, but recent occurrences and particularly the Villa raid the other day, persuaded me that it is necessary for America to show a strong, courageous front to the family of nations. I do not feel that the Villa raid was of Villa's initiative. He was probably backed up in it by someone else.

I think that Wilson is in the main right in his diplomatic policy, and I cannot help but feel that the Republicans and some of the Democrats are playing politics with a national issue.

I am very strongly for the government ownership of all plants making arms, armor plate and munitions of every kind. I do not believe that our peace should be at the mercy of a lot of agitators who profit by our warlike activities. I think that the new secretary of war [Newton D. Baker of Cleveland, Ohio] will probably push that plan. He is a great municipal ownership man and I look to see him go into the munition trusts with a hickory club and smash them. . . .

The party-mindedness of the people and their concentration on the war, as described in this letter, reveals that the Progressive party could expect little success in 1916.

[164]

MY DEAR NORMAN:

The book went forward today and I trust you will like it.* It was written as a sort of running start to get back on a novel that I have been working on four or five years and which I hope to get off the block within the next six or eight months.

What you say about politics, I suppose brings it before the house. I have never seen so rotten a state of public opinion as we have at present in all the thirty years in which I have been observing it. I think perhaps that the fear of war has filled public sentiment full of blowholes, and it does not ring true. I cannot account for the fact that the people are not working out a national view of anything. Their attention seems distracted, and they can hold it but for a moment on any one thing. They are tremendously party minded. I have never seen so much tooth-chattering fear of getting out of party alignment, and it is true as much in the Republican party as it is in the Democratic party. The curious thing about the Moosers is that they are infected with it too. We are a feeble folk, but I believe we are building our homes in the rock. As nearly as I can see by testing out our state organization in Kansas, it is as good a state as it was last year when we polled around 100,000 votes, but I have not the slightest hope of polling one vote more, even though Champ Clark were nominated for president against Weeks and even though we ran the Colonel or Gifford Pinchot or Hiram Johnson at the head of our ticket [Champ Clark, conservative Missouri Democrat; J. W. Weeks, conservative Republican senator from Massachusetts; Gifford Pinchot, Pennsylvania Bull Mooser who had been involved in the Ballinger-Pinchot controversy; Hiram Johnson, Progressive governor of California and United States senator]. Folks are just hamstrung with the fear of war and huddled together in their parties without much sense. I do not think in all Kansas there is a Republican, whose name would reach beyond his county line, who would announce for Wilson today. And I do not think there is a Democrat of any importance who would not be for Wilson. The folks are not thinking. They are just dreading.

Naturally I feel that this is a temporary panic, but it is here—a fact and that is about all there is to it, and I don't see what there is to do

---

* *God's Puppets*, a series of political short stories that White wrote and published in 1916.

about it. It may be a lull before the storm or it may be the first stages of insanity. I give it up.

·

Muckraker Lincoln Steffens's handwriting was unbelievably difficult to decipher. As White was writing the following reply to one of Steffens's letters, one can imagine his blue eyes twinkling in merriment and a smile curling on his lips.

To Lincoln J. Steffens, New York City, April 11, 1916

My Dear Stef:

I have just had a quiet session of communion with your letter. In a general way I can see that you seem to approve of my book. I get the name of Lindsey of Denver, and Tom Johnson of Cleveland [Judge Ben Lindsey, who was gaining fame for his juvenile court work, and Tom Johnson, reform mayor of Cleveland], and Jesus of Palestine, but there I lose track and come out somewhere down in Mexico, which doesn't seem to have any relation to anything else, but nevertheless interesting.

I am glad that matters stand as they do, and I wish you to believe me—

Theodore Roosevelt had a passionate hatred of Woodrow Wilson. He wrote White many times that Wilson was a danger to the moral fiber of the American people. Roosevelt wanted to declare war on Germany and felt that Wilson's restraint and diplomacy were cowardly. Frequently, he publicly denounced Wilson in bitter language. The recipient of the following letter had written White protesting Roosevelt's attacks on President Wilson.

[166]

MY DEAR MR. FIELDER:

I thank you most sincerely for your frank letter of April 12. I have been a rather staunch supporter of President Wilson and have believed that his preliminary correspondence with Germany and his preliminary maneuvering with Mexico during the year 1914 and most of the year 1915, would lead to some real adjustment and some climacterical event which would settle in our favor the international difficulties that confront us. Reluctantly and with great sorrow, I have been compelled to accept the belief that his type of mind, argumentative, logical and persuasive, is not the type of mind that will settle such events as now are stirring in this mad world between us and our hostile neighbors.

This preface is necessary to explain my feeling about Colonel Roosevelt. He has another type of mind. It is dynamic, instinctive, given to conclusions, and, on the whole, direct and passionately earnest. I have written to him many times expressing my feeling of disagreement with his public attitude toward President Wilson.

You speak of his violent barroom language. He feels violently, more violently than I feel, doubtless more violently than you feel. He expresses himself true to character. But we should not judge a man by externals of language or by his minor vices. During the Civil War, thousands of people, good honest patriotic people, were shocked out of supporting President Lincoln because he told in the White House stories that would not now be permitted in any saloon in the country during a busy hour. He was given to what is known as unclean similes and metaphors, but they did not prevent him from being a great, a good, a kind and wise man. I am sorry that he told disgusting stories. I am sorry that Colonel Roosevelt cracks down on President Wilson as he does, yet I do not regard a man's manners as an essential part of his fundamental character. During the 30 years in which Colonel Roosevelt had been in public life, his course has always been forward. It has always been honest. It has always been toward good, worthy, important things. He, more than any other man in the country, is responsible for our awakening of civic righteousness. He turned us from the materialism of Hanna into a larger and more spiritual life. A man must have some vices, I suppose, and if he wants to take a club and go out and rhetorically hammer the daylights out of the President, why it is his royal American privilege to do so, and I have a theory that it hurts the Colonel a lot more than it does the President.

At the Progressive convention in June, 1916, White, Gifford Pinchot,
Harold Ickes and other militant Progressives wanted to nominate
Roosevelt quickly and, then, leave the Republicans with the possi-
bility of nominating Roosevelt too, or facing sure defeat if a Repub-
lican, Roosevelt, and Wilson all ran for the presidency. George
Perkins, however, stalled off the nomination of Roosevelt until after
the Republicans had nominated Charles E. Hughes. Then, Roosevelt
refused to run, since this would aid the re-election of Wilson. Roose-
velt's refusal killed the Progressive party. White was heartbroken
at Roosevelt's decision, but his admiration for Roosevelt was such
that he could not criticize Roosevelt for the decision.

To Theodore Roosevelt, June 15, 1916

My Dear Colonel:

This is written in St. Louis where I came directly after our convention. I am reporting this Democratic convention, which is my idea
of a sedentary pursuit.

I expected to write to you as soon as I returned to Emporia, but I
read in the paper this morning that you are ill, and I hasten to write
to let you know how anxious I am for your speedy recovery. Politics
after all is such a small segment of life, and the big splendid things
of life outside of politics and beyond it mean so much more than the
differences of politics (or agreements of politics, for that matter)
that any menace to your well-being touches me far more deeply and
quickly than the things that may happen to your political fortunes.
I shall count among my permanent assets, gathered in the journey upon
this planet for whatever further stage of the journey may lie ahead, the
joyous satisfaction I have had in your friendship. It has lifted me up
in every material and spiritual way, and has left me a bigger and more
useful man than otherwise I should have been; so when I read that
you are ill, I am troubled and turn to you with a friend's sympathy.

And really I have nothing to offer but sympathy. Whatever advice
I may offer is quite intimate and personal, and brief: Don't worry. It
will all come out in the wash. God's chiefest blessing to man is, after
all, change. A year's turn of the wheel will bring new opportunities
and new duties. Rest and wait. The personal differences between
Hughes and Wilson are on the whole too unimportant to warrant
much excitement over the present situation. It will be a good time to

loaf and invite your soul. Possibly your body needs some attention also. Don't spend yourself too lavishly. Don't get in a place where you will be held responsible for Hughes as you were held responsible for Taft. There is too much judicial mind and Wall Street broker's caution in the whole situation to warrant you fretting your spirit or mortifying your flesh over it. One manly word for the general cause we all believe in is enough. Then go away somewhere and let the cistern of life fill up. Don't even bother to answer this note, but know that whatever you do, at least one friend's heart is with you.

White's grief over the collapse of the Bull Moose party is well demonstrated in this letter to another Kansas member of the party.

To RODNEY ELWARD, Castleton, Kan., June 24, 1916

DEAR ROD:

I am weak and weary, sick and sore. I am without star or compass politically and am up in the air and a mile west. I have no blame for anyone. Victor Murdock and I agree better than anyone else, I guess, and I suppose I can let you in between Victor and me.

The whole trouble with our humanitarian platform, as I see it at the moment, is that it hit war. Kaiser Bill blew it up. You cannot get humanitarian progress on the first page when humanitarian retrogression is occupying the headlines. You cannot get people interested in minimum wages and laws for hours of service and equitable railroad rates in the face of the news from Verdun.

My interest in these things is as keen as it ever was, and I have no doubt yours is, but the average man has his attention focused on the headlines on the front page and you cannot budge him. . . .

George Perkins, former Chairman of the Bull Moose Executive Committee, did his best to rally active Progressive support behind the candidacy of Charles Evans Hughes. Many Progressives, however, suspected that neither Hughes nor Perkins had any real progressive sentiments.

To GEORGE PERKINS, New York City, September 26, 1916

MY DEAR PERKINS:

I have your letter of the 14th asking me to give you some idea of the campaign. As nearly as I can see the situation, most of the Progressives, I should think as many as 80 to 95 per cent, are going to vote for Hughes. They wish him well and they are looking forward to him to produce by the reaction of his character upon future events, some real vital issue, which will indeed, and in truth, reunite the Republican party. As matters stand, the party is not united. They can all vote in one box for Hughes, and they can vote in one box and elect a Republican Congress, but the party will be no more united now than it was in 1913, unless Hughes unites factions by bringing to the progressive viewpoint with the prestige of the presidential office some issue that will drag the standpatters of the old guard to our position. A repetition of the Taft administration will produce a repetition of 1912 automatically. Our fellows know the way out of the back door, and they know the way into the front door again, and they would just as leave go round again as not.

There is no enthusiasm and small interest in the campaign. I think the Progressives have all made up their mind to take their medicine like a little man, and I believe it is a waste of time and energy to appeal to them further. But I also believe that they are no more united with the Republican party today than they ever were.

Kindly give my regards to Colonel Roosevelt. I should write to him myself, if I did not think it would annoy him and bore him unnecessarily.

I see by the papers that your sweet and beautiful daughter is to be married. I wish her much joy and you all the comfort that comes with the consolation of religion, for I suppose nothing else will comfort a man under those circumstances. Eugene Ware [favorite poet of Kansas] once said to me after a wedding in his family, "Daughters-in-law I find easy to assimilate, but with the average man, I believe the son-in-law is an acquired taste."

Hoping this will find you the same, I am—

Norman Hapgood and many other Progressives supporting Wilson's re-election tried to get an endorsement for Wilson out of White. But now that White was back in the Republican party, he was never again to bolt the national ticket. He was unhappy, however, about the entire campaign. In a letter to Henry Haskell, of the Kansas City Star, November 1, 1916, he wrote that "as the election draws near my hope for an earthquake which will destroy us all becomes more and more ardent."

To NORMAN HAPGOOD, Wilson Independent League,
New York City, October 10, 1916

MY DEAR NORMAN:

I am in a rather sad position politically this year. I have no enthusiasm for either cause.

I notice that the Democrats are using my kind words about the President, all of which were true when they were written and none of which would I change in the least today. Yet I do not feel under the circumstances that I wish to take a partisan attitude at all. Hamlin Garland [novelist of the rural Middle West] wanted me to sign a statement along with a number of Republicans, but I did not seem to care to do that.

I am giving genuine support to the Republican state and county ticket out here and so letting it go at that—carrying the entire Republican ticket at the head of our paper, getting a sort of an alibi for next year when I believe the fighting will be well worth while along some line that I probably don't see now. But I can't work myself up to any sort of sweat in this campaign. I trust this will answer your telegrams and explain why I did not meet Bainbridge Colby [former

[171]

Bull Mooser who supported Wilson and served in Wilson's Cabinet in 1920] in Omaha.

Theodore Roosevelt wrote White on December 18, 1916, denouncing the Middle West as "yellow" for casting its vote for Wilson. Roosevelt stated: "The feeling about Wilson that 'he kept us out of war' did not have the slightest particle of foundation in morality. The man or woman who voted for him for that reason did not in the least object to going to war with Santo Domingo and Haiti, and killing and wounding some hundreds of badly armed black men in those countries; he or she did not care for the fact that some gallant fellows of our own were killed there. All they meant when they said 'he kept us out of war' was that he kept their own worthless hides safe."

To THEODORE ROOSEVELT, December 27, 1916

MY DEAR COLONEL:

Man! you are clean, plumb crazy; wild as a bedbug about the West. There wasn't any yellow streak in the West at the election. I am getting letters from all over this part of the country about my recent article in *Collier's* ["Who Killed Cock Robin," *Collier's*, December 16, 1916]* from Progressives who would fight at the drop of the hat, men who hate the Wilson foreign policy as they hate poison, and they are chuckling and chortling at the defeat of Hughes. You may remember eight or nine years ago, I received cords of letters from you telling me what kind of a man Hughes was—and you were right. He came out here in the West and revealed himself as exactly that kind of a man, and do you think for a moment that the West would stand for that kind of a man! It wouldn't and it didn't.

Your opening paragraph seems to indicate that the West was to blame for not getting into the Republican Convention.

* White contended in this article that the West refused to vote for Hughes because of his lack of progressive utterances.

[172]

Holy Smoke, man, there wasn't a fighting Republican last May between the Mississippi River and the Pacific Ocean. They were all a lot of pussyfooting harmonizers whose highest ideal was the nomination of Hughes because he didn't stand for anything. The fighting bunch was still sticking to the Progressive ship. You were registered as a Progressive. We believed then and you seemed to agree with us that the bigger noise we could make in the Progressive Convention, the more show we could make of nominating you in the Republican Convention. We would either get you in the Republican Convention or an acceptable compromise. So the whole kit and boodle of us here in the West turned in and began holding precinct and county and State Bull Moose conventions and hip-hip hoòraying and shooting off blank cartridges, and we certainly did make some considerable noise, and we certainly did scare the daylights out of the Republican National Convention, and it gave us Hughes which was the best we could hope for.

And then Hughes caved in. Instead of coming up to his milk like a good little kitty, he squawked and backed off and began playing to offend neither side. In every western town there is a pro-German bunch, and that pro-German bunch mostly was Democratic, but it was vicious in its denunciation of you, and [ardent in] its support of Hughes, and Hughes never for one moment did a single thing to take the curse of that pro-German outfit off his candidacy. And the more that pro-German bunch abused you, and the more you lit into the pro-German bunch, and the more Hughes grinned like a Cheshire cat, the surer and firmer was the die cast against him. It wasn't yellow, it was the best kind of Americanism. And you must quit scolding the West. Here live the kind of people who support you and your ideals. Here live the men who are going to work out the economic and political problems that will confront this country after the war. And, if there is any fighting to do, here are the men who are going to do the fighting. The thing for you to do is to back off and get a little perspective on this election. Get clear out of sight of the Wall Street ticker and the munition makers' public sentiment, and then you will see that the West did the only thing it could do with self-respect.

There were two milk-and-water candidates. If Hughes had been elected, the rank and file of the people saw no reason to believe that he would get very much further than Wilson, and they did not propose to build up a united party on any cambric tea basis and Hughes was a cambric tea candidate as against a kind of a skimmed milk candidate.

[173]

For instance: I voted for Hughes because I was in a manner bound to do so by the action of the Progressive National Committee. Sallie, who loathes Wilson's foreign policy, who believes in universal military service, who is a National Union suffragist and a radical economic progressive, voted for Wilson. And she did so because during the campaign Hughes slipped clear out of her imagination, and she feared the Wall Street taint upon him, and she did not want to encourage by her vote anything that had any connection with the group that controlled the Republican Convention of 1912 or that throttled the Republican sentiment in 1916. There never was a moment when Hughes gave any indication that he was any better than Taft, and she didn't see him any better than Taft.

When you go west, if you do go west to the Fiji Islands, why not stop off for a day or between trains in Emporia? I should like to see you and will not bother you with politics. . . .

You must not assume that because I think you are a fit companion for the March Hare and the Mad Hatter, politically, that we do not both love you to death and would not go along wherever you would lead. But we are entitled to our opinion, and at the moment a conservative statement of our opinion is that your letter indicates that you should be in the madhouse; in the padded cell of the madhouse; chained in the padded cell of the madhouse; where we should send you our affectionate seasonal greetings.

Ray Stannard Baker was one of the leading muckrakers of the day. Upton Sinclair in The Jungle *(1905) had graphically described working conditions in the Chicago stockyards, and now White wanted a book written about the monopolistic control of the industry. In addition to his muckraking work, Baker wrote delightful stories under the pen name of David Grayson.*

MY DEAR BAKER:

Here is a letter from our friend Stubbs [former Kansas governor, W. R. Stubbs] which rather explains itself. It seems to me that there is a splendid chance here for someone to go into the matter of the food trusts—or particularly the meat trusts of the United States—and make a splendid and informing article. I can't do it because I am still busy on my interminable novel [*In the Heart of a Fool*]. When I get that novel done, I am going to do a lot of things, but I can't do it now, and Stubbs and his friends are keen to have this thing done soon. Dwight B. Heard, president of the National Live Stock Association, is a very dear friend of mine, and a former Bull Mooser, and has a lot of stuff which might interest you. I wish you could consider this a six months' job. I believe you could make a series of articles and a splendid book out of it, a book that would have considerable historical value as indicating, fifty years from now, the time when the food of the nation was held from the people of the nation more or less at the whim of certain rich men of the nation. Fifty years from now this will be as astonishing and unimaginable as slavery I hope, and I believe a series of articles in a book from you on this subject would hasten this thing to an end.

Recently I saw something that made me perfectly green with envy. It was the lovely little limp-leather volumes of David Grayson. I am going to bend nobly to my work and hope someday to save up enough money to own one of those sets, which of course is not very important. Anybody with money can own one of them, but only a sweet and beautiful soul could have written them and only a kind . . . publisher could have issued them.

Please remember me kindly to Mrs. Baker. I do wish you and she would come west. Come to Kansas, or come to Colorado where we are in the summer, that we might loaf and invite our souls together.

You know Stubbs well enough to write him directly about this beef trust matter. I wish you would do it. Send me a copy of your letter and I will govern myself accordingly.

I see that our beloved Ider M.* is to be on the Tariff Commission. Mrs. White, who voted for Wilson, says this really justifies her vote, though she is generally grouchy and sore on Wilson and voted for

---

* White frequently spelled Ida M. Tarbell's first name as Ider as a midwestern gesture of scorn for eastern pronunciation.

him to get as far as possible away from the stink of the Hughes environment.

When you see Steff [Lincoln Steffens], give him my love.

In January, 1917, Germany announced that it was resuming its policy of unrestricted submarine warfare. Immediately, the United States broke off diplomatic relations with Imperial Germany. Wilson, however, still shrank from war. As the following letter indicates, the war was still remote for Midwesterners, geographically cut off by mountains from the Atlantic and Pacific highways. The recipient of the letter, Lord Bryce, had published a distinguished study of the United States, The American Commonwealth (*1888*).

To JAMES LORD BRYCE, Sussex, England, February 19, 1917

MY DEAR SIR:

What a lovely letter yours of the 27th was about my "Cock Robin" article [*Collier's*, December 16, 1916].* I am delighted to know that you felt its essential truth, and I believe myself that it was fairly true.

... The West as I read it is strongly pro-Ally, but the war is not a first-page story in the West. A score of things interest the West, and Wilson won chiefly as a refuge from the crowd that dominated the two Chicago conventions.†

Second, you ask does the West approve the policy of complete abstention in Mexico? I don't know. I would say that the opinion of the West on the Mexican subject was not formed. Our people tremendously dislike intervention of any sort. They were aroused over the Columbus raid and would have justified a counterattack, but that was nearly a year ago and, as you know, public attention over a minor

* White had stated that the West had not voted for Wilson because "he kept us out of war," but because the West trusted his progressive spirit and had felt that Hughes was a conservative.

† George Perkins, in control of the Progressive Convention, and the Republican organization that nominated Hughes were looked upon as too conservative for the old Bull Moosers.

[176]

event may not be held tensely for a year, and Columbus has more or less vanished into the dim past.*

It is, as I see it, largely a matter of leadership. If Wilson had led us into Mexico after the Columbus raid, we should have followed, but he did not lead us, and we did not push him. If Colonel Roosevelt had been president, and had occupied one or two of the northern states of Mexico after the Columbus raid, the country would have justified keeping them. But a democracy has no foreign policy of its own. It accepts whatever responsible leadership seems to be in charge. The Republicans made a vast mistake in trying to make a campaign out of foreign policy. You can't stage it. It doesn't get across in a country where balance of power lies at least a thousand miles from any border.

Third, you ask what the radicals or progressives of the West really want? I should say quietly that they want government ownership of railroads, but are not vociferous about it but rather determined. They want rather drastic inheritance taxes, and they want the proceeds of the inheritance taxes spent in internal improvements under expert direction. They want to break the power of the alliance between politics and big business. They want to equalize opportunity much more than it is equalized, for instance, on the Atlantic seaboard. They have a rather definite opinion that federal old-age pensions should be established, and that the natural resources should be operated along socialistic lines—the coal, the oil, the water power, the forests and the minerals. They desire the tariff put out of politics into an expert commission, and they desire a rural credit law which will take care of the tenant farmer.

These, of course, are merely measures and not principles, but I should say, as a principle, they desire a genuine redistribution of the wealth of the country without waiting for such an opportune time as will come only in the dreams of the conservative when a readjustment will not hurt business. The radicals and progressives desire the readjustment now, and at any commercial cost, realizing that, after all, business will function, commerce will not be suspended, and that humanity will be fed and clothed and housed during the crisis that

* The civil war that threw Mexico into turmoil, during these years, prompted some Americans to urge intervention. Following Pancho Villa's raid on American soil American troops were temporarily sent into Mexico. Less than two weeks after this letter was written, a German note was published offering Mexico the return of the Southwest if Mexico would join Germany, should war break out between the United States and Germany.

may occur, and that after the crisis a new and better condition will prevail.

In the present state of daze and confusion following the suspension of diplomatic relations, I should say that the crying need of the times is leadership in America. There is no strong voice to which the people will listen. Colonel Roosevelt was crucified by bad stage management at Chicago, and the people have turned from him temporarily, as I see it. He could lead if they would listen, but the last Chicago convention was such a tragically sad piece of business that today he is not in a position to lead. I do not think he was to blame for the tragedy at Chicago. I think Mr. Perkins and a group of stockbrokers, who were keen for a unified party, were to blame. But, nevertheless, the Colonel suffers and will suffer until some new turn of events places him on the stage in a rather different light. And with him off the stage, we have a leadership fit for discussion, an academic leadership, a leadership, wise and scholarly and cautious, when we should have a leadership strenuous and certain and aggressive. The people are in the mood to follow, but alas, they were compelled to follow without knowing how miserable it is to follow the wrong kind of leadership. The more I read of the conditions in '58 and '59 and '60, the more I see them duplicated in our life today in America—fumbling, befuddled, idiotic optimism. Of course, when the flash of light does come, when the thing strikes, when the tragedy of our nation is dramatized, we will read the drama aright and will rise to a noble part. But just now, we are having a period of national blind staggers.

This letter has been dictated at odd times and between whiles during my work editing a daily newspaper and trying to write a novel, and it may be more or less disjointed, but it is my view of the situation, and I trust you will discount it ninety to ninety-five per cent, and realize that it is only one man's views.

Mrs. White, who remembers our pleasant hour with you and Mrs. Bryce at luncheon six years ago, wishes particularly to be remembered in this note.

When peace comes, I shall probably represent a syndicate of American newspapers at The Hague or wherever the peace conference is worked out. Possibly I may see you then. I shall look forward to the possibility with keen anticipation, and until then, good-bye.

Dorothy Canfield, daughter of White's favorite professor while he was a student at the University of Kansas, wrote to White expressing alarm over the Middle West's lethargy toward the war, and the apparent failure of this great region to understand the vital need of checking autocratic Germany. White's analysis, that this was largely a result of the remoteness of the Middle West plus the fact that Wilson shrank from taking the final step, has a great deal of validity.

To Dorothy Canfield Fisher, Paris, France, March 13, 1917

Dear Dorothy Canfield:

Your letter has come, and I am sending you herewith a bundle of Gazettes and some other papers from this middle western section. I think you got the wrong idea of the Middle West from the pacifist statesmen. The whole trouble with the country, of course, is the academic leadership. We need, of course, positive, aggressive leadership, and we are having a rather calm, judicial and impersonal leadership, and it is too bad. But it is the leadership the people chose, and in choosing it they misinterpreted themselves, I think rather seriously and sadly. But don't be discouraged about your West. It is as true as steel and as sound. In a crisis it will develop its own leadership. The whole trouble is we do not see our grave danger as a crisis. We are too remote from the war. But when we see it we shall rise.

Sallie and I look forward eagerly to the day when you may come west and see all of these things.

On April 2, 1917, Woodrow Wilson appeared before Congress and read his war message. Four days later Congress, in the small hours of Good Friday morning, declared war on Imperial Germany. White enthusiastically supported the declaration. For some time he had felt that Wilson was dilatory in making his request. On May 1, 1917, White editorialized: "Great times make great men. The great man who has come out of these times is Woodrow Wilson. If democracy— which is but another name for Christian brotherhood—makes a long forward stride in humanity out of this world crisis, more than to any one individual in the world credit should fall to Woodrow Wilson. . . ."

To Joseph Tumulty, White House, Washington, D. C.,
May 2, 1917

Dear Mr. Tumulty:

Some time when the chief needs jollying along, kindly poke under his Presbyterian nose, the editorial from yesterday's Gazette and tell him it came from a man out west, who has not always agreed with the President, and who has sometimes fretted because things were not going fast enough.

White was greatly annoyed at certain Progressives and Socialists denouncing the war as a Wall Street international bankers' war. As he understood the war, it was essentially a struggle to prevent autocratic Germany from attempting to dominate Europe and the rest of the world. In Kansas his old friend, ex-Senator Joseph Bristow, was opposed to the war and to raising an army through selective service.

To Rodney Elward, Castleton, Kan., June 8, 1917

My Dear Rod:

I wasn't jawing at Joe for exposing graft. What I was jawing at Joe about was for sneering at the war as a Wall Street war and trying to belittle conscription as an unpatriotic thing while it is, as it seems to me, the only scientific way to get soldiers. Heaven knows, if Joe wants to go in and expose the graft of the administration, I am with him, heart and soul, but he weakens his graft exposition when he exhibits such evident malice against the war. I wish America might have been able honorably to keep out of the war, but America was

[180]

not honorably able to keep out of the war, and I am glad America is in the war. There is only one way to get out of the war, and that is to fight out, and we will flunk out a lot quicker if men like Bristow, sneering at the motives of the war and the purposes of the war, justify all the mollycoddles and sapheads in their weak and wobbly attitude toward the war. But in cleaning up grafters, I am with Joe, heart and soul. The best way to clean up grafters is to start on the basis that this is a righteous war, and that the grafter is doing an unholy and unrighteous job in a righteous war, and not to assume that this is an unholy war, which in a way justifies the grafter whom Joe is yelling at.

I hope this explains my attitude.

The United States entered the war before White had finished his progressive novel In The Heart Of A Fool. *He revised the book to include America's entrance into the war, which he viewed as the natural culmination of the progressive desire to base human relations on a fair and democratic foundation. Now, according to White, instead of solely carrying this out in the United States, the entrance of the country into the war made this an international program.*

To GEORGE BRETT, The Macmillan Company, June 29, 1917

MY DEAR MR. BRETT:

...I have tried to set forth a thesis: the thesis being that this is essentially a spiritual not a material world and that in this spiritual world only spiritual rewards and punishments come as a result of spiritual virtues or spiritual lapses, and that material gains and losses are in no way connected with a man's spiritual attitude.

Of course, it seems to me that the crux of the whole war is the struggle of the world away from the gross materialism of Germany to a certain higher spiritual standard of life contained in the word Democracy. And in that far the book is tremendously timely. But I fear that the average reader may not detect the trend of the book.

[181]

*In August, 1917, White and Henry J. Allen sailed for Europe to in-
spect the work of the American Red Cross. Before White returned
in October, he and Allen had toured the front lines as well as investigating conditions behind the lines in France, Italy, and England. He
published the story of the trip in a somewhat light and gay spirit in*
The Martial Adventures of Henry and Me *(1918).*

To THEODORE ROOSEVELT, July 30, 1917

MY DEAR COLONEL:

I want you to read the Vernon L. Kellogg piece in the August
Atlantic. Kellogg and I grew up as boys together in Emporia and went
through the University of Kansas together, and when I went into the
newspaper business, he went into academic life and got more or less
enamored of Doctor Jordan [David Starr Jordan, chancellor of Stanford University and vice-president of the American Peace Society]
and fell into the pacifist way of thinking. Then, he went to Belgium
with Hoover as director in charge at Brussels and in French-occupied
territory [Herbert Hoover was chairman of the Committee for Relief in Belgium, 1914–1919] and saw the fighting machine of Germany
close up. It cured him of his pacifism, and his article, it seems to me,
would be called "The Confessions of a Pacifist." It is really worth
reading.

Kellogg came home a changed man. He had the academic pickle
pretty well soaked into his hide before he went, and was a tremendous
believer in the egoistic system of philosophy and believed in the exalted individual, and he came home thoroughly humanized and socialized and believing in a number of important things outside ourselves that makes for righteousness. And so I want you to read his
piece.

With the example of LaFollette and Bristow before me, I have
leaned back in my support of the President, but it did not seem to me
that I had leaned too far because undoubtedly the pro-German propaganda, neatly concealed in attacks on the administration, is a dangerous propaganda.

The Middle West is doing its part. Kansas, which is 20th in population, was 11th or 12th in the size of its donation to the Red Cross. We
filled out our naval quota in May, and we are sending our National
Guard recruited to its full strength, and are having no trouble with

the draft. When they begin to bring home our dead, we will wake up, but we are so far from the seaboard, so far from actual hostilities, that the war will not be a very personal matter with us until it becomes so through our personal losses. Then, the West will come to itself. But don't worry in the meantime. We are going to do our full share and do it bravely.

I haven't written to you for a long time, and I thought these few remarks submitted above might be in order. Don't forget Kellogg's piece.

I may see you in ten days or so. I have just been asked by Mr. Davison [Henry P. Davison] of the Red Cross to go to France for him on a trip of inspection and expect to do so. I do not know my sailing date now. . . .

It has seemed to me that since the 4th of March he [Wilson] has done well, not perhaps tolerably well, but what might be called intolerably well. He has got the declaration of war; he has got the conscription; he has got things moving, not rapidly, but I should say on the whole in the forward direction even if in more or less confusion, but still moving. And after all, he is about the only man who can act. So it has seemed to me wise to stand for whatever good he has done, and stand rather vigorously for those things, because there is a cult here in this country which wants to flunk out of the war, and is trying to make the war unpopular by calling attention to the mistakes of the administration. If we flunk out of this war, as I see it, we will have it to fight again. Only by fighting out of this war can we hope to settle the issue with Germany for this generation and the next. And it has seemed to me that Bristow and LaFollette and Cummins [J. L. Bristow, R. M. LaFollette, and A. B. Cummins] and that group which is forever bellyaching around about the council of defense, and the graft, and the favoritism at Washington are really making a sentiment not so much against graft and corruption and favoritism as they are making a sentiment against the war. And I have feared that too much anti-Wilson talk, now that we are in the war, would justify the pro-German pacifist and would not help matters at Washington.

To WALTER LIPPMANN, War Department, Washington,
November 20, 1917

MY DEAR LIPPMANN:

... I want to take this opportunity for thanking you for the letters you gave me. They were very helpful. Since I have been home, I have been out making speeches to farmers for the last two weeks every night. They don't seem to get the war, and I have avoided all big towns and have been talking in schoolhouses and country churches. Incidentally, I have been soliciting for the Y.M.C.A. and using that as a reason for the meetings, but what I have been trying to do is to get this war to the farmer. Of course, he is the last man who socializes, and as this war is the greatest social adventure, he is the last man in. But I think he is coming, though slowly. ...

On his return from Europe, White wrote a series of syndicated newspaper articles to publicize the work of the Red Cross to the American public.

To SENATOR CHARLES CURTIS, Washington, D. C., December 5, 1917

MY DEAR CURTIS:

... My articles reached forty newspapers from Boston to San Diego, with a total circulation of over five million, and I hope they are doing some good. I am also writing a series of articles for Collier's Weekly, and the publicity department of the Y.M.C.A. and the Red Cross are making demands of me, and the Treasury Department asked me the other day to get up some kind of a screed to help them sell the baby bonds. I can't carry a gun, and I know if I were given command of troops I would probably make some fool blunder that would kill half of them, and I wouldn't have the nerve to take a commission. But I suppose every fellow can do his little damnedest in the line for which he is fitted, and I am trying to do mine. In this war I am going to know

[184]

no politics or religion or friends except the successful conduct of this war to a decisive end. . . .

World War I brought increased governmental control of business far beyond the expectation of the most hopeful progressive. Our economy existed under a form of war socialism with government boards in control of production, shipping, railroad operation, prices and rationing, and labor relations. White hoped that after the war, rather than permitting the relaxing of controls, the progressives would fight to retain them.

To Mark Sullivan, *Collier's Weekly*, January 28, 1918

My Dear Mark:

The California Outlook [organ of the California progressives] busted because there seemed to be no particular need out there for it just now. The war swallowed the progressive issues. You say you would like to have my views of affairs in general. I think the big thing to do now is to quietly organize a hundred or so fellows who are dependable and who may take such steps as are necessary after the war to serve all the economic and social campaigns that the war brings to us. I think price fixing should be permanent, but not done by Wall Street. I think the government should tighten its control either into ownership or operation of the railroads. I think that labor arbitration should be a permanent thing, and that we should federalize education through universal training, making it a part of the system of education, and making camps permanent in every section of the country to which young men from eighteen to twenty-two could be sent for from six weeks to three months of every year for military and educational training. And that this training should be universal and that a part of the education incident to the training should be the shipping of young men from one part of the country to the other. So that after his four years' course every boy in the United States will know something of California, something of the

[185]

South, something of the Michigan, Wisconsin and Minnesota countries, something of New England, and something of the Middle Atlantic seaboard. To support that, I think the income taxes should be ninety per cent on all incomes over one million dollars a year, and that they should be graduated down from that, so that no man can have a permanent income of over two hundred thousand dollars, and that no inheritance over ten million will pass. With these two last clauses written into law, we will have plenty of money for our national training, and we will nationalize our young men and make them citizens as well as potential defenders. What do you think about this?

To E. W. Howe, Editor of the Atchison (Kansas) *Globe*,
February 19, 1918

My Dear Ed:

Since your letter of December 8 came to hand, I have been just too busy to spit. I finished up finally for the press a novel called "In the Heart of a Fool." I have been working on it seven years. I have written it through three times, and I revised it entirely from the last of January until the other day when I came back to my desk. Also, during the month of December and part of January, I wrote a sixty thousand word story entitled "The Martial Adventures of Henry and Me." This is the story of our trip to France, and in it I have added a little fake love story to carry the book. I wanted to catch the young man who wraps up a book and a box of candy in his overcoat pocket and goes out to see his girl Sunday night, and the love story is added for that purpose. . . .

Throughout the last forty years of his life, White continually advised groups, with which he was affiliated, to broaden their base in order to include leaders from other parts of the country than the

[186]

eastern seaboard. He was confident that New Yorkers, particularly, had no conception of the rest of the United States.

To CHARLES NORTON, Vice-President of the National City
Bank of New York, February 21, 1918

MY DEAR NORTON:

... I have been thinking more or less of late that the Red Cross should broaden. The war council is too much Atlantic seaboard, and too much rich man. Out here in the Middle West, I hear a good bit of quiet, good-natured complaining, and the time will come when the complaining may not be so good-natured. Assume a military reverse temporary, but ugly; assume then some inadequacy of transportation between the front and Paris; assume some unnecessary suffering of our wounded, and the grumbling will become acute and vicious. It seems to me it will be better for the Red Cross if, instead of having a war council made up practically of one kind of people from one part of the country, it can have in the crisis, which may be expected naturally, all kinds of people from all parts of the country to do the explaining. I have no doubt that the explanation will be adequate, and that it will be entirely satisfactory as to the facts, but folks have a curious habit of weighing testimony through the witness rather than by the facts. We shall have no trouble with the coming Red Cross drive. It will go through beautifully, but if we have a long war, that is to say, a war two or three years in length, just as sure as guns, the folks in the Middle West are going to demand some sort of democratic control of the Red Cross. They are going to demand state organizations, which shall elect delegates to a national organization and which shall elect the national officers of the Red Cross. Unless they find that the national officers of the Red Cross come from not merely rich men along the Atlantic seaboard, not merely bankers, even from all over, but men representing all walks of life. This does not mean that it should be Bolsheviki and I.W.W. [Industrial Workers of the World], but it does mean that it should be constituted about as the national committees of the majority parties have been constituted; not more than one man from any particular section and not a majority of men from any particular class.

I am writing to you this in the most friendly spirit. I have entire faith in the war council of the Red Cross. I believe in its efficiency, and I believe in the men who serve on the war council, but on the other hand I do know the folks, and I know that the devil will be to pay with no pitch hot some of these fine days, if the control of the Red Cross is not extended through the country and not merely through the country, but throughout every vocation of life in the country. . . .

White always retained a close personal friendship with Chauncey Williams, the publisher of his first book of short stories, The Real Issue *(1896). Chauncey Jr., to whom this letter was written, had visited the Whites during summertimes in their vacation home in Colorado. The young man was now ready to leave for Europe as a soldier.*

To CHAUNCEY WILLIAMS, March 13, 1918

MY DEAR CHAUNCEY:

I received a letter from you a few weeks ago, and was delighted to hear from you. Your father says that you are going to be home for a few days after your commission comes. You don't know how proud I am of you. You are going into the most beautiful experiences a man may have, the chance to serve in a great cause and in a great way, and withal to serve in the most wonderful environment. You will see France at its best, because the soul of France is keyed higher than it ever was keyed before in the world. You will see men, literally hundreds of thousands of men, at their best and noblest and you will see the world in the midst of a great change. I believe that historians will look back upon this epoch as the most dynamic epoch in the world; the time when the greatest social, political, industrial, and spiritual changes of men were made. It seems to me in two thousand years there have been only a few great episodes; the birth of Christ, the discovery of America, and the contest that began with the battle of the Marne have marked the three greatest changes of the world. And you are going forth to be a soldier of this great change.

It is a high and blessed privilege, Chauncey, and I am glad that you are taking my friendship with you. God bless you and keep you, my boy, and bring you back safe to your beloved.

Rolla Clymer, one of the newspapermen trained on the Gazette, left to operate the paper in El Dorado, Kansas. White's advice as to the method of establishing the paper as a powerful instrument of good will in the community throws light on his own newspaper ethics.

To ROLLA CLYMER, March 29, 1918

MY DEAR ROLLA:
    ... Now as to the news policy. Of course, the first job of the newspaper is to print the news, but on the other hand after you have piled your paper full of names, you must have a policy, and I should say that policy should be the material and spiritual improvement of all El Dorado, and do not forget the spiritual improvement stands for dozens of things. You may have to tear up your city printing contract, but do it. And you may have to tear up your county printing contract, but do it, and do it in a cold-blooded way. You will find that the confidence of the community in the paper's integrity is worth three times as much as the contracts which you lose. And you will only lose those contracts temporarily, for when your integrity is established, they will come back, and then they will stay with you. A newspaper's good name is its chief asset, it brings not only circulation, but power and prosperity.
    There isn't anything else in the newspaper business as sacred as that axiom. You will find it hard to preach spiritual things in a material-minded town. You do not want to be longfaced about it and sanctimonious, but you do want to stand for brotherhood and the Golden Rule. And the best way to get brotherhood and the Golden Rule in that community is to preach for a municipal band and auditorium where it can give free concerts; and a park system where the band can give concerts; and a Y.M.C.A. with gymnasium and swimming

[189]

pool and dormitories to make it self-sustaining; a trolley line going to the various oil camps of the county and running into El Dorado; a welfare association with a free employment bureau and a scientific care of the poor of the community, and many other such propositions as will give the poor devil, who has not much of a home, a chance to move around in the community to enjoy himself and to live decently upon his wages. And stand for a clean town. Insist on law enforcement. Make them drive out the prostitutes and the gamblers, no matter whose building they occupy. Brace up your courage, and do not be afraid that a small loss of today is going to weigh against the great good of the paper, by having it proved to be loyal and brave and fair. . . .

The Denver, Colorado, police wired White: "Are you dead? Man of your name 35 died here of pneumonia. Relatives unknown." He replied in the following spirit.

To THE DENVER POLICE (telegram), April 13, 1918

Your wire asking if I am dead here. Opinions differ but my closest enemies feel that I am. Personally, I doubt it, but have no conclusive evidence either way.

When White returned from Europe, Henry J. Allen remained in Paris working for the Red Cross. In February, 1918, White launched a successful primary campaign for Allen as governor. He helped run the campaign through the November election, at which time Allen was elected.

My Dear Colonel:

You may have seen in the papers that Henry Allen has left the Red Cross and gone to the Y.M.C.A. Here is what happened to Henry. Last April, I received a letter from George B. Case of the war council of the Red Cross saying in effect that I would have to stop Henry Allen's criticism of the administration if he continued his service with the Red Cross. Mr. Case explained that the Red Cross was a military organization, and that the President was the commander in chief of it as well as the army, and that criticism of the administration was insubordination. I had read all of Henry's letters and for the life of me I could not remember one which had even remotely criticized the administration. I talked to Ralph Stout of the Star and he could not at first, but upon thinking it over remembered that Henry wrote an article for the Star and mailed it on ship board, contrasting the psychology of Washington with the psychology of Paris, London and Rome, the other great war capitals of the Allies, showing how calmly and with what strength and efficiency they were working as against the confusion which was the necessary result of the first year's entrance of an absolutely non-military people into a great military undertaking. There wasn't a line that could not have been written by George Creel [director of the Committee of Public Information] himself. I wrote a properly crawling letter to Mr. Case, and gave bond for Henry's good behavior, and wrote to Henry who I knew wanted to serve more than he wanted to criticize.

In early June, I received a letter from Ivy Lee, head of the publicity of Rockefeller and head of the publicity of the Red Cross, offering me, as Henry's close friend in Kansas, this alternative: either Henry should resign from the Red Cross or abandon his race for governor. I was in the Northwest at the time, and wired Lee asking for a protocol until July 1. He wired back that it would be entirely satisfactory. His reason for demanding action on Henry's part was that the Red Cross was being criticized for allowing one of its workers to run for office. There was no charge that Henry had tried to capitalize on the Red Cross in any way. The actual facts are that I am in charge of his publicity campaign and I have kept down all reference to the Red Cross knowing that it would be rotten bad taste. When I got back to Kansas I stumbled, accidentally, into a large chunk of information. It came confidentially, so that I may not put it into the letter, but it is absolutely reliable. It is that a man high in the Democratic party demanded of the Red Cross that they tie the can to Henry for political reasons. His nomination was practically assured. If he was nominated and elected, while away from Kansas serving the Red Cross, his personal strength would add greatly to the strength of the Republican ticket. The Democrats have a senator to re-elect, and Henry's popularity would make it hard sledding for the senator. Also, the Democrats might lose two congressmen. Hence, they seem to have put the screws to Davison [H. P. Davison, chairman of the Red Cross], who had appointed Henry to his Red Cross job, knowing that he was a gubernatorial candidate and formally wishing him success in his candidacy.

This was the situation that I found when I got back late in June. I tried to get into communication with Mr. Davison, but he was up in Canada, fishing, without a postoffice address. The Red Cross at Washington, I was satisfied, was under the control of the man that was after Henry. And then I learned that a man had been sent from Washington to Paris to relieve Henry, and that my protocol with Ivy Lee had been violated. I cabled Henry that the jig was up, that the Democrats were after him, and the devil was to pay, but he made a wise jump from the Red Cross into the Y.M.C.A., rather than be humiliated by a peremptory discharge just before the primary. In the meantime, I was in Camp Funston yesterday spending the day with General Wood. The announcement of Henry's jump to the Y.M.C.A. came just before we were going in to lunch. After I had told the General the story of how the Democrats had tried to junk Henry, he looked up in one of those sad, retrospective moments, and said: "White, don't you think that it is my turn to write a volume on 'The Martial Adventures of Henry and *Me*'?"*

Hoping this may find you in the same blessed state, I beg to subscribe myself, my dear sir, your most affectionate and obedient servant, always—

White's fear that the Republican party might become a destructive, conservative party rather than a constructive, progressive party was

* This refers to Wood's disappointment at being passed over as head of the American Expeditionary Force.

*borne out in 1919 and 1920 when the Republican party, under the
leadership of Henry Cabot Lodge, defeated the League of Nations
in the United States Senate. During the 1920's the Republican party,
also, repudiated progressive principles and through its leadership
prepared the way for the crash of 1929 and the resulting depression.*

To WILL HAYS, Chairman of the Republican National Committee,
September 17, 1918

MY DEAR MR. HAYS:

I have your note of the 11th saying you wanted my suggestion and
active co-operation, and you were kind enough to enclose your
speech at the Indiana Editorial Association, which I read with care
as I read everything you have been putting out since your election.
With most of it I agree heartily. With some of it I disagree rather
fundamentally. You are going to drive away from the Republican
party a lot of former Progressives by forever harping on the fact
that after the war we are going back to the good old days. Now,
these Progressives were not so much interested in Roosevelt as they
were interested in exactly the sort of thing that is being badly done
by the Democrats, the federalization of transportation, food, fuel,
and labor. There are four million of them, and they are going to
quit the Republican party colder than a mackerel when they are convinced that the Republican party wants to go back to the laissez
faire days before 1912. I wouldn't stay with the Republican party
overnight if I didn't believe that it was going to stand for a rigid
unification of all the railroads of the country under one railroad
system, strictly controlled by the government and probably operated by the government, if not owned by the government, and if I
thought that price controlling was to be abandoned, and if I thought
that federalization of labor under labor conciliation boards was to be
abandoned. I know my crowd, and no man can lead them back into
the Republican party unless they are satisfied with the Republican
party as a radical party.

I am very much against the present Democratic administration. It
is doing badly, things that should be done well. But to say that the
things should not be done at all makes the average Progressive see red,
and you cannot do it if you want to reorganize the Republican party.
This letter is confidential and not at all for publication.

[193]

Following the signing of the Armistice, November 11, 1918, White decided to attend the peace conference and write feature articles for a syndicate of American papers. He took his son, W. L. White, with him on the trip. They sailed for Europe on December 14, 1918, and did not return until June, 1919. On the day of departure, White went to see Theodore Roosevelt, who was in a New York hospital gravely ill. Roosevelt died while White was abroad. During his time abroad, White wrote regular letters to his wife, Sallie Lindsay White, about their experiences. The following excerpts are from these letters:

Aboard SS *Transatlantique*, to SALLIE LINDSAY WHITE, Dec. 21, 1918

. . . I walked the cold wet deck for a time with Norman Angell [Norman Angell, British publicist and author]. I must tell you about him. . . . He is highly intelligent, widely informed and very fine. He talks beautifully. . . . He is going to spend some time in Paris. He has a semi-official invitation from Colonel House [Edward M. House, confidential adviser to President Wilson] to the peace conference and offers to help me wherever he can. . . . He thinks the imperialists will beat Wilson out of his game. He feels they will not tolerate the Wilson program. He says Northcliffe [Lord Northcliffe, owner of the London *Daily Mail*] is the dominating European figure now, and that he is extremely imperialistic. . . . Angell likes the fool book [*In the Heart of a Fool*, just recently published]. He hasn't finished it yet. The first part puzzled and confused his British mind. He could not understand why the book did not begin after the first hundred pages. But he was greatly impressed by its sincerity and thinks it an A 1 book—a big important thing.

Paris, to SALLIE LINDSAY WHITE, January 7, 1919

. . . This is the day when we heard of Roosevelt's death, and all day I have been on the verge of tears. (If I just had you here we could talk it out and I should be happy.) As it is I am very sad. All the Americans are sad here. They feel that a great world loss has come. I don't feel that way so much. God will take care of this world, I suppose, but where will we have such another friend! Did I write you that when I came away from him in the Hospital I felt that I had seen the last of him. The last of the robust vigorous Roosevelt that I met way back there in the old days, when I came dancing in to you to tell you about the wonderful man I had lunched with! He was going very fast that day when I saw him at the Hopital. The man I saw was gentle, and was very kind. . . . It seemed ended, all the work of the man that was, all his works and ways. Today I feel a big impulsion to write about him, but it may pass with the month. You know I have always wanted to do that thing, "The Life and Times of Theodore Roosevelt." I think I could do it well—understandingly, humanly! But I don't know, possibly it is not my job. If you think so when you get this, write to Mr. Brett [George Brett of The Macmillan Company] and ask him to have someone take it up with Mrs. Roosevelt. . . .

Paris, to SALLIE LINDSAY WHITE, January 8, 1919

. . . I had a talk and half an hour's walk along the banks of the Seine with the Colonel [Edward M. House]. We talked—I guess I did most of the talking—most frankly. For I wanted him to know what bunk we—Baker [Ray Stannard Baker, who was in charge of public relations for the American Peace Commission] and the liberals here generally—think the League plan is. . . . I found House rather radical, more than one would expect. He is the force that has kept Wilson abreast of the times. He is quite candid. He says things in short direct sentences and is rather engaging in his manner. He told me that the weakness of Wilson is his inability to get on with people who disagree with him. House said he urged Wilson to use Roosevelt in the war, to send him to Russia as the head of a Commission and give him full power. But Wilson could not bring himself to see it. I talked straight from the shoulder, a veritable flood of talk for me, and he followed me closely. I never caught his attention wandering. He is for the economic phase of the League but Lansing [Secretary of State Robert Lansing] and the President, I guess, don't see it. Lansing is quite reactionary about that phase of it. But I feel that House will get it to Wilson some way.

From time to time, as the peace conference negotiations dragged on, White went on trips to see conditions in other parts of Europe. On one trip, he and his party drove through Verdun, Alsace-Lorraine, and to the German Rhineland. Here, he wrote, they saw beautiful, prosperous towns already booming with activity. Prophetically, he warns in the following letter of the danger of the autocrats coming back into power.

Coblenz, Germany, to SALLIE LINDSAY WHITE, January 25, 1919

. . . There in the night we saw all their furnaces ablaze, all their big cities flashing with lights, all their great industries working day and night. It was a horrible contrast to the hours and hours of desolation that we had seen the day before as we went through France. The peace should not be written until the delegates to the conference see not merely the devastation in France, but the unpunished Rhineland. They are parts of the same picture! Germany is the same Germany; changing the government, sending the Kaiser to Holland, is not enough. The fellows here along the Rhine, the Americans, feel that the whole democratic movement in Germany is a mere trusteeship for the autocracy which will come back in a few months or a few years as the exigency of the politics of Europe demands.

On the way back from the Rhineland, White's party visited the Hindenburg Line and the battlefields of Château-Thierry, the Argonne, and Belleau Wood. Then they returned to Paris, where White found some welcome letters from home. The proposed Prinkipo conference between the Allies and Soviet Russia, at which White was to head the American delegation, never took place because of French opposition.

. . . I had the letters in my arms when we met Ray Baker. He said, "We have been trying to get you at Coblenz for a week. We've got something on hand for you." But I had your letters unread in my hand and said, "All right—I'll see you later," and left him. When I rounded the corner, I found Colonel House toddling around and he grabbed me to say, "I'm glad you are going to take charge of this Bolshevik thing for us!" I answered, "Oh, am I," and he laughed and said he supposed so. Then I knew what Baker wanted. But I hurried on with my letters and spent the hour with you, and what an hour! What grand letters. . . .

I told Col. House yesterday I would go to Prinkipo only if they let all the newspapermen go who wanted to go. The Bolsheviks demand the fullest publicity, and it is my only safety. For the French do not want to confer with the Bolsheviks. The French feel their military safety is with a strong centralized government in Russia, one which will assume the Russian debt largely held by France. So French statesmen are fighting the whole conference. House and the President are very much for it and in my talk with House he told me he had just two things to ask of the Bolsheviks. First, that they devote their propaganda to their own country; and second, that we establish peace. He said he did not care what kind of a government they had, if they devoted themselves to it and didn't go around disturbing the industrial peace of the world with it. But the French will send no envoys to deal exclusively with the Bolsheviks, so there we are—blocked! . . .

Paris, to President Woodrow Wilson, April 28, 1919

Sir:

The Conference is almost over. I believe I have known something of the inside of almost every great movement, something of what you have done. And as one American belonging to the cynical profession of the press, it may hearten you to know that every great move you have made has seemed to me wise and just and strong. I shall go home to support your course here with enthusiasm and with what force I can command.

I realize the tremendous inertia of the French in resisting publicity. Yet, I genuinely believe the world response, which has come from your Italian stand,* which after all was strong chiefly because it let publicity into the Conference, will well be duplicated, if you insist that when the Allies meet the Germans, to give the enemy his terms, the press of the world shall have some representation at the meeting. Such representation when the Covenant, which has been made in the open, is finally arrived at in the open would absolutely vindicate point number one. And the humble people of the world, who have looked so eagerly to you for championship, would feel that in this final crisis you have stood by them. I hope you can feel that even an extraordinary effort to overcome the French inertia will be worth while in this final struggle for the open consummation of a just Covenant. But, in any case, I have the honor to subscribe myself in this splendid adventure of yours into world politics.

Paris, to SALLIE LINDSAY WHITE, April 30, 1919

. . . He [Wilson] really has done wonders here, and how he has done it is past me. I give him up. He is more mysterious than ever. All so vague and remote and impersonal and colorless, yet tremendously powerful. He has really dominated this situation, and that all alone. No one has helped him. His own delegation has helped him more by guiding him away from the blunders it made. He has no friends, no cronies, no advisers. I give him up. . . .

In May, White and his son left for England. White wrote his wife that it seemed like home to be in England again, and he observed: "The English language and English ways and simple, kind-faced people more than make up for the English cooking!" Norman Angell took him to meetings of the British Labor party.

* Refers to Wilson's successful opposition to Italian demand for territory inhabited largely by non-Italians.

London, to SALLIE LINDSAY WHITE, May 31, 1919

... The free frank incendiary way that these British radicals talk about revolution would make your hair curl, only they don't expect bloodshed. They expect to have a chatty revolution and then all go home to tea.

I have another article in my head about the peace—the hard malicious French peace, full of revenge and of materialism that would shame the Kaiser. When you think of what Grant and Lincoln did, this peace makes you ashamed. Not that the Boche does not deserve it and more. Not that he would not have done much worse, but we were supposed to be fighting in a noble cause, more interested in setting him and the world a good example, than in following a wicked one. ... Wilson is not to blame, assuming that he decided to stay and bargain his soul away for the League of Nations. He has made the best trade he can. But it is none the less a shameful bargain and will rise to damn us all in another generation.

White was a bad prophet. He did not realize that in 1920 the American people, emotionally worn out by war, would go back to a reactionary America—"normalcy" it was called.

To WILL HAYS, Republican National Committee, August 6, 1919

MY DEAR MR. HAYS:

Thank you for your letter of July 30. I have no doubt of your genuine desire to elect a ticket. But, on the other hand, don't ever think you can elect anybody who is an incrusted old reactionary. It cannot be done. The country does not want a mere business man for president. A business man with vision, who realizes that this is a changing world and that the changes must come as well from the heart as from the head, will get somewhere. But no one who thinks in the terms of Lodge, Penrose, Lowden, Goodrich, Harding, and Watson [Senator Henry Cabot Lodge of Massachusetts; Senator

[199]

Boies Penrose of Pennsylvania; Governor Frank O. Lowden of Illinois; Governor J. P. Goodrich of Indiana; Senator Warren G. Harding of Ohio; Senator James Watson of Indiana] is going to get anywhere in this country.

The summer and fall of 1919 found the people of the United States vigorously discussing the League of Nations. Although the League was defeated in the Senate, in November, 1919, public sentiment seemed to be for American participation. White, back home in Emporia, did his best through editorials and correspondence to get Republicans to ratify the League of Nations. As the record of course shows, he was not too successful.

To Senator Arthur Capper, August 21, 1919

My Dear Arthur:

. . . Here is the political situation as I see it. Sixty per cent of the Kansas people are against the League today, possibly more. But if the League is defeated, we will have to go ahead with a strong military program, which will mean universal service and a big navy. The threat of universal service, either as an accomplished fact or as a Republican program, thrown into the campaign of 1920, combined with the fact that the Republicans defeated the League of Nations, and are standing for a big navy, and have probably got a candidate who voted against the League of Nations, would give us a fat chance to win.

Just imagine what the women of this state would do when the Democratic orators went around and told them that their boys would be taken for universal service, because the Republicans wouldn't establish a League of Nations. We can quite easily justify a military program after having adopted the League of Nations, by explaining that it is a temporary expedient to be used while we are trying out the strength of the League. But to use a military program as a permanent, everlasting policy of America would lick the Republican party worse than it was ever licked before, and it would be the last licking it would ever get. I would vote for the League with certain restrictions and reservations, but I would never vote for an amendment to the League which would be unacceptable to the President. He is too smart. He is a singed cat. You think you can play politics all around him, but he fools you. And he can pretty nearly be elected to a third term in this country, if the League is defeated and the Republicans make a record for universal service and a big navy and nominate for president any man who voted against the League.*

There again you have trouble. If the Republicans defeat the League and nominate a man who was against the League, the League becomes a vital issue in politics. If they defeat the League and nominate a man who is for the League, they haven't a leg to stand on. The only way to get the League out of politics is to adopt the covenant and go on with the economic and industrial program which is yawning before us for settlement. I should write this to Senator Curtis [Charles Curtis], except that I don't know him quite well enough to butt in with these suggestions. But if you want to tell him what I think, or show him these suggestions, go ahead.

The Non-Partisan League [a left-wing farm organization founded by A. C. Townley] is organizing in the Fourth Congressional District. They are not getting anywhere. But, my dear boy, assume a defeat of the League of Nations, an economic mix-up in which farm prices would be confused and unsettled, and Democratic orators going about telling the farmers that their boys are to be taken away from them, and that the threatening war in Europe will involve us, because we have no League of Nations to stop wars; and combine all that with the Non-Partisan League, and Senator Curtis would have a fat chance to go back! The thing that happened to Ingalls would happen to him [Senator John J. Ingalls, defeated by the Populist uprising in 1890]. "Now is the time for all good men to come to the aid of their party." I wish to Heaven, Curtis could see this and realize that, if we defeat the League of Nations, we are in the Devil's own box for next year. You can discredit the old man this year, but he will turn up smiling next year, and Heaven knows that the country has had so much Democratic incompetency that another term of it would swamp us. Yet all the talk of incompetency would fall on deaf ears in front of a military situation.

* Woodrow Wilson's illness removed him from the 1920 situation. The League was defeated by the technique of adding reservations to the Covenant that were unacceptable to Wilson.

[201]

To Charles F. Scott, Iola (Kansas) *Register*, October 27, 1919

Dear Charley:

. . . I note that you ask if the country is going to hell. Before you read any further, close the door and let me tell you something in dead confidence, and for Heaven's sake don't let it get out that I said so, but I really don't know. Tuesdays, Thursdays, and Saturdays, I think it is. Mondays, Wednesdays, and Fridays, I am more hopeful.

We are certainly going through a tremendous change. The world, and particularly the American part of the world, is adopting a brand-new scale of living and a brand-new scale of prices all at the same time. It has given us the worst case of social bellyache that it has been my misfortune ever to see or hear about. By a prodigal wave of the hand, somewhere along during the war, we have raised the laboring men into middle-class standards of living and he is not going back. But he cannot stay where he is unless we cut down profits in some way, to pay him his increased wages. Or unless we tax away incomes, inheritances and rents so that the state-owned industries can afford to do badly and at a loss, a lot of the things that private individuals are not doing well at a profit, and which must be done in order to keep the new standard of living going. It is a mess. We have jumped about a hundred years in less than ten months in our economic growth, and I will give the whole thing up. . . .

White's suggestions, in this letter, that there should be a national minimum wage commission and jobs for the unemployed provided by the federal government were not carried out until the days of the New Deal. The Republican party in the twenties viewed such recommendations as "subversive" and "communistic."

To Paul V. Kellogg, *Survey*, December 2, 1919

My Dear Kellogg:

I have your letter asking what is the way out of the industrial tangle into which war economics have thrown the country. You ask how should the public go about it and what should be our practical objective. It seems to me that our practical objective should be to keep every man who wants work in a job three hundred days in a year, and that he should be kept at work at a living wage, that is to say a wage upon which he may maintain a family of six in the enjoyment of all the comforts of our civilization, electric lights, central heat, and power, modern plumbing, convenient fuel for cooking, decent housing, good clothing, clean and exhilarating amusements, time for reading, and money to make profitable reading possible, some leisure for seeing his city, his state, and his country, and at least a high school education for all of his children and a college education for such of his children as desire it. That should be the first practical objective of society. I believe it can be secured without overturning the present economic and industrial order, and may be obtained under our present institutions as they are now organized in the government. The first thing I should do would be to secure a constitutional amendment, giving Congress unlimited powers over commerce and industry, and under that amendment I should establish a national minimum wage commission with full powers, and provide for federal employment agents who would take up the slack in our labor situation, thus securing so far as possible regular employment for people in the seasonal industries. This would soon wipe out the revolutionary ideals of labor. I should not fight Bolshevism with guns, but with steady employment. This program may seem far in advance of today's conditions, and yet some forward movement must be taken, and taken quickly, or the situation will become vastly more dangerous than it is now.

White served on the committee that wrote the Republican platform in 1920. The plank on foreign affairs was a meaningless straddle of the League of Nations issue. Henry Cabot Lodge was largely responsible for this ambiguous plank calling, in vague terms, for an international association of nations. By the time this letter to Murdock was written, Wilson was a sick man. He had collapsed in September, 1919, while on tour advocating the League.

To Victor Murdock, Wichita *Eagle*, February 4, 1920

My Dear Vic:

. . . I am going to try to go to the National Republican Convention. I want to see the wheels go round. Will Hays put me on the Republican Platform Committee. He has about twenty or twenty-five former Bull Moose on that committee and about twenty-five others who are as near progressives as Cummins or Kellogg or men of that type. But he also has on Murray Crane [Senators Albert Cummins, Frank B. Kellogg, and Murray Crane] and a lot of old high-binder standpatters who haven't had an idea since the fall of Babylon and who, while they agree with the general justice of the fall of Babylon, think it was hasty and ill-considered.

What do you make out about Wilson? Is he stubborn, or sick, or stupid, or what? I had a great crush on him in Paris, but I haven't had much taste for what he has been doing the last two months. . . .

White was a middle-of-the-road thinker. He never considered himself to be a pioneer like Socialist Eugene Debs or Senator R. M. LaFollette. To do so, he argued, would cost him his hold on middle-class America, which was always wary of too much "radicalism."

To F. Dumont Smith, Hutchinson, Kan., February 26, 1920

Dear Mr. Smith:

. . . I think Lincoln was the right kind of a radical—a radical who moves with the main body of the troops, but keeps moving forward.

The scouts, the pioneers, and snipers of radicalism, of course, are needed, and they leave their bones on the field to mark as much the way we should not go as to mark the way we should go. And great, forward-thinking men like Lincoln, who carry with them in their revolutionary movements the sound opinion of their generation, are heroes. . . .

Before the Republican convention, White denounced Harding as a man who would out-Taft Taft in reaction. Yet, after the nomination White threw his support to Harding. Somewhat naïvely he hoped that, as president, Harding might listen to progressive advice. Just the opposite happened under Harding's presidency. Reactionary business forces dominated the government and increased their monopolistic control of business.

To Senator WARREN G. HARDING, July 10, 1920

MY DEAR SENATOR HARDING:

Your letter of June 30 finds me upon my return from California. I see by the paper that a number of Progressives headed by Walter Brown [former chairman of the Bull Moose party in Ohio] talked to you the other day. No doubt they said what I should have said, and it seems to me that your conference with them makes a further conference with me at this particular time only a burden upon your time. I am quite sure I could add nothing to their general counsel.

I feel that your election is fairly assured by the weakness of the Democratic nomination. The women of the Far West and of this Middle West are tremendously against Cox [Governor James Cox of Ohio, the Democratic presidential candidate] because of his Tammany support and of the support of Nugent [Senator John F. Nugent of Idaho] and of the New Jersey wets. If he dry-cleans his reputation, it will have to be with a straightforward, clear-cut, unequivocal declaration for the Volstead Act, which, of course, I doubt if he will give. But he can't get away by saying that he is in favor of the enforcement of the law or any such wishy-washy statements.

The Progressives, such as are party-minded and are not running more or less on their own schedules, are inclined to vote the Republican ticket this year, from top to bottom, but that does not mean that they are going to be easy to handle after the election. They feel very definitely and quite strongly that their views of reconstruction must be heeded, and they will make the fight for their views after the election for the next Congress.

My mail is full of cantankerous letters saying they are going to vote the ticket, but are going to have their say later. They don't like this "back to normal" business. They don't like you to be called a man of the McKinley type, because they feel that the McKinley day was the least satisfactory day in the history of the Republican party. They have little use for school-reader Americanism and resounding phrases of that sort. But they will want specific, progressive performance after the election, and I feel sure that you will see the wisdom of their course and ask them to state quite specifically exactly what they feel should be done. That being done, and if counsel is asked of them, I have no doubt that you will be able to unite the Republican party. But, as you know, the Progressives are not a very party-minded bunch, and we are voting now in the affirmative for a rather obvious purpose of voting for a reconsideration if we don't like the way the motion carries.

I assumed you want frank, man talk, and I am giving it to you as I would want you to give it to me. I know that pussyfooting and polite phrases are of no value at this time and I am speaking frankly as man to man, that we may have a clear understanding in the coming election and administration.

Wishing you every success in the campaign, I am—

The reaction of the twenties was a nightmare to White. Feeling that he had to choose between evils—Harding or Cox—he chose Harding. In the Gazette, September 3, 1920, *White rationalized that the Democratic party, made up of big city bosses and the Solid South, was a menace to the nation. Therefore, the public should vote for the good old Republican party. "The issue," said White, "is one of parties, and not men." In his correspondence, White was not so strong for Harding—as the following letter to a California Bull Mooser shows—as he was in his editorials.*

To Myer Lissner, Los Angeles, Calif., September 3, 1920

My Dear Myer:

Here are the Roosevelt letters. I have been away for three months and have neglected your letters.

Politically I am unhappy. I poured my heart out to Victor Murdock and got this reply:

"My dear Will: I am glad you are still able to feel pain. Yours, Vic."

Enclosed find an editorial on Harding from tonight's paper, which is the best I can do. I can't get out and whoop it up for him, and I have written a letter to Harding substantially what I put in this editorial. I am not a bandwagon artist.

The New Republic, *militant liberal weekly, asked White to write an article on the campaign. His lack of interest in the campaign is revealed in this letter. Actually, he did not write an article for the* New Republic *until March 9, 1921. It was entitled, "We Who Are About to Die."*

To Herbert Croly, the *New Republic*, September 11, 1920

My Dear Mr. Croly:

I will try and work out something for you, but I am low in my mind and may not be able to do it. I am so low in my mind that I wouldn't laugh at Charlie Chaplin throwing a whole custard pie at Cox or Harding or both. I think that the only honest vote either a Republican or a Democrat can cast should be a spite vote against his own party. And it all comes out of trusting our politics to professional politicians. We have got the same propositions going here that they had in Jerusalem two thousand years ago. The Pharisees are running the temple and bossing the religion and handling the caucuses and the people are getting the worst of it. But so long as the folks think the worst of it is the best of it, there doesn't seem to be anything to do. We who feel like going in and making a roughhouse in the temple will only be crucified in the attempt.

I am delighted that you liked my convention stories. I really am tremendously interested in the situation and was deeply moved by the vainglory of the spectacle of the conventions. Possibly my reaction was serious. I'm not humorous. I couldn't be humorous in this situation.

In about a week or ten days I will send you something about the political situation, if I have anything on my heart worth writing.

Edna Ferber and the Whites were intimate friends. Miss Ferber's autobiography, A Peculiar Treasure, *contains delightfully human sketches of Will and Sallie White. The Whites, as this letter indicates, spent the summer in Moraine Park, Colorado.*

To Edna Ferber, September 14, 1920

My Dear Edna:

... We had a beautiful summer, Sallie and I, in Colorado. ... We had some company, an average of nine, I think, at the table was our rule, sometimes it ran up to fourteen, but never lower than seven. Bill and Mary were both there. I suppose it will be Bill's last all-summer trip in the Park. He is going to work next summer. Just at the moment Bill is in Lawrence [at the University of Kansas] attending "rush week," but he is going to Harvard next week, and he thinks he will go to work next summer on the paper. He has been working now for three or four years, and he makes a pretty fair fist as a reporter. I wish you would give me your Chicago address. Bill would like to stop and see you if he goes by the way of Chicago, and I want him to. I expected to go with Bill to Cambridge, but Sallie being away,* it will be impossible for me to leave because my mother cannot be left alone. And, of course, Mary, too, has some rights that a white man is bound to respect.

Mary seems to have come into a new era in her life. Last year and the year before she was mighty carefree, as you know, but this year she is bucking into her studies, doing all sorts of stunts, taking five subjects and is clamoring to take six; has an ambition to make grades and is tremendously impressed with the idea of going to Wellesley. She has forgotten all about the horse, except in odd moments, when the horse complex returns, but it only holds her attention a few minutes a day. The horse and all that goes with the horse is in the past with her. She is reading serious books. She got her great stimulus to work at the Y.W. conference at Estes Park, where she did remarkably well and met a lot of girls from different colleges, mostly eastern colleges. . . . She reads all sorts of tremendously serious, high-brow stuff, and at the same time she does love to put pins in the teacher's chair. She is taking charge of the house, now that her mother is gone. We lay out the program for the meals, and she balances up the ration and orders the stuff and bosses me around, and really is a wonder. She is so rotten good that I'm always afraid that when she takes off her corset cover her wings will sprout out and she'll fly away.

Having disposed of the rest of the family, I now come down to father. Father has had a beautiful rest. I didn't take the cover off my typewriter while I was in the West. I left all my letters unanswered, as you have reason to suspect, and just naturally loafed. Bill drove us around in the car a good deal. . . .

As a result of my summer's siesta, I feel quite fit and want to go to work. I have the Roosevelt thing on the block and will probably get rid of it right away. It is hard to work when Sallie is out of town because she shields me from the telephone and from callers and from various pests that are roaming abroad. But I've got to buck in and do the best I can. . . .

* Mrs. White was taking care of a sick brother.

Ed Howe, publisher of the Atchison Globe, *was a distinctive journal-ist and writer. His novel,* The Story of a Country Town (*1884*), *was a grim, powerful, dismal picture of a midwestern town. None of his other books ever equaled this first novel in popularity or in reality of presentation.*

To Ed Howe, October 29, 1920

My Dear Ed Howe:

I had bought your book [Anthology of Another Town] two weeks ago and had read it through. I think it is a great book. How square and honest and true you are when you take your pen in hand and sit down and write. I shall write something about the book in a few days. It is really as big a book as "The Story of a Country Town." Of course, it never will be so popular because it hasn't the sustaining interest. Only a man who loves and appreciates and knows the life which you depict will be attracted to it. The fact that there is no love interest will someway fail to hold a lot of readers who ought to read it. It is funny about this love interest business. It will hold a lot of people to a poor story and the lack of it will keep them away from a really good thing. There ought to be a law against love. Why don't you run for the legislature on the platform: "Down With Love"? It's worse than whiskey. There's nothing except the weather causes such a large economic loss in the United States. If love and the weather were adjusted, what a heaven this earth would be. Why don't you do something about it?

The Gazette *for November 23, 1920, hailed Sinclair Lewis's* Main Street *as "a most glorious book" and rated it as one of "the great novels of American life." Although living on Main Street himself, White always was able to see the limitations of small-town life* as well as its *better qualities.*

[210]

DEAR MR. LEWIS:

Mrs. White and I read aloud and have just finished "Main Street," and I hasten to tell you what a noble thing you have done. It has been years since I have read anything so splendidly conceived and so skillfully executed as "Main Street." I am sending herewith a little editorial from the Gazette which I hope you will like. With all my heart I thank you for Will Kennicott and Sam Clark. They are the Gold Dust Twins of common sense. I don't know where in literature you will find a better American, or more typical, than Dr. Will Kennicott. Of course, Gopher Prairie is my habitat. I was born in Emporia and grew up in a town which grew with me from 100 to 4,000 people—the little town of El Dorado, Kansas. But it had a boom in the eighties, and with that boom came a lot of college people: a Yale man or two, and some men from Harvard and from the midwestern universities; and they colored the town, as I think they did most of the boom towns of Kansas. There are many Gopher Prairies in Kansas, but also there are a lot of towns here around three thousand that have done some notable things. After a Kansas town passes five thousand, it becomes a considerably better town, has some civic spirit and is striving consciously to be just and beautiful in its outward expression. The struggle is pretty hard and sometimes the town loses, but still it is struggling. . . .

Emporia is a town of ten or eleven thousand and is a typical prairie town. Kansas towns are, for the most part, coming into the Country Club stage, and one or two have publicly owned golf courses as a part of their playground equipment.

However, all this is beside the point. What I really wish to do is to tell you how much Mrs. White and I enjoyed your book. I want to use your book for a Christmas present, and I am enclosing a blank check. Would you be good enough to ask your publisher to send me upon receipt of the check, books to cover the names which I enclose on another slip and will you then be kind enough to autograph those books with your name and my name, as for instance, "To Dr. Will Mayo with Christmas Greetings from W. A. White" and whatever greetings you wish to send him, signing your name with the date, Christmas, 1920, and fix the others up somewhat similarly.

If I were a millionaire, I should buy a thousand of those books and send them to my friends, and then I would go and bribe the legislature of Kansas to make "Main Street" compulsory reading in the public schools. No American has done a greater service for his country in any sort of literature, than you have done.

To VICTOR MURDOCK, Federal Trade Commission,
Washington, D. C., December 20, 1920

MY DEAR VIC:

I haven't written to you for a long time, and I haven't heard from you in a long time. The other day I told Sinclair Lewis, who lives at 1639 Nineteenth Street, N. W., Washington, to send you a copy of his book, "Main Street," autographed, with my compliments. I thought you would enjoy it. Sallie and I read it and had a lot of fun out of it. I thought maybe you and Pearl would also. It is a pretty good country-town book. Of course, there is the other side of the story. He does not tell the other side, but at that, the side that he does tell is well worth telling. It is the sort of thing that puts discontent into the hearts of folks. And I think that contentment is worse than "red" any day.

I, of course, am very unhappy politically. I suppose any man is, who has any love of country or faith in its institutions, or hope for its future. I don't think we have come to the Slough of Despond yet. We are going down further. But what I fear is, or perhaps not so much what I fear as what I hope for, is that we will dam the waters of progress up so that there will be a tremendous breakover flood. And, in that wave there may be some real gains for progress, even after the receding waves of reaction at some future time have come. I feel that our splurge from 1903 to 1914 was well worth while. We did get a lot of things done. Things that are well worth doing; things that are permanent. But I feel also that nobody much is paying attention to those things now. And as Christmastime draws near I grow lonesome and want to see you and long to have a talk with you to get the stimulus of your own reflections. But I can't do anything else but sit down and write this letter. Accept my love and Sallie's love for you and Pearl and Marcia and Kathryn [Mrs. Murdock and their two daughters].

My Dear Baker:

What a God-damned world this is! I trust you will realize that I am not swearing; merely trying to express in the mildest terms what I think of the conditions that exist. What a God-damned world!

Starvation on the one hand, and indifference on the other, pessimism rampant, faith quiescent, murder met with indifference; the lowered standard of civilization faced with universal complaisance, and the whole story so sad that nobody can tell it.

If anyone had told me ten years ago that our country would be what it is today, and that the world would be what it is today, I should have questioned his reason. . . .

The "Roaring Twenties," or the "Jazz Age," brought a new frankness into American life. The old Victorian ethical code, which frowned on the mention of the word "sex," to say nothing of a discussion of its meaning, was destroyed beyond recall. Novels like F. Scott Fitzgerald's Flaming Youth *and* This Side of Paradise *had the heroes and heroines openly discussing sex problems in a way that seemed obscene to the older generation.*

To Marco Morrow, Topeka *Capital*, February 7, 1921

My Dear Marco:

I have been out of the state for a month since your letter came asking me to contribute to "I've Been Reading." Here goes:

I have been reading Flaubert's "Madame Bovary." This is an old book and I sometimes think one gets on farther with the new books by reading the old ones than he does by reading the new ones. For upon books of this old French school the new realistic or naturalistic American school is building upon a foundation. And incidentally I believe I have stumbled onto a rather important truth, probably old, probably you will find it in Solomon. Probably Solomon uttered it when he said, "Stay with flagons, comfort me with apples; for I am sick of love." Solomon was bored to a crisp. Madame Bovary was bored to a crisp and so she went out and had three successful adulteries. And I am satisfied that Madame Bovary was not a very bad woman. She was simply bored to extinction. I think that a good deal of immorality of one sort and another—business, political, and one might say social—is due to the fact that people are bored. If they lead interesting lives, they are less likely to those lapses which require excitement. And the excitement, not the immorality of the excitement, is the source of their chief desire. The next time I hear of a man or a woman going wrong, either socially or politically or commercially, I am going to look and see if that man or woman isn't bored to a nice, crisp brown and see if he wasn't seeking excitement rather than anything else.

My dear Marco, I hope this won't stop the readers of the Capital.

Organized labor had a difficult time during the "normalcy" of Harding. In the wave of uncritical reaction which swept the country, anti-union employers smashed unions and proclaimed that the open shop was the only American plan. White was a frequent reader of Lincoln's works and undoubtedly remembered that Lincoln had once said: "Labor is prior to, and independent of, capital. Capital is only the fruit of labor, and could never have existed if labor had not first existed. Labor is the superior of capital, and deserves much the higher consideration."

To C. H. Howard, Commonwealth Steel Company, St. Louis, Mo.,
February 10, 1921

Dear Mr. Howard:

Thank you very much for the copy of John Wesley Hill's "Abraham Lincoln, Man of God," which I am reading with great interest. I note particularly your suggestion that I might find material for editorial discussion of Lincoln as a man of God. I note the chapter on

[214]

the Christian view of labor. I wonder if Mr. Hill is not trying to give the impression that if Lincoln were alive today he would stand with the open-shop movement. Someway I feel that Lincoln would do no such thing. I feel very strongly that his deep sympathy and understanding for the man who is down and is trying earnestly and intelligently to rise would impel Lincoln to realize that the unions have done more for labor than any other one force in the last hundred years, excepting, perhaps, universal education. I feel that the Christian view of Lincoln would try to encourage the unions to give them more and more power and make their membership more and more intelligent. I feel that the great struggle of our century is to take it to the middle class, that submerged group commonly known as labor, and give it an intelligent co-operative interest in industry. By this I do not mean in commerce at all, but in the production side of industry. And I feel that Lincoln would have welcomed such a rise on behalf of labor. . . . An arrangement by which labor will have actually a voice in setting wages, considering shop conditions, and other details of production. I do not think labor even remotely hopes to have anything to do with the commercial side of industry. But on its production side, I think labor may well be consulted now. And if a brotherly instead of paternal attitude be taken, I believe this thing could be worked out. And I am tremendously sorry for all the bitterness and rancor which are spreading through the country in the open-shop movement.

Thanking you again for sending me this book and for giving me the opportunity to intrude upon you at this time, with views which probably do not entirely meet your agreement, permit me to subscribe myself—

Mary White died early Friday morning, May 13, 1921. The previous Tuesday her skull had been fractured by a blow from the limb of a tree while she was riding her horse. Her father was in the East. When Mary's condition became serious, it was too late for her father or brother Bill at Harvard to arrive home before she died. On the morning following the funeral, her father shut himself in his office and wrote a beautiful tribute to his daughter. This obituary was widely reprinted in newspapers and magazines and Christopher Morley included it in his book Modern Essays, *published later that year. Since that time the piece has been reprinted in over two hundred books.*

To J. J. DUNCAN, JR., Estes Park, Colo., May 28, 1921

MY DEAR YOUNG FRIEND:

I have received letters from all sorts of people—from members of the President's Cabinet and from the wife and daughter of Colonel Roosevelt, sending sympathy to Mary's mother and to me for our loss in her death, but no letter I have received brought the clutch to my heart as poignantly, and as joyously too, as your letter. I know of nothing that would make Mary more happy than to know Cricket was in good hands. She loved Cricket. From the time that she was twelve years old until her death, I think she loved Cricket the donkey better than any other inanimate [?] thing in the world. I am so proud and glad that you have Cricket and that you and Mary were good friends.

We may not be in the Park this summer, but if we are, Mary's mother and I would be pleased beyond words to have you ride Cricket up and take dinner with us.

I know that it was hard for you to write that letter, and I want you to know that you gave Mary's mother and father a real throbby jump of joy in the midst of our tears, and I want to thank you for your thoughtfulness and for your cheery words.

To WALTER ARMSTRONG, Salt Lake City, Utah, June 3, 1921

MY DEAR WALTER: *

Thank you so much for your beautiful letter. Sallie and I have read it, and it was indeed good of you. I am glad you saw the piece we wrote about Mary. It may interest you to know that the piece has been copied by newspapers all over the country. As nearly as I can figure out, it has gone out in papers aggregating a total subscription of two and a half million, probably a wider circulation than anything

* Walter Armstrong was an old college friend who had introduced Mr. White to Sallie Lindsay.

[216]

that has ever been published in the Gazette. And I cannot help feeling that some place along the line her life has reached out and touched other lives through this article, and I hope it has touched them for good. That immortality is sure. And it heals my sorrow somewhat to know that I helped her to that wider influence.

Mary was a joyous child. We can't think of her for five minutes consecutively without breaking into a laugh. And you can't go around weeping your eyes out and laughing at the same time. We have to laugh if we think of Mary and we love to think of Mary. Which is my idea of rather a sad mixup in one's emotions. But I don't want people to get an idea that I was sorry for myself when I wrote the piece, for really I was not. Mary on my books is a net gain, however hard the loss. A profitable proposition who has more than paid her way in the joy she has brought and the memories she leaves, and if this is the end, still as the books stand I am away ahead. I suppose to you, my dear old friend, I can say something personal; something about the problem of immortality. It doesn't bother me. If Mary is alive and conscious, she is happy. She was always happy and always useful. If she is not alive and conscious, then she was most useful and most happy, and in either event it is all right.

J. J. Davis, newly appointed secretary of labor, inquired of White as to suggestions on employer-employee relations. White's reply naturally was based on his own experience in the Gazette shop. Through the remainder of his life, particularly when labor gained a more equitable status in the 1930's, White believed that the greatest problem in the situation was the intolerant, somewhat money-mad boss.

To JAMES J. DAVIS, Secretary of Labor, Washington, D. C.,
June 18, 1921

DEAR MR. DAVIS:

I have your letter of June 15 and am greatly honored by the request you make in it. I don't know that I can qualify as an expert, as the

[217]

lawyers say, upon labor matters. I have a small payroll of six or seven hundred dollars a week in my printing office and in building for the last two years, at the peak of prices, I have carried a payroll in the neighborhood of a thousand dollars and have been able to borrow, beg, earn and steal enough money to keep it going. On all my jobs, whether printing or building, I run a closed shop. And I have found that it pays. I find that, if an employer takes a personal interest in the men; there is no trouble with labor laying down on the job. It is the boss that provokes absent-minded laborers.

You ask me what you can best do in your job to promote "the best interest of the American workman and to secure his co-partnership in the country." My feeling is that, in the job of getting the American workman to take an interest in his co-partnership in the progress of the country, you want to get the American employer also to take an interest in the co-partnership of the American workman. Somewhere between forty and sixty per cent of the trouble with the workmen is in the boss. I should try to get it in his big noodle that the one thing which will make dividends and make profits for the stockholders is self-respect in the man who works. Anything that will bring self-respect into the heart of the worker will increase his production and thereby increase the profits of the boss. I have made what little money I make in industry by a small labor turnover. The average time of service in the Gazette office of twenty-five people is between nine and ten years. That doesn't just happen, and it doesn't happen because I pay more cash wages than anybody else, though I keep from fifteen to twenty per cent ahead of the union scale. My small labor turnover comes from the fact that I am forever cultivating self-respect in the men. Self-respect in the men speeds up production. If the boss can get it into his head that the more responsibility he can put on the shop, the more interest he can get the men to take in their work, the more he can promote unions and organizations of all sorts—shop committees and co-operative devices for increasing output—the more money he is going to make. He will begin to see the first principles of modern industry.

But the boss who feels that he has to hire spies to know what his men are doing, the boss who feels that the labor market is like the cattle market or the cotton market, the boss who goes at industry with an ax, generally gets the ax in the back of his own neck before the transaction closes.

Having educated the boss, I should go after the men, hammer and tongs, and tell them this: Now here is this boss that wants to keep down the labor turnovers and is treating you like human beings and is giving you a share in the management of the back room, and it is up to you to make good. It is up to you to increase production. It is up to you to keep down strikes. It is up to you to make profit for the boss, so that he may feel that his investment in your self-respect is justified. I should say I would encourage labor leaders like Sidney Hillman of the Amalgamated Garment Cutters [Amalgamated Clothing Workers], and I should cultivate leaders like the men who run the big brotherhoods, and I should talk to labor in terms of increasing, rather than decreasing a day's work and show them how much more money there is in it for labor to be efficient than there is for labor to be inefficient. But I should go to labor only after I had convinced the boss. He is the man you are after. Convince him and it will be easy enough to convince labor. In the meantime, while I was talking to the boss I should talk to both labor and capital about the advisability of placing more and more shop responsibility, and hence shop control, in the hands of labor committees. Teach the men to be responsible, and you will teach them to be effective. Teach them what the finished product means. And by all means don't try to buy out, or crush out, or wipe out their organizations, whether they be A. F. of L. unions or shop unions, or whatever. Give the men any form of expression they will take, and trust to the common sense of the average human critter to make the organization, with which he chooses to affiliate, work to ends which are for the common good.

I have faith in the goodness of God and the general decency of men, and I believe it will work in the labor problem as well as anywhere else, at least I have seen it work on a small scale. It might not work in mass production, but I believe that the unit of hiring and firing should be small enough so that the straw boss should know his men, should be of them and with them and for them and have as much interest in them as he has in the brass collar above him. I believe that then industry would thrive more than it does under the present system.

Pardon this long letter. I am greatly interested in your work and I have great faith in what you do. If at any time I can serve you, please let me know. I am more interested in the labor situation in America than in any other problem.

The New York World carried a series of revelations about the Ku-Klux Klan, an intolerant "one hundred per cent American" movement. Editor Swope asked White to telegraph his judgment on the Klan. Until the demise of the Klan as an important organization, Editor White wrote scathing editorials about the stupidity and bigotry of such hatemongers as the members of the Klan.

To HERBERT B. SWOPE, New York *World*, September 17, 1921

An organizer of the Ku-Klux Klan was in Emporia the other day, and the men whom he invited to join his band at ten dollars per join turned him down. Under the leadership of Dr. J. B. Brickell and following their own judgment after hearing his story, the Emporians told him that they had no time for him. The proposition seems to be:

> Anti foreigners
> Anti Catholics
> Anti Negroes.

There are, of course, bad foreigners and good ones, good Catholics and bad ones, and all kinds of Negroes. To make a case against a birth-place, a religion, or a race is wickedly un-American and cowardly. The whole trouble with the Ku-Klux Klan is that it is based upon such deep foolishness that it is bound to be a menace to good government in any community. Any man fool enough to be Imperial Wizard would have power without responsibility and both without any sense. That is social dynamite.

American institutions, our courts, our legislators, our executive officers are strong enough to keep the peace and promote justice and good will in the community. If they are not, then the thing to do is to change these institutions and do it quickly, but always legally. For a self-constituted body of moral idiots, who would substitute the findings of the Ku-Klux Klan for the processes of law to try to better conditions, would be a most un-American outrage which every good citizen should resent.

It is to the everlasting credit of Emporia that the organizer found no suckers with $10 each to squander here. Whatever Emporia may be otherwise, it believes in law and order, and absolute freedom under the constitution for every man, no matter what birth or creed or race, to speak and meet and talk and act as a free law-abiding citizen. The picayunish cowardice of a man who would substitute Klan rule and mob law for what our American fathers have died to establish and maintain should prove what a cheap screw outfit the Klan is.

To C. T. Start, Kansas City, Mo., October 7, 1921

Dear Mr. Start:

I shall try to write the editorial which you desire, but the trouble is that I do not feel that we need much of a "line of defense against the advance of radicalism." The radical is a poor fish who doesn't get anywhere. The real danger is your conservative, your reactionary, and he is getting somewhere. He is liable to have this country by the throat, and if I were getting up a first line of defense, I would line it up against the highly respectable politician who bolsters up the big grasping profiteers of high finance, rather than against the poor simp, who rages aroundabout overturning the country. The country will not be overturned, but it is liable to be put to sleep, and I wish the Legion [the American Legion] would get a little more excited about the dangers of respectable conservatism and insidious reaction and run out a first line of defense against some of those ginks. But I will try and do the best I can.

Douglas Fairbanks and Mary Pickford were the leading motion-picture idols of America during the decade following the war. As this letter indicates, White met Doug Fairbanks and was very favorably impressed with him. Fairbanks was a handsome, romantic, athletic actor while Mary Pickford had the title of "America's Sweetheart."

[221]

My Dear Frank:

... The "Doug" was there but the "Pickford" was not, at least, she was invisible in her car, which was no great matter. I liked the "Doug" very much. Direct, casual sort of cuss, and as you say not professionally unspoiled. The professionally unspoiled is a sad lot, isn't it? It is like the absolutely pure. I have always had a low opinion of Royal Baking Powder on that account. . . .

W. L. Huggins, fellow Emporian, never could understand White's support of labor unions and liberal causes in general. Huggins, a product of pioneer Kansas, was unable to adapt his thinking to the changed ways of urban-industrial America.

To W. L. Huggins, March 30, 1922

My Dear Huggins:

I have yours of the 27th. Glad to get it. Glad always to hear from you. I note the quotation from a part of the letter from your friend on the Pacific Coast. He calls the New York Nation a Socialist paper. I should hardly call it Socialist. I should say if it had any "ist" to it, it was pacifist, and in so far as the Socialists are pacifists, it agrees with the Socialists, and then, of course, the word Socialist is tremendously broad in its definition. The left-wing Socialists believe in communism at a jump with a revolutionary propaganda. The right-wing Socialists are about where the Bull Moosers were ten years ago. They believe in evolutionary, step at a time, organic changes of the government which will put the means of production in the hands of labor, whatever that means. It doesn't mean much to me.

The letter speaks of a certain Miss Svecenski in an article in the Nation declaring that "liberals and radicals will I hope give more attention to the colleges." I really see nothing wrong in that. I was in a Republican meeting about two years ago, in which we were trying to work out some plan to help the party, and I myself stood up and advocated giving more attention to the colleges on the behalf of Republicans. I should say that colleges should be the large propaganda fields of not only liberals and radicals, but conservatives, and I see no reason why any boy over eighteen should be denied hearing the doctrine of Taft, of Debs, of Harding, of Wilson, of the Nation, of the reactionary New York Times, of the Appeal to Reason, or of the organ of the National Chamber of Commerce. In fact, I think the more he gets from all sides the better boy he will be, and I know that both sides are going after the colleges just as hard as they can, the liberals and radicals on one side and the conservatives and reactionaries on the other, and I should say that it is an open fight and a clear field and the fellow that convinces the boys and girls is entitled to them.

. . . I suppose there never was a college in the world in which all the professors agreed, and when I went to the University there were sharp fundamental disagreements about pretty nearly everything among the various members of the faculty. If everybody agreed about everything, it would not be a university. It would be a cannery. A university, as I figure it, is mostly for discussion, and out of discussion will come wisdom.

I am glad to talk these things over with you, Bill, not because I hope to convince you, but because I want you to see how I feel.

White took an extremely active interest in the Emporia Young Men's Christian Association. He frequently headed up fund-raising drives and devoted a great deal of time improving the Y's standing in the community.

To The Alabastine Company, April 1, 1922

Gentlemen:
This is a begging letter. I am president of the Emporia Y.M.C.A. We are going to redecorate our building. I want it done in Alabastine,

and I want you to give us the Alabastine. The labor unions have agreed to put it on without cost. If you will give it to us, I will give you in advertising in the Emporia Gazette dollar for dollar. You can write the advertisement, or I will write the advertisement, and you will put your dealers' names in this district in the advertisement. We have a building of thirty-two bedrooms, three stories, with three halls and a lobby, and you can estimate it from that.

I suppose there is no use talking further. You know how poor a Y.M.C.A. is in a little country town. Here we have to scratch gravel, and dig our toes down into the earth beneath the gravel to come out even every year. You can just charge this off on your income tax, and take credit with the Lord, presuming that the advertising in the Emporia Gazette will do you no good. I cannot guarantee the value of the advertising in the Emporia Gazette, but I believe I can guarantee you some standing with the Lord. Anyways I will bet you twice the price of the Alabastine that you will be happy about it, if you do it.

H. L. Mencken carried on a one-man crusade against "bluenose" Puritans during the twenties. He particularly went after the supporters of the Eighteenth Amendment and the fundamentalists of the Bible Belt.

To H. L. MENCKEN, Baltimore *Sun*, April 29, 1922

MY DEAR MR. MENCKEN:

Mr. Edward Murphy, managing editor of the Sun, sent me your piece, "What Ails the Republic?" I enjoyed it very much. There is so much truth in what you say that I don't know how to extricate it from the matters with which I am constrained to disagree.

My boy Bill, who is in Harvard, admires your work very much. He spent his good money in subscribing for the Smart Set for his mother and me so that we might see it, and I always read your books as they come out. I think one of the smartest, among the many smart things you ever said, was that the reason why they lynched the brownie down in the South is that it is so deadly dull down there that they have nothing else to do. For much the same reason, I fancy Madame Bovary indulged herself in surreptitious flirtations.

One thing I think you misread, and that is the motive of prohibition. Back of it all there isn't any jealous feeling of the fellow who wants to soak his hide full of coffin varnish, and more or less diluted carpet tacks, but instead a feeling that when his hide is so saturated he does things which cripple him as a producer of worldly goods and make him a burden to the taxpayers, either through his own desires to tear up sidewalks, or to take an ax and go home to make clam chowder out of the children, or to get on the taxes as a pauper. Your puritan is essentially, therefore, a thrifty cuss, and he is willing to curtail his own joy for the sake of increasing his bank account. If he can save his bank account by reducing crime, and hence his taxes, he is tremendously interested in taxes and makes a great to-do about crime. It is not because he is a bluenose, but because he is a tightwad. He is not envious. He is just near.

You ought to read Webb Waldron's book, "The Road to the World." It is a faithful picture of several phases of this midwestern country.

Why don't you come west and spend a few days in Emporia—"fairest village of the plain"? Mrs. White and I would be mighty glad to show you the town, and I would get police protection for you from the governor down to the city marshal, so that you could bring in a bottle of life-sustaining hooch, and hang on to it as long as you wanted to, and as often as you pleased.

Will Hays, after serving as Postmaster General in Harding's Cabinet for about a year, went to work for the motion-picture industry as its arbiter of morals and of taste. This step was taken to offset the storm of criticism from church organizations over pictures which were considered lewd.

MY DEAR WILL:

I have been wanting to write you for some time, but have not got around to it. I was sorry to have you leave the Cabinet. Of course, being so far out in the West I have never known just why you left it, but knowing you, I know it was for some good reason.

I note from time to time that you try to get some order out of the moving-picture business. I have my own ideas about that, which are briefly this: That until you grade the theaters very sharply you will not get very far reforming the movies. The spoken stage does grade its theaters very carefully. You know what kind of a play to expect in certain houses and from certain actors and certain producers, and what kind to expect from others, but as it stands now in the moving-picture business every picture has to appeal more or less to all kinds of people in the audience. So it doesn't rise very high. It cannot rise high, and as the result the highbrow avoids the movies, and they are given over largely to the lowbrows. If you would have a highbrow theater, a middle-grade theater, and a lowbrow theater, the patron then would know where to go to get the kind of a show he wanted. He doesn't know today. And as a result, a story told on the moving-picture screen has to be obvious, trite and melodramatic, no matter what its accessories are, no matter who is acting it. There should be a moving-picture theater where life can be portrayed as life, without being obvious, trite and melodramatic, and where the happy ending is not necessary, and where the patrons would get up and walk out if such a gooey, sticky, glutinous picture as "Smilin' Through" were put on the screen. "Smilin' Through" is beautifully photographed. It is admirably staged. It is probably expensively done, but the producers would no more dare to tell that story truthfully with realism and genuine art, if they told it in the movies, than they would dare to put on an obscene play. The movie audience is obsessed by the moron, because every picture house expects a moron to be a patron. Until you can segregate your moron, and make plays, and consequently playhouses, for the fifteen per cent of people whose intelligence scores over thirteen years old, you won't get very far purifying or uplifting the movies.

Pardon me for these extensive remarks, but they have been on my heart for some time. With most affectionate personal regards, I am—

Kansas was swept by a strike of railroad labor in July, 1922. The Kansas Industrial Court forbade any posters expressing sympathy for the strikers. White immediately wrote an editorial denouncing this order as an "infamous infraction of the right of free press and free speech." He then put a card in the Gazette *office expressing sympathy for the strikers. White got a tip that a warrant for his arrest was being issued. He didn't want to be arrested early in the afternoon so he took a ride in the country. From the standpoint of wide news coverage, it was better that the first news of the arrest be carried in morning papers. After his arrest and while he was waiting trial, he wrote the Pulitzer prize-winning editorial "To An Anxious Friend" to his friend Governor Henry J. Allen. After his arrest, too, he withdrew his poster and asked the strikers to do the same.*

To SENATOR W. E. BORAH, August 3, 1922

MY DEAR BILL:

I was mighty glad to get your letter and knew when it didn't come that you were just busy. I want you to know all about Henry and me on the free speech question.

I have nothing to gain in this protest. I have a newspaper and have free entrance into any newspaper or magazine in the country. But what hurt me was my friends on Commercial Street, business men, bankers, doctors and private citizens who own no newspapers and who were muzzled by the governor's order.

I was arrested for exposing a poster on the Gazette bulletin board. The poster declared: "We are for the striking railroad men fifty per cent. We are for a living wage and fair working conditions." This was modified from a poster issued by the strikers committee declaring: "We are for the striking railroad men one hundred per cent."

I did not go one hundred per cent because I honestly believe that the strikers have a good cause but an unfortunate strike. But the governor and attorney general, however, felt that my poster was incendiary, and I felt that I should defy their order to take it down, in order to test the question whether or not in a state wherein no martial law has been declared, where no gun has been fired, and wherein there has been no blood shed, the utterance of any opinion about a strike, temperately made and issued in an orderly manner, is not a citizen's right. That is all there is to my arrest. It is a question for the courts to decide. It has nothing to do with wages or with the industrial court law. I am indicted with two men I never saw and never heard of, two strikers, and we are charged with a conspiracy to stop the Sante Fe trains. It's too much for me to understand if that is a good law. And this is not an ex parte statement, but the whole truth so far as my own connection with the case. The state administration holds that this placard is picketing, and it is with violating the anti-picketing law that I am charged.

I defied the law because, the legislature not being in session, I could not take part in a fight to repeal it. Annulment was my only course. But after the test case was filed, I took down my poster. It had achieved its end. And I wrote to the strikers in Emporia and elsewhere to take down their posters while the court was considering the test. In Emporia every sign came down. I got more signs down by moral suasion in one ninety-word letter than the state was able to get down with all its proclamations.

We are coming into serious times. The industrial question—the difference between the man who owns the machines and the man who runs them—must be settled by reason, not by force. And if it is settled by reason, we must guarantee to every man free utterance of what he finds best suited to his place in the world. We must make him be temperate. But granted temperate utterance—and fifty-fifty surely is not wildly rabid—the right of every man to speak his mind and express his sympathy with any man or cause should be granted. It is the one base upon which men can reason together and get at the truth. And in times of stress, the right to temperate utterance of a citizen's views must, of all times, be free. For only in times of stress do we feel deeply, and come to our convictions upon matters of public policy. A government that suppresses its citizens, fearing for the peace, is not greatly interested in justice, and yet only as a government is founded upon justice, upon an intelligently convinced majority, and a minority satisfied that its cause has been fairly heard, can we have peace in a modern world. Force will only require more force and more until questions are never settled by reason.

I am enclosing herewith a little poster that Henry will allow me to put in the window though it is much more dangerous than the one he took out.

In the meantime, the relations between Henry and me are most cordial. He believes that peace is more important than justice, and I believe that justice is the only thing that will bring peace. And we are going to have it out on that clear up to the Supreme Court if necessary.

Give my sincere regards to Mrs. Borah. Mrs. White was asking about you the other day and if she were here, I'm sure she would join me in affectionate good wishes.

The case never came to a trial. White did his best to prevent a dismissal, but the state administration did not dare go through with it. Political enemies of White and Allen charged that the entire thing was a frame-up to get publicity for the two men. This was one added reason why White wanted a trial.

To Richard J. Hopkins, Attorney General, November 7, 1922

My Dear Dick:

The election is now over and I can address you about my case without any implication that anything I might say might have a political significance. I'll probably never be able to help you politically again because in the Supreme Court you won't need it. But I think you know what your friendship has meant to me, and if there could be any selfish return from me to you, I'd not write you now.

In all good faith, I courted that arrest so I might test in the courts, up to the highest if need be, that picketing clause of the industrial court law. As you know, my whole heart is in the industrial court law, but I believe it will be a stronger law if it does not rest so entirely on force and repression as the picketing clause seems to base it. I believe an outsider, who has no immediate interest in the strike, should be able to go personally to the strikers or the employers and state decently and temperately any views about the strike, for or against it, that he has in his heart. Moreover, I believe he should have a right to utter temperately in any newspaper or on a billboard or in a store or on his office or home windows any honest sentiment about the strike, the employer or the employee.

Now that was my contention when I put up the poster. It seemed

[229]

to me you restricted the right of free utterance by the order against the posters.

I did not conspire with the railroad men. The posters were up in Emporia and none was in the window of the Emporia Gazette until after I read the governor's order. The strikers did not ask me directly or indirectly to put up a poster. When I saw the posters on Commercial Street in Emporia, I came to the office and asked a reporter to go out and get one of the posters for me. He said he knew where he could find one—I think he said in a barber shop. He went out and got it, and I put it up with modifications. There was absolutely no conspiracy in the act.

Now what I want is this—a trial, an immediate trial. By waiting eight years, you can't get any more evidence nor a different law. Don't dismiss this case. Don't fail to appear. Don't give the effect of laying down. Go to it. Try it with all your heart and let's see where the right and wrong is in this matter. If I am convicted, I'll appeal to the Supreme Court and there will have fairly able counsel. . . .

And I beg of you with all earnestness and all the friendship we have had, not to let this thing seem to be a farcical frame-up by dismissing it now or failing to let it come to trial November 22nd when it is set.

To RICHARD J. HOPKINS, Attorney General, December 5, 1922

MY DEAR DICK:

I think you could write some such letter as this either to me or to the county attorney:

"It is a matter of common knowledge that the defendant in the case has been clamoring for a trial of his cause. It is but fair to say that this case was brought against the judgment of the attorney general's office. He did not believe when it was brought, there was sufficient cause for action in this case; we did not believe the facts would warrant conviction of this defendant for any offense against the laws of Kansas.

"The warrant was served out by an employee in the governor's office and the governor differed with the attorney general's office from the beginning. In ordering this dismissal against the unmistakable demand of the defendant for a trial, this explanation seems advisable in the interest of justice to all parties in the case."

This could be put in the third person and addressed to the county attorney or could be put in the second and addressed to me as a letter from you to me. Something of this sort is due me. Your name was associated with this sentence, and we have been friends for a long period of years. I feel I'm being shanghaied, and I do not want my friends to say as good a man as Dick Hopkins participated in this wicked and cruel treatment of a citizen who was his friend.

I don't think I am asking an unfair thing but I am asking this with all my heart.

This case will come up for dismissal on the 8th and this letter should be there by the 8th. A day or two later, the 9th or the 10th, will be too late for circulation. But when the case is dismissed, with the news of the dismissal, your letter would help and at the same time I intend to make a few remarks on my own account—not about you but about those directly responsible for bringing this case.

With kindest personal regards, I am—

In February, 1923, the Whites sailed with Mr. and Mrs. Victor Murdock on a cruise in the Mediterranean area, during which they met Mr. and Mrs. Guthrie. White was never in sympathy with the "Red Scare" of the early twenties. He particularly did not like the refusal of the New York legislature to seat duly elected Socialist members.

To W. D. GUTHRIE, July 10, 1923

MY DEAR MR. GUTHRIE:

Your book, "The League of Nations and Miscellaneous Addresses," has been on my desk two months now, and I have finished reading it. Until now I did not feel like writing to you, for I dislike more than anything the man who acknowledges a book I send him by saying he will greatly enjoy reading it. What I want him to say is that he *has* greatly enjoyed reading it. And that is what I can say after reading your "Problems of the Bar," the last article in the book. It was more than kind of you to send it to me.

Naturally, you would expect me to disagree with some positions you maintain, but my disagreement is not so fundamental as perhaps you might expect. I more than nine-tenths agree with you in your position about the League of Nations. The golden moment has passed when America has any business going into the League of Nations as it is today. Sometimes I persuade myself that the world had reached a height of aspiration between November 1918 and January or February 1919 when it might possibly have been wise to unite the nations of the world in an altruistic enterprise. But alas, that day is a memory and the memory of it only an illusion. Perhaps there was no reality to that day but only an emotional fizz. . . .

All of your splendid patriotic addresses . . . excite my ardent admiration. What I am unhappy—and I suppose you realized I would be—about is your address at that annual meeting of the Association of the Bar of New York upon the "Suspension of Socialists," and your further report as chairman of the Committee on Political Reform of the Union League Club, though in the latter address I found much less for disagreement than in the first.

Here is something of my reaction, and I am sure it will interest you. The Ku-Kluxers in Kansas are objecting to the Catholics receiving nomination and election to the legislature for exactly the same reasons that you set forth against the Socialists. In Kansas, the Catholics are in a sad minority—"They are a feeble folk but they build upon the rocks." The Ku-Kluxers tell us we must not admit the Catholics because they are not amenable to the usual influences which control men in their public acts. The Kluxers tell us that the Catholics are subject to control of the Catholic hierarchy in their legislative votes on certain questions and that, therefore, they should be barred from the Kansas legislature. It is my blessed privilege to answer, first, that the statement is not true, and even if true, it is not important because only if the Catholic people of the state are in a majority can they affect seriously the settlement of any mooted question between the Catholics and the Protestants. And, if in a majority, they have a right to settle these questions. And, moreover, the Catholics are human beings like the rest of us, subject to the influences of human reason, and the same give-and-take. Opposition and pressure, which move one human being, will act on another quite independent of his religious and political affiliations, and in the end the average level of intelligence in the community will realize itself in government. So that the political

[232]

ostracism of the Catholics is wicked and un-American but—more important—quite futile.

I should say that the same arguments affect the Socialists. It seems to me they are more powerful as martyrs than as reasoning protagonists, and I believe in this country we are safer wrestling with any form of political opposition than we are in suppressing it. Of course, when a man commits a crime, he should be punished even if that crime is incendiary language. But the statutes covering incendiary language, it seems to me, are sufficient to cover any infractions of the law which the revolutionary propagandists may commit. I would not make a special case of their propaganda unless it actually violated the peace and dignity of a commonwealth or a nation, and when a man did violate these laws, I'd make short shift of him, and until he did, I'd let him alone.

... With the kindest personal regards, to which I hope I may join personal remembrances to Mrs. Guthrie, remembrances in which Mrs. White joins me to both of you, I am—

The western farmers suffered greatly in the postwar world. Many of them were in the slough of depression when the rest of the country was enjoying a prosperous boom. The Pittsburgh-plus transaction refers to the policy of the steel industry in quoting prices as of Pittsburgh-plus transportation costs.

To W. S. CULBERTSON, Federal Tariff Commission,
Washington, D. C., July 26, 1923

DEAR BILLY:

I have your letter asking what I think the election of Johnson of Minnesota [Magnus Johnson, elected to the Senate from Minnesota on the Farmer-Labor ticket] signifies in political and economic terms. I have been thinking it out pretty carefully for several days. In fact, for more than a year I have been feeling that the economic conditions here in what might be called the western Mississippi basin would take a strongly marked political turn.

Basically, our trouble is the old trouble we have had for forty years —transportation. We have to ship everything we sell to a buyer and put transportation in everything we buy from the maker. We are overloaded with freight rates. In every Pittsburgh-plus transaction which governs American prices and makes every industry a national instead of a local industry—steel, lumber, fuel, food, and clothing— the Missouri valley and environing communities have to pay the price for nationally stabilized industries.

In prosperous times, there is enough margin in agriculture and those local industries dependent upon agriculture here in the Middle West to give the farmer and his friends a profit. So he is peaceful. But when the economic pinch comes, the farmer feels it, and he is intelligent enough to realize that he is suffering from a remedial wrong. He may be unwise in looking to politics for his remedy, but he does look to politics for a remedy, and when he gets into politics he raises the very devil. The middlewestern farmer of Iowa, Minnesota, and Wisconsin was responsible for the Peter Cooper movement, and the Greenback movement* nearly fifty years ago. The railroad legislation of the mid-seventies was rightly called farmer legislation. Thirty years ago, the farmers of Kansas, Nebraska, and the Dakotas gave backbone to the Populist movement and ten years ago, as you know, the Bull Moose found his best pasturing out here.

Each of these movements, futile in itself, left a permanent impression upon the politics of the country and its institutional life. This part of the world is responsible for national prohibition, it pioneered in woman suffrage, gave impetus to the demand for direct election of United States senators, the passage of the income tax amendment, the adoption of the direct primary, and a lot of propositions of that sort.

It is a curious thing that when the farmer gets mad, because he is unfairly treated in the matter of transportation, he forgets more or less about the transportation question and does something else.

Now this is a long way around to Magnus Johnson. But Johnson's election, taken with that of Shipstead, Frazier, Ladd, Brookhart [Henrik Shipstead, elected to the Senate from Minnesota on the Farmer-Labor ticket; Lynn J. Frazier, elected to the Senate from North Da-

---

* Peter Cooper, wealthy industrialist, was the Greenback party's candidate for president in 1876. The Greenbackers demanded an increased amount of paper currency and the regulation of the railroads.

[234]

kota on the Republican ticket; E. F. Ladd, elected to the Senate from North Dakota as a Nonpartisan Republican; S. M. Brookhart, elected to the Senate from Iowa as a progressive Republican] and the tremendous majority given LaFollette, the victory of Ferris [W. N. Ferris, elected to the Senate from Michigan on the Democratic ticket] in Michigan and the obvious complex of Nebraska and Kansas as revealed by the recent election, proves very definitely that the Middle West is on the rampage again. The only thing on earth that will hold them in the Republican ranks next year is prohibition. The Middle West is going on the war path. The leadership of the towns is for Harding. He will carry the college ward in every county seat, but he will lose the railroad wards and lose every township in the county.

It is hard to see who will get the recalcitrant vote. I don't believe it will be the Democrats. Ford [Henry Ford, whose name was being mentioned as a possible presidential candidate] might get it; a third party even without Ford. I don't think there is a remote chance to get a Republican delegation from these states. LaFollette on a Republican ticket would carry these states. They are in more or less of a LaFollette mood, but the machinery of politics will keep LaFollette men off the Middle West delegation. By all the rules of the game, Harding should have a renomination. If voting were a matter of intelligence and not of emotion, he would win, but we seem to be headed for an emotional campaign, and I genuinely fear that an honest, decent, courageous, intelligent man is going to get an awful licking.

And this is what I think the election of Johnson means in Minnesota.

The publication of Raw Material *by White's old friend, Dorothy Canfield Fisher, prompted the following letter.*

To Dorothy Canfield Fisher, August 21, 1923

My Dear Dorothy:
What a delicious book it is—your high-water mark. I read "Fairfax Hunter" and "Professor Paul Meyer" and "The Ideas of M. Brodard" this morning to Edna Ferber, and she cried enough tears on her new dress to spoil the front. I read the whole book through at a sitting Sunday, and it refreshed me like a tragedy. You have never done such splendid work before. If Harcourt wants me to review it I will, and

[235]

have him tell me where he wants me to put the review. I would be mighty glad to do it. You and Willa Cather and Edna Ferber are doing better work than any three men on the American continent.

We poor men are having a really hard time. First you take our ballot from us; then you deprive us of our booze; and it looks as though you are going to rob us of even the alphabet.

President Harding died on August 2, 1923. His health had broken as he had become aware of the scandals and corruption participated in by some of his close friends. Weeks before Harding died, W. L. White wrote an editorial about Vice-President Coolidge referring to him as "the little runt of a man" who "quacks" when he talks. The editorial was left to be used when needed. As White wrote later, "the evening before Harding died, by some devilish streak of luck that editorial appeared." At once, White received protests from a number of people he did not know.

To CARL JACOBSEN, Glen Ridge, N. J., September 10, 1923

DEAR SIR:

You are a persistent old witch-burner. I suppose you want me to get out on the housetops and lament in sackcloth and ashes. The whole truth is this: I was out of town during the President's death, and the article was written by my son, a Harvard student. Would you have me fire him and humiliate him before his community? Why not go on and serve the new president? Won't my actions in the next two or three years speak louder than any retraction of words that I might make, which words would humiliate a young man who has been talked to privately? I don't seem to get excited about this, and I can't work up any bitter burning sense of remorse, but every time I see that young man how he squirms. I get a good chuckle out of it and think he has learned a good lesson.

Governor Pinchot of Pennsylvania was instrumental in solving the anthracite coal strike of 1923. President Coolidge, always cautious, kept away from this strike of national importance.

To GIFFORD PINCHOT, September 11, 1923

MY DEAR GIFFORD:

I have had a curious feeling about your splendid coal victory, and I suppose I ought to tell you about it that you may govern your actions accordingly. You know, of course, that I was pleased beyond words with what you did in every detail, but the country wasn't. Big newspaper people soft-pedaled it, they didn't like your wage increase and the eight-hour day. The country is reactionary—against labor, middle-class conscious. The red-baiters have so thoroughly scared the people, with the bogie of Bolshevism, that any public man who takes any public attitude in favor of organized labor, or any other kind of labor as far as that is concerned, does so at his tremendous peril politically. A dozen or fifteen years ago your actions would have made you a heroic figure in American politics. Idealism, altruism, or whatever you want to call it, was on an ascendant wave. Now the tide is washing out. The net result of your splendid victory is that you are a subject of dislike and distrust by the forces that are leading the Republican party and dominating the nation. I want to support you for president. I would rather get licked with you than win a victory with anyone else who can possibly be in the running, but we shouldn't kid ourselves, if we go in, the current must change or we'll have a rough voyage.

I thought we had reached the nadir last year. Signs in the Northwest have been hopeful, but the danger of the hopeful signs lies in the fact that most of the men who have won so signally there are some rather cheap demagogues. When the people respond to demagogues, it's dangerous for the honest man to venture abroad. There is no sane, strong, progressive undercurrent out here. There is rural rage, and a sort of fascists hatred and suspicion and a paralyzing poison of supernational patriotism, which responds to the touch of the scoundrel in the Ku-Klux Klan, and makes it rather difficult to get ideas of constructive progressive change into the hearts of the folks. All this may change soon, and I hope it will, and if it does, I'll see it and tell you, but you'll have enough fellows filling you with hot air, and I'm trying to get the truth to you. You did a righteous act and a fine service to your country, but you certainly did put the trimmings on your presidential boom if you ever had any. Hinc illae lacrimae.

In the spring of 1924, The Macmillan Company published a volume of White's Gazette *editorials entitled* The Editor and His People. *These were selected by Miss H. O. Mahin. The preface which she wrote about White underwent some changes at his hands.*

To HELEN MAHIN, Lawrence, Kan., December 1, 1923

MY DEAR MISS MAHIN:

I like your preface very much, but I made some changes in it, changes which are in the nature of repression. After all, you can't go around singing my praises at the top of your voice in this preface without prejudicing people against me. Repression is always the strongest form of propaganda. So please be a good girl, and let these changes stay as they are, even though they do take the fortissimo out of your piece. But fortissimo is merely confusing. The soft pedal will get the air across.

Isolationism made no sense to White's logical mind. He realized that technology had reduced the world to a neighborhood. When he was asked whether he would support Hiram Johnson for the presidency in 1924, he told the recipient of this letter, a former Bull Mooser, that he could not because of Johnson's isolationist position.

Dear Mr. Ewert:

I was mighty glad to get your letter and recall the good old days of 1912. I am sorry I can't line up for Hiram Johnson. I am so entirely opposed to his position on foreign relations and am so thoroughly convinced he will make that the major issue of his campaign and if elected, make it his major activity—his isolation policy—that I can't go with him.

Heaven knows, I'd like to! I admire his courage and am proud of his character and admire him greatly personally. But I feel nearer to Pinchot [Governor Gifford Pinchot of Pennsylvania] on the whole than Johnson.

Robert M. LaFollette, Sr. was sick at the time of this letter. He, however, recovered and ran on a third-party ticket for the presidency that year. In spite of the kind words in this letter and his own independent candidacy for the governorship of Kansas, White supported Calvin Coolidge.

To Robert M. LaFollette, Jr., Washington, D. C., March 29, 1924

My Dear Bob:

Having known you since you were in knee breeches when you came to Emporia in 1908, I suppose I am licensed to call you Bob. Anyway I want to and so it goes. Tell your father to make the fight of his life for his health. Never before have we needed him so badly. It seems as if the army amassed around the idea of a just government for all Americans is mobilizing fast and getting in training for the fight. We cannot lose the General without confusion, discouragement and a long time of waiting, perhaps another generation. I have fought so long that I am anxious to see even in the sunset some sign of victory. Tell your father he must fight for health now in the name of his loyal and affectionate friends. . . .

Although Alfred E. Smith put up a powerful fight for the Democratic nomination in 1924, the Democrats nominated John W. Davis after a long convention wrangle.

To Henry L. Mencken, May 14, 1924

My Dear Mencken:

Wouldn't it be grand to have a campaign between Cal and Al, with the conservatives supporting Al and a wide-open town and the radicals supporting Cal, and a limp and busted bung starter? You and I could make enough money to pay the national debt by chautauquaing the country in a joint debate, changing sides every other day.

As to my rage. The only thing that makes me mad is the modern American poetry. I could write a beautiful article under the title "To Hell With Pegasus, He's a Goat" or perhaps "Why does the Pierian Spring Flow Only Red Raven Splits?" but I won't.

During much of 1923 and 1924, White worked on a biography of Woodrow Wilson which was published in the fall of 1924. He also covered the two political conventions for a syndicate of newspapers. The Mediterranean novel mentioned in this letter as well as the book on Theodore Roosevelt were never published. White was very unhappy over the Kansas political situation, since both candidates for governor refused to repudiate Ku-Klux Klan support.

To Victor Murdock, Wichita *Eagle*, August 14, 1924

My Dear Vic:

...I have finished my Wilson story, that is to say, written it through and have revised the whole thing once. Sallie and I are now going over it again and then we will go through it in the proof, giving it four good revisions. If you have a last-minute thought about Wilson, trot-er-on, I want it. We hoped to get down this week, but I think I ought to stick on the job until we get five or ten chapters ahead for the printer. The book will be about a hundred thousand words, something less, not much, and should be out in October if everything goes well with me. In the meantime, I have put my articles from the two conventions in a little book that will be out in ten days or two weeks. I shall send you a copy [*Politics: The Citizen's Business*]. I have my Mediterranean novel ready to spring next year after the Wilson thing has shot its wad, and I have a book on Roosevelt also two-thirds written, so that I am going to be pretty busy in the writing business for the next eighteen months.

Henry [Henry J. Allen] called me up on the phone and wanted me to run for governor as an anti-Klan protest, with no desire to be elected. The devil with that proposition is that I might really be elected, which I don't want to be. But if you have a notion that you want to go against Curtis [Senator Charles Curtis] two years from now, I wish you would tell me because I might take a notion to run this year and go out and lick the two of them to help you. I have no ambition except for my friends. I think I would rather see you win the Senate than anything else in the world politically. Personally I would rather see you in Wichita. Bill is writing editorials for the paper now. I enclose a couple that may interest you.

To GEORGE MARBLE, Ft. Scott, Kan., August 26, 1924

MY DEAR MR. MARBLE:

... I am full of rancor and east wind about the gubernatorial situation. I won't vote for a klansman, and yet I want to vote for someone. I wired Bristow [former Senator Joseph L. Bristow] telling him if he would run, I would finance his campaign myself or see it done. I would do the same thing with Stubbs [former Governor W. R. Stubbs]. Do you know how Stubbs feels? Clyde Reed* thinks that Henry Allen would be a good man. What do you think about it? Some of the fellows want me to run. I don't want to run if there is any hope of being elected, for I don't want to be governor of Kansas, but I might run to give a few thousand fellows a chance to vote for someone who was not a klansman and so purge their souls of that sin.

* Clyde Reed was defeated for Governor in the Republican primary by Ben S. Paulen.

[241]

On September 20, White decided to file his independent candidacy for governor. This announcement brought widespread offers of volunteer help. It attracted nation-wide attention as well. Rollin Kirby drew a cartoon for the New York World *depicting White chasing the Klan out of Kansas. Ernest Gruening wired that, "nothing in your long career is as important, essential and far-reaching as your splendid stand in opposing the Klan-controlled old parties today."*

To OSCAR FAGERBERG, Olsburg, Kan., September 24, 1924

DEAR MR. FAGERBERG:

Thank you very much for your kind letter. I am trying to assemble enough votes from men who believe in the fundamental principles of our government, without regard to party, to scare the daylights out of the managers of both parties so that they won't tie up with the Ku-Klux Klan again in Kansas for a generation. To do that it is necessary for me to run for governor. It may be necessary to serve as governor. Office holding and seeking has not been in my line, and I don't like it. But I am willing to do even that for this cause.

I am sending you herewith 150 of my announcements which you may distribute among your friends. Thank you so much for your kindness.

The Republican papers that supported Paulen, the Republican gubernatorial candidate, attacked White for dividing the vote, and thus aiding the Democratic candidate. White avoided national and state issues except the issue of ridiculing the Klan. Fred Trigg of the Kansas City Star *helped White's campaign with plenty of publicity. White kept Henry J. Allen and Clyde Reed from endorsing him for fear of hurting their political futures. The support of Charles Scott of the Iola* Register *he welcomed, since Scott, a conservative, had been an opponent in the past and this action now, White thought, wouldn't hurt him. Victor Murdock's support, too, was welcomed, since Murdock had not been a regular Republican since Bull Moose days.*

My Dear Henry:

I am in for Sunday, and find your letter here. I am asking Amrine [Milt Amrine, who ran the White campaign headquarters] to forward all those Paulen Ku-Klux matters to Fred Trigg to use. Fred is getting it out in good shape, and I think we will release it.

I felt that you were wrong about the program because I felt that it gave me an opportunity to pledge myself not to have a radical administration. And the fear of that administration was holding off certain support which I had a right to expect. The program has released that support and it is coming in fine shape, it seems to me. Clyde Reed offered to come out for me the other day, but I wouldn't let him, I have asked him to denounce the Republican State Central Committee, which does not affect his regularity, nor spoil him for a candidacy two years from now. I think the last thing I said to you in Wichita that Sunday at your house was that I wanted to go out into this thing all by my little lonely against the Klan, and if I was defeated, not put the stigma of defeat on anyone else whose political future might be affected by my defeat. Scott came to me himself, without asking, out of his own conscience, and he is far enough removed from me politically so my defeat would not affect him any more than my election. But I have said all along that you and Clyde should be held in reserve and not called out to go down with me, so I did not accept Clyde's offer, and have not asked your editorial support, nor thought it wise for you to make speeches. With Victor, it is different, he is a free lance and has no regularity to conserve, so I felt justified in asking his help.

In this connection, as I go about from town to town, holding these whacking big meetings, I am affected with a curious sense of dual personality, as a candidate hermetically sealed from the truth, outside my friends I am sanely assured that I shall win. As a reporter who has seen other men equally crazy and unhappily licked, I am as cynical as Voltaire. The net result of these conflicting personalities is this, I am like the man who knows mighty well beyond all question, that he actually is Napoleon Bonaparte, but who refrains from saying so for fear of being locked up in the booby hatch. In the meantime, I know what a terrible lot of fun the crazy people have, I am enjoying it to the full. If sometime you hear of me running out in the middle of the street and yelling the surplus air off my lungs, in sheer joy, you will be able to explain it—but don't.

White ran third in the campaign, but he drew so many votes from Paulen, the Republican candidate, that Paulen's vote ran a hundred thousand behind the Republican ticket. White gathered approximately 150,000 votes largely by his own efforts. During his campaign he supported the candidacies of C. B. Griffith, candidate for re-election as attorney general; Frank J. Ryan, candidate for re-election as secretary of state; and Jess W. Miley, candidate for re-election. These Republican officeholders were anti-Klan and, therefore, in danger of being defeated.

To Senator Charles Curtis, November 10, 1924

My Dear Charley:

When I saw you there in St. John your words stuck in my mind for a long time, because I know they came from your heart. I realized when I went into that race exactly what it meant to a lot of men like you who had been hoping against hope that I could stay around the Republican premises long enough to give me a standing and fellowship. But I felt profoundly about that Klan evil and still do. It is a menace to our politics, and I think even the most conventional conservative will admit now that if I hadn't got in the fight Ryan, Miley and Griffith would have been defeated. In every one of my speeches I asked my friends to vote for them. Out of the 150,000 votes I got, I think at least half of them went to Ryan, Miley and Griffith, Democratic votes that they never would have got.

I also made it easy to defeat Davis [the defeated Democratic candidate, Jonathan Davis], for I took from him the votes of those prosecuted by the Klan which he ordinarily would have got, though he didn't deserve any of them, for he was a straddler. So I think from a purely partisan standpoint my race was a good thing, and incidentally I think it was a good thing from your standpoint, personally. In a lot of places where I went I found that these Klansmen were talking about having a white United States senator, meaning a reference to your Indian blood. They are just that bigoted. And, while their leadership is usually controlled, yet it is dangerous.

I don't want to look too far ahead, but I think I can say this surely, that if the Klan should ever get after you for any racial reason, you would not have a more valiant champion than I. I don't know who is going into the Senatorial race next year, but I don't think Henry

[244]

Allen is; I don't believe Victor Murdock would; Stubbs might. I have no enthusiasm at the moment for Stubbs. He is the sort of man who, in a race against you on purely racial grounds, the Klan might indorse. In which case, what I have said above stands. I hope the results in Kansas, some of which I have just enumerated, will ease your heartbreak at my action, but alas I would do it again if the situation was duplicated. The way the Catholics and Jews and colored people were persecuted by the Klan in Kansas was a dirty shame, and I couldn't rest under it. It has nothing to do with the result of the primaries, but when Paulen stopped the anti-Klan resolution which Griffith and Ryan wanted, leaving only the two Klan-indorsed candidates for the people to vote for, I put on my war paint and feathers and went out. I was very much inclined to support Paulen the first few days after the convention, but not a minute after the party council.

I write this because you and I, who have been so far apart in past years, have been getting together in recent years and this is the longest political letter I have written to anybody for months.

P.S. I hardly need tell you, Charley, that I didn't want to be governor, and didn't expect to be at any stage of the campaign. I don't want any political office, elective or appointive. I want my freedom, such as it is.

To A. E. HOLT, Chicago Theological Seminary, November 11, 1924

DEAR DR. HOLT:

Thank you for your fine letter. I feel proud of my fight. It was worth while. I had my say. Before I started on the campaign, while I was testing out sentiment, I got a letter from a Jew in southern Kansas who told me how his business had been hurt by the Klan and how his children had been bedeviled in school. It is one of the things that put steam in my spiritual engine when I went out. Well, I had a letter from him the other day enclosing fifty dollars for my campaign fund, and he indicated in the letter that since I had made my campaign he had been living in a new world. The fact that I could get out and spit in the face of the Klan, and had done it, had cleared up the atmosphere, had sent people in his home town to his defense, and he was very happy. I am very proud of it all and to my pride your letter adds joy....

[245]

Nationally, Calvin Coolidge won an easy victory. LaFollette, however, running on a progressive platform calling for public ownership of water power, farm relief, abolition of the injunction in labor disputes, and a federal child labor amendment, gained almost five million votes. This indicated that there was a strong undercurrent of liberal sentiment, but over fifteen million were happy with Coolidge and eight million were content to stay with the Democratic party.

To O. G. VILLARD, *The Nation*, November 19, 1924

MY DEAR VILLARD:

If I had come out for LaFollette, I would have lost half of my strength. Here was a funny thing: labor in the Middle West is shot through with the Ku-Klux Klan. It voted for Coolidge, a lot of it, because Coolidge was right on the Pope. I didn't get much of it because I was wrong on the Pope. And LaFollette lost about forty per cent of his normal vote because of the Klan. If I had a million dollars, I would devote some part of it to proving or disproving a theory that I have; namely, that the big business interests of Wall Street, "Nordic, Protestant, Gentile" might have put up some money to the Klan in Georgia, financing their high-powered salesman to make trouble for the Jewish international bankers and also to smash the labor movement by diverting it and dividing it. Certainly nothing has hit labor such a smash in my memory in politics as the Ku-Klux Klan. All over this Ku-Klux territory, labor was voting for Coolidge because he was against the Pope. It will be a decade before labor recovers what it has lost by flirting with the Ku-Klux Klan.

I realized rather early that I might have to make the fight or at least lead the fight against the Klan in Kansas, and I didn't want to be handicapped by any outside political indorsement, so I went to it all by my lonely.

White was intrigued by Calvin Coolidge. He wrote a series of articles on Coolidge for Collier's *in 1925, which were printed in book form later that same year. During the decade of the thirties, he worked arduously on a fuller biography of Coolidge, which came out in 1938 under the title* A Puritan in Babylon. *White hoped that Coolidge would lead the country away from the isolationism of the Senate group, but as Sumner Welles points out in his book* The Time for Decision, *Coolidge was the most provincial of our presidents and little interested in world affairs.*

To CALVIN COOLIDGE, January 27, 1925

MY DEAR PRESIDENT COOLIDGE:

I have always felt that a man's life was the visible manifestation of his inner faith. In writing about you, I have talked to various people about the dominant creed of your life, and it seems to me that I can find a profound belief in the moral government of the universe which has motived every important thing you have done. I talked to a Congregational preacher in Holyoke who happened to be at the home of our mutual friends, the Dwights, the editor of the Holyoke Transcript. The preacher's name was, as I recollect it, Robinson. Anyway he spoke beautifully of your faith which ripened into a definite conviction. My remembrance of what he said was that you came at the definite development and expression of your faith through conscious study, earnest reading, and self-searching about the time you became president; though, of course, the whole creed was latent in you more or less motiving your life for many years before.

This seemed a reasonable story. I joined the Congregational Church myself about ten years ago in some such fashion and about the age you were when you joined in Washington. But now I read a story by George Harvey in the North American Review which says in effect that the Washington Congregational Church, quite to your surprise and thus manifestly without consulting you, made you a member by election with no sort of profession of faith.

I should greatly appreciate the facts, of course with the understanding that I am not to quote you directly in anything. I am sorry indeed to be bothering you this way, but to write accurately one must know definitely what he is talking about, and all my life I have striven for accuracy.

Now for another matter: I am deeply interested in your endeavor to work out some kind of a definite foreign policy; in your endeavor to get along with Borah [Senator W. E. Borah] and the Foreign Relations Committee. All my life I have been interested in the practical end of politics, and wonder if you will permit this suggestion: While

[247]

you may not care to use the Democrat members of the Committee to make a majority of the Committee, yet if you have them definitely and obviously ready to use, you may find it unnecessary to use them because you have them. Such is the paradox of politics. There is one man in the United States who quietly and without any advertisement can produce that situation. He is Colonel House [Colonel E. M. House, Woodrow Wilson's confidential adviser]. I have known him for years. He is absolutely trustworthy, as close-mouthed as a mole. I happen to know that he is exceedingly anxious to help you. I saw a good deal of him in New York recently. A word from you would bring him to your side and only you and he need know about his activities. You might address him directly or through any mutual friend. I think Mr. Dwight Morrow knows him, though I am not quite sure. Certainly Lamont [Dwight Morrow and Thomas Lamont, both members of the firm of J. P. Morgan & Co.] knows him if you would care to ask Mr. Lamont to do it. Naturally I should be only too glad to ask him to come to you and you might be quite sure that he would elude any reporter however vigilantly he might be watching at the gate. I merely make this suggestion because I know it is one of the ways that you can work out a solution in the Senate Committee.

I shall be in the East at a meeting of the Rockefeller Foundation* in late February, from the 21st to the 25th. I might come a few days before if there was anything I could do to help you in any way. Command me if I can help.

Henry J. Allen's suggestion that White accept an invitation to speak before the Wichita Junior Chamber of Commerce provoked the following letter.

* For many years White served as a trustee of the Rockefeller Foundation.

My Dear Henry:

As I told you, I am going to Honolulu the 17th and cannot accept McGraw's invitation. I couldn't accept it anyway. The Chamber of Commerce business and the whole crowd of top hat go-getters make me progressively tired. They are the trouble with the country. . . . The fellows that don't want justice in industry are . . . the manufacturers' association, the associated industries and the like. They are the outfit that cleaned out the Child Labor amendment.* They are the outfit that has to be put in its proper place in this country, taken down from the throne, and made ordinary voting American citizens instead of assuming to rule the land by their eminent respectability.

A Junior Chamber of Commerce makes my feet hurt. Why not let the young people have a little indiscretion, a few years of gay irresponsibility? Why harness them to a plug hat early in life? If I should go down to talk to Jim McGraw's bunch, I would probably insult them which I don't like to do.

Pardon this outburst. Give my love to Elsie and Henrietta [Mrs. Allen and their daughter] and believe me—

When this letter was written, the beloved William Lyon Phelps of Yale University was spending the summer in a small Michigan town.

To William Lyon Phelps, August 31, 1925

Dear Mr. Phelps:

As one country correspondent to another, I greet you. As one country preacher to a better one, I salute you. As one picnic visitor to a fellow marauder of fried chicken, I kowtow before you and challenge you to a contest of prowess. You may beat me writing, you may beat me preaching, but I will beat you eating fried chicken at

* In 1924 a child labor amendment was sent to the states. It has never been ratified.

[249]

any picnic between the Alleghenies and the Rockies north of Thirty-six, for money, marbles or chalk.

Anybody who will take a dare will steal a sheep!

To W. S. Fitzpatrick, Independence, Kan., November 24, 1925

Dear Mr. Fitzpatrick:

... I note what you say about Coolidge. As far as I can see now there is no opposition to him in the Republican party. If the convention were to occur tomorrow, I should be for him. He represents exactly the mood of the people. In a different mood he would not represent them of course. In the Roosevelt days he would have been impossible and out of line. But he is an honest, courageous, cautious, kindly conservative, and that is what the people want and they are entitled to have it. ...

White was an American delegate at the Institute of Pacific Relations held at Honolulu July 1–15, 1925. Among the other American delegates were Ray L. Wilbur, Chester H. Rowell, Mary E. Woolley, Stanley Hornbeck, and Payson J. Treat. This letter contains the general American attitude that the world was moving toward a peaceful society. The major European nations had just signed a pact at Locarno guaranteeing existing frontiers. What those who welcomed this pact did not comprehend was that there was no power present to check any nation which violated the Locarno Pact.

To the Members of the Pacific Institute, December 29, 1925

Dearly Beloved:

This note goes out a few days after Christmas, with the old year closing and a most profitable year in every sense for America and the world, with the prospects of peace on earth among men of good will

[250]

brightening with every day's news. Locarno has made a great difference in America. That difference is evidenced in our president's attitude toward foreign affairs, reflecting a certain kindness in the American heart. Our institute is, of course, a mustard seed which is still in the earth but which is by no means dead and is working powerfully. I feel its effects all about me.

Personally, I have had a most enjoyable half year since we parted. I have written a book about Calvin Coolidge, which I tried to make honest, and I think possibly succeeded as well as one does with the ordinary run of his ideals. I have been, two or three weeks, in New York, attended a meeting of the Rockefeller Foundation and saw prospects for great plans going forth to conquer disease in the world, to spread scientific information over various parts of the Orient. I attended a meeting of the Woodrow Wilson Foundation from which later in the year the world may expect some significant spectacle that will help toward peace. I also attended a meeting of the Nominating Committee of the Institute of Pacific Relations, and of a group of members of the Institute which was most helpful and inspiring.

The Middle West is in fairly good economic condition. We are still, out here in the western Mississippi Valley, an agricultural people. Agricultural conditions are improving but are, by no means, satisfactory. Out of this western side of the Mississippi trough may come, next year, a political unrest that will unsettle things a bit. It is the only ominous part of the country. The industrial section is prosperous and happy, more than contented.

I am looking forward eagerly to the next meeting of the Institute and hope it may be my good fortune to be with you all again.

With heartiest greetings of affection and good will, I am—

White never completed his manuscript on Theodore Roosevelt, nor did he ever write a biography of W. J. Bryan, although he has a sketch of Bryan in Masks in a Pageant *(1929). The recipient of the following letter was a prominent Kansas Republican.*

My Dear Jim:

I was mighty glad and proud to get your letter. What a wonderful diagnostician you are. The Coolidge book was born about as you suggest. Collier's Weekly wanted an article about Coolidge. I went east to get it without much thought of him, merely to fill an order, got interested in him, was baffled by him, and bedeviled by his evanescent character, wrote four articles then made it six, then concluded there was a book in it, went back east, got more material and concluded that Curtis and Borah [Senators Charles Curtis and W. E. Borah] were contrasting figures out of the west more or less needed to bring Coolidge out by comparison, submitted them as special articles to Collier's, toned them down and rewrote them for the book. Hence and so the Coolidge book.

You guessed it. The Wilson book was a labor of love. I disliked the man tremendously, but was rather fond of his type. So in affection and trepidation and a certain amount of pious scorn, I wrote the Wilson book.

I have two other books that I want to write, one about Roosevelt, which I started four years ago and when my daughter was killed, stopped. I don't know why, just because I did, I guess, and I couldn't go on. The other is about Bryan. Bryan has interested me tremendously as a study of a man without a brain. He had vast emotional qualities, quick, rather impromptu perception, but profoundly bad judgment on all public questions and on most private ones. He who never thought in his life had the quality which makes others think. His discussion of the money question in '96 was vapid, emotional and erratic, but it did set people to thinking about the problem before the nation and that campaign was a good campaign to have been waged. I think one of the best campaigns I ever knew largely because Bryan put his heart into it and others put their heads into it and got a final truth out of the combination.

I am sending you a book that will have a very small circulation, published by the University of North Carolina Press, growing out of a series of lectures that I delivered out there last year [*Some Cycles of Cathay*]. It will interest you, I hope, without too deeply irritating you.

What a little while it seems since we were all back in the Kansas

Day Club* thirty-four years ago, with our past all ahead of us. I don't know but that it is pleasanter in retrospect than it was in prospect. Anyway, we have done the best we could, haven't we?

With affectionate greetings for the New Year, I am—

Frank Munsey was a newspaper entrepreneur who treated the newspapers that he bought like shares of stock. He consolidated many of them and wrecked others. When he died, White wrote the following editorial: "Frank Munsey, the great publisher, is dead. Frank Munsey contributed to the journalism of his day the talent of a meat packer, the morals of a money changer and the manners of an undertaker. He and his kind have about succeeded in transforming a once-noble profession into an eight per cent security. May he rest in trust!"

To Nicholas Murray Butler, January 6, 1926

Dear President Butler:

Probably I was a little rough on Frank Munsey but the whole tendency of the times in newspaper consolidation and standardization, I think, works badly. I would rather have the press as it was in John Milton's time, or Benjamin Franklin's time, when a man with the proverbial shirttail full of type could express himself, air his views, and get it off his chest, rather than to have the mass production of newspapers owned by investment bankers and filled full of stupid syndicate matter and conventional opinions as they are today. It is a bad thing for the newspaper business, and it is a bad thing for the people. And Munsey and his kind are getting halos for doing a bad thing. I have no quarrel with Munsey, personally, but I had to say what I said for the craft I loved.

* Launched in 1891 by young Republicans like White to infuse a new spirit into party ranks.

[253]

My Dear Milt:

I don't know how you look at Lewis' books, but I think they're splendid, poetical things, dramatizing the struggle of the human heart toward the ideals. "Main Street" was not so good as "Babbitt," but "Babbitt" was a tremendous poetical satire of American life, striving to find something in itself worth while, turning futilely from politics, business, formal religion, and women, unsatisfied, with the striving in its heart for beauty, for truth, for the unrealized ideals.

So I thought "Arrowsmith" was a noble book. It dramatized a soul's struggle for freedom, for the right to self-expression. It was in short the story of the prodigal son. This man who went out to dwell with the swine, came to himself and went back to his father's house where he could have freedom and peace and the joy that these things bring. I am sure they are all in the book, and if you would only read it without being offended by its externals, you would see them. . . .

To Eleanor K. Edwards, Princeville, Ore., March 17, 1926

Dear Miss Edwards:

I have your note asking me for my favorite recipe. Here it is: "Orange au jus."

Take a large ten cent orange, gouge your thumb in the top, peel it without a knife, bust it with the grain and eat it so, with as much pianissimo on your intake as possible.

Harold Ickes could find little to approve in Calvin Coolidge or in White's biography of Coolidge. Unlike White, Ickes never became a good Republican after the collapse of the Bull Moose party. Ickes's own story can be read in his Autobiography of a Curmudgeon.

DEAR HAROLD:

I didn't expect you to like the Coolidge book, and yet I do think the old man is a mystic. Old Scrooge was a mystic. He had faith in the divine character of wealth as much as Lincoln had in the divine character of man. He and Coolidge both believe that Commerce is a sacrosanct matter. They are whirling dervishes of business, just as blind in that faith as Roosevelt and LaFollette were blind in their faith in the people and in the nobility of man and the righteousness of the judgments of God.

The fact that I don't agree with this thesis doesn't blind me to the fact that he is crazy about it, sincerely, genuinely, terribly crazy. . . .

The Book-of-the-Month Club, Inc., was organized in 1926 with White, Dorothy Canfield, Heywood Broun, Henry Seidel Canby, and Christopher Morley as members of the editorial board. Over the years the Book-of-the-Month Club through its selections was to exert a powerful influence on American letters. From the outset, the principle set forth in this letter was rigidly adhered to by the board.

To ROBERT K. HAAS, Book-of-the-Month Club, Inc., May 15, 1926

DEAR MR. HAAS:

I am in the midst of the books and have one or two fairly well lined out, but here is one complication which we ought to settle right now. I should certainly recommend Christopher Morley's book "Romany Stain," if it were written by any other author. It wins easily on its merits as one of the books, perhaps first—a beautiful thing. But Mr. Morley is one of the judges. If we include his book on this list, and certainly if we include it as the "Book of the Month," then every time a book by any of the five of us appears on the list an embarrassment might arise. Certainly I should not want any book of mine submitted under any circumstances. I think the money we get for this service should be sufficient to keep all of the judges from submitting their books. I realize that Mr. Morley probably does not know this book has been submitted, and has nothing to do with the submission, and yet I feel rather strongly about it. Will you kindly communicate with the other members of the committee about this matter? You are quite welcome to quote my letter.

A motion picture depicting the life of Woodrow Wilson was not released until 1944. The following letter is an interesting insight into Woodrow Wilson.

To WILL HAYS, May 15, 1926

MY DEAR WILL HAYS:

Allen Kander was in Emporia not long ago to talk to me about a moving picture production of a book of mine called "In Our Town," and while he was here I took up with him a project which has been on my mind for sometime. It is a film life of Wilson. I wish as a penance for your sins you would order from the Houghton Mifflin people there in New York, a copy of my Wilson book and read it. It has in it the basis of the story I would like to tell of the real Woodrow Wilson.

The thing should be opened by a prologue showing the blood of his ancestry in him—a gay Irish preacher for a father, who adopted the South in his early manhood and became one of your eloquent pulpit orators, witty, amiable, kind of a Ladies' Society gladiator, given to a clay pipe by way of democracy; a punster, a story teller, who loved a little toddy now and then and who was not above talking too much on occasion; who came out of an Irish editor in Steubenville, Ohio, a prominent citizen, member of the legislature, member of the state senate, once director of what afterwards became the Pennsylvania Railroad, a man of parts, whose wife, Wilson's grandmother, was an implacable hater who refused to make up with her own daughter after an elopement. So much for his father's side.

[256]

For his mother's side—preachers, scholars, theologians, wranglers, contenders, shy people, punctilious, proud, aloof from the herd, intellectual, aristocratic, Scotch than whom there is no whomer in the matter of opinionation. So much for blood.

For boyhood—a frail, freckled, red haired, shy, wistful youth. Tremendously bookish, and so set apart from the herd, who never went to public schools in his life. Tutored at home by his preacher father and his preacher's daughter mother. Who had to put on glasses at nine and so was spotted in boyville for a bit of a sissy. Bad tempered, of whom tradition says that he threw down the bat and walked off the field when he thought he was being unfairly treated. As a youth, rather a girl's young man, bookish, given to few but passionate friendships with young men, his fellow students. Leaving college on account of ill-health in his teens, studying at home with his father whom he adored; not mixing with the boys of his age. Going back to school, this time to Princeton, and because of his excellent mental equipment being a regular fellow, a contender for prizes and a debater, manager of the baseball nine and forever bragging about his baseball prowess but never playing very much, but a good accountant and a good manager. Then he had a try at law, and failed because he could not mix with folks. Then a young professor at a girl's school; didn't like it. Went to a boy's school, coached the team, became a hero, tried to mix, was exceedingly pious, didn't quite belong, not quite adjusted to life, married a maternal type of woman who soon regarded him as she did her other babies, a subject of shielding care, coddled him, shielded him. Went back to Princeton to teach; became popular as a lecturer. His father came to live with him. The two complemented each other; both Irish, both gay, but in young Wilson's heart certain implacabilities that came from his Wilson grandmother, and certain dour, shy, opinionated qualities that came from the Woodrows, his mother's people. President of Princeton. There for the first time he struck executive work. The essayist, debater, lecturer bred feuds, factions and intrigues. The popular idol of the classroom, as an executive, had noble ideals of democracy for his college but instead of instituting his ideals, he stirred up a tremendous row, had the faculty by the ears, the trustees by the nose, and the alumni involved in a general riot in which his ideals went to pot. But they were noble ideals and afterwards prevailed in the college when Wilson was gone. Quit the college in despair at the end of defeat while his ideals, which were righteous enough and just enough, rose from his defeat under the guidance of others. Was nominated governor by the Democrats

[257]

looking for a respectable, frock-coated gentleman with which to beat another respectable, frock-coated gentleman. Was imposed upon the party by the bosses who expected to fool him but who did not know the Woodrow iron in him. Impressed his program on the legislature, disowned those who made him, but disowned them in a good cause and righteously, but cold-bloodedly and apparently without regret. A gay spirit with his friends, a black and implacable spirit to his enemies. The two forces of blood working in him forever desiring popular acclaim and popular love, yet offering only intellectual qualities in return for affection outside of his narrow circle. Then the presidency after less than twenty months in politics. The evolution of a liberal from the professorial days when he was an academic conservative. The death of Mrs. Wilson. And right here it seems to me you will find in the book the account of the Peck episode which could darn well be put on the screen. The courtship and second marriage, certainly affording a certain element of delicious comedy, but never pharisaical before the tragedy of the war. The two sides of Wilson working on the war; the executive side of the Woodrows, assembling the greatest physical force ever gathered on this planet in proportion to the time spent gathering it—a tremendous job in which the genius of the people took over the administration of the White House—and then on the other side Wilson the debater, the lecturer, the academic wrangler, taking charge of the spiritual forces in the upper air that finally broke the German morale; the slogan builder, the phrase maker hammering away putting courage into the Allies, taking heart out of the enemies, a great struggle in the upper air. And then Paris, the Versailles Treaty, compromise, inability to do team work, Princeton repeated, intrigue everywhere, miserable surrender; swaps, even trading his immortal soul and letting loose of minor principles for what he regarded as the great ideal, the League of Nations. The tragedy of the inept. The great democratic spirit wrestling with the immemorial traditions of Europe bringing forth his ideal in every human form, full of faults but containing his ideal. And because he had sacrificed so much for it, even his soul's integrity, clinging to the outer form, a mere phraseology, like a vain child, petulant.

A little boy with glasses, wistfully looking at the game that he could not play, and even in trying throwing down his bat and coming off of the field. His quarrels with men, breaking with House, breaking with Lansing, scolding Hoover [Colonel E. M. House, Secretary of State Robert Lansing, and Herbert Hoover]. The shadow of his physical breakdown thrown across him even in Paris. The home-coming to a disillusioned people. The quarrel with the Senate. The dinner at the White House with the Foreign Relations Committee. Repeating over exactly what happened at Princeton with the treatises; taking a noble ideal of democracy, making it a personal quarrel. The appeal to the people. The fell blow of fate. His breakdown. Struggling with petulant phrases and impatient rhetoric for the cause to which he had consecrated his life. The home-coming to Washington. The isolation. The refusal to accept the compromise which Hitchcock [Senator Hitchcock of Nebraska, Wilson's spokesman in the Senate] and the other Democrats would have made. The whole miserable failure of his ideals because of his personality. The nobility of his soul beneath the sublimity of his aspiration. His vast incapacity to get on with people, to do team work, to give and take. The little boy in the Presbyterian Manse who had never had a fight, never been knocked down or given and taken blows, there defending futilely, and knowing no rules of the fighting game, the ideal which might have saved the world. The attempt of House to see him. His isolation surrounded by Grayson [Admiral Grayson, the President's physician], Mrs. Wilson and family. And finally the exclusion of Tumulty [Joseph Tumulty, presidential secretary]. The defeat of 1920. The inauguration of Harding. The lonely days in his home on Connecticut Avenue. The last tragic attempt on Armistice Day to speak. And then the end; with a hopeful note closing it showing the meaning of his vision, the nobility of his purpose, his exalted ideals for peace.

I think, Will, that there is a big moving picture in this. You have got a lot of library stuff of Wilson's various public appearances, from his Princeton days to the end, and the moving drama of his life, which really is one of the most dramatic figures in modern history, somewhat like the classic figures of Greek mythology, not unlike Promethesus Bound, will make a powerful picture. And it is not propaganda either, even if his ideal of world peace is emphasized.

It is highbrow stuff, I know. And you know also I have contended that you fellows are not making any audience for highbrows. You are getting the morons into your houses who chase the highbrow stuff out, and you won't segregate the morons. But I believe, properly worked out, here is a big movie story, and I want to do it. I know nothing about the art of screening, absolutely nothing, but I do know what makes a tragedy, and I do know that there is an intellectual audience in this world that is deeply refreshed spiritually by a consistent tragedy.

Please, Will, if you love me, go and get my Wilson book and spend a couple of evenings with it before you say thumbs down on this proposition. If you people can stand for reality instead of fluff and can make a hopeful and beautiful tragedy without shrinking, here is your chance.

I shall be in New York, at the National Arts Club, sometime in the afternoon of the 20th, until the afternoon of the 26th. When you have read my book, if you want to talk to me, call me up, but don't let me intrude on you until you have read the book. Pardon this long letter and believe me—

To Brand Whitlock, Vichy, France, July 15, 1926

My Dear Brand:

I was glad to get your good letter upon my return from a trip to Rochester, Minnesota, where Mrs. White and I spent four weeks. She went through the Mayo Clinic, and they told her she was tired and worn out, but not to worry about her health. So I am happy along that line.

I didn't expect you to bother with my book on the President until you were tired out. I am sending you another book which is lighter and easier reading, called "Some Cycles of Cathay." I hope you will not feel that you have to say that you have read it.

I notice that you suggest that I write a book about Harding. You know I would give anything to do it. It has fairly tantalized me for a year and a half. It isn't Harding's story; it is the story of his times, the story of the Prodigal Son, our democracy that turned away from the things of the spirit, got its share of the patrimony ruthlessly and went out and lived riotously and ended it by feeding among the swine. God what a story! The story of Babylon is a Sunday School story compared with the story of Washington from June 1919 until July 1923, and so far as that goes, considerably later. We haven't even yet got back to our Father's house. He can't see us even from afar off. It's invisible. And the whole thing is epitomized by the rise of Harding. If ever there was a man who was a he-harlot, it was this same Warren G. Harding. But I suppose it ought not to be written now. It would hurt too many hearts. I don't know. I could write it and I dare to write it, but it would be a bitter and awful thing. . . .

Mrs. White and I were coming over to France this year if it had not been for her health. We expect to get over either late this year

[260]

or early next. Please let me know where you are all the time for of course we want to see you. Remember me affectionately to Mrs. Whitlock, the dear girl. Always let me know what you are doing.

To Theodore Roosevelt, Jr., July 15, 1926

My Dear Colonel Roosevelt:

It was good indeed to get a letter signed with your initials. Your handwriting is like your father's somewhat; indeed very much. Once or twice he initialed a note to me, but generally he signed his name in full.

I am pleased, greatly pleased, that you are unhappy and dissatisfied with the times. Of course, times are made more or less by leadership, but there is the other half of the equation, the times develop leaders. It would have been an uphill and terrible struggle, possibly a futile and tragic struggle, ending in sad defeat for your father, if he had lived in these times. Perhaps if he had lived, he would not have permitted public sentiment to sag as it has sagged. One doesn't know. Nothing is as futile as the ifs of history.

I feel that we have not come to the turn of the lane. The manifestations in Iowa, in the Dakotas, and in Wisconsin are sporadic, much like the manifestations of the Grangers in the seventies, or the Greenbackers in the eighties. Those are little isolated dust storms on the desert, whirling spitefully, but meaning little except as evidence of a gathering storm which is not yet even upon the horizon. I don't want to be gloomy, for I am not. I am most happy. But the nation has not yet been shocked out of its materialism. And, of course, Coolidge is a tremendous shock absorber. His emotionless attitude is an anesthetic to a national conviction of sin which must come before a genuine repentance . . . I do not see anyone on the horizon who is going to shock us into a realization of our deadly lethargy. Jim Watson [Senator James Watson of Indiana] can't; your brother Dick can't; Nicholas Murray Butler [President of Columbia University] can't. We have just got to grind along and develop our man, and it is a slow task calling for all our patience.

God, how I would like to get out and raise hell for righteousness! Instead of which I sit in my office and write unimportant editorials and go to my house and write unimportant books, with the gorge in me kicking like a mule all the time.

[261]

Six years ago I started and almost finished a book called "A Friend's Chronicle," telling in a gentle, amiable, and I hope modest way, of some of the gay and happy things that happened to me in the shadow of your father's life. My daughter died. It happened that while I was writing she was in the room a good deal, studying and reading. We were talking a good deal about it, and since then I have never been able to take up the work again. Sometimes it calls to me. Your mother once wrote a letter saying that I could use the correspondence between your father and me in the book. I don't know where the letter is. If I should want to take the work up again, perhaps she or you would write to me again confirming the old correspondence. I should be glad if you would. It is one of the things I want to do before I die, but someway I hate to do it at this time. I feel as the children of Israel must have felt in the Babylonian captivity. I have hung my harp on the willow, I suppose, but it has to come off sometime and that book should perhaps take it off.

Your letter is responsible for this long dissertation. Would you mind passing it over to Mrs. Roosevelt and to your mother, with my affectionate regards.

To C. G. Christgau, Westerville, Ohio, July 29, 1926

Dear Mr. Christgau:

I have your circular letter asking me what influences, I think, are having an unfavorable effect upon the attitude of the public toward prohibition. My feeling is that the whiskey rebellion in the Atlantic seaboard states has reached a stage where it is in danger of spreading across the United States, not among the middle classes but among the upper classes, using the word upper in its economic, not in its moral and spiritual significance. . . .

Unfortunately that leadership is also, under our present condition of world disillusionment, more or less the moral leadership. This is horribly bad, but it is true. Rich men lead the world, and rich men in the East are making this great rebellion, not industrial leaders but social leaders, the idle rich whom Roosevelt denounced. Just one thing will stop it—a blast from the White House, nothing else; possibly industrial leaders like Rockefeller, Gary, Davidson, Ford [John D. Rockefeller, Judge E. H. Gary, G. A. Davidson, and Henry Ford], and others who are not in what is known as the society, if they would join in a terrible blast against the potential danger of weakening law and order and good morals. But if the White House does not give out that blast, then prohibition is pretty badly up against it in the East. We, in the West, are safe no matter what happens. It will do no good for editors like me to rave. I don't appeal to the socially exalted classes, neither do the preachers. But the White House could appeal and so could Wall Street, if it cared to move.

On October 23, 1926, White wrote to Professor John Ise praising his book on the oil industry, observing: "Your chapter on the Teapot Dome scandal will probably be classic. . . . You have done a service to the American people." White offered his help if the oil people in Kansas threatened his teaching position at the University of Kansas.

To Chancellor E. H. Lindley, University of Kansas,
October 27, 1926

My Dear Chancellor Lindley:

The other day John Ise, of your Economics Department, sent me his book on "Oil," printed by the University Press. The title attracted me and the fact that it was done by a University man gave me an interest in it, and I picked it out of a dozen books that came for review that day, and having poked my nose into it read and read and read for three hours at odd times during a busy day.

Here is a fine piece of academic research but also it is research into dynamite. I should not be surprised to find the oil interests of this part of the country making a secret drive on Ise. His views on conservation, which are well buttressed by facts, will offend the more predatory and less thoughtful element of the oil industry, particularly that part that goes out west. I should not be surprised to find that Young John D. Rockefeller, whom I know well, is more or less in agreement with Mr. Ise, but the drilling companies, the big refining companies, and their political attorneys are liable to land on you and on the University.

[263]

Also Ise's chapter on Teapot Dome, which I regard as the best statement I have ever seen anywhere except Judge Kenyon's [W. S. Kenyon, of the United States Circuit Court] opinion from the Circuit Bench, that chapter is liable to get Ise into trouble with the Republican politicians in Kansas. It seems to me Ise is right. It seems to me also that he is well within his rights as an academician investigating a subject of current interest. But to tell you the truth, because of what I sensed in the first few pages, I read the book more carefully, being lured on by the fact that I should know about it in order to defend it when the shock of attack came, if it did come.

But of course I wouldn't want to see it come, hence I am not going to review it with any very great candor. It is a book that should be read by academicians, and of course it is not popularly written, nor is it intended as a shocker. Its tone and attitude are not those of the muckraker but those of the scholastic investigator.

All of which is rather borrowing trouble perhaps, but I thought you would be better prepared for trouble, if you could know about it in advance. This letter, of course, is confidential. . . . Maybe we will have an opportunity to talk things over. I am sure the better element of the Kansas press should stand by you in any gesture of academic freedom that might be required by the situation.

Mary White continued to be uppermost in the thoughts of her parents throughout their lifetimes. As the following letter indicates, the Whites gave Emporia a park in Mary's memory. Peter Pan Park, as it is now known, is Emporia's favorite recreational spot.

To The Emporia City Commissioners, October 28, 1926

GENTLEMEN:

We are herewith handing you a deed to the tract of land along the Cottonwood River west of Neosho Street known as the Randolph tract. This tract, together with a small addition adjoining it, comprises about forty-two acres, most of which lies on the north side of the Cottonwood, but nine acres lies south of the Cottonwood as the description in the deed will show. This tract we have deeded to the city as a free gift in memory of our daughter, Mary White, who was born in Emporia June 17, 1904, and who died May 13, 1921. To this tract we expect to add by purchase or to furnish funds to the city to condemn a twelve-acre tract known as the Brown tract, lying immediately east of the Randolph tract, extending from Neosho to Congress Street and south toward a ravine emptying into the Cottonwood River. We expect also to purchase another small tract of an acre or so to straighten out the boundary line of the park. We have no restrictions to add to the gift save these:

First, that it shall always be used as a park, and that the park shall not be commercialized.

Second, that the name of White shall never be used in connection with the park.

Third, that we be allowed for five years to spend as much as we can afford, of our own money, probably something like a thousand a year in improving the park and bringing it up to a plan submitted by Hare & Hare, landscape artists of Kansas City.

We hope to be able to enclose the park in a suitable fence or hedge and at the end of five years to turn it over to the city with no further restrictions than those named just above. We shall try to effect the purchase of this additional land above mentioned reasonably soon, and failing that shall turn over to the city what seems to be an adequate sum, and ask the city to begin condemnation proceedings and pay for the land out of the sum which we shall furnish.

White was a firm foe of American interference into the affairs of other nations in the Western Hemisphere. Relations with Mexico were particularly strained during Coolidge's administration because the Mexican government was starting to curb absentee landlordism and foreign oil producers. It looked for a time as though Coolidge would support military intervention in Mexico, but the public was so opposed to this step that instead he sent Dwight Morrow as a goodwill ambassador. Relations quickly improved.

To Dwight Morrow, New York City, February 4, 1927

Dear Mr. Morrow:

... I wish I could take our dearly beloved President and persuade him that the friendship of the Latin nations is on the whole and in the long run vastly of more cash value to America than the money that he would make in forcing our view of the Mexican situation upon Mexico at this time without arbitration. If he would only go to the World Court, or The Hague, with our case and let it rest there. America would make billions in that imponderable thing that produces capital known as good will. Pardon this outburst from an anxious heart.

White was a firm supporter of the Prohibition amendment. Nowhere are his reasons for this attitude better explained than in the following letter to an opponent of his views.

To Gabriel Wells, New York City, February 26, 1927

Dear Mr. Wells:

It all comes down to the definition of liberty, doesn't it? I have tried to indicate my feeling that liberties are inexorably restricted as civilization becomes more complex. This liberty to drink what one wants to drink, and to buy it where one wants to buy it, is a perfectly defensible liberty in a simple civilization. But in a complex civilization, that liberty is not defensible because, although we will both admit that not more than ten persons drink to excess, the presence of ten persons in a hundred, a hundred persons in ten thousand, ten thousand persons in a million who are drinking to excess, this number endangers the lives, property, and security of too many people. Machinery requires a calm, steady nerve. Poisoned nerves at throttles, levers, and key places make a tremendous waste in a complicated civilization, hence it is the duty of the nine people who do not overdrink, as it seems to me, to give up their liberties so far as drink goes for the good not of the one man who abuses the privilege but for the ten

[266]

thousands who are his potential victims. That is the whole philosophy of prohibition. If it cannot stand on that, it goes. That is my answer to your question about the relation of the soul of democracy to personal liberty.

As I said in my last letter, I am beginning to raise the question whether or not, with the many substitutes for boredom which civilization is presenting, that is the radio, the moving picture, the cheap automobile, and a diverting environment, man may not lose his vicious appetite for alcohol and use it as wisely as they do around the Mediterranean where they have become immunized to alcohol. If new conditions have changed the relation of man to booze, then of course our legal attitude toward it must change also.

There is no such thing as an essential liberty. Liberty, as I see it, is the largest use of one's personal desires consistent with the common good. The liberty to sell the milk of one's cow, which looks like a primitive liberty, is now being restricted, and very properly. The liberty to sell the flesh of one's pig when one will and where one will and how one will is properly restricted, because it conflicts with the right of the majority to clean milk and undiseased pork. Once a man had a right to dispose of his daughter as a chattel, a right which he doubtless cherished as sacredly as the bootlegger cherishes his right to sell his liquor, but another element entered in. New conditions make new morals. No liberty, as I see it, is stable. Morals, after all, are customs.

Thank you for your patience with me, and also I thank you for your kind words about my article in Harper's ["Cheer Up, America," *Harper's*, March, 1927]. I have enjoyed tremendously having your letters.

At a banquet in Salt Lake City in March, 1927, White made the statement: "As a Kansas farmer said to me, 'No man will ever tell his beads in the White House.' " The Inter Mountain Catholic (the official publication of the Diocese of Salt Lake) editorially attacked White, asserting that "Mr. White's remark was wholly uncalled for and most unfortunate; it reflects bigotry." The campaign of 1928 demonstrated the validity of the prediction.

[267]

My Dear Mons. Hunt:

I want to assure you and the people of the Catholic faith in and about Salt Lake City, that I was hiding behind no subterfuge when I said that the sentiment of the Kansas farmer who told me: "No man will ever tell his beads in the White House," is not my sentiment. Obviously, however, if the remark gave offense to my hearers of the Catholic faith, it was an ill-advised remark, and in the future I shall be happy to change the phrasing of it. The remark that the man made, however, represents in its rustic phrasing a political fact. You and I may deplore this fact, but nevertheless I am afraid the fact exists.

I am a Republican and came of Yankee stock, but if there was an honest and courageous Republican candidate for governor in Texas and someone would return from Texas with the report that the old unreconstructed Southerners were saying: "No damned Yankee will ever be elected governor of Texas," I would not be offended at the man who reported the remark. I should laugh at the prejudices of the South with the man who reported it. I shall be more than happy to see the day come when an honest and intelligent Catholic will have an equal chance as a candidate for president against an equally honest and intelligent Protestant. Among intelligent thinking men religion has no place in politics. When I made the remark I was simply calling attention to the fact that unfortunately there are enough bigoted and unintelligent men to prevent an honest Catholic from being elected. As there seems to be in Salt Lake City a more or less general feeling among Catholics that I was in sympathy with the Kansas farmer who made this remark, I wonder if you could find space in your publication for this letter or for at least a part of it.

To Guy Stevens, Association of Producers of Petroleum in Mexico, April 21, 1927

Dear Mr. Stevens:

The fact that I haven't replied to your letter of April 7 does not indicate that I was not greatly interested in what you said in your letter, and that I am not convinced that you have a real case to submit to whatever board, commission, court or governmental agency shall finally settle the matter. I have always felt that the Mexican Government should recast and reform its contention in these oil disputes, and in stating my position in previous letters I have tried to put myself in the place of the contending Mexicans. Not that I thought they were right for I do not, but that I thought they had a side, a contention, an issue, if you will, which we should consider. And there is the whole point between us. I believe very earnestly that this is an arbitrable matter. I'm not sure that word is in the dictionary, but you know what I mean. My quarrel with the policy of the State Department has been that the State Department has been too quick to show force to a weaker nation; has been too rigid in following a diplomatic procedure which would have been all right with Great Britain, Germany, France or Italy, because a show of force could have been met somewhat by a show of force. My feeling is that when we Americans through our State Department found that our insistent policy of justice to our nationals in oil disputes and other grievances about American property in Mexico was meeting with evasion, quibbling, and delay, we should have brought the matter to a crisis by demanding immediate arbitration, calling in our neighbors and friends internationally, setting forth our whole case before the world, and demanding a showdown and a settlement, not through force but through publicity and arbitration. Such a course would not have cost us the friendship of the South American Republics. Such a course would have got all that we will get by a show of force, if our cause is as just as it seems to be.

I have presented through the Gazette the side of Mexico merely to show that they had a "side"; that they had an issue, and so to make sentiment for arbitration. This whole case affects property. There is no moral issue that cannot be arbitrated at stake. My criticism of the State Department has been that in a matter wholly affecting property they have brought our country perilously near a political and international crisis. And I should say that it would be unbelievably wicked to go to war with Mexico without first offering to arbitrate the issue at stake. The sad and miserable part of the whole business is that by inflaming the issue of property between the two countries, we then make it terribly likely that violence against life will come in and so precipitate war, not on the issues as they first were made, but upon other issues arising from the property issue which will inflame the people and so produce a war. The war will buy with American blood your property for you, but it will stink through all time and shame you to eternity—you who own this Mexican oil and are pressing our

[269]

government through your insistence upon your rights in such a way that your insistence will eventuate war.

It is a quibble, it seems to me, to say that the interests which are doing this are not the interests which have disgraced America in the Harding administration through the Teapot Dome and Pacific oil scandals. Ownership may pass, change, insinuate in and out of various corporations, but the great leaders of the oil industry who tried to rob the Government under Fall are now trying to buy their property in Mexico by the blood of American boys. They who tried to steal are now trying to murder. These are short and ugly words, but they represent a feeling in the heart of the American people which may within a decade turn a conservative, patient, and complacent people into a turbulent unreasoning majority which will work through Congress such a wreck and ruin upon stable business and honest industry as this country may not repair for a generation. I have seen mobs rise in our politics. It was my honor and distinction to oppose free silver in '96 with all my heart. I knew and admired Mark Hanna and helped him win the election of '96. He was kind enough to say that I contributed a pamphlet used more than any other pamphlet for the success of that election. And I had my choice of many high offices and refused them all. Then I saw the triumph of an unbridled plutocracy turn and two decades of agitation follow which certainly you would not like to see repeated in the coming thirties and forties. Do not mistake the calm and inertia of today for a license of public approval. Underneath the waters that are so smooth are terrible dynamic forces. And you who are the guardians of vast interests, honest interests I should say as the word goes, must pause and consider whether it is worth while to insist upon a show of force and to fight against arbitration in Mexico at this time. If you get your war and your property in Mexico, you will probably lose it in the decade that will follow when an angry people, seeing the truth, will clamor for revenge.

I believe with all my heart in the present economic system, the capitalist's system, to use a phrase coined by its enemies. It is the only system which will work with the world in its present state of moral and intellectual development. But it is in grave danger, not from the forces below, but from the mad, greedy folly of the forces above.

I hope you will receive this letter in the spirit in which it is written and know that I am not one of those who would tear down, but I hope I am among those who would defend and construct. And I feel that any policy a newspaper or a public man can pursue now which gives the side of the Mexicans in this controversy and thereby forces arbitration is the conservative policy, is the constructive policy, the only policy which in the end will save all of the rights of your stockholders and will stabilize the present economic system.

To CALVIN COOLIDGE, April 25, 1927

DEAR PRESIDENT COOLIDGE:

I know that it is no part of your job to read current literature, but occasionally I drop into a book that is real. I've dropped into two books in the last ten days that are most illuminating—Frank Simonds' book on "How Europe made Peace without America" and M. Tardieu's book on "France in the United States." I am so impressed with this book that I am making bold to send you a copy which I have ordered from the publisher. Tardieu is a pretty hard-boiled conservative, but he has an understanding heart and an open mind, and, it seems to me, his book is worth an evening's notice. Frank Simonds' book, it seems to me, is one of the great books that has come out of the war—understanding, illuminating and prophetic. Pardon this intrusion but when I find such books as these I'm eager to pass them on.

Unless some political cataclysm occurs you need not worry about the Kansas delegation. Forces are beginning to work now quietly in your behalf—forces of harmony rather than division.

The Sacco-Vanzetti case attracted world-wide attention. During the height of the great Red scare these two labor organizers were sentenced to death, on very flimsy evidence, for the shooting of a paymaster and his guard. Public opinion forced Governor Fuller of Massachusetts to review the case in 1927. After an investigation, Fuller refused a pardon and the men died on the night of August 22, 1927. Since they died in the electric chair, increasingly more people have come to believe in their innocence. Felix Frankfurter of the Harvard Law School suggested that White write this letter.

To Governor A. T. Fuller, Boston, Mass., June 1, 1927

Dear Sir:

I sprang from New England stock—as old New England stock as there is. I have just returned from New England, where I have been talking to college groups, and I was surprised beyond words to find the bitterness and hate which had sprung up in New England, particularly in Massachusetts, among those who fear that Sacco and Vanzetti will not be executed. Until I went into Massachusetts, into the home of my ancestors in fact, I had no idea that men could let their passion so completely swamp their judgment into fears and hatreds; so deeply confuse their sanity. I now know why the witches were persecuted and hanged by upright and godless people. I hope in going through the evidence in this case you will realize that we, who do not know the law, sometimes do not see the implications of evidence nor interpret its significances accurately. And as one human being to another let me urge that you will turn to your personal attorney, whoever he may be, whenever the case seems vague and the issues confusing. This is a tremendously important case for America. It seems to me that our courts would be vastly more discredited before the world if we executed innocent men than they would be if we refrained to execute innocent men when there was even a shadow of doubt as to their guilt.

Pardon this intrusion but this case seems to be wider than your state. It is America and America's justice which is on trial.

White's letters to his former Bull Moose friends like Gifford Pinchot are the best indication that the Emporia editor was not too pleased with the days of Republican supremacy in the 1920's.

DEAR GIFFORD:

... I don't think the dawn of the better day has come. We have got to sink lower before we rise higher. Prosperity must break. We must get out of our timidity complex. Lord! Heaven! How scared we are of change for the better. Stability is our God and until we change our Gods we won't change our attitude toward living. I'm pretty hopeless. I wish I could have seen you. I have so many things I wanted to talk about even if I am one of Job's comforters.

It was inevitable in view of the reactionary spirit of the 1920's that White would be attacked as a Socialist or Communist. Such a charge did not disturb him when it was made by "lunatic fringe" groups, but when it came from a fellow newspaperman it caused him great alarm.

To Hugh Powell, Coffeyville (Kansas) *Journal*, July 6, 1927

DEAR HUGH POWELL:

Did you know that you hurt me with the editorial saying I had stood for "socialistic and communistic measures"? It happens that my pet aversion is socialism, and I suppose all sane Americans scorn communism with a deep and bitter scorn. In political measures I have indeed advocated the initiative and referendum which are now successfully operating in every state bordering Kansas and in something like half the states of the Union including the conservative state of Massachusetts. I have stood for the primary which is practically universal in its use all over America. I never cared for the recall and differed with Roosevelt about the recall of judicial decisions. In economic measures I have not gone as far as LaFollette, and have stood with what is known as the Roosevelt group, and every measure I ever advocated has been adopted and is either now in successful operation or has been repealed like the Fugitive Slave Law because there is no longer need for it. In matters of foreign relations, peace, disarmament, etc., I have never put my toe one inch farther forward than Elihu Root, Chief Justice Taft, and Charles Evans Hughes have already gone. I am not now any farther than they are toward pacifism. I supported Coolidge's battleship program, do not believe in disarmament, believe in military education but not compulsory military education, believe in preparedness but only so far for instance as Coolidge himself would go. I would not advocate a peace treaty that goes farther than America has already gone with other nations looking to the outlawry of war.

I have thought carefully over all the measures I have ever advocated and so far as I can see there is not one either political, economic or international which could by any stretch be called socialistic or communistic. I am a Republican, and have in my desk a letter from the President of the United States commending me for my Republicanism in 1924. I contributed that year to the Republican National Committee, supported all the ticket except Ben Paulen, and three members on the state ticket have written to me that I was responsible for their election that year. I have bolted candidates no more frequently than the average man. I have just been noisier, but there never has been a year except 1914, when I supported Allen and Murdock [Henry J. Allen and Victor Murdock], when I did not support a great majority —an overwhelming majority—of all the candidates on the Republican ticket from top to bottom.

And it hurts like the dickens when you, whom I admire and respect, use the words "communistic and socialistic" about my political activities. Call me a liar if you will; crazy if you must; coy, uncertain, hard to please if you have to; but, my dear Hugh, please don't stick that dirty phrase "communist or socialist" on my name. I value my patriotism as I value nothing else in this world.

On July 19, 1927, White gave a dinner for Kansas editors with Secretary of Commerce Herbert Hoover as guest of honor. It was part of a successful build-up which landed Hoover the Republican presidential nomination the following year. White long had been a Hoover booster. In the 1920 Republican convention he had cast his vote for Hoover on the ballot which gave the nomination to Harding.

[274]

To Herbert Hoover, August 2, 1927

MY DEAR SECRETARY:

I am sending you herewith all the clippings that I can find. I particularly wish they would go to Mrs. Hoover that she may get some idea of what a really important person she has married. I find that clippings like these help me in my domestic status, and I'm not above lending a hand to another poor struggling mortal.

The clippings were particularly interesting. I commend particularly to Mrs. Hoover the ones from the Lyons News. I've only sent you the first crop of clippings. There is another crop going around, comment on the comment of the editors, and even a third cutting of the editorial alfalfa in which the various editors who heard you talk are appearing at Rotary, Lions, and Kiwanis, and Chamber of Commerce luncheons and dinners all over the state, telling the story of your prowess. I know of no one for many years who has made such good copy in Kansas as your visit made.

If Vernon Kellogg [close college friend of White's, who served under Herbert Hoover in Belgium during the war, and was now secretary of the National Research Council] is in the West I'd like to have him look over these clippings after Mrs. Hoover has glanced at them. He will know something of the towns in which the papers are printed. Always command me when I may serve.

Nan Britton, Warren G. Harding's alleged mistress, published her confessions in The President's Daughter (*1927*). *Nan Britton claimed that, as president, Harding was supporting an illegitimate baby born hardly a year before his election.*

To Henry J. Allen, August 10, 1927

DEAR HENRY:

Your letter of the 8th found me in bed entertaining some castor oil, which would be a grand place and a perfect time to read the Harding book. I note that you report that Long believes that the Harding story puts "Harding in the class of the early English Kings." Possibly. My view of the face cards would be that it puts him in the class of the late English Jacks.

Hoping this will find you the same, I am—

To JOHN MACK, *Kansas Republican*, Newton, Kansas, August 24, 1927

MY DEAR JOHN:

... In 1923 the Victor Murdocks and Mrs. White and I spent two months on a cruise with the Judge [E. H. Gary, chairman of the United States Steel Corporation], going around the Mediterranean. Victor and I were young huskies in our mid-fifties, and the Judge, rather frail in his late seventies. He was a spare, soft-voiced, reticent little man who wore more suits of clothes on that trip than anyone aboard ship. I was greatly consoled by the fact that he wore a cloth hat to match a suit. I had such a hat, but my son Bill, who was in Harvard, sniffed at it and wouldn't let me wear it. But when Judge Gary, who was the glass of fashion, put it on, I came home and ignored Bill. But to return to the Judge. On the trip, at every landing point, he was forever busy with the nobility and the gentry, and didn't have a very good time. Apparently the steel trust and the State Department had sent word ahead that he was coming and so the Minister's yacht or the Consul General's boat always appeared in any harbor we made for the Judge, and he was carted off to talk to officialdom. The Murdock and the White families were not on leash. We ran wild, saw whatever good shows there were—and as you get around near Suez there are some good ones—shopped in the bazaars, ate ungodly food in the restaurants, and enjoyed life to the full. When we came aboard after each stop, the little Judge would come pattering up to us in a self-deprecatory manner, and ask us in a low voice to tell him what we did and what we saw and about the fun we had, and would look wistfully at us out of his blue eyes. And I remember once, as we put off from Naples and told the Judge about some particularly gala experience we had in a show and a restaurant, he massaged his old jaw sadly and said:

"Well, well, you certainly had a good time. But when I was in Rome day before yesterday, for just one day, I had to see the

[276]

King, and the Pope, and Mussolini, and Stinnes, all in one twelve hours!"

He shook his head sadly and went away bemoaning his unfortunate lot.

I don't think he ever had a very good time. He was too busy and too bedeviled by his position. The boat was filled with wealthy bankers who hung on Gary's slightest word when he talked to one of them, and rushed off to tell the other bankers all about it, possibly to cable some stock buying order in New York. Always one felt the Judge guarded himself against stock broker's gossip. He liked to talk to Victor and me apparently because, as far as he could see, we were the only two men on the boat who didn't give a tinker's large yellow resined obstruction about what the Old Judge thought about anything pertaining to the market. We were not property minded, and he knew it and often hunted us up to talk to us. He and Victor talked a lot about the Bible. Victor read the Bible as a guide book when we went into Egypt, Palestine and that part of the world. The Judge also was a Bible addict. We met the Judge one day in Jerusalem. He was being steered around by a gorgeous Arab guide in a wonderful silk robe and some kind of a gaudy headpiece. The guide was bedecked and bedizened and bedamned with every kind of decoration that ever came off of a Christmas tree. Our guide, whom I had nailed down myself from the Tourist Agency, was a meek-mannered, smart preacher politician, who used to live in Smith County, Kansas, who knew all there was to know about the Holy Land and talked a blue streak. But this gorgeous caliph of Bagdad, who was towing the Judge around, spoke such broken English that the poor Judge got precious little out of him except his blue blood and his lineage, and came nosing into our party for a few scraps of information about the Tomb of Abraham, or Rachel, or somebody, who was lying in the sepulcher before us.

The last time I saw him was on a train near London. I was wandering around, trying to get a drink of water, a hard thing to do in Europe. The Judge called me into his compartment, pressed the button, and bought a large quart bottle of mineral water for me. . . . He had an Irish twinkle in his eye and was a splendid listener. I have seen him in various struggles and under various stresses, and he had a most remarkable nerve. Nothing could shake it. I heard Sam Gompers [head of the American Federation of Labor] stand up and bellow at Judge Gary for an hour and twenty-two minutes, and the Judge sat there, still, solemn, unflinching. He crossed his left foot over, his right foot under, once in all the ordeal, and I watched him like a cat, being a reporter on the job. And I know that he didn't so much as drum with a finger, or moisten his lips, and he glared right back at Sam Gompers and tried to keep his eye all the time that Gompers was talking. . . .

The Daughters of the American Revolution subjected themselves to an attack in the press for circulating a pamphlet The Common Enemy *and labeling middle-class liberals like William Allen White as dangerous Reds. The D.A.R., also, had a blacklist of important Americans including Dean Roscoe Pound and Felix Frankfurter of the Harvard Law School, President Mary E. Woolley of Mount Holyoke College, Clarence Darrow, Rabbi Stephen S. Wise, and Editor White. The following letter was an attempt on White's part to drive some sense into the D.A.R. and stop the charge of Red and the blacklist.*

To Mrs. Alfred Brosseau, President General of the Daughters of the American Revolution, August 11, 1927

Dear Mrs. Brosseau:

I have your letter of August 4, commenting upon an editorial in the Gazette in which we criticized the officers of the Daughters of the American Revolution for joining in the red-baiting endeavors of the ultra-conservative organizations centering around Washington. You make the point that your circular "The Common Enemy" did not name the persons—Mrs. Catt, Florence Kelley, Jane Addams, and others—who were the subject of the most bitter, unfair, and evidently malicious attacks of the red-baiters. Of course you are right. "The Common Enemy" did not name names. But your Organization has sponsored the circular which does name names, and it is hardly a defense to stand upon your circular and not also stand for its implications and recommendations and endorsements.

Moreover, I happen to know that your membership out here in the West has received, after reading "The Common Enemy," the objectionable circular for which you deny responsibility. Surely intelligent editors, like the editor of the New York Times, the New York World, the Kansas City Times, are making no mistake in putting directly at the door of the National Officers of the D.A.R. the odium which attaches to the assault upon good citizens and useful Americans who happen to differ in their political beliefs with these reactionary red-baiters in Washington.

I happen to know personally, very personally, a case in point. I am, and always have been, a Republican. I contribute money to the Republican organization. I am a member of the National Republican League. I have supported President Coolidge in his army program and in his battleship program and I have a letter from him thanking me for my political activities three years ago. I am on terms of fairly good standing with my party in my town, in the state, and in the nation. Yet I am listed in the circular which you endorse as a red. Moreover, when I have been billed to speak at various places, members of the Daughters of the American Revolution have formally protested against my appearance in behalf of the Daughters of the American Revolution. Their protest has come solely because of the action of the National Officers of the D.A.R. in giving endorsement to that red-baiting circular. More than that, I was asked by Mrs. Cora Wilson Stewart [chairman of the Illiteracy Commission of the General Federation of Women's Clubs], to head an organization to combat illiteracy. Every other woman's organization in the United States which Mrs. Stewart has approached has given its sanction, extended its co-operation to Mrs. Stewart's work, excepting the D.A.R. When Mrs. Stewart asked members of your National Council in Washington, why they could not co-operate with her "Crusade for Illiteracy," they replied that it was on account of me. When she pushed them for an answer, she was referred to a retired General of the Army who told her that the charge against me was that I had contributed to the New Masses. I give you my word and honor I never wrote for the New Masses. I am a subscriber to the New Masses, as I am to the Nation's Business, and the Economic World, and a dozen other publications which we use in the Gazette Office in getting in touch with all sorts of opinion, radical opinion as well as conservative and reactionary opinion. I dislike very deeply the editorial policy of Life and Judge, being a Prohibitionist. But I do not refuse to subscribe for them on that account any more than I would refuse to subscribe for the National Economist whose hard-boiled, high protection views are not held commonly out west. But I never wrote for the New Masses

[279]

nor contributed anything to it except my subscriptions. And the allegation against me submitted to Mrs. Stewart by the army officer speaking for the D.A.R. was utterly false. You say in your circular, which you were kind enough to send me, that you "are for national defense." So am I. The Gazette, which I own and control, gives columns of free advertising every year to the Citizens Military Training Camp. Our men belong to the National Guard and their time is not deducted when they go to the training camp, and I have offered certain of my men full wages to attend the Citizens Military Training Camp. While standing for the national defense, I also believe tremendously in peace and believe in the League of Nations, the World Court, the Hague Tribunal, and every organization or institution which tries to promote international understanding and good-feeling, and which would substitute reason for force wherever it can be substituted in our international relations with humanity, constituted as it is and will be for our lifetime, at least, and possibly for many centuries hence. I hate war as I used to hate the open saloon. But when war came, being too old to fight, I went into the Red Cross without salary and my boy went into the training camp as soon as he was old enough.

I mention these things to show you how unfair it is to have members of the D.A.R., when I go into a community to talk on education, or literature, or to support Calvin Coolidge, and his policies, rising up sputtering at me because of a circular which your National Council has recommended to your membership in which I am denounced as a red.

You will find pretty generally over the United States that editors and public men will not endorse this foolish and malicious attack upon people like Jane Addams, Mrs. Catt, Florence Kelley, and others, merely because they disagree with men who are ardent believers in the national defense. It takes all kinds of people to make a world, and I can understand how a philosophic pacifist like Jane Addams does her most necessary part in offsetting the deeply reactionary attitude of, say, our army friend in Washington, who is overzealous in his belief about the necessity of force and the folly of reason in our international relations. I happen not to agree with either of these distinguished Americans, but I would not set out to make a list of those with whom I disagree, and circularize the country protesting against their right to have their say in any public meeting and discuss the truth as they realize it.

You will find this attitude of American tolerance fairly general, at least in the Mississippi Valley. The Mississippi Valley will be the first to respond to the call to arms as it was in 1917, but it will be the last to endorse a red-baiting attitude which denies honest, conscientious, God-fearing Americans of any faith the right to have their say in any public assemblage. And certainly members of the D.A.R., influenced by the circular which you endorse, are doing that over the United States today. So long as the endorsement of that circular stands, so long will the D.A.R. continue to find itself the subject of gay quips and merry jibes in the American press. It is quite possible to be enthusiastic for national defense without pillorying those who disagree with the ultimate expression of that excellent doctrine.

Kindly pardon this long letter. I have always honored the D.A.R. and have believed in its tenets and respected its officers. I, myself, am from colonial stock. The White family came to Massachusetts in 1639. My great-grandfather was a Revolutionary soldier, and my grandfather was born during the Revolutionary War. I love my country, believe in the capitalistic civilization which prevails in Christendom, and value my good name just as highly as the members of the D.A.R. value their status and standing. There is no reason why men of my type, liberals who hate communism with a deep loathing, should not work with the D.A.R. But at one stroke of the pen, when you endorse the circular which puts under the ban the officers of every women's civic organization of the country, most of the interchurch organizations and the missionary boards, the D.A.R. has isolated itself in the work of making a better, fairer, lovelier America and must not complain if its isolation draws upon it the fire which is directed to those superpatriots who see no good save in their own endeavors and tolerate no associations except those of their own caste and class and kind.

All of which is submitted in the kindest spirit, with all good will and in the hope that you as president of the D.A.R. will understand why it is that our American newspapers are making disagreeable comments upon an organization which heretofore has had only their most generous praise.

Governor Alfred E. Smith was the logical Democratic nominee for president in 1928. His record as governor of New York had made him the leading figure in the Democratic party. White had written a friendly sketch of Smith for Collier's, *August 21, 1926. Smith was unable to accept the invitation mentioned in the following letter.*

To FRANKLIN D. ROOSEVELT, New York City, February 11, 1928

DEAR MR. ROOSEVELT:

Audacity is a concomitant to success for other things besides oratory, and I have my nerve as will appear in about one second. I want Al Smith to come to Kansas to address the Kansas State Editorial meeting at Emporia, the last week in April, or the first week in May.

You may now pause a moment to get your breath, and I will tell you why.

Smith is supposed to have horns and a tail out west. Kansas is one state, possibly the one state, that has made prohibition a success. But in general Kansas is the center of the world which Smith does not know and which does not know Smith. This Editorial Association is Non-Partisan. I am requested to invite him by editors of both parties. If he comes to Emporia, to Kansas, the center of everything that is foreign to him, a rural population, an agricultural civilization, a population ninety per cent American-born of American parents, and sixty-five per cent born in Kansas, he will be facing a different audience, but naturally will be speaking from a different rostrum from any rostrum that he might mount in the Atlantic seaboard or even in the South. It would do more for him politically than any other one thing he might possibly do to come with his message to a liberal state like Kansas and say it to our faces. Incidentally, he would be probably saying it to our hearts and make more hay than he could make with any other political gesture.

I am writing to you because I don't know another soul in New York City who could present this matter to Smith as you can, and I hope you can do it. I would write to him, but he doesn't know me, never heard of me. I am, as you know, a Republican, but I admire Smith greatly. I think his is one of the important brains now functioning in American politics, and I believe with all my heart it would be a good thing for him and a good thing for Kansas if he could come here. This is no Ku-Klux territory. They have passed out of Kansas because we grasped the metal hard and crushed them early. But it is a state of English stock, Protestant religion, and of almost entirely agricultural pursuit.

Please be my minister in this matter.

The Nation magazine held a Blacklist Party for all those whose names were on the D.A.R. blacklist. The invitation read in part: "Dear Fellow-Conspirator: We notice that your name appears on the Roll of Honor drawn up by the Daughters of the American Revolution and their allies, the Key Men of America. Some call this Honor Roll a blacklist. It includes United States Senators, Communists, Ministers, Socialists, Republicans, Editors, Housewives, Lawyers—most of us, in fact." Although White was unable to attend the party, he sent the following telegram.

To RUTH STOUT, Secretary of Blacklist Party, *The Nation*,
May 4, 1928

Unworthy though I am to stand before the kings and queens of courage in the true American aristocracy, yet because some fumbling fool has placed me there, I none the less appreciate the great fortune I have had in this distinction. Some people have all the luck. I am one. If a good name is rather to be chosen than great riches, a place on the D.A.R. blacklist is better than a license to steal in a mint, or to have a hand in the Continental Trading Company's jackpot. I am sorry that I cannot be with you at the dinner tonight. However unworthy I may be to sit there. But I have noticed that what you grab and what you keep is all to the good, so I shall grab and keep this distinction as among my most precious laurels.

White was a delegate to the Republican convention where he served
as a member of the subcommittee which drafted the platform. White
opened the Republican campaign in Kansas with a speech at Olathe
on July 12. Although he respected Al Smith as a man, he opposed
Smith's Tammany Hall background, his wetness, and his urban con-
nection. White charged in his speech that Smith, as a member of the
New York legislature, had voted against bills to curb saloons, gam-
bling, and prostitution. Eastern papers carried these charges, and
Smith denied them. White employed two investigators to comb the
journal of the legislature and released the findings on July 29 and 30.
Then, Walter Lippmann explained to White how the charges of pro-
tecting gambling and prostitution had grieved Smith's family. Lipp-
mann told White that Smith had voted against these reform bills be-
cause he sincerely believed they were unconstitutional, unenforce-
able, and unworkable. White withdrew his charges on gambling and
prostitution, conceding to Smith "the purity of his motives which
always should be granted in any political controversy." After this,
the Whites went to Europe on a six weeks' trip. When White re-
turned in October, he spoke in the South under the auspices of the
Republican party, but he made no further comment on the gambling
and prostitution charges.

To Edward J. Woodhouse, Chapel Hill, N. C., July 20, 1928

Dear Mr. Woodhouse:

I have your letter of July 16. I am now compiling Smith's record.
I hope to have it compiled in detail showing the page and paragraph
and parliamentary status upon each motion upon which he voted in
a long line of Tammany votes in Tammany block during his entire
legislative career with the liquor interests. This he cannot deny. His
official biographer, Mr. Moskowitz [Henry Moskowitz], husband of
the lady who has been and is Smith's most keen political adviser, declares in that official biography exactly this:

"The liquor interests were friendly to Tammany Hall and Smith
stood for legislation favorable to them which Tammany sponsored."

The Moskowitz biography is an officially inspired biography used
for campaign purposes by Smith's own campaign managers. In his
record you will find that Smith voted not only with Tammany on
the liquor question but on questions controlling gambling and prosti-

tution. This does not mean that Smith is a low fellow. On the contrary, I have the highest respect for his integrity, his courage, and his intelligence. But he is thoroughly Tammanized in spirit and in a moral point of view. And his courage, wisdom, and honesty will not prevent him from making such a record in the White House as Tammany would desire wherever he and Tammany can agree without losing too many votes.

First, he can Tammanize the federal courts by appointing men opposed to legislation unfavorable to the various Tammany interests of our great cities.

Second, he can and will put on the Supreme Court men of his own kind and will use his remarkable political acumen to get those men confirmed by dealing and bickering with the Senate as every American president has dealt and dickered with his Senate to get confirmations since Jefferson's day.

I do not apologize for Teapot Dome, nor Sinclair, nor Doheny, nor the little house on K Street [Harry F. Sinclair and Edward L. Doheny, involved in the Teapot Dome oil scandals. The house on K Street refers to the headquarters of the "Ohio Gang" during Harding's administration]. They were rotten. They came as the reaction of war probably, in which the Republicans tried to steal as much as the Democrats had wasted. But in national politics, barring the Grant administration, and the scandal in Cuba, and in the Post Office Department following the Spanish-American War, these scandals were sporadic. Tammany is always in scandal. Five scandal investigations are now in progress in New York City against Tammany men for things done, not eight years ago, but less than eight months ago.

Pardon me for not continuing this long letter. I have many others to answer. But this is the basis of my faith that Smith is a menace to the country, for all his high qualities and in spite of them.

To Walter Lippmann, New York *World*, October 15, 1928

Dear Walter:

I have two distinct reactions when I read my mail. The girl in the office divides it into two piles: those who agree with me and those who do not. When I find a long line of lousy kluxers agreeing with me, I want to go out and be a repeater above seven times for Smith. But when I get mail from the lowbrows among the Catholics, who insist that to oppose Smith at all is to inject the religious issue into the campaign and abuse me for mudslinging, when I have only read the man's record, I want to go out and set up my ward so solid for Hoover that there won't be a scattering vote. ...

To Myron S. Blumenthal, Universal Trade Press Syndicate, New York City, October 18, 1928

Dear Mr. Blumenthal:

I am sorry to have neglected so long your letter of October 6, which I have read with great interest. I was glad to get it, and will be glad to give you what seems to me the answer. You ask whether I condemn Hoover for sitting in a corrupt Harding Cabinet and remaining silent. Of course, in the Cabinet meetings no corruption is ever discussed. And, of course, each Cabinet member's department is entirely isolated from every other Cabinet member's department, and there is no way of knowing that corruption is going on until it is exposed.

When corruption was exposed in the administration, Coolidge immediately set the wheels going to punish the corruptionists. It was no business of Hoover to leave the Cabinet because Coolidge was prosecuting the corruptionists. Everyone must admit that Smith had no more hand personally in the corruption of Tammany than Hoover had in the corruption of the Harding administration. But the corruption of Tammany is a system. It isn't the big stealing of Tammany. It is the little oppressions, backsheesh, grafts, petty holdups of business concerns that makes Tammany dangerous. The big thieves, both in the Republican party and the Democratic party, can be taken care of, but no man ever rose in Tammany fighting Tammany corruption. But a man can rise in both the Democratic and Republican parties fighting corruption. In those two parties witness Bryan, Roosevelt, and LaFollette. It is the Tammany system, not the sewer scandals or milk scandals, which makes Tammany a menace, and corruption in the Republican party is being handled by Republicans who are not afraid to fight it. But Al Smith has never complained against the corruption in Tammany, indeed he said in his speech on the Fourth of July that Tammany was all right. If Hoover ever says that Sinclair, Doheny, Fall, and Daugherty [Harry F. Sinclair, Edward L. Doheny, Secretary of the Interior Albert Fall, and Attorney General Harry M. Daugherty, all connected with unsavory episodes in the Harding administration] are all right, and their stealing is all right, I shall change my mind about him.

I hate the religious fight being made on Smith. I have denounced it time and again. He seems now doomed to defeat. I shall regret that part of his defeat, though not all, nor indeed not much is due to bigotry. But I hoped he would be defeated on the wet issue with Tammany symbolizing it.

I hope I have made myself clear. Of course in this brief space it is hard to do so. I think the New York World is right in denouncing any attempt to inject the religious issue in this campaign. I have always found the World a fair opponent.

To HAROLD ICKES, Chicago, Ill., October 20, 1928

DEAR HAROLD:

I was glad to get your letter, and curiously enough I was not as badly shocked as probably you presumed I would be when I read that you were going to vote for Al Smith. Why not? This is a free country and one man's judgment, given a reasonable amount of intelligence, is as good as another's. I see a lot of reasons why I could vote for Smith, but I see more why I could vote for Hoover.

I hope to see you in the next few months. Meanwhile remember me to Mrs. Ickes.

To FRANK R. KENT, Baltimore *Sun*, November 27, 1928

DEAR MR. KENT:

. . . Here's where I go into reverse. I am so constituted that when I get in a fight I am more worried about being fair to my opponent than I am about anything else, and sometimes I get maudlin in trying to be square. So I wound up this campaign with that pity for Al Smith which is akin to love. The poor devil didn't have a Chinaman's chance. Someone ought to have told him. He just did everything wrong. And he apparently had no one around him who had the faintest conception of the United States. It was tragic. And so, having a soft spot for heroes of tragedy, I heard the radio story of his night at

Tammany as the returns came in and caught myself thumbing my
eyes as the tale unfolded. . . .

*For the first time since Reconstruction days the Republican party
split the Solid South. Al Smith's wetness, his Tammany history, and
his lifelong urban existence hurt him in this dry, rural, Protestant area.
Smith's life and ways were alien to Main Street America. In spite of
White's suggestion that the Republicans build up a southern branch,
election returns since 1928 have demonstrated that the South is still
solidly Democratic.*

To COLONEL HORACE MANN, Republican National Headquarters,
December 26, 1928

DEAR COLONEL MANN:

Your Christmas card came today and reminded me that for some
time I have intended writing a letter to you. I am one of the men in
the United States to whom Hoover could give no office under any
circumstances. Yet I shall be in politics all my life. I like political
power, and have found that you get much more political power by
taking monastic vows against office holding and office seeking than
you do by holding and seeking office.

The thing that is uppermost in my mind just now is the South.
There is a good chance in North Carolina and Tennessee to make
them doubtful states at every election, and a fine chance in Florida.
I have been in Texas for two weeks since the election, from Dallas
south to Houston, and then northward to Lubbock and Amarillo,
scouting around on my own hook. In northwest Texas and in the
Texas cities there is a real opportunity to establish a Republican
party, definite, permanent, and reasonably successful, and I know of
no other purely political problem that will rise in the Hoover administration which is so important as the problem of establishing in
three or four southern states a real Republican party. It can't be done
on the old line. We musn't forget that our victories this year have
had some relation to the decreasing proportion of colored voters in
the states we won. In Northwest Texas there are about as many col-

[288]

ored people as there are in Kansas, Colorado, and Missouri. They are good, self-respecting, property-owning colored people who are sensible and amenable to reason, and they should be taken in the party as any other citizen, given no more consideration and no less, as we do in Kansas and as they do in Colorado and Missouri. But white leadership should be allowed to develop just as colored leadership should be allowed to develop, if it can develop independent of race. The problem is intricate and it requires time, patience, and intelligence to solve it. At the proper time you and others who know the situation should take it up with the President. A blunder would be expensive of course. Mr. Hoover carried the South on prohibition. It wasn't religion. I was down there and I know. Probably the nomination of some southern Democrat to some important office, possibly the Cabinet, possibly in due course the Supreme Court, would be a just recognition of the politics of the situation. But it would be a terrible blunder and hinder a new Republican organization in the South beyond telling to appoint a wet Democrat, or a Democrat who had been lukewarm on the subject of prohibition. As I see it, we should make it plain to the dry element in the South that, in so far as party gratitude is concerned, to begin with we wish to make some gesture that will indicate our gratitude to the dry Democrats, that will make it possible for us to function as Republicans, because after all, the exhibition of common sense in leadership is the surest guarantee of party integrity and the best omen for success, and we must persuade these dry Democrats that we are square, if we wish to make some of them over into active Republicans.

I know you will pardon this long letter and let my interest in party success be my excuse and mitigation. I have no candidate for any office. I wouldn't have the slightest idea where to go or how to begin if the subject of patronage came up and am not greatly interested in patronage. But I do feel that a service to our country of the first magnitude may be achieved by holding something of our gains in the South. I am satisfied that we carried Georgia and Alabama. The ballot there, about which I do not need to tell you, and a ruling permitting the split ballots for Hoover to be assembled not in the Court House, but in the State House did the trick for the Democrats, first by allowing them to throw out a large percent of Republican ballots as spoiled ballots, and second, by allowing them to change the ballot counting away from the precinct where it was polled.

In Alabama another situation with which you are familiar prevailed. I think we were counted out there. I would not put Alabama into the doubtful column for all this, and have very little hope of Georgia, except as industrial conditions there repeat those in North Carolina and Tennessee.

This letter is in no sense personal, though of course it isn't for publication. It may be used in any way you think it wise to use it, except publicly. With kindest personal regards and the season's best wishes, I am—

To Justice Louis Brandeis, January 12, 1929

Dear Justice Brandeis:

Thank you for your kindly note. You ask, "Shall we soon have another 'great rebellion'?" Probably not, I should say. We shall probably have a slow evolutionary adjustment of the blessings of prosperity, an evolutionary movement toward justice in which greed shall be overtaken; righteousness not in what you might call criminal action but in equity. I hope with all my heart that the Hoover administration will mean just this, for I see no other immediate hope. The people were not in a rebellious mood this year, but I think thousands of western progressives balked at Smith, first because he was going too fast; second because he zigzagged on the wrong side of traffic on prohibition; and third because he represented a strange, unfamiliar, and to many narrow minds, an abhorrent tendency in our national life. Partly it was religion that symbolized the distrust. But I think it was chiefly an instinctive feeling for the old rural order and old rural ways, the tremendous impact of a desire for the good opinion of the old lady next door. I think inevitably in this century we shall see another moral censor than she, new moral standards. But still the old order holds fast in spite of our urban and industrial development.

Mrs. White joins me in sincerest regards and kindliest wishes for you and yours during the coming year.

To Henry S. Canby, Book-of-the-Month Club, January 21, 1929

My Dear Canby:

A letter from Mr. Haas indicates that the Book-of-the-Month Committee has asked to have Walter Lippmann's book [*A Preface to*

Morals, which finally was selected by the Book-of-the-Month Club] held over for consideration next month. In view of the fact that we have picked "Cradle of the Deep" [by Joan Lowell], an obviously light and rather trivial book, it seems to me that we could well afford to take the Lippmann book. I think it is Lippmann's high tide. It is a serious book but beautifully written and simply written. There isn't a paragraph in it that the average intelligent American cannot understand and to me that is everything about a book. After all, books, when they sell in hundred thousand lots, should be aimed at the ten thousand and not at the five thousand crowd. We cannot deal much in caviar now. We are in the sauerkraut stratum.

Which brings up the subject of Ed Howe's book [*Plain People*]. I think that's a splendid book, a tale of America, a plain man's story with a Franklinesque philosophy, and interesting on every page. I wish you could think about it and consider it.

To WALTER LIPPMANN, New York *World*, January 21, 1929

DEAR WALTER:

Several times while I was in New York, I had your telephone calls, but I made a very short stay and was tied up pretty well before I got there. It wasn't important that I should see you, for I spent a day and a half coming home reading your new book in the proof for the Book-of-the-Month Club. It stands as your highwater mark, and I am glad that your best work is your latest work. I recommended it as the book of the month. I believe they agreed on another book this month, but are holding yours over for consideration next month, and I hope we will take it. I am writing the other judges to be particularly careful in reading it. It seems to me that it is one of the big important things done in America in recent years.

As I read it, I thought when I got home I would write you a letter telling you that I felt you should get out of the newspaper business if you could and lead the literary life, and now Ralph Hayes [New York banker and author] tells me that you have been made Editor-in-Chief of the World, and so I won't write my letter. I suppose it is better to be Editor-in-Chief of the World and so move the masses than it is to be a philosopher and appeal to the leadership of the country and the world. In your new book you do both because it is easy reading. I have never been able to read John Dewey. I have tried and tried and failed. I have no doubt he has something important to say, but I don't know what it is. I know what you are trying to say. Someone should print an interlinear edition of John Dewey, translated by Harold Bell Wright, or Eddie Guest.

But your sentences and paragraphs are as crystalline as Emerson. You have a great talent and your life is well before you. How proud Fay must be of you! I envy you the happiness of the coming years which I have seen myself in passing them.

Henry J. Haskell, publisher of the Kansas City Star, *was on intimate terms with the White family. The* Star *was the most powerful paper circulating in Kansas and was generally allied with White and Henry J. Allen in political affairs.*

To Henry J. Haskell, London, England, April 29, 1929

Dear Henry:

I thought a line might help. Things are going on splendidly. The Star looks healthy. Kansas politics are in the throes of naming a Federal Judge. Fred and Clyde and Henry and I seem to be for Hopkins [Fred Trigg of the *Star*; Governor Clyde Reed; Senator Henry J. Allen; and Richard J. Hopkins], and Capper [Senator Arthur Capper] is willing to go along, but the Attorney General and the President seem to balk. After all, I suppose they will have the last guess.

This is going to be a grand year for spirea and unless we have a frost it will be grand for strawberries and apples in these latitudes. The iris is coming along and looks healthy and it has been a great year for tulips. The tulips in Emporia have never been so lovely because of the long backward spring without heavy frosts.

I was in Washington at the editorial meeting and saw a lot of your friends who asked for you, from the other papers; also went to the White House. There is another atmosphere around there from the Coolidge atmosphere. It is the Roosevelt atmosphere stepped down through a vast transformance, but still Rooseveltian, muffled but quite as vigorous. At the table Hoover lets the conversation die. Roosevelt never did. But at the desk I fancy Hoover gets more done than Roosevelt. And both are going in the same direction. White House intimates are Vernon Kellogg and Henry [Vernon Kellogg, director of the National Research Council, and senator Henry J. Allen], different from Stearns [Frank W. Stearns of Boston, close friend of Calvin Coolidge] and the Massachusetts crowd.

I hope you will not hurry home.

White earnestly sought the appointment of Richard J. Hopkins to the federal bench in Kansas. Hopkins was backed by both Kansas senators, too, but President Hoover and Attorney General Mitchell had adopted the policy of appointing federal judges without considering political endorsements. White's contention, in this letter, was that that was an excellent ideal for machine-ridden states, but that in rural states it meant going to vested interests for the appointments. On May 6, White sent a three-page telegram to Hoover containing the same sentiments that are expressed in this letter. After months of pressure, White and his political friends succeeded in persuading Hoover to appoint Hopkins. Those opposed to Hopkins charged that he was a tool of the Anti-Saloon League. Hopkins's nomination was bitterly opposed in the Senate by a minority of senators.

To ATTORNEY GENERAL MITCHELL, Washington, D. C., May 4, 1929

DEAR MR. ATTORNEY GENERAL:

This letter is about the Kansas Judgeship, and I hope you will bear with me while I discuss the theory of appointing Federal Judges outside of politics. The theory looks like copybook perfection. But this Kansas case affords a perfect example of the fallacy of the hypothesis. What you are getting is something worse than political indorsements, and what you will get if you neglect entirely political indorsements, is the indorsements of interested litigants.

Let us take this Hopkins case as an example. I believe it seems to

[293]

have become a celebrated case. Someone who looked at the files said that there were six thousand indorsements for Lilleston [W. F. Lilleston, a corporation lawyer]. Lilleston represented, as of course you know, the interests which had gathered around the Pollock Court [John C. Pollock, United States district judge since 1903] in a regime where every legal safeguard was thrown around public service corporations until a scandal was created which might easily have resulted in a movement for impeachment, a scandal much more flagrant than that in New York. The Lilleston candidacy represented at the outset the perfect type of what you would get when you turn from politics to lawyers. The attorneys for interested litigants, the public ultiities companies, oil, gas, power, had money to spend, had connections all over the United States and filed this tremendous bulk of indorsements for this perfectly decent though practically unknown young man. I understand that Lilleston is not being considered, but you will pardon me if I discuss his case. It is so typical. His supporters divided themselves into two squads, the supporting squad and the squad attacking Hopkins. The attorneys for oil, natural gas, electricity, and the railroads were able to get not merely hundreds but thousands of letters for Lilleston from men who know nothing about him, and they were also able to get, which is more important, big men in the profession in Indiana, Ohio, and Illinois to take Hopkins's standing on the estimate of their colleagues, who are employed in Kansas by the great interstate public service corporations. They made an impression. It seemed as though there was one body of opinion among the distinguished lawyers of the Middle West that Hopkins was not a good attorney and that Lilleston was.

The plain fact is that neither of them is a particularly good lawyer. Neither is any man who is being considered by your office for this job, an outstanding lawyer; McDermott [George McDermott, former judge of the Kansas Industrial Court], whom you recommended for the circuit bench, was not an outstanding lawyer; merely a good average state capital corporation attorney, with a corporation training and corporation slant, but square and decent—certainly not a bad appointment. As for Lilleston, he has been in the firm that handles the Standard Oil business, is a clean, decent square fellow. But, if he had been made Federal Judge, he would have been beholden to exactly the same crowd that scandalized the Court under Pollock.

Now about Hopkins: He is what you call politically indorsed. He will get no great lawyers to front for him because he has been on the other side of public service lawsuits. As attorney general that was inevitable. But his previous practice had come as the result of his service as lieutenant governor in the old Bull Moose days, and naturally he got the other side of these public service lawsuits. And equally naturally he had honestly earned the gratitude and friendship of those who, as public officers and public men, were indignant at the wicked encroachment of the great public utility organizations. Governor Allen directed Hopkins in most of his fights. Before Allen, Capper and Hopkins were friends and political allies. Our Supreme Court is divided along the old line, the Progressive line. Justice Burch and Justice Dawson believe with all their hearts that Hopkins is a poor lawyer because he is a Progressive. The Chief Justice who has kept the Court a free Court, maintains that Hopkins is a good lawyer, and he is as country lawyers go, but no great shakes compared with the leaders of the Bar who, being leaders of the Bar, are able to command big salaries from rich and often predatory clients.

Take the case of Allen, Capper, the Star which has always supported Hopkins, and myself. If we did not know that Hopkins was a square man, that he gives these public service corporations a square deal, we would not be urging him. We have no desire to be unfair. But we do not want the Judge of our Court beholden to these great predatory interests for his appointment. And when you get outside of politics entirely to get indorsements, you are not leaving politics at all, but you are going into another kind of politics. And you will find in too many cases, and in this Kansas case almost exclusively, that by ignoring politics you are letting interested litigants name the Judge. And in any case you will find, where you depend finally upon legal endorsements, that source is tainted by the fact that our commercial life tends toward larger and larger units of capital which employ automatically all the good lawyers, or so nearly all, that the residue is negligible.

Every state has its own peculiar situation, but it resolves itself into something like the Kansas situation, where railroads, oil, gas, and the Hamiltonian conservatism that believes in the divine right of property to rule, are all on one side, and on the other side are the citizens struggling through the agency of politics to maintain some sort of righteous balance, and are endeavoring to hold something like an adequate control over their public service corporations. To hamper that control will mean state socialism. It is the only alternative, and I hate it and so do you. But, if the Courts are named by the lawyers of this country without the veto of politics, you will remove the one

[295]

check which the people have in their fight for justice, and they will turn to public ownership like a mad mob.

You should know something of the Kansas situation as it is distinguished from others. Kansas lies at the northern edge of the southwestern oil and gas pool. Pipe lines must cross our state, must serve our people with oil and gas, and must serve the people of other states further east, even into Ohio and Indiana and north to your own state. The status of pipe lines and interstate pipe line business is not defined. It must be defined rather by courts than by legislatures and congresses. It is too delicate and intricate a situation for more than the broadest legislative guidance; hence the terrific struggle to control this court; hence the six thousand indorsements of Lilleston; and hence men knocking on your doors to tell you about Hopkins, who live five hundred miles from Hopkins, and whose Kansas clients, being used to the Pollock regime, fear him and fear him unfairly, fear him only because they want a man who sees their clients' rights with an eye-single to theirs. More than this, Kansas is in the trough between the Missouri River rate and the Rocky Mountain rate. We are doomed by our position under the long and short haul clause, which I am inclined to believe is fair at that, to be an agricultural state. Probably Kansas, Nebraska, and the Dakotas which lie in this trough are the most purely agricultural states in the Union. In this trough, if you include Iowa, the incipient agricultural unrest of the last fifty years has been started. In the Greenback days, in the Granger days, in the Populist days, this trough, a sort of slough of economic despond, has bred political mosquitoes that have stung and poisoned American business and politics at fairly regular intervals every twenty years. The culmination of the whole agricultural problem piles up here between the Missouri River and the Rocky Mountains. And Kansas is peculiarly agricultural in its economic status.

President Hoover's farm plan is bound to be finally challenged in the Courts. It may be challenged in the Courts of Kansas, probably will be. There again it is necessary to have a free man on the bench, not a radical. Hopkins is no more radical than I am despite what the railroad attorneys may say, though I believe they think I am a wool-dyed Bolshevist. But Hopkins will not face the agricultural problem, when it enters his Court, with suspicion and distrust. In the balance between Hamiltonian conservatism and Jeffersonian democracy, I should say that Hopkins was more Jeffersonian, but not a Jacksonian rabble-rouser. He has stood for prohibition as an economic rather than as a moral issue. He has an open mind and a clear head, and it seems to me, if the Kansas City Star could support him through more than a dozen primaries and elections, and if Senator Allen and Senator Capper, both square conservative men, are backing him, and if in addition to that you have the President of the State Bar Association and his predecessor in office, the Attorney General, the Chief Justice, and the County Bar Association in every county in which he has practiced, and nearly half the District Judges, and more than half of the prosecuting attorneys testifying to his legal qualifications, you need have no fear that he does not measure up to any man whose candidacy is before you. As for a compromise, the winner of a successful compromise will have before his eyes this significant fact: that with all the political support a man can have, two senators, his party organization, and a host of witnesses to his legal qualifications, the compromise was effected by the sinister influence of aggrandized capital seeking more than it should have in our Courts. And this will be true in many states.

I quite agree with you that you should go outside of politics to investigate your men. But I don't believe that you can follow the leaders of the Bar in America as the Bar is now organized; particularly when they are so unanimously lined up for one man and against another as they are in this case. Go to the Bar surely, but beware of the high salaried leaders who have interested litigants. Be sure that you make a fair and intelligent balance between political influence and legal testimony.

My excuse for writing this letter is that I have been in practical politics for more than forty years. I sat in a convention before I could vote. I have been accused of being a boss in this state. Patronage does not interest me. Allen and Capper will tell you that while they were governors I never asked either a patronage favor, though I had some influence at the time. I should never ask Hopkins for a favor. But this thing is more than patronage, deeper than patronage. It goes into the foundations of our present commercial organization, and while I am writing this I suppose primarily for the Hopkins case, I am also coming to you because I want to discuss the whole matter of ignoring politics in naming Federal Judges. Sometimes you must ignore politics; sometimes you must not. But I should say when you have two senators who have never established or tolerated a machine as governors, who owe to no machine their place as senators, and who bring you adequate testimony of the legal qualifications of their candidate, it would be a sad mistake to enforce against them a rule that you would enforce in a machine-ridden state like Pennsylvania or New York, where patronage is the nest for corruption as it never has been in Kansas. We have never had a major patronage scandal. Money is negligible in our primaries. I know this because I have won in the primaries seven times out of nine in the last twenty years and have never spent money.* Your aspiration is commendable to take your Judges out of the patronage machine. But it should be wisely applied, or it will pack your Courts with men of the plutocratic cast of mind.

And now in closing, let me beg your pardon for this long letter. My intense desire for justice in this case is my only excuse.

The campaign of 1930 in Nebraska found George W. Norris running for re-election to the Senate as an independent. He was vigorously opposed by the overwhelming majority of the papers of the state. White wrote editorials in his favor, and then sent bundles of Gazettes *into Nebraska to aid in Norris's re-election. The Republican organization did its best to defeat Norris since he had bolted the party to support Al Smith in 1928.*

To George W. Norris, November 2, 1929

Dear Senator Norris:

Enclosed find three exhibits: A—the editorial from the Gazette which I promised; B—an editorial from the Kansas City Star, better than mine; C—a letter from someone who seems to be an old acquaintance of yours, when you were both young, and he may have been handsome.

I wish you would feel free to come to me at any time during the coming campaign to help you. If there is any phase of your candidacy, in which you would like to have any particular thing said coming from a Republican neighbor on the south, please be candid with me and tell me what you want and let me do it. And remember this: that while I am in a general way Republican, I bolted my ticket as a candidate in 1924 and, as you know, went out with Roosevelt after

* This statement is ambiguous, since the primary campaigns that White had run did cost money.

I had been elected Republican national committeeman, chucked that job, became Bull Moose national committeeman, and stayed on the reservation until 1916, and wrote nothing for Harding in 1920.* So I am not particularly regular and have much sympathy with your attitude.

Nothing pleased me more last year than the publication of my letter expressing faith in you after you had bolted Hoover. I didn't agree with you in bolting Hoover, but I did respect your courage and your conscience, and I was immensely pleased that my testimony for you got into the campaign. Not that I wanted it to help Smith, but that I wanted it to help you. If the Democrats had only known that they were not embarrassing me in the slightest by publishing that letter, but delighting me, they might have taken another attitude. I don't know.

Anyway, I am for you and I want to serve you, and you **can** tell me best how and when and where.

White had excellent insight into President Hoover's inability to stir people and lead them in times of stress. The grim depression days required a leader who could appeal to the mass, but President Hoover failed in this undertaking. The following letter was to a former Emporian who was now a White House intimate.

To David Hinshaw, December 3, 1929

DEAR DAVE:

. . . The President has great capacity to convince intellectuals. He has small capacity to stir people emotionally, and through the emotions one gets to the will, not through the intellect. He can plow the ground, harrow it, plant the seed, cultivate it, but seems to lack the power to harvest it and flail it into a political merchantable product.

* After the Harding era, White frequently told his liberal friends that he had not written any editorials for Harding. Actually he wrote a number.

Probably he would fail terribly if he tried to do the other thing. He must be what he is. What he is is important and necessary, but I don't think he can sublet the job of emotional appeal. People going around talking to luncheon clubs don't get very far. Public sentiment isn't made that way. The intellectual appeal finally will win. It is a slower process, but probably surer. . . .

American troops occupied the island of Haiti in 1915. In 1930, President Hoover appointed a commission to investigate American occupation of the Negro republic. White was a member, and in its final report the commission recommended the termination of American occupation. White was assured by a source close to the White House that he had been included on the commission "as a guarantee to the public that the investigation wouldn't be a whitewashing affair." Other members of the commission were James Kerney, W. Cameron Forbes, Henry P. Fletcher, and Elie Vezina.

To Thomas Butcher, Emporia, Kan., February 12, 1930

Dear Tom:

Thank you for your nice note about the Haitian thing. I am terribly scared about this job. The only thing I can contribute to the Commission is a virgin mind. If the President realized how little I knew, he would take me off the Commission. The Haitian problem, as I see it, is just one phase of the problem of the tropics. Vast riches needed for the sustenance of the temperate zones, riches in vitamins, carbohydrates, and minerals, all tightly locked away from their usefulness in jungles, marshes, and the wilderness, requiring capital to unlock them; capital that only may use its key to unlock this wealth in the hands of a stable, intelligent government; and alas, a population reared in the tropics, de-energized in the tropics, with no need to develop the habits of thrift and industry and foresight, which would produce their own capital and without tradition, need or desire for a stable, intelligent government. That is the problem as I see it of all

[300]

the tropics. And the question for the white man is: shall he develop the tropics quickly by force or wait another hundred years while he educates and inspires the tropical peoples into some sort of capacity and aspiration for the kind of government necessary for unlocking the treasure of the tropics?

This is a mere hypothesis. Heaven knows, my knowledge of the facts is a blank, and I am willing to admit when any strong man looks me in the eye and begins quoting facts my hypothesis is blowed.

Hoping this will find you the same, I am—

When this letter was written, White was waiting to meet with the rest of President Hoover's commissioners. Shortly after this was written, the commission sailed for Haiti.

Palm Beach, Fla., To SALLIE LINDSAY WHITE, February 22, 1930

. . . Here I am all landed and the first thing I am doing is to write to you. It seems ages since I left you on the platform. I never seemed so lonely in my life. . . . The Frisco railroad people met me at the train and escorted me in state and style to their train where they took my picture. They had reporters meet me at Memphis and Birmingham. I read all the way down and have got a lot of information about Haiti. The problem is not as simple as it seems. But it looks as though the first thing to do is to get a civilian governor, and the second thing to do is to get someone to help us let go of the bear's tail—say Brazil or Chile—and to organize a Pan-American wrecking crew for this sort of service. . . . This is a nice decent little 3rd class hotel, for which I am paying $10 for a room next to the elevator. The minimum at the other places is $25! But this is better than I was raised to! I had a nice dinner in lone and solemn state—cold consommé, pompano, broccoli and a baked apple. $3.15! I shudder to think what food is at the other places. I had a long letter from Josephus Daniels who as secretary of the navy put the marines here. He passes the buck to the State Department—which was Bryan and later Lansing. But the whole business is a mess and probably he is right that the State Department is most to blame, for the Wall Street connnection is *through* the State Department . . . anyway out of it all we may light a

lamp of experience to *guide* our feet in the future and may begin to
formulate a new policy and so bid good-bye to dollar diplomacy! ...
Palm Beach is just a great big stinking bawdy house of the rich and
the pretended rich; all sham which should be shame! It has neither
beauty nor distinction and what's more it rained so hard this afternoon that it soaked through my trunk. ... It's no place for us honest
men, and so mostly I think they avoid it. ...

Port-au-Prince, to WILLIAM L. WHITE, Emporia, Kan.,
March 3, 1930

DEAR BILL:

Of all the places I have ever been this is the most curious and interesting, and in some ways this is the most important thing I have had
to do. ...

I saw a curious thing at the Governor's reception the other night—
a man about forty or fifty, a dark, swarthy mulatto suddenly flashed
across my face the living spitting image of Charlie Curtis as he was
thirty years ago. I never saw such a remarkable resemblance; the way
he held his head, his physical mannerisms, his bodily form, his eyes,
his mustache, his cheekbones, which we think in Curtis are North
American Indian—all are just as marked in this man. ... I noticed even
his complexion is like that of Curtis. Somewhere back in the sixteenth
or seventeenth century, maybe the early eighteenth, when Louis
Papin, Curtis's grandfather left France, he probably left a brother,
or a cousin, or a grandfather and the old grandfather had more breeding vigor than a white-faced bull because there it is—the French of
Curtis and the French of this man breeding through two races true to
form in this generation. ...

I have been with them [the ruling elite] a good deal, in their homes,
at their clubs, and the other night I went to a country club dance. ...
I never saw such manners in my life; three kinds of wines on the
buffet side table and nobody taking more than a few tablespoonful
occasionally in a little glass. I had the devil's own time because we
commissioners are officially on the waterwagon, we drink nothing—
at least all abstain publicly and so far as I know privately except
purely ceremonial champagne—and I had to explain to these people
why we do not drink wine being officials of a dry government. Of
course I do not smoke and, of course, I do not dance, and I had to

[302]

convince them that I was an ungodly liar, and I fear I left them with the suspicion that my other vice was wife-beating. But they were too subtle and sophisticated to show their disapproval, if they had it. But they must have thought I was a strange bird. . . .

The whole population feels that its liberties have been trampled down. They honestly feel that we are tyrannical, and the fact that the occupation is honestly trying to serve the Haitians does not get to them, because we are not serving them in the Haitian way. However, we are trying to serve them after the manner of American civilization and American ideas, which they loathe. We are in the 20th century looking toward the 21st. They are in the 18th century—with the ideals of the Grand Louis always behind them as models. We are pointing the way for them to enter the modern world. They love the old regime.

Write me the news of city politics. . . .

Hoover's Haitian Commission found an impossible situation when they reached the republic. American marines were keeping a president in power who had little support from the vocal leaders of Haiti. The commission forced the incumbent's resignation and set up the machinery to allow a president to take office who had the support of the Haitian opposition to American occupation of the island.

In HAITIAN WATERS, To SALLIE LINDSAY WHITE, March 16, 1930

. . . Of all the funny things I have ever done, the funniest is signified by the words above "in Haitian waters"! For on it hangs a tale of five elderly gentlemen commandeering a first-class cruiser of the United States all armed and manned and deliberately sailing out of port with her entirely without orders from either the State or the Navy Department, and heading for home. It is the undiplomatic climax of two weeks of undiplomatic negotiations which include the setting up of a president of Haiti without warrant of law and providing for a government without sanction of constitution. Here is the story: Thursday it became clear that if we called our election for the new permanent president before January, 1932, we should have to have a decision from the State Department at Washington declaring that the department would not object to it on constitutional grounds. For days we wrangled by wireless and finally got clearance. But probably grudgingly. Someone's technical views in Washington seem to have been overruled. And the message we had from Washington began to develop uneasiness: a lack of belief that our plan would work, an evident feeling that we were taking a lot of things for granted that we could never put through. We were told to get everything in writing. We were instructed as to details which rightly should have been left to our judgment—at least considering that Forbes [W. Cameron Forbes, governor of the Philippines from 1909 to 1913] was chairman who had 30 years' experience in colonial affairs and Fletcher [Henry P. Fletcher, undersecretary of state from 1921 to 1922] was with him who had been 27 years in the services of the State Department and ended his career as assistant secretary of state. So carefully and painfully meticulous was the department in our instructions that I got the laugh of the day by saying: "Gentlemen, from the tone of these dispatches lately I should say that the young men there feel that control of this commission has passed entirely out of the hands of Forbes and Fletcher into the hands of White!"

We began to say Friday that we were leaving Saturday night and inference desired orders. In the meantime the captain of the ship began to ask for orders to go to Guantánamo for coal. He got no reply. We got in reply more insistence on care, and a desire to have all documents submitted upon which we based our settlement. Nothing was left to our judgment. We then wired that documents would follow in a few hours as soon as they could be coded—a long process—and said we would proceed on the ship to Guantánamo—a day voyage— while the documents were going through the code and would start at ten Sunday morning with the department's permission and return from Guantánamo, if the documents submitted were in any way deficient in the department's opinion. The reply came: "Documents not here, too late to read them before ten o'clock Sunday." In the meantime we had made our farewell calls on the old Haitian President and had conferred with the new one, bade farewell to the press, and our allies of the opposition, and if we stayed in the bay of Port-au-Prince it would mean just one thing—the desertion of Washington. And the fat would be in the fire. In the meantime the orders had not come from the Navy Department! And of course the marines and the Navy Department have charge of this Haitian show. We filed the documents at 9:30 Saturday night. At ten o'clock Sunday morning not a word from the State Department. Not a word from the Navy Department.

No orders—nothing. The captain of the *Rochester* was somewhat under our control. We knew the shore was watching. The Haitians had asked us Saturday to allow them to "demonstrate" for us—a big parade with bands and banners and flowers and speeches—Sunday morning before sailing, but I, to whom this came, said no; that we were going to the ship Saturday night and would sail Sunday morning at ten. So at ten we had to go. And we sat in the cabin five old grayheads waiting for the clock. At ten we sent a wireless to the State Department saying that we would be cruising Haitian waters during the day and night in the direction of Guantánamo, and asking for further orders. So here we are five old men in charge of a battleship sailing down the Spanish Main at sunset. . . .

White's major role on the commission was to win the confidence of the Haitian opposition, which at the beginning was hostile to the commission's presence. As a first step in winning confidence, White persuaded the military not to ban a procession that was to protest American occupation. The details in this letter to one of his ex-reporters explains how from the time of the parade the opposition co-operated with the commission. When this letter was written, White had returned to Emporia.

To CHARLES M. VERNON, Pacific States Saving & Loan Co.,
Los Angeles, Calif., April 2, 1930

DEAR CHARLES:

It was indeed a terrible shock to see your signature on the letterhead of a financial institution. Little did I think when I wrapped the comforter about your neck and kissed you and sent you out into the wide world to earn your fortune by the sweat of your fingers that you would go trailing off under the bushes into the primrose path and become a banker. But it's all right with me. I suppose you are doing publicity and not handling any of the dirty money so that I shall never have to take your meals to you in jail. Sit down and write me the whole story of your sin and downfall.

Now about the dusky damsel who got mixed up with me in the newspaper report. It happened this way: I was caught quite acci-

[305]

dentally in front of my hotel trying to duck in and avoid a procession which was being held somewhat because I intervened to lift the ban on it. And I stood for a moment curiously viewing the parade which was just heading by. It was a woman's parade and as you know they are all colored people in Haiti; absolutely no white voting population. The elite of Haiti were heading the parade which means mulatto, octoroons, quadroons, and other multiple roons into the sixty fourths and ninety sixths, but all frankly calling themselves Negroes, though some of them were blonder than you and a few had light straight hair with blue eyes. They were—if I must say it—good looking and in many cases most beautiful women. This church parade was a woman's parade and started in the swell neighborhood of the town at the aristocratic Catholic church. Suddenly from out of the line, or out of the sidewalk, or out of the crowd, I never knew which, appeared a gaunt, wrinkled, poor old peasant woman in a blue cotton dress. She ran toward me and either fell, or kneeled, or prostrated herself, Heaven knows which, it was so quickly done, before me. The parade stopped and began to jam and form a crowd around her. The fashionably dressed leaders began to glare at the old woman. I reached down and helped her up with both hands. She thrust toward me as she rose a little homemade Haitian flag made of two pieces of paper pasted together. She said something to me in either French or Creole or Patois, which I couldn't understand and which I knew I must not assent to for that reason, being there more or less in an official capacity. But I smiled my prettiest smile and shook my head, and then she ran back into the crowd toward where the line should be and was glared at more or less by the well-dressed women. She stood for a second or two trembling and frightened, and to reassure her and to reassure the crowd that I was in no way embarrassed by the incident, I waved at the crowd touching the tips of my fingers to my lips in as affectionate a gesture as I could make and conciliatory withal. For as much as two or three seconds the crowd stood dumb in amazement that any white man from America, and that white man with ambassadorial rank who had just taken a salute with nineteen guns, would do such a thing. Then a roar of applause broke out and the reporters knew that an incident had happened. They didn't see it, being well back of me, but they saw me stoop over to the old lady, and thought I had kissed her hand. They said so. The A.P. a day or two later asked me if I wanted a correction when the boys found exactly what had happened. I said no, for the story was essentially correct. If I had thought of it I might have kissed her hand to assure the crowd that the incident so far as

I was concerned was not untoward. The U.P. reporter was not there. He heard the truth several days later and sent the other story, and that's how the two myths got to going. I am willing to stand on either, or if necessary both, that I kissed the old lady's hand and that I threw kisses at the crowd. God knows I am not proud nor race conscious, and something had to be done to restore good feeling. After that it was pie for the Commission. We could do anything we wanted to with the Haitian opposition which had been teetering on the brink of revolution and bloodshed until that hour, having somewhat lost faith in all Americans.

As I said at the beginning, I wasn't much use on the Commission except as a contact with the ruling classes among the Haitian people, who were of course all colored in various hues. The language and usages of diplomacy were all strange to me. I couldn't function in that medium. I have been an agitator all my life whose business it has been to make himself plain and convincing and not to construct compromising and inoffensive formula. So I suppose I was more or less a fifth wheel there except as herein before noted.

Pardon this long letter and believe me always—

White cast himself in the role of interpreter for the American middle class. Literally thousands of people that he had never met wrote to him asking his views on a wide variety of subjects. During the troubled days of the depression, this flow of letters increased immeasurably.

To CHARLES E. MORGAN, New York City, November 26, 1930

DEAR MR. MORGAN:

...If my own view of my political philosophy is correct—and it may not be—I suppose I have two or three strong political convictions: first, a thorough distrust of the proletariat when it is organized on its own exclusive basis; second, a thorough distrust of the plutocracy when it is organized or when it tries to influence the political activities of the middle class. I distrust the proletariat because it is ignorant and selfish, and the plutocracy because it is cunning and greedy. As a corollary of those beliefs, I feel, and I use the word feel advisedly, without much logic to back it, that given time for discussion and for facts to work their way, the middle class will be able to protect the proletariat from destruction through its own ignorance and the plutocracy from destroying society through plutocratic greed. It seems to me that the rise in economic standards and social status which we have seen in the last twenty years warrants us in believing that through that change of environment which comes from enlarging income, large sections of the proletariat may be assimilated, even merged into the middle class losing through generations of education and environment much of their ignorance. . . .

To J. GARDNER COWLES, Des Moines *Register-Tribune*,
December 5, 1930

DEAR MR. COWLES:

It falls to my lot to get up the January Bulletin of the American Society of Newspaper Editors, as a member of the Board of Directors. I have been thinking that perhaps it might help if we could let the Bulletin discuss for one issue some of the dangers and temptations that beset our job. We have fairly well eliminated direct corruption in American newspapers; that is to say, government subsidy, venal sale of views or news, the control of policies by a too raw connivance with the advertising department. Of course, a few papers do these things, but they are the black sheep of the profession and are well marked and known. But we are developing unconsciously other faults.

Rich owners are too much inclined to forget that ours is a profession and not an industry. Their previous ethical standards were founded on buying and selling material things and not upon dealing with the unsubstantial but highly valuable good name of a newspaper which is rather to be chosen than great riches. Also with the coming of the demagogue into public life, we, as editors, are too much inclined to play him up as news, forgetting the devastating influences of the power which we give him by publicity. Again I think we are inclined too much to invade individual privacy for the sheer purpose of circulation, and are liable to breed a venality in our sensationalism which is little less wicked than the venality of editors in the seventies and eighties who sold their policies for cash. To build up circulation at the expense of good taste and public policy is as bad as to put money in our purse through the more direct method.

Well, anyhow, along these very lines I have been discussing, I wish you could write me something from the angle of a man who controls the newspaper situation in his town. The Emporia Gazette, for instance, dominates a little town like Emporia just as your papers have a sort of spiritual lordship over Des Moines, yet you and I both know that we have terrific competition. Every monopolist has his competitors if he is smart enough to know it, in the ruthless sense of justice that inheres in his patrons, the public. If a man goes wrong, they know it. If he gets rotten at the core, they feel it! And one way or another his monopoly is a chain of sand unless it is strengthened by his own moral purpose. I wish you would say something of that kind. It is a problem of our modern journalism, which is more and more controlled by absentee owners, that is to say, owners who come into the business from banks and bond houses and are not trained in the ethics of the profession. I wish you would write something which might be called the confessions of the monopolist, or something of a similar type, indicating the powers and the tremendous responsibility and the inevitable failure under certain circumstances that must come to the man in the newspaper business who does not play the game like a fighting gentleman. I know all of the boys will be glad to read it, and I should be personally deeply obliged. I would like the copy in about Christmastime. Make it long or short, anything from 200 words to 1,000 or 1,500, if you get to going good.

If you have any suggestions about whom else I might get to handle some of the topics touched upon above, I should be pleased to have your suggestions. . . .

When Wisconsin put a statue of the late Senator Robert M. LaFollette in the National Hall of Fame, White editorialized in the Gazette, *April 26, 1939: "LaFollette was great as a practical law giver—a man who crystallized noble ideals into reality, a statesman who clinched like a wrestler at the neck of wrong, and downed it. He fought without surrender, without mercy, without compromise—a warrior for the justice of God. A great man was 'Fighting Bob.' " When this letter was written, W. L. White was in the Kansas legislature fighting for an income tax bill.*

To Mrs. Robert LaFollette, Madison, Wis., December 26, 1930

Dear Mrs. LaFollette:

I was writing to your son Philip a moment ago and found myself thinking of you and of him whom we all affectionately know as old Bob. God bless him. I was asking your son to come to Kansas on Lincoln's birthday to put enthusiasm into a group of young men whom my boy Bill is associated with; youths in their twenties, thirties, and early forties who are where we were a generation ago. Our generation made a bad fist of it. Through no fault of your husband and in spite of his warnings, we compromised too much. The half loaf attracted us. I hope that the younger generation will know better. I have tried to teach my boy this out of my own experience. I wonder if we can transmit our spiritual experiences from generation to generation or does this generation have to acquire its own spiritual qualities, its own courage, its own faith, its own technique of attack and defense. I don't know.

But I hope you will pardon this sentimental letter of a sedentary old gentleman looking back on the past. If by any chance your son Philip talks over the Kansas adventure with you, I trust you will advise him to accept my son's invitation. He is in the Legislature leading the fight for an income tax. He voted for Senator LaFollette in 1924, his first presidential ballot, and was proud of it then and has flaunted it in pride ever since.

With the season's warmest good wishes, I am—

The increasing deterioration of the economic structure and President Hoover's lack of action, prompted the following letters:

[310]

To M. F. AMRINE, Lansing, Kan., February 4, 1931

DEAR MILT:

Here is Henry's [Senator Henry J. Allen] letter. What Henry overlooks is that from forty to sixty per cent of the power of the presidential office is not in administration but in morals, political and spiritual leadership, quite apart from party responsibility. He is, after all, President of the Nation and a servant of God as well as head of the Republican party, and as President of the Nation and servant of God, he has much more to do than to run a desk as a head of the greatest corporation of the world. He has to guide a people in the greatest adventure ever undertaken on the planet. For without leaders the people grow blind and without vision the people perish.

I am not saying this in public because I know Hoover is Hoover, but nevertheless I don't think his friends should fan him and sing to him on a flowery bed of ease made by his temperament. The bed should be made just as thorny and the racket just as unbearable as possible to get the most possible leadership out of him in this crisis. But I haven't the heart to crash in and yell bloody murder. I'll let somebody else do it.

Hoping this will find you the same, I am—

To VERNON KELLOGG, National Research Council,
Washington, D. C., April 4, 1931

DEAR VERNON:

I think Hoover is in a little better condition than he was six months ago, and I think if he can keep Congress out of Washington, he will be better still. Congress and he are temperamentally subject to chronic maladjustments, and I still think, as I wrote Charlotte [Mrs. Vernon L. Kellogg], that the major blunder of his administration has been his incapacity to forget the mean things the progressives said about him and what Norris did to him in '28* and meet them on friendly terms, jolly them along, get their affection, for they are on the whole an emotional crowd and through their affections blunt the edge of their opposition. This was the sort of thing that Wilson could not do but Roosevelt could. Politics after all is one of the minor branches of harlotry, and Hoover's frigid desire to live a virtuous life and not

* George W. Norris supported Al Smith in 1928.

[311]

follow the Pauline maxim and be all things to all men, is one of the things that has reduced the oil in his machinery and shot a bearing. . . .

To BURTON BRALEY, June 5, 1931

DEAR MR. BRALEY:

You bet I'll read your book [*Shoestring*]. I see by the blurb that your heroine goes out west and falls in love with a mining engineer. She took an awful chance. America did that not long ago and now look at her.

Hoping this will find you the same, I am, my dear Braley, proud indeed to subscribe myself—

The great problem of how to achieve security without a resulting loss of freedom weighed heavily on White's mind as the unemployment rolls increased in numbers and a wave of foreclosures and bankruptcies swept the farmers and small businessmen. In this letter, he refers to what is needed to achieve security, but at the same time to retain freedom, as capitalistic socialism. During the days of the New Deal he was to call it benevolent capitalism.

Estes Park, Colo., to CHESTER ROWELL, San Francisco *Chronicle*, July 14, 1931

DEAR CHESTER ROWELL:

It was kind of you to send me your dissertation on what might be called capitalistic socialism, which I read with great interest. It seems to me to have struck a good lead. I have been wishing for some time that the President would find it in his heart to evangelize a little upon the duties of the great industrial leaders and teach them that duties go with rights. It seems to me that so long as our form of government throws such tremendous safeguards around the invested dollar, the privileges of safety call for certain duties; notably to secure by custom and practice for the man who works, the same right to his investment in his craft as the dollar has for its investment in business.

I believe this century will see the struggle for a new equality among men; at least in what is broadly known as Christendom. We have secured for humanity religious equality founded upon the open Bible and freedom of thought and political equality through the ballot, and educational equality through the public schools. Each of these rights, which are really equalities, has come after a definite struggle. Now we are up against the struggle for economic equality, and the clash is coming quickly; in terms of decades rather than of centuries between the communists who will guarantee economic equality to all without individual liberties, on the one hand, and, on the other hand, capitalism which must give the individual a certain minimum of economic equality if he is ready and willing to work, and at the same time give him liberty to rise above the minimum by whatever qualities of industry, energy, talent or genius he may possess.

The minimum which our capitalistic organization should somehow guarantee to the capable and willing worker, in good times and bad, should be decent food, housing, clothing, and the educating of his children not merely until they are fourteen or sixteen, but until they are twenty-one. Also this minimum standard should provide for security against poverty and old age. This economic equality, it seems to me, should not come through government, not through the dole, not through politics in any way, as a right sometimes becomes a potential menace after it is politically guaranteed. But rather this economic equality should come through the organization of industry or commerce, the thing you seem to feel is socialized capitalism.

Now after we do secure, through organized industry, this minimum standard for the capable and willing worker, we have then changed the economic motive from fear to hope—hope for better things. I think this new equality will form a security which will remake human psychology. Every time we have changed man's attitude toward his environment, we have made a new man, and this economic equality plus religious, political, educational and social equality, all of which we have fairly well secured, will regenerate man by broadening his self-respect, which, as I see it, is the only way through which the Kingdom can come on this sad old earth.

[313]

Now I have not set all this down merely to air my views, but to ask you in all sincerity why we cannot get the President to stand for some such program; to stand not as a political leader, but as the leader of an industrial nation, the mouthpiece of the new capitalism which shall guarantee, along with the new equality, every individual's liberty to rise? Surely he has enough progressive friends to warrant trying this. The greedy forces of the privileged dollar have no hesitancy in going to the White House with their demands. Could not a group be formed of industrial leaders, college men and earnest souls like you and me, to present some such a program to the White House, not for its political adoption, but for the purpose of evangelization?

It seems to me the situation between the Caspian Sea and Honolulu is sufficiently critical—even acute, so that from the forum of the White House such a clarion call as I have indicated is needed. The President has stood bravely and effectively for the privileges of the invested dollar. Now is the time for him to stand also for the duties of the invested dollar. . . . Why can't a half a dozen of us quietly call on him, ask him for an evening and talk this whole thing out and urge him to front for it? I have no desire to be known in the matter, but I feel that unless a definite hope is held out to the average wage worker in this country, he is liable to listen to the siren call of the communist who will promise him security without liberty. I feel we are living in a dangerous age.

I hope this finds you well and happy. For three or four months I have been out of the fight. I worked too hard last winter on a local unemployment problem, worried too much, and the doctor ordered me out like Nebuchadnezzar to eat grass, and here I am up in Estes Park thinking up trouble for our good friend in the White House. I expect to go all the way with him in the convention and in the election, realizing that his many weaknesses as a popular leader with Congress hamper his hand, but proud that he has done so many noble things as an executive and as a leader in international matters. When you have nothing to do dictate a page or two and send it in. I am greatly interested in your reaction to this problem.

White realized that it would take colorful leadership to stir America out of its economic impasse. In this letter, he urged David Hinshaw, a presidential adviser, to persuade President Hoover to head a national emergency relief corporation.

DEAR DAVID:

Here is what I was trying to tell you about the emergency relief problem that last day. I was so inarticulate that perhaps I didn't make myself clear.

It seems to me that as things stand there is no normal economic solution of the present acute emergency in American industry. Hundreds of thousands of men, women and children are going to suffer terribly this winter in spite of all that the natural laws of economic change can do, however soon it may start, however rapidly it may move. Yet the situation is not hopeless, for if we can re-create the dynamic altruism outside of government which moved us during the war, we can harness forces that will bring relief and make us a better and nobler people. We are faced with two evils, a glut and low prices for agricultural products particularly wheat in the West, and secondly, starving workers who cannot get at the food in the bins. My thought was to organize a national emergency relief corporation with a capital made up of organized subscriptions of as many millions as it will take to buy enough of the farm board's wheat to feed these hungry people; not merely wheat but other foods such as potatoes, fruits, and any food products whose prices are sagging in any locality. Prunes, for instance, in California, vegetables in the Imperial Valley or in the Gulf states. This food having been bought by the national corporation above mentioned may then be passed on and paid for by state organizations and in turn distributed by county or city organizations, not as a gift or as charity, but in return for work performed by the unemployed on projects outlined, supervised and designated by the cities and counties; road work, public improvements, park work, bridges, any of a score of different kinds of public work. I believe that if the President himself would lay other things aside for a few months and head this national corporation, he could arouse the public conscience and awaken the latent altruism of the American people so that any amount of money asked for by this emergency corporation would be subscribed, as we raised the Liberty Loan, Red Cross and Y drive funds during the war. Here is something the President could do to dramatize himself in his own peculiar field of effectiveness, using his lifelong training altogether outside of politics. His presence in the fight to save the self-respect of the American workman and keep him from the shame of charity and the dole would encourage the millers to mill the wheat and the bakers to bake the flour at

[315]

cost if not absolutely free. Moreover, I believe the packers and the cattle industry would contribute meat either at cost or gratuitously to such an endeavor and the value to the movement to awaken idealism and sustained individualism would be a baptism of fiery faith which would harden this nation to greater strength in future years. . . .

President Hoover created in August, 1931, the President's Organization of Unemployment Relief. White and William Green were two members of this commission. Throughout the Hoover administration, although numerous commissions were appointed to deal with the problems arising from the depression, very little actually was done in a positive manner to check unemployment or to prevent the recurrence of abuses in the economic structure.

Estes Park, Colo., to WILLIAM GREEN, American Federation of
Labor, September 1, 1931

DEAR MR. GREEN:

Yours of August 28th is before me. . . .

Now about the relief situation. As I said, I am anxious to work with you. There must be ten or a dozen men out of the sixty who feel as you and I do that the need is not for charity but for employment. I wish I knew who they were; perhaps you know better than I. If you have a hunch about it, will you look over the list, which I have not before me here in the hills, and give me your judgment if I can serve you in any way. It seems to me that our relief program should be divided into industries rather than into states. Most of the industries are merged, amalgamated, or closely associated and by making appropriations from surpluses accumulated or from dividend funds, each industry could arrange this fall, winter, and spring for enough jobs—odds and ends cleaning up, betterments, maintenance, and the like—to keep at least the skilled worker in the industry away from want. And here's another thing that I feel strongly. By organizing relief through industries rather than through states and regions, a better knowledge of the actual conditions and needs of the men will be available than if relief is offered outside of industries. For instance, from weathered experiences in my little town at home, I have learned that there are two distinct classes of men in want. One class is the unskilled class: those on the lower fringe of unskilled labor whose improvidence has kept more or less in the bread line or near it, even in the best times. These men in the winter, chronically or at least occasionally, make no bones about asking for charity and accept it with no wound to their pride or self-respect which, alas, must have been cauterized early in life. The other class is composed of the skilled labor: men in the building trades, railroads, and in the major industries. These men have never accepted charity, and I don't blame them if they would steal before they would beg, and rob before they would steal. They should not be asked to accept charity under any circumstances. If they need help, and if finally in the crises of cold and hunger, work is not available, then some arrangements should be made so that they may borrow on their personal notes the money they need to ward off want.

Which brings me back to my first proposition. We should organize by industries, because in the industries the two types of men will be fairly well known and loans could be made intelligently. If, for instance, the rich investors in railroads could cooperate with the railroad union, and the rich investors in textiles could cooperate with the textile union and the rich investors in mining could cooperate with the mining unions to see that the unemployed in each of these industries who had maintained their self-respect might not lose it, but borrow without interest or at one or two per cent, if they could save their self-respect, then as I say, the jobs could be done through the industries rather than through the states or regions vastly more effectively and vastly more intelligently and with a more sympathetic understanding of the problem.

Your voice will carry far. If you feel as I do, I wish sometime or some way you could talk the matter over with . . . the President, and see if this kind of an organization could not be worked out to save the self-respect of men, which is for the perpetuity of this government just as important as to save their bodies from hunger and want.

Count on me to join in any way, publicly or privately, in this endeavor which seems to me the major goal of this whole relief movement. It is the only way to keep down barricades in the streets this winter and the use of force which will brutalize labor and impregnate it with revolution in America for a generation. I am deeply afraid of the coming six months.

Dear Mr. Daniels:

... We are going through strange and awful times and I fear worse ahead. Our business here has slumped twenty per cent but we are teetering along in the high water up to our chin, hoping we have reached bottom and will begin to climb up. I appreciate a line from you from time to time. Mrs. White joins me in most cordial regards.

I hope to see you at the next Democratic convention. I have been reporting conventions now since 1896 and trust I will die at it. A national convention is really the greatest show on this Continent, combining for me all the thrills of a prize fight, a bull fight, a gladiatorial exhibit, and a house afire.

Are you fellows down in Dixie going to take your stand lying down or on your feet?

John S. Curry today is recognized, along with Thomas Hart Benton and Grant Wood, as one of the great artists of the Middle West. White was able to interest enough Kansans to support a project which made it possible for Curry to paint a series of murals in the State House at Topeka depicting the history of Kansas.

To R. A. Holland, Director of Kansas City Art Institute,
November 12, 1931

My Dear Mr. Holland:

I met, in New York the other day, John Curry, a young Kansas artist who seems to be making his way pretty rapidly in the eastern art circles. I saw his exhibit at the Ferargil Galleries, and talked with men who know about art, and they say Curry is a comer.

I have been wondering why the West cannot make some show of recognition of Curry. What is the prospect of getting Kansas City to take charge of the thing? I believe if I would urge it, Curry would come out and talk to various western groups, and I am sure we could make a place for him out here.

Our politicians and our freaks get so much advertising that when a man from Kansas lifts his head to the higher realm of artistic creation, it seems to me the West should do something to recognize and reward him.

I shall be glad to have your views on this, and if I can help in any way to promote Curry's Kansas fortunes, I will be glad to do so.

To President Ernest H. Wilkins, Oberlin College,
November 26, 1931

Dear President Wilkins:

I have your letter in which you ask me what I would say to a young man about to graduate from College who desires to make his life count in public service.

It seems to me this is the most important question that can challenge a man coming out of College. Never in America before has the need been so great for unselfish, effective, intelligent, courageous men to tackle our political and social problems as today's need presents. Times cry for young men from our colleges in public life and the answer is a fairly faint squeak.

Of course, the obvious thing for a boy to do is to run for office. But I should say that the obvious thing is not the wise thing. I should advise him to get into his party machinery, to bore from within for his ideals—precinct committeeman, district committeeman, county committeeman, state committeeman, chairman wherever he can, heads of delegations, work into the machinery for a few years until he is known, and until he has the confidence and esteem of the rough-and-tumble rank and file around him. Then, if he can take a minor office without salary and with power and influence, as, for instance, the City Council, member of the legislature, or work on purely honorary commissions and boards, there is his chance for another year or two. Incidentally, he should be making his living as he can. And, if he is a lawyer and has to take corporation cases, he should take them with mental reservations that he will not let the corporation attitude and point of view warp his mind away from the public interests. If he is a newspaperman, he must keep his own soul intact. If he works on an honest paper, he can do it. If he works on a crooked corporation

[319]

owned or mob appeal sheet, he can't do it any more than he could work in a gambling house and keep straight.

Assuming that the boy makes a fairly good living from his graduation until he is in his early thirties and has tied up with his party organization and is well known as a square shooter among his fellows, loyal but not blindly partisan, apparently ready to kick over the traces but really slow to do it, the time will come when he can be placed officially where he can do some good, possibly in office, possibly at the head of his organization, possibly merely as an agent provocateur of righteousness in his community. From then on he is on the vitriol sea of politics and Heaven help him unless he has wisdom, courage, tactful sympathy with the weaknesses of humanity, and a moral sense that will make him honest in the thousand oblique temptations that come to a man to lower his banner.

After this, no one can advise him. He is the captain and crew of his own brig, "the cook and the officers too."

I wish I could be more specific, but in a general way that is how I feel about public life.

The School of Journalism at Drake University asked White to write a message to its students. The following letter is an excellent analysis of his views on newspaper ethics. To his dying day, he had nothing but scorn for lurid, yellow journalism.

To the Students of Journalism, Drake University,
February 5, 1932

To the Students of Journalism:
And so, best loved, you are thinking of entering Journalism. I am old-fashioned. I like the phrase "the newspaper business" better than Journalism, because after all we are newspapermen, we Journalists, first, last, and all the time. We are direct descendants of the king's herald and of the bell man. When man lived simply and primitively, the business of disseminating news was done simply and primitively.

But now in a complex civilization, among peoples highly sophisticated, the newspaper business has become complex; indeed it is so complex that broadly speaking there are many kinds of newspaper business; kinds which broadly speaking reduce themselves to two kinds, the honest kind and the dishonest kind. But like all generalizations, this one which presumes the absolute black goats and the absolute white sheep of Journalism, is not such an easy classification to make as it seems. Yet as a working hypothesis it must stand.

Therefore, you are confronted with your choice between two kinds of Journalism, that which accepts no social obligations, which regards no moral scruples, which has for its object merely the financial returns. The get-the-money crowd in Journalism has produced a type of newspaper which has become a form of blackmail softened here and there by mendicancy and which is no more respectable than any other form of prostitution. This group of newspapers appeals to a low type of readers, the morons, who learn nothing and forget everything, who reason with their emotions entirely and will accept anything without question which is stated in sensational terms. This business is highly profitable and entirely crooked. So in the end it has only the satisfactions that come with the possession of money in its rawer forms. To be a member of the profession which is interested only in getting money, one must have a certain psychology; a psychology rising from an utter disbelief in anything except that a sucker is born every minute and that the chief end of man is to relieve him from his money. Deception in all its subtle forms, from downright lying to the higher realms of prevarication, is required in every phase of this kind of a newspaper. Its advertising columns are open to every swindler who cares to enter. Its news columns may be perverted for money paid indirectly by the beneficiaries of its deception or subtly through financial gains to the owners of the newspaper. Sensational headlines, sensational language, appeals to fear, hate, envy and cupidity are the tools in this kind of a journalist's workshop. He must brag about himself. He must lie about his opponents. He must flaunt and advertise himself in every cheap way known to the harlot. And in the end, his is the harlot's success. He gets the money. He loses the respect of his fellows. Go in for that kind of Journalism, if you are anxious for quick, flashy success. But keep out of that kind of a newspaper, if you prize your self-respect as the pearl of great price, even though you walk the streets and dig ditches and wash dishes looking for another job.

The other kind of a newspaper is engaged merely in selling the news, gathering it from the ends of the earth, gathering it from the immediate environment, setting it down carefully, avoiding sensational headlines, avoiding sensational language, interpreting the news truthfully without fear or favor; without fear of sensational competition, without favor to any party, faction, group, or class. This is a hard job. It requires intelligence. It requires moral sense, and above all it requires moral courage. Time and again you have to risk the dollar, let your competitor have it, to gain the esteem of the wiser, decenter group in your community. There is money in this branch of business, in the end, I think, more money than in the other branch, certainly more success, certainly more satisfaction, certainly more ultimate happiness.

So think it over, dearly beloved; make your choice. But know this: You have just one place where free will operates. When you stand at the crossroads, you can go either right or left, but having entered either path, it is hard to change. If you take the crooked path, you will be enamored of its glamorous success. If you take the straight path, when you go crooked you will hate yourself. But assuming that you decide for the strait and narrow path, there is a lot of fun down that way, a lot of joy, a lot of pleasurable satisfaction. But these satisfactions are spiritual. Material rewards do not follow spiritual excellence, nor do material punishments follow spiritual delinquencies. In our civilization no one is going to starve. But you can go hungry, and you can go shabby, and you can go weary and footsore along the narrow path and you will have to take your satisfaction out in self-respect. If you are not prepared to do that, well and good. Take the primrose path of dalliance, eat, drink, and be merry and die a cynic with a big funeral.

The appointment of Benjamin Cardozo to the Supreme Court of the United States was widely acclaimed by forward-looking people. During his years on the court, Cardozo brought a realistic vision to the court's decisions.

To Senator George Norris, February 19, 1932

DEAR SENATOR NORRIS:

I have not had a good drink since I left Kansas City to come to Emporia to make my fame and fortune nearly forty years ago. What I have taken has been more or less surreptitious, medicinal, against my best judgment and with a strangling conscience-stricken feeling that I was drinking the bootlegger's blood or his widow's tears.

But this seems to be an extraordinary emergency, and I want you to do me a favor. Hunt up the Senate bootlegger, get a good long brown drink of nose-choking, hair-raising, gullet-gagging hard corn liquor and then and there take one happy untrammeled drink for me in celebration of the appointment of Judge Cardozo. I can't get safe and satisfactory liquor out here, or I wouldn't impose this on you.

If, on the other hand, you feel there are any physical or spiritual reasons why this imposes too much of a burden on you, please ask Bill Borah, or Ed Costigan, or Senator Couzens, or Senator Cutting [Senators W. E. Borah, Edward Costigan, James Couzens, and Bronson Cutting] to do the job for me.

This occasion shouldn't go uncelebrated. And hoping this will find you the same, I am—

The deepening course of the depression and the failure of any leadership to chart a way out of our economic difficulties prompted White to write this letter to Columnist Walter Lippmann.

New York City, to Walter Lippmann, April 19, 1932

DEAR WALTER:

I have been in town ten days or so, and everywhere I hear convincing evidences of your success. You are a vogue. Your leadership in these days is unquestioned among the people who think. You must be careful; incidentally, perhaps, "Beware when all men speak well of you."

What a mess this busy Babylon is in. The thing that pains me in it all is that we aren't thinking in terms of a better tomorrow, but merely trying to make a bridge back to yesterday.

If out of this thing can't come some permanent peace of mind and economic security for the average man, the manual worker, the small fellow who has other talents than the acquisitive faculties, we will have lost the world as well as our own souls. If the fear motive is to persist on and on as the prod in the pants of humanity, if we cannot supplant hope and joy for fear, if the capacity for financial reward is to be the sum of all the virtues, what's the use of all this travail, all this shot in the arm of financial stimulation to start up the circulation in the rotten old carcass? My heartbreak at liberalism is that it has sounded no note of hope, made no plans for the future, offered no program.

I haven't bothered you because you are busy, and I have been attending meetings of committees, and I hear your voice in your writing, but I want you to know how proud I am of you, how proud we are of you, and to caution you to watch your step. Don't let the Bankers get you.

Samuel Insull built up a powerful utility empire by unsound pyramiding of holding companies. By 1929 his and five other giant financial groups largely controlled the power production of America. Insull's empire crashed in 1932. Thousands of innocent investors saw their earnings wiped out.

Chicago, to WILLIAM L. CHENERY, *Collier's Weekly*, June 13, 1932

MY DEAR BILL CHENERY:

There is a story lying wide open here in Chicago spreading from Chicago across the whole eastern end of the map. The story of Samuel Insull, his rise and fall. Insull in the last ten years has gathered up the control of the public utilities of the eastern half of the United States. He conducted a big campaign in Maine on some sort of a referendum.

He tried to steal the beautiful Falls of the Kentucky River. He is a power in Kansas politics. He was the boss of Indiana. He was actively in the politics of at least twenty states. Moreover, he had to be in the politics of at least twenty states in order to hold his great financial web from being torn to pieces. He typifies all that went wrong in October, 1929. He was greater than the others, but morally he is typical.

It isn't a muckraking story—the tragedy of it—Insull, broken, down and out, power gone, his faith shattered, his own age has gone. It is a tremendous story, not for one or two articles, but for a book and it is a Collier story. I can't write it. I am not strong enough. Wouldn't tackle it under any circumstances, but get some young man—one of these young reporters who have done their economics well in Harvard. Know what they are talking about and put one of them on the job. Tell them to give you the core of it, but to make of it—a human book. There is a fellow named Dennis Tilden Lynch, I believe, who wrote the story of Grover Cleveland and Brigham Young. He is the kind who could do it. I am down here writing for N.A.N.A. [the North American Newspaper Alliance] about the Republican convention. I am staying at the Blackstone, and I shall be in New York next week probably for a day or two at the National Arts Club, but I won't write the story—I am just telling you.

Harold Ickes and I have been talking it over. We think it is a God-given opportunity for a national weekly and a smart and handsome editor.

During his long newspaper career, White was critical of the anti-labor, antiliberal bias of the Associated Press. The particular instance that prompted this letter was the AP's unfavorable story of a liberal writers' group which called at the White House to protest the administration's inaction toward the depression.

My Dear Kent Cooper:

I have your note of the 22nd in answer to mine of the 19th, concerning the crack taken by the Washington Bureau at Waldo Frank, et al.

This case is typical of what may develop into a real weakness in the Associated Press. If these dull days continue, and I see no let-up for several years, inevitably the discontented and defeated will grow class conscious and they will develop an inferiority complex and will be touchy. Moreover, in just the proportion they are misreported or ignored or goaded by such inaccuracies as our Washington Bureau developed in just that proportion will they gain strength and become a menace to the orderly evolutionary growth of our economic system. Our organization is peculiarly suspected by these people. We are the prosperous, the well fed, the contented in their minds, however low our balance may really be, however hard hit many of our individual members may find themselves. Therefore, it seems to me that one of the major aims of our organization should be to give these under-privileged and their leaders an absolutely square deal. We can afford to lean back. In the case of Waldo Frank and his group at the White House, there the spotlight played and there the boys fumbled the ball, and there the Associated Press got one nice, juicy, well-deserved black eye. And again and again it will get it, if our reporters are not specifically instructed about these matters.

It is so easy for a reporter, copy-reader, the city editor, and the staff of our prosperous papers to take the Country Club attitude, the boss's slant, toward those who for one reason or another are whacking the established order. But the easy thing must be avoided, if we retain any value as a news agency except such value as may come to us as a purveyor of journalistic fodder for contented cows.

Please consider these things, not as criticism but as the earnest conviction of one who wants to see our game win but who knows how easy it is to gum the cards by good intentions.

The 1932 election, as was customary, found White supporting the Republican ticket. His progressive friends like Gutzon Borglum, the sculptor, found this incomprehensible in the light of Hoover's innate conservatism. White, as he himself points out, favored a low tariff, aid to the farmers, and government operation of the Muscle Shoals power project. Yet, his Kansas background and his desire to influence the party in Kansas led him to support Hoover rather than Franklin D. Roosevelt.

To Gutzon Borglum, Stamford, Conn., October 13, 1932

Dear Gutzon Borglum:

I have your letter and am glad to get it even though you are unhappy about my political attitude. All that you might say about the tariff I have said, and said more bitterly than you, and am still saying it. I criticized those who voted for the tariff bill and criticized the President for signing it, and I have not let up in my protests against it. But on the other side of the picture is Hoover's peace program, which is good. His efforts for world understanding, in spite of the tariff, have been constructive and important. If one assumes that his theory of attack upon the depression is a good theory—that is to say, the expansion through government agencies of credit to institutions which hold the savings of our people—no one can question that he has averted great panic in this country and perhaps throughout the world. For that, it seems to me, he deserves support of good citizens. His sincerity and his honesty cannot be gainsaid.

I don't agree with him on Muscle Shoals. I don't agree with him on the farm problem. I am probably a little more to the left than he is in many ways. But balancing all in all it seems to me I have a right to my opinion as a progressive and that others should be tolerant of my opinion as I am tolerant of theirs. I greatly admire George Norris. I supported him two years ago and when he had no papers in his state sent my own papers up there free. I should support him four years from now in spite of the fact that he supported Smith four years ago and is supporting Roosevelt now. I don't agree with him on many matters, some of which are important. But in the main and on the whole, Norris has made his life count. I think the same is true of Hoover; in the main and on the whole, he has made his life count on

[327]

what might be called the side of the angels, with all his faults, and they are many, and I know every one of them.

I don't believe Franklin Roosevelt is going to give us a new day or a new deal. I fear that he will take us down rather than up. It may be that we have to go down in order to break the stiff necks of the Pharisees, but I would rather hope we could work it out without a cataclysm.

I have written this letter frankly, and of course not for publication, because I wish you to understand how I had come to certain conclusions which I can quite understand deeply offended you.

Whatever you do, come and see me the next time you are west.

To Miss L. Grace Shatzer, Cumberland, Md., January 23, 1933

Dear Miss Shatzer:

A note from Dr. Canby, Editor of the Saturday Review, encloses your note to him calling his attention to the fact that in the Saturday Review of Literature two years ago, the word "gallaptious" is used either by Mr. Morley [Christopher Morley] or by me. I note that you wish to know the meaning and origin of the word.

I wrote the article in question. I coined the word, only I think it was "galluptious" instead of "gallaptious." I intended to convey by the sound of the word a feeling of gaiety, voluptuous delight, and gusty writing. I have used the word many times. I like it. Probably it will die with me. But it is a good word so far as I am concerned, and after all I am not a purist or a stylist, and if I desire to coin a word this is a free country and the counterfeiting laws are easy in the writing business, and I feel free to do so. I hope I am not corrupting the grand old English language to any extent.

White looked to the leadership of President-elect Franklin D. Roosevelt with hope permeated with good Republican doubts. His analysis of Hoover's qualities and failings throws light on the Hoover administration. Theodore Roosevelt, Jr., a distant cousin of Franklin D.

[328]

Roosevelt, told a friend just before March 4, 1933, that he was Frank-
lin's distant cousin—just about to be removed.

To GOVERNOR THEODORE ROOSEVELT, Philippine Islands,
February 1, 1933

MY DEAR TED:

Thanks for your letter. I hope I have the right steer on this Philippine situation "which I am agin it." If I am wrong, I am sorry.

Your distant relative is an X in the equation. He may develop his stubbornness into courage, his amiability into wisdom, his sense of superiority into statesmanship. Responsibility is a winepress that brings forth strange juices out of men. I don't know. I can't prophesy. But if he fails seriously, watch out for the fireworks.

Then we shall need a leader and where will we find him?

President Hoover is a great executive, a splendid desk man. But he cannot dramatize his leadership. A democracy cannot follow a leader unless he is dramatized. A man to be a hero must not content himself with heroic virtues and anonymous action. He must talk and explain as he acts—drama. I hope when you come home, and I expect you will be home before frost, I may see you.

This world is certainly full of a number of things.

Allan Nevins, professor of history at Columbia University, wrote
White on March 11, 1933, praising his article, "Herbert Hoover, Last
of the Old Presidents or the First of the New," Saturday Evening Post,
March 4, 1933. White's feeling was that in many ways Hoover as
president had set forth on many new paths and should not be classed
with the Harding-Coolidge type of president.

MY DEAR NEVINS:

Your letter saying "don't trouble to reply" is here, and of course I am glad you liked my Hoover piece. Originally I got to going good and made it too long for the uses of the Post, so they had to cut out about a fifth of it. But it stands up pretty well as it is. I got most of my material from the White House, so I feel that the President on the whole is going to be pleased with it, yet I didn't shrink from writing the truth, for I saw it was the truth about him.

Among the things cut out were several chunks that I regarded as diamonds in the rough. Of course every man feels that way. Paul Anderson* in The Nation seemed to think I was trying to set up some sort of a defense for Hoover, which I was not trying to do. I have not heard a word from him and shall not hear. He says thank you in great pain and always under an anesthetic, at least laughing gas. But I wonder if there is much historical value . . . in the sort of thing Paul Anderson has been writing in the last two or three years. To set out with a thesis about a man or an event, and then to string on your hypothesis only the facts which will fit it, does not seem to me to be fair either way. I have admired Anderson and still do. I think he is courageous and fine, and I have applauded so much that he has done. But he and a lot of the young fellows, who are dissatisfied with the social order and things as they are, are getting so miserably bitter about it. Bitterness will get them nowhere. Human nature is what it is and not what it should be. It moves slowly; faster in the middle perhaps than either in the proletarian or plutocratic sides of the stream. And I don't think malice hurries it up. Maybe I am wrong. Heaven knows.

Anyway the real thing I want to answer the letter about was to say that I liked your letter. I have had twenty or thirty, and I prize yours more than all because you wrote it.

As you say, Roosevelt has captured the American people. I am sending you two or three editorials from the Gazette that may indicate how a Hoover Republican is reacting to the Roosevelt stimulus. It seems to me that in this crisis democracy is sick abed. Which does not mean that it should be knocked in the head with communism nor stood against the wall by fascism. But it does need a shot in the arm of temporarily centralized power which always can be removed and

* Paul Y. Anderson had been writing critical articles about President Hoover for the past several years.

the danger is that will be removed too soon. Hence my feeling about Roosevelt that it is not so much what he does as the way he does it. The people will forgive mistakes. They will not forgive inaction, debate, cowardice, dilettante hesitation, splitting hairs.

Pardon these philosophical meditations. Charge it to the doddering habits of an ancient of days.

With kindest regards—

A Puritan in Babylon, *published in 1938, was written at various intervals over a period of years. The recipient of this letter was the author of* Lincoln; A Psycho-Biography.

To Dr. L. P. Clark, May 12, 1933

Dear Dr. Clark:

I was tremendously interested in your Lincoln book. I wish such a study might be made of all our presidents. More or less they are all enigmas, as of course every man is.

My particular reason for writing to you is to interest you in Calvin Coolidge. I am writing a biography of Coolidge. I once wrote a small book about Coolidge, but I am trying to go into his life more definitely and deeply than I went into it before. And I am turning to you for help. Of course, I am not a psychiatrist, just a country editor who lives with people and tries to understand them. But this man, Coolidge, while a country-town man, indeed one who goes back of the country town into the rural neighborhood, strikes me as being habitually controlled by the defense motive of a country boy to the town, to the city, to urban civilization. I have talked with Coolidge many times. Once he told me that he was inhibited by shyness as a child, and it never had left him. His childhood was punctuated by sorrows. Death came to him early. His grandfather, who was his companion and baby chum, left him when he was six. His mother went when he was twelve, and he was like her, one of her people. He was not a Coolidge as I trace the heredity, except in certain Indian traits; silence, and gentle

[331]

saddish streak, and a mischievous habit that made him, in the White House, ring all the bells at once and then disappear to fool the servants—made him do many things like that—a hold-over puerility which never lessened its influence in his life. . . . In his autobiography, which is tremendously revealing, one finds that he declares that he deliberately suppressed his wit and humor and talent for sarcasm in his youth because he found it did not get him anywhere and made enemies. In his autobiography, it seems to me he is always rationalizing his conduct forty years after the fact. But I am not so sure that he did not lay out his life pattern pretty deliberately, some of his so-called rationalizing may be actually remembrances of a plan. It is hard to say. But I have never read an autobiography which seemed to rationalize his conduct, which seemed to present a man as a planned and deliberated career, so consistently as Coolidge's autobiography presents him and his career as such.

I hardly know how to say what I wish to say here. But I want your advice. I wish you could tell me how to proceed to get at the kernel of this spirit. He was mean as the devil sometimes to those whom he loved, in outbursts of meanness. He was kind beyond words to casual people, some of whom might reward him, some of whom never could reward him. I cannot quite find the string of hypothesis on which to thread the man. You have done so admirably with Lincoln, so convincingly, that I turn to you for advice.

I have not proceeded far with the actual writing. I am still collecting material. I must go to Europe to report the International Peace [Economic] Conference and probably shall be gone all summer. So you need not be hurried in reaching your conclusions about Coolidge. I would be glad to send you his autobiography and my small book about him, written ten years ago, which by the way he liked and which his friends, Morrow [Dwight W. Morrow, banker and ambassador to Mexico] among others, thought was the best explanation of him that had been written. The biography I am writing is in no sense an official biography, or a family biography. I am striving earnestly to make it the truth and nothing but the truth. And I suppose my whole desire in this matter is to have your guidance in finding it. I have no desire, of course, to quote you in any way. But if you can help me see into this spirit, as its remains reveal it in his life and biography, I shall be more than grateful, and if I can express my gratitude in any substantial way I shall be pleased to do so at your suggestion.

[332]

The editor of the Gazette *was captivated by the activity of the New Deal during its first three months of power. In the* Gazette, *April 6, 1933, White observed: "Strange things are moving across this American world of ours. The country seems to want action—dramatic action. Roosevelt is supplying the want."*

To E. M. Hopkins, Dartmouth College, May 17, 1933

My Dear President Hopkins:

Of course I was glad to get your letter. And I was particularly happy to know your attitude about President Roosevelt. I was one of those who went the distance with Hoover, knowing his faults, realizing his many temperamental shortcomings, but also believing in his honesty, his intelligence and his rather cautious courage. But his temperamental defects made it impossible for him to lead the country, and the country demanded a vocal leader. They wanted drama, which means intelligible action in politics. Hoover never could explain himself. It is the glory of this man in the White House that he can explain himself, that he has carried the people with him. He has burst out of some sort of chrysalis since March 4. We in the Gazette and my friends among the liberals in Kansas, which include Senator Capper, are going the whole distance with the President. But a fear is lurking in the back of my head that some time in the future either some calamitous failure or an excess of success may switch him back to the Governor of New York in whom I had no great faith. I am always looking subconsciously for him to drop his White House disguise and appear as was. Which Heaven forbid!

There is, of course, the ninety-nine per cent probability that I just did not know him in New York.

Anyway, all of our speculations last fall about the needs of democracy for leadership were temporarily set aside by this man. Maybe it is that way always with democracy; that need growing excruciatingly painful brings the leader to birth. There are more things in Heaven and earth than we dream of in our philosophy probably.

It may interest you to know that I am trying to write a full-length biography of Calvin Coolidge, who interests me deeply as an individual, the last of the Puritans. If you know anything about him, or know of anyone whom I should see, or to whom I should write, this is an S.O.S. call for help. I am trying to solve him as a man and fit him

[333]

into his time, the Golden Age. My book might well have for a subtitle, "A Puritan in the Golden Age."

Pardon this long letter. You brought it on yourself. I must go to London two weeks from tomorrow to report the International Economic Conference. So you will have plenty of time to think over Coolidge before I begin to resume my work next autumn.

Old Bull Mooser Harold Ickes was keeping the kettle boiling in Washington in his post as secretary of the interior. The White-Ickes correspondence during these New Deal days is a veritable gold mine of information on the changing American scene. Shortly after the following letter was written, the Whites sailed to Europe not to return until the early fall.

To Harold Ickes, May 23, 1933

My Dear Harold Ickes:

I am sailing for Europe on the *President Roosevelt*, May 31. I have a job reporting the International Economic Conference for the N.A.N.A. [The North American Newspaper Alliance], a good string, the outfit that has been handling my convention stuff for some time. And I am writing this because I won't see you nor you won't hear from me until maybe midautumn. I want to tell you how splendidly I think you are doing.

You have given me two major kicks, fine high-voltage thrills, first in the appointment of Glavis [Louis R. Glavis, whose discharge precipitated the Pinchot-Ballinger controversy in the Taft administration]. There is a certain poetic justice in that. And Lord, if you could have taken back the little stenographer who floored Root [Elihu Root, former secretary of state] when Root asked him if he wasn't betraying his employer, and he retorted that he was protecting his country —my cup would have foamed higher than a 3.2 mug of beer! But my second kick was also fine when you named Harry Slattery [Harry Slattery, secretary of the National Conservation Association, 1912–

[334]

1918, and head of the Rural Electrification Administration under the New Deal]. I watched his work for twenty years. His friends have been my friends. I have seen the moon of reaction eclipse him and he kept his faith and fought on.

If you can use Judson King [Judson King, director of the National Popular Government League], do so. Dear old Jud! For twenty-five years he has been on the firing line. His guts must be heavy with lead but his heart is light. And I should like to see him be where he can throw back some of the shrapnel that the crooks and conservatives have tossed at him.

Your Big Boss is doing a splendid job. I am scared stiff about him. Every day, as he handsprings lightly over the first page, tossing the world on his toes, I am jostled by a fear that he will fall down, but he has not fallen down so far. And the fine thing about it, of course, is that he has established good will enough now so that he can make some mistakes. March 4, the American people did not care what a man did so long as he did something. And since March 4, there has been something doing and mostly something doing in the right direction. But if his foot slips now they are not going to count it against him.

These are grand days, worth living for!

How do you account for him? Was I just fooled in him before the election, or has he developed? As Governor of New York, I thought he was a good, two-legged Governor of the type that used to flourish in the first decade of the century under the influence of LaFollette and Roosevelt. We had a lot of them, but they weren't Presidential size except Hiram Johnson, and I thought your President was one of these. Instead of which he developed magnitude and poise, more than all, power. I have been a voracious feeder in the course of a long happy life and have eaten many things, but I have never had to eat my words before. I shall wait six months and when I get back from Europe—if they are still on the plate, down they go with a gusto. And I shall smack my lips as my Adam's Apple bobs. . . .

While the Whites were in Europe, Kansas was rocked by a great bond scandal. Warren Finney and his son Ronald of Emporia were

*indicted for forging of bonds and for manipulation of depositors'
funds. The Whites had the Finney daughter with them on their trip.
William L. White has written the story of the Finney bond scandal
in novelized form in* What People Said.

To Erwin Canham, *Christian Science Monitor*, October 27, 1933

My Dear Mr. Canham:

We came through New York in a rush and could not get down to
Washington. Mrs. White bought a little memento for Mrs. Canham.
Where shall I send it? We are so grateful to you for all your kindness.
Please write and tell us how things are going.

Our homecoming was one of the saddest of my life. For twenty
years and more, for the last fifteen years especially, I have enjoyed
the friendship of a man named Finney in this town, telephone manager and banker. I knew him as a fine, public-spirited, generous, intelligent, courageous and sometimes cantankerous man. But like all bankers, he was leading some kind of a double life. What, I don't know.
His son went wrong, probably so far as I can figure it out, forged a
million dollars' worth of municipal bonds and scattered them like a
drunken sailor's money all over the lot in this part of the West. There
are two theories of the crash and the disgrace that followed. I can
subscribe to either. One is that the son is trying to protect the father;
the other is that the father is trying to protect the son. Both seem
doomed for the penitentiary. It is a hard life. When you get along in
your sixties you like to feel the stability of your friends. The girl
who was with us when you saw us last is the daughter of this house,
a nice child who developed tremendously during the European trip.
During the last six weeks of it, we kept entirely the knowledge of
what was going on at home away from her, and not until she landed
in New York did she know her brother was in jail and her father
probably on his way to the penitentiary. She took it like a lady and
did not bat an eye. That helped a little.

I was summoned by both sides of the case as a witness. Six years
ago, I helped arbitrate some differences between Finney and the telephone company. After they summoned me, I suppose they are not
going to use me, but I had to be here just the same. The trial started
Monday. It is all sad and breaks my heart.

We had a wonderful time in Europe. We went from London on

[336]

the Soviet ship through the Kiel Canal to Leningrad and then to Moscow. We stayed there two weeks—two gorgeous weeks—and saw the world turned upside down. From Leningrad we went into Warsaw and then into Vienna where we saw the world starving to death, wasting away with the threat of the Nazis on the German frontier and the threat of the old Royalty within. Then we spent the month of September happily in Italy, ranging from Naples to Trieste, and sailed on the Cosulich Line which devotes the first week of its homeward journey to a cruise of the Mediterranean, stopping also at Lisbon and the Azores. The trip was a delight.

While the Whites were in Moscow, they met a high member of the Communist party who told them: "I was a constant reader of the Emporia Gazette for two years." Quite startled, White asked him where he read it. The man explained that during the war he had been in jail at Leavenworth, Kansas, because of his sabotage activities as a member of the Industrial Workers of the World. A copy of the Gazette was going to a conscientious objector at Leavenworth, and the Communist had thus had access to it. White later observed that this highly placed Communist granted the Whites many courtesies in Russia that they otherwise might not have had.

To HAROLD ICKES, November 14, 1933

MY DEAR HAROLD:

I have returned from five months in Europe. I spent some time in Russia and have written some stuff about it. Russia is the most interesting place on the planet. Their experiment is colossal. Their success is only approximate. But they are happy and on the whole contented. They have no liberty, never have had, wouldn't know what to do with it if they had it, and probably don't want it, preferring other things, security and peace. But they are the most stable government on earth. I talked with Mussolini and told him this. He batted his eyes and leaned forward and said: "What?"

Being of a mischievous disposition, I answered:

"Because they are still shooting them in Russia. They are quicker on the trigger than you people are and are good for a long time."

I came back here to find strange things. I am more than ever convinced that the people should rally around the Roosevelt leadership. It seems to me things, by which I mean conditions in general, socially, economically, politically, are better than they were when we left. I can see a distinct improvement. There was an upswing in July and August, checked in September, started again in late October, and still going strong in our part of the Middle West. I cannot see that the farm agitators got anywhere. I am against it and have been. I came back to find the Blue Eagle [the emblem of the National Recovery Administration] all over the Gazette. My son has been supporting the President and since I came home I have written a few editorials, one or two of which I enclose. You might be interested in some of the things I have written about Russia for the Gazette, not the N.A.N.A. stuff which was for the big daily papers, so I am wadding that in herewith. . . .

To Paul Jones, Lyons (Kansas) *News*, November 16, 1933

Dear Paul Jones:

I am in three minds about the N.R.A. One, that it is leading us to Fascism; another that it is leading us to Communism; another that it is leading us to the boneyard. In addition to which I have a sneaking subconscious hope that the thing will work, that it will pull us out of the hole. I'm like the fellow who owns a dog and doesn't know whether he has distemper or is mad and hates to shoot him because he may get well and be a good dog.

So I am going to pet the N.R.A. and feed it and watch it.

I hope you are well and happy. These are parlous times.

Frederick C. Howe was another prewar progressive who became a significant figure in the early days of the New Deal. Howe's auto-

biography, The Confessions of a Reformer, *is a stimulating and provocative work.*

To FREDERICK C. HOWE, Agricultural Adjustment Administration,
Washington, D. C., November 27, 1933

DEAR HOWE:

As I see it, the President is our only hope. Right or wrong, he is trying earnestly, honestly and courageously to do something, and if he makes five good hits in twelve, it is better than the human average. Of course, I shall see you when I come to Washington.

Kindly give my regards to Secretary Wallace [Secretary of Agriculture Henry A. Wallace] in whom I have every confidence and for whom I have the highest respect.

On February 19, 1934, Postmaster General Farley canceled all air-mail contracts on the basis that his predecessor, Walter F. Brown, had been in collusion with the air-mail companies.

To SENATOR GEORGE W. NORRIS, February 14, 1934

DEAR SENATOR NORRIS:

. . . Remember this: the Postmaster General of the United States was the chairman of the Democratic National Committee. He is an avowed partisan. It was his job to beat the Republicans, and in his heart he probably feels that it is his job to keep them beaten. When he stirs up a row that reflects on the administration of his predecessor, it should not be forgotten that his predecessor was a Republican, and that the harder Farley can smear Brown, the harder it will be for any Republican to come back to Washington four years from now.

So don't join in the cry "Stop thief!" until you know, first, whether there has been a thief; second, how much was taken; and third, how much politics there is in all the sustentatious investigations of the Democrats. But until the present contracts are annulled the Democrats cannot get the contracts.

Graft is wicked. It is the result of the spoils system in politics. The Democrats are as ruthless in their adherence to the spoils system as the Republicans. Neither is better or worse than the other; and this form of graft, which is inevitable under the spoils system, is the price of democracy. Rarely does it amount to a considerable sum, nor a sum bearing any considerable relation to the total sum spent for taxes. Probably it doesn't amount to one per cent of the gross.

But, at that, the graft of democracy is better than the robbery of special privileges under the "favorite" system. It comes with a dictatorship—whether he be a premier or party boss. Our form of government has its drawbacks, but they are light compared with the drawbacks of any other system—fascism, communism, or absolute monarchy.

So, when our friends the Democrats are, what they call, "uncovering the wickedness of the Republicans" let us bear in mind that they are, after all, Democrats and, in the main, patriots, but also Democrats just the same.

Always remember that, and stop, look and listen!

Secretary of State Cordell Hull's reciprocal trade treaties evoked enthusiastic response from the editor of the Gazette. *He wrote innumerable editorials hailing the idea as a step in the right direction toward a better and more peaceful world.*

To CORDELL HULL, Secretary of State, February 20, 1934

DEAR MR. SECRETARY:

Enclosed I am sending a short editorial from the Gazette which might interest you. It occurred to me that this might be printed in Tennessee papers to your advantage, and if your secretary will send me a half a dozen names of your editorial friends in Tennessee, I shall write a little note to each together with the editorial suggesting republication.

It seems to me you are growing in strength all over the country, and I am most happy to see it. I felt that fate was giving you a hard deal in London.* I wrote something of the kind for my North American Newspaper Alliance syndicate, and when I came home through Russia, I found considerable response to my suggestion. I earnestly hope your tariff ideas will be given administration approval. Can see no other way for us to return to normal trade relations in the United States. A narrow nationalism will plant weeds on hundreds of millions of acres that might be raising food, and will set looms and spindles to rusting, douse the fires in thousands of furnaces that might be humming and glowing with activity. The world needs what we can grow and make so tragically that it seems to me it is spiritual suicide— and incidentally material decay—to allow a shortsighted tariff policy to restrict our influence in the world of industry and delay human progress for another half century. If I can help you in any way, please let me know how and when and where.

Although White had left the Board of Trustees of the University of Kansas before World War I, he had kept himself informed on educational matters. He was particularly concerned about the status of the Presbyterian College of Emporia. Many times he had assisted in fund-raising campaigns to aid the college. The New Deal assisted struggling colleges through the National Youth Administration, which made it possible for students to work part time at tasks set up by their institutions and financed by the government.

* President Roosevelt sidetracked any agreement at the London Economic Conference for the stabilization of world currencies by declaring that the United States must go its own way. As a result, the conference failed and Secretary Hull, who had headed the American delegation, had to see his hopes for the reopening of world trade temporarily delayed.

My Dear Mr. President:

I feel that my special knowledge of the academic situation in this part of the Middle West justifies my addressing you at a time when I know your desk is buried in correspondence. The denominational colleges in this part of the world are in the midst of serious crisis. Kansas has fifteen such institutions. Each of the bordering states has its quota, Colorado less, Missouri and Iowa more, Nebraska about the same, Oklahoma perhaps a few more. Texas and the Dakotas and Minnesota, the whole Trans-Mississippi country is dotted with these small and ordinarily fairly well-established denominational colleges. Ninety per cent of them are up to the scratch educationally with their curricula properly supervised by central authority. Their degrees or their credits are accepted by the larger Atlantic seaboard universities, Princeton, Yale, Harvard, and these western schools though small are circles of light and learning in their communities. Also, this is true between the Mississippi and the Alleghenies north and south. But I happen to know the Trans-Mississippi educational situation and so far as these small colleges go it is lamentable.

I presume at least ninety per cent of them are passing their faculty payroll. They are cutting down curricula. Students are being aided by the CWA [Civil Works Administration, a temporary federal relief organization] which is fine, but in the last four years these colleges running behind trying to maintain their standards and meet their payrolls all have piled up a staggering burden of debt. They cannot meet it much longer. This debt is financed in the local banks. Trustees are on the paper. Mostly it is secured by farm mortgages, sometimes taken out of endowment which is being milked dry. Ordinarily again in good times, these colleges can go to the people—their denominational supporters—and wipe out their debts and increase their endowments. Those doors are closed today and probably will be closed for some time, perhaps for several years and the colleges cannot live under the status quo much longer.

They all have adequate plants, substantial buildings. They are going concerns with the student body from three hundred to seven hundred, in a few cases a thousand, and west of the Mississippi these denominational colleges offer academic opportunities to probably fifty thousand students within three hours' automobile ride of home; opportunities that the young people could not take elsewhere. Living standards at state universities are too high; tuition fees at the larger eastern universities prohibitive. But here at home this student body can get a good grounding in what might be called academic fundamentals. From these small colleges they go into professional schools in the East and for their Master's degrees to better schools. They are doing a real job—these small midwestern denominational schools. If you could arrange to have the R.F.C. [the Reconstruction Finance Corporation], or some similar organization refinance their debts for a long term at a low rate of interest with annual amortization, it would save the situation. I know of nothing else that would. As credit, I should say, having been a College Trustee nearly all my life, these small colleges are as good as any bank, mortgage company or any other going business concern. They have back of them a definitely substantial and dependable clientele. It is obvious why the clientele is unable to rescue them now. Hence this letter, and I most earnestly beg of you to give this matter your serious consideration. . . .

With kindest personal regards, I am—

After the following letter was written, White served on a committee that secured an appropriation for the Jefferson Monument.

To W. C. D'Arcy, D'Arcy Advertising Agency, St. Louis,
March 28, 1934

Dear Mr. D'Arcy:

I have learned that you are to present to a Congressional Committee the proposal to erect a Jefferson memorial monument at St. Louis. For a long time I have wondered why the Nation's lasting memorial expression to Jefferson was not created there at St. Louis, overlooking the West. Jefferson and his ideals of democracy have been the ideals of the West in this country for a century. Today the West is Jeffersonian in its ideals much more than Hamiltonian. It is in the West that the great uprisings of the people have occurred translating into modern terms the Jeffersonian ideals. St. Louis is the only gateway to this great West which Jefferson added to our domain. Here he raised his

[343]

Ebenezer. Here on the west side of the Father of Waters should rise a grateful Nation's memorial to the Father of a great ideal, to a new experiment in human government—democracy.

I earnestly hope that this memorial will be erected and erected now and erected in St. Louis. The part of the Louisiana Purchase from which this letter is written will certainly be happy to see this memorial erected.

In a speech at the University of Kansas Commencement in June, 1934, White stated that by and large he was for the New Deal. "It is neither communism nor fascism. Much of it is necessary. All of it is human. And most of it is long past due," he declared.

To ALLAN NEVINS, Columbia University, May 24, 1934

DEAR MR. NEVINS:

. . . You and I agree about the New Deal and Roosevelt. I am concerned about the danger to the Bill of Rights. Of course, it is not manifest yet. It seems to me the New Dealers are still depending upon the courts and due process of law after having got their toe smashed when they stuck it across the deadline in the airmail contract case. There is no hint or threat in Washington of cramping our political liberties. But nevertheless, there is a feeling that the assumption of all this economic power will develop an arrogance that will seek to support itself by tyranny; tyranny begets arrogance, and arrogance requires tyranny in human nature, being what it is. I was in Washington recently. I feel there is no "plan" either concealed or conscious. The President goes on one running board after another headed for his evident desire to get out of the morass. He hitchhikes with the inflation boys, then with the silver boys, then with the Johnson [General Hugh Johnson, head of the National Recovery Administration] crowd who evidently intend to perpetuate and institutionalize the NRA, then with the apple-cheeked, starry-eyed brain trusters in the Agricultural Department, most of whom are decent fellows but few of whom are in agreement about anything. Felix Frankfurter [professor of law at Harvard University and intimate adviser to the President] has great influence, but it is countered by other young men of equal importance who do not hold with Frankfurter.

It is obviously a case of trial and error all along, with the President the greatest hitchhiker since Andrew Johnson, going a little piece down the road with anyone, backward and forward, zigzagging, covering and recovering. And yet I am persuaded he is earnest and honest in his endeavor to get us out of the mess, though not intelligent. I'll bet he is mooching his intelligence from his younger associates. Essentially he has courage, but I fear courage without intelligent purpose, if it sticks, will become arrogance, and if he wobbles as he may, assuming his honesty, his very courage can become devastating.

He had the National Society of Editors at the White House, Thursday evening, April 19, the editorial writers, managing editors, a few Washington correspondents, not many, and the editorial directors of the newspapers in the larger American cities. He talked for two full hours, sitting down, in the dining room which was cleared of tables and filled with chairs. For an hour and a quarter I should say he talked directly and without a break. Then he answered questions. I had not seen him for nearly ten years. I was struck by the change that had come over him. He shakes his head a good deal and gestures from the neck up when he talks. He is facile, and his facility under duress may become recklessness, but under normal conditions is somewhat the basis of his charm. He frankly confessed his currency tinkering had been a failure; said so almost in those words; declared that it had not done for commodity prices what he expected it would do. He complained about the silver group ganging him and in several instances when he was explaining the basis of certain actions and certain policies, he exhibited what to me seemed a dangerous tendency to reason from one to many. He has a habit of generalization and simplification which is not scientific and sometimes is disillusioning, at least to me. His mind is quick and superficial. Of this I am dead sure. He still smiles too easily for one who shakes his head so positively. I fear his smile is from the teeth out, though I am not sure how much the unconscious arrogance of conscious class is back of his smile. Away down in my heart I am scared. He is a fair-weather pilot. He cannot stand the storm. This is, of course, the futile blundering that all gratuitous prophecy is. Take it for what it is worth.

I saw and talked to some of his young men, notably Tugwell [Rexford G. Tugwell, Roosevelt "Brain Truster," appointed head of the

Resettlement Administration in 1935] whom I liked. He is at least candid. He believes in planned economy, and I think his obeisance to democracy is not mere lip service. I think he hopes to achieve his goal, retaining to the people the right to withdraw, to change, to modify, to overturn in the traditional American manner through parliamentary channels. I hope one can do that, but I distrust the power he would generate in any human hands that are around this administration or that have been around any other administration that I ever knew. I believe politicians on the whole are as honest and effective as business men, but I never knew a business man or a politician whom I would trust with all the power they are generating around the White House there in Washington. They are liable to be as wicked, as ruthless, as greedy as those men in Wall Street who had in a small group all that power which Tugwell would give to government in the third decade of the century. They took us to hell, and I doubt if the politicians would be much better. I cannot see how they would get us out. But we are in it and we have to get out. I would like to see the Wall Street crowd dehorned and unclawed, but I don't see much sense in gluing the horns and claws of Wall Street on the politicians. They still remain predatory weapons.

Lord, I don't know!

The Republicans of course are without leadership. Vandenberg [Senator Arthur Vandenberg of Michigan] is a good bet, but there is real fear that he will be defeated in Michigan, which will put him out of the picture. There is no hope for Mills or Wadsworth [Ogden Mills and James Wadsworth of New York] as national leaders. Young Teddy Roosevelt is trying to find the spotlight. I saw him in New York; tried to get him to take his stand on the Bill of Rights, and then not to be economically reactionary. The danger of so many of these fellows who are howling for the Bill of Rights is that they want to use it for reactionary purposes to stop many of the necessary changes and reforms which must come eventually when we recover, if they cannot come along with recovery. The Bill of Rights, I fear, in the bright lexicon of Young Teddy is to be the bulwark of privilege rather than a defense of democracy. There again I may not sense it right.

I am sending you something I wrote about Tugwell. And I am making a Commencement Address at the University of Kansas, which will more or less express my views about the challenge to democracy, which we must meet sometime in the next decade or two. I am not

[346]

fearful of it under Roosevelt. The challenge will come more danger-
ously from the right than from the left. . . .

The recipient of the following letter was a former Gazette *reporter.*

To WHITELY AUSTIN, *Hutchinson* (Kansas) *News,* June 13, 1934

MY DEAR WHITELY:

The impatience of young men like you with the slow, sure processes of democracy—which solve problems, not in terms of years,
rarely in terms of decades, sometimes in terms of generations—that
hot-foot haste to be a godsaker, is what has landed Germany back
of Hitler, Italy back of Mussolini and Russia back of Stalin; and no
good will come of it.

The gorgeous thing about a dictatorship is that it furnishes a damn
fool a sure, quick way to take his country to hell and prove what a
chump he is. Watch for the Hitler and Mussolini fireworks. Democracy has its checks and balances. We elevate dubs and boobs and tear
them down because we are free to do so, and never fail to do so. But
the dub and boob of the dictatorship are permanent. They stick until
they crash.

As I love you, let me beg of you to be patient with the chumps,
with the half-baked emissaries of an even-less-baked and more gooey
constituency. Because, someway, in the mysterious alchemy of time,
out of this hell-brew rises the essence of truth.

*The Theodore Roosevelt Medals for 1934 were awarded to Judge
Samuel Seabury of New York "for distinguished service in the pro-*

motion of social justice" and to William Allen White "as an outstand-
ing interpreter of the American mind." The awarding committee said
of White: "A keen observer, a genial student of his fellow-men, a
writer of gracious and effective prose, his influence in two generations
has been largely due to his ability to keep in the company of millions,
the neighborly point of view, the kindliness, the realism and the tol-
erance of a man who knows the best and the worst about every man
in town, and is neither deceived nor embittered."

·

To Henry J. Allen, Wichita, Kan., June 28, 1934

Dear Henry:

Thanks for your note about the Roosevelt medal. As I figure it out
in perspective, the thing that we were all trying to do twenty years
ago was to enlarge the middle class by beating down the ears of the
big crooks who were robbing us all by penny-pinching, dishonest
devices of corporate financing, and operating on the one hand and
on the other hand by making the way up easier for what might be
called the under-privileged—the fellow without much acquisitive
faculty who had other good qualities, industry, loyalty, good will,
intelligence outside of business and an aspiration for better things.
More or less we did what we started out to do; we did enlarge the
middle class, bringing privileges to millions in the first two decades
of the century who were under-privileged, but we did not knock
down the ears of the big crooks and they played hell with our civilization in the third decade, and here we are.

Through it all, I have never given a tinker's damn what might happen to me politically, and I have been any kind of a damn fool that
I wanted to be in any given time, sacrificing myself for causes that
interested me and glad of it, and no regrets at the end. For most of my
causes have won, which was all I was after. That I have been able to
hold a few friends like you proves that men are divine as well as
human and can forgive and forget and overlook and have patience. So
it's all right! And I am glad we are here.

*Until the day of his death, White devoted a large amount of his time
to a futile attempt to capture control of the Republican party from
the reactionaries.*

To CHESTER ROWELL, San Francisco *Chronicle*,
September 11, 1934

MY DEAR CHET:

I was glad to get your form letter and the editorial enclosed which
has my prayerful approval. The only thing I should change in it is
that I would lead off with the warning that the Old Deal is dead and
emphasize that a little more than you did.

After that you are dead right about the Republican party. If it can
only break itself of the habit of grave robbing, trying to exhume a
"day that is done," trying to preserve "the sound of a voice that is
still."

There is utterly no sense in being licked by this Roosevelt outfit,
if we lay present and definite plans in opposition. I should say that
here is a plan that would work:

First of all, old-age pensions, unemployment and sickness insurance, under some sort of federal control, regulation, support and en-
couragement. This would furnish economic security to the common
man.

Second, I should revise the N.R.A. into a permission for any industry or any unit of any industry to organize without coercion for
the purpose of controlling output and hence prices. And, in return for
this privilege, I should require these organizing industries to submit
absolutely the question of wages and ultimately the question of prices
to a federal board with absolute power. And, also, I should require
them to recapitalize under government supervision, squeezing the
water out and starting over with a greatly reduced capital structure.

Third, I should get some smart guy like you to write the financial
plank.

And fourth, promise to submit a constitutional amendment, taking
the tariff out of the hands of Congress and putting it in the hands of
the executives with the veto power in Congress by a two-thirds vote
on not more than one schedule at a time.

About the best thing that this outfit has done, it seems to me, is to
try, although futilely, and it would almost seem insincerely, to estab-

lish the right of collective bargaining, and I admire tremendously the Labor Board's decision that collective bargaining is to go by majority rule.

The trouble with our beloved party is that it is shot through with the plutocratic conquest. If it can get rid of that, the party can revive. But it cannot live with fatty degeneration of the heart.

You don't know what delight your signature at the end of a letter gave me, even a form letter. I have missed you. I hope you are well and that things are going fairly well with you.

I have just returned from the Mayo Clinic where I had a minor operation that five years ago would have required a major operation. And I seem to be well and as happy as I can be in a bewildered world.

To JAMES A. FARLEY, Postmaster General, October 6, 1934

DEAR MR. FARLEY:

I have your letter of October 3 suggesting that you would like to read my letter of September 20 to the President, indicating that he "sure would get a kick out of it."

All right, go to it. Anything that will give any president of this country a smile should be encouraged. Boy and man, reporter and editor, for nearly 50 years I have known them all, in and out of the White House, since Harrison. I think I know the job. It was conceived of the devil who in one of his large, jocular moments, wishing to get even with humanity, squeezed the old bean and thought up the ballot box and then laughed for a hundred years. After which the devil invented the presidency by combining all the futile despair of Sisyphus with the agony of Tantalus and shaking in a jigger of the nervous irritation of a man with ants in his pants. I have done a lot of mean things in my life, but I never wrote a mean article about a president while he was in office, and precious few after they ever left office, though I did drop some silent tears for Harding with a dash of caustic acid in them. But of all the men I have known, none has had such a hard task as the present incumbent, and while I don't agree with a lot of things he has done, God knows he has done his best, and better than I could do or any friend that I know of could have done. So if any gay quip of mine can give him a second's surcease, pass it along. I am also enclosing a clipping which may give you a giggle and him a grin.

[350]

White spent a hurried week in Washington just before this letter was written. As the letter reveals, he was worried that the reactionary Republicans would make an agreement with Huey Long, the Louisiana Kingfish, whereby Long would run on a third-party ticket to draw votes away from Roosevelt. Long, in White's eyes, was a dangerous demagogue with a fascist hue.

To Harold Ickes, February 7, 1935

My Dear Harold:

· Herewith enclosed is an editorial that I wrote in the Gazette, not particularly to be passed around but for your own eyes.

I had a letter from a man who has recently been in Louisiana, a man fairly high in the eastern organization of the party, who wrote this:

"Getting close into the picture, one catches a pipeline direct to Huey and this is his strategy: To run for President in '36 with no expectation of being elected, but hoping to draw enough radical votes from Roosevelt to permit the election of the Republican nominee. Long's price will be the dispensation of southern patronage by which he expects to build an invincible machine in 1940. Should Long run and should he be able to get the Townsend,* the Sinclair,† and other such elements back of him, the Republicans could slip in. But that frightens me because I don't believe they have been sufficiently chastened to be worthy of power."

This man is level headed. I cannot tell you his name. But there is something in it.

And the more partisan politics you inject into this administration in the next two years, the more liability there is that this plan will win and it would be terrible. Hasn't someone around the shop down there got it in his head that Roosevelt can't win next year without the progressive Republican votes of the Middle West from Ohio to the Coast, but particularly the Mississippi basin north of Tennessee?

Whatever you do, don't bother to answer this. But I fear that a reactionary victory in '36 would be followed by a Fascist victory under some demagogue like Long in '40, and then the devil would be to pay.

* Refers to the Townsend Plan for pensions to everyone over sixty years of age.
† Refers to Upton Sinclair's End Poverty in California movement.

It was a beautiful evening by the fire out in Spring Valley [Ickes's home in Washington]. Thank you for letting me sit there a while.

Remember me most cordially to Mrs. Ickes.

Congressman Hamilton Fish of New York wired White on February 19, 1935, that he wanted to know why the Gazette attacked his speech at Springfield, Missouri. Fish, at this point, was carrying on an attack against a supposed Communist menace to the nation.

To Congressman Hamilton Fish, February 22, 1935

Dear Mr. Fish:

I am sending you, herewith, the editorial which appeared in the Gazette. It had no reference to your Springfield speech.

It was written in Cambridge, Massachusetts, by my son ten days before your Springfield speech. I haven't read your Springfield speech.

Where you and I part company is on this red-baiting business. You are walking right straight into Fascism. I hate both Communism and Fascism because of their denial of free discussion of any subject whatever at any time or any place. I think this bill which purports to stop distributing subversive material to soldiers or sailors could easily be used and would probably be used to muzzle a paper which denounced the strike when soldiers were sent to stop the strike. You know and I know that soldiers are often sent into a strike area to bolster up a weak cause of the bosses. And a newspaper that wished to denounce that cause could not do so under this proposed law.

In general, the way to keep the army loyal is to keep the government wise and just in industrial relations. And, if the government sends troops out in a wicked cause as it might well do and has often done, the government and not the people who denounced the cause are to blame, if the army lays down its arms. I have no fear of the common sense of the common soldier. In any just cause he will shoot

[352]

and shoot to kill, as he should. But in many industrial controversies he is asked to shoot and shoot to kill where the right is in his victim.

The whole red-baiting business, the whole matter of substituting force for reason, guns for argument, the whole business of denying fools their folly instead of letting them prove their folly, is the core of my general objection to your attitude. I have the greatest respect for your economic social liberalism, but unless it includes political liberalism and the right of free discussion on any subject at any time, I part company with you and that most sadly.

The fear of communism was successfully used by Adolf Hitler and Nazi Germany to scare the Western democracies from co-operating with Soviet Russia before 1939 to check the menace of fascism. It was not until Germany plunged the world into war for a second time that leaders like Prime Minister Neville Chamberlain began to awaken to the menace of Hitlerism. In the United States, many sincere and patriotic Americans, according to their own light, played into the hands of Hitler through their constant attacks on communism.

To I. V. HORNER, Tulsa, Okla., March 21, 1935

DEAR MR. HORNER:

I am sorry to have neglected answering your letter of the 15th so long, but I have been out of town. I recall very well our pleasant association nearly a generation ago. I was glad to get the material which you sent me about your debate with The League for Industrial Democracy.

As a debate, you have got them licked. But I am afraid you have gone a little further than the truth would justify. On the extreme right and the extreme left of social endeavor, both sides are wrong. The middle ground holds the truth. The I.L.D., on the one hand, and the National Republic and George Lockwood,* on the other, just can't tell the truth about one another. They get the facts straight,

* The National Republic was a superpatriotic group headed by George Lockwood. J. R. Carlson's *Under Cover* describes some of this group's work.

[353]

but the facts are often a long way from the truth. For instance, a man might be "chief of the flying squadron" in the textile strike and be a pretty good citizen. It all depends upon the merits of the textile strike. My recollection of the textile strike* is that the strikers were right and the bosses were wrong. Neither of them was 100 per cent right, and you have got to figure it that way. Powers Hapgood [Powers Hapgood, author of *In Non-Union Mines*, 1922] is a believer in cooperation as a cure for our industrial ills. He thinks it is a cure-all. It is probably one of a dozen more or less necessary panaceas. But maybe none of them will work. I don't know. No one knows until they are tried.

It seems to me about the best attitude in this whole matter is the attitude of patience and tolerant suspicion.

Whatever will happen, we will not go communist. We have too large a middle class. There is a danger of fascism. Fascism always comes through a vast pretense of socialism backed by Wall Street money. Both Hitler and Mussolini were Socialists, and both were backed by the big business interests of their countries. They shed their socialism as soon as they got in power. Huey Long is the type we must fear. Huey Long backed by the Wall Street money on the quiet, rabble-rousing the morons into a belief that he was going to give them pancakes three times a day, is a menace.

I wouldn't put much faith in Matthew Woll [vice-president of the American Federation of Labor]. He is a professional red-baiter. He believes it. He is sincere. But I think he sees ghosts where there are none.

I suppose you might as well be warned that I have been on the black list for ten years of Woll and all the red-baiting nervous Nellies of the country. Yet, while I have been on the black list, I have been a delegate to two Republican National Conventions, served on the Resolutions Committee that wrote two Republican platforms, and on the small sub-committee that had the final say about the whole Republican program.

But because I laugh at the threat of communism, I am supposed to be a sympathizer of it, and God knows I think it is the funniest doctrine that has ever been presented to the American people, and has just about as much chance of winning converts or making any real headway in America as Mormonism, polygamy, or the doctrine of the transmigration of souls.

* Refers to the great Industrial Workers of the World strike in 1912.

Don't think from this letter that I didn't enjoy the way you landed on your opponent. It was fine. I could hear the old shillala whacking on their tails with resounding whacks. And as one who enjoys a fight, I enjoyed your polemics, but I don't believe that things are as bad as the National Republic and the professional red-baiters make them out. But as I say, you want to discount me 40 to 90 per cent, for I am on the black list myself and enjoy it.

It was good to see your letter and to recall old times. I hope soon our paths will cross again. With kindest personal regards, I am—

Congress, in an isolationist mood in 1935, passed the Neutrality Law which placed an embargo on goods of war to both parties at war. President Roosevelt, with more foresight, urged an embargo on the aggressive nation only. White, in 1935, supported the Congressional bill. At this time he did not realize that this position handicapped the European democracies facing the menace of Hitler.

To J. J. Buchanan, Pittsburgh, Pa., May 24, 1935

Dear Dr. Buchanan:

I would reply to your letter of May 21st that the best way for America to avoid war without dishonor is to redefine our rights as neutrals by a Congressional enactment which will empower the President to at once declare as contraband of war any raw materials or manufactured goods or munitions which either belligerent in a foreign war shall declare as contraband and refuse shipping permits to any ship carrying out of American ports such contraband.

There is absolutely no other way to keep out of war. The President who does it would have to be a superman for courage, wisdom and honesty. He would have to fight organized minorities of farmers, labor leaders, manufacturers and munition makers. He might have to face panic and depression at home. But even that is better than war. . . .

[355]

A presidential boom for Governor Alf Landon of Kansas was already on the way by the summer of 1935. He was portrayed as a governor who had balanced the budget—a Kansas Coolidge, someone remarked. Landon and White were members of the same wing of the Kansas Republican party.

To W. S. Fitzpatrick, New York City, July 19, 1935

Dear Mr. Fitzpatrick:

The photograph is going on today's mail. I don't know why it hasn't gone before. There are two opinions about Roosevelt in Kansas. Mine is this: that he has slipped. But not enough to lose the state against anyone we are now considering against him. As Ingalls [Senator John J. Ingalls of Kansas] said—"Not now." But a year from now it may be different. My opinion, which differs from the best opinion in the state, is that if times get good, people vote the Republican ticket, and while times are bad, they are going to vote Democratic. I have a notion that times are going to get better. If they get better enough, Roosevelt will lose Kansas. That's my opinion. Right next to yours on my desk I had a letter from the Governor, to whom I had expressed my opinion that if times get better Roosevelt will lose Kansas. He writes:

"Milt Tabor [Topeka *Capital* editor] is just back from his vacation, and he brings in an interesting statement. He spent his time visiting solely among the farmers, away from the court houses. He reports a big change in sentiment toward the Roosevelt administration. This time a year ago the state was burned up; the farmers didn't think they had anything left. They were glad to take the allotment checks, etc., and still are for that matter. But with the improvement in crop conditions and finances they feel that they have some property now and are viewing optimistically once more their prospects for owning more property, so the waste and the extravagant expenditures are shocking to them now as property owners."

There is no politics going in Kansas just now. It is dead in the shell. If I were suddenly asked to pick a gubernatorial candidate for the Republican party here, I would throw up my hands in despair. We have a lot of fine men, but not the kind of vote-getters that we need. And we have a lot of fellows not so fine who are vote-getters, and would make a mess of it if elected.

[356]

Now, about Landon. He is keeping his feet and using his head so far as the presidential talk is concerned. I saw him the other day and had a pleasant talk with him at a barbecue. I think I have not been in his office since he was elected. Certainly not for more than two years. I haven't his confidence. Certainly not in matters of patronage. We are friendly enough, and I like him, for his father was my dear friend. He has grown in every way since he came to Topeka. The really best thing about him is his capacity for growth. I have never been able to visualize him as president. I suppose the friends of Coolidge in Vermont and in Northampton, Mass., and the friends of Grover Cleveland in Buffalo used to laugh when they heard these men talked of for president. But responsibility does a lot to a man. If he has any iron, it becomes steel, any quartz, it becomes gold. If I were guiding Landon's destiny, I should give him four years in the Senate and see what happens.

I wish you were back in Kansas. You would enjoy it. We need rain, but we always do at this time of the year. Yet it may be a serious scorch. Not, however, the drouth of last year. Mrs. White, to whom I showed your letter, sends her best regards and her most cordial remembrances to your family.

During 1935, White aided the Landon boom for the presidential nomination to the extent of writing many letters, similar to the following one, to people all over the nation. In October, however, the Whites left for a trip to the Far East. By the time they returned the Landon candidacy was in full swing. The Whites attended the inauguration of the government of the Philippines on November 15 as guests of the Philippine government. From there they traveled to China and returned to San Francisco on January 15, 1936.

To E. BEN JOHNSON, Spokane, Wash., August 19, 1935

(Confidential)

DEAR MR. JOHNSON:
I have your letter of August 16th inquiring about Governor Landon. I am glad to give you what information I have.

Let me begin with his father, who was an original Bull Mooser even before the split of 1912. I was national committeeman of the Bull

Moose party in 1912, having resigned as a Republican national committeeman for Kansas. I decided not to accept any money from George Perkins, the chairman of the Bull Moose National Committee. So we raised our own money in Kansas. Governor Landon's father raised $1,000 in Montgomery County and sent me a check. He was at that time receiver of the Prairie Oil and Gas Company in Kansas, an honest, upstanding man, a leading citizen of Kansas. I knew his son when I was Regent of the State University in 1907 or '8, when the boy was a student there. When he got out of college he went into the oil business. His father's business. I watched his career with interest and pride. He has worked with the progressive faction in Kansas consistently for twenty years since his first vote. He is honest and courageous. He was chairman of the Republican State Committee from 1928 to 1930. And was elected governor in 1932 and 1934. I supported his gubernatorial candidacy through two primaries and two elections with all the ardor I could command.

Now comes the but—

The office of the Presidency in this crisis requires a man of great experience, of wide and high vision, of rather gigantic size. You will notice that Governor Landon has not thrust himself forward in this crisis. He recognizes, as I suppose I do, and all earnest men must recognize, that his gubernatorial experience in Kansas would leave a long, wide step to the White House. His modesty is commendable.

He has had almost as much political experience as Coolidge had when he was elected vice-president. And Landon is a bigger man than Coolidge was the day he went to the White House. But Coolidge took the job when it was merely a job of executive leadership. Economically, we were on an ascending spiral. He faced no serious problems. He instituted no crucial policies. If Coolidge were called to the White House today, I believe he would make a conspicuous failure. He is not the man for this hour.

The impact of the job in the White House is tremendous. If a man has any latent subconscious powers, they are aroused by the overwhelming responsibility. Few men fail to respond to this awful challenge. Taft rallied slowly, Harding failed. McKinley only partially rose, but he was growing when he died. I think Wilson met it in a way, though sadly handicapped by his temperamental peculiarities. I am inclined to believe that Landon would rise to it. I don't know. No man knows. I don't think he knows. I think this is the reason why he is modest. He stands in awe and fear of the terrible consequences of a failure to rise. I have talked very little with him about the job.

[358]

Though we have been dear and close friends since his boyhood. I have not sounded the clarion note for reasons which are obvious in this letter. I fancy if he should come to me and say "I am ready to go. I think I can do the job," I could conscientiously lead out. But perhaps this is not the time. All I know about Landon is good. It is a question of size, and the Lord knows he outsizes most of the Republican aspirants.

While in China, White, who was a trustee of the Rockefeller Foundation, spent some time investigating the various Chinese projects of the foundation. When he returned home, he sent his opinions of the foundation's work to John D. Rockefeller, Jr.

To JOHN D. ROCKEFELLER, Jr., February 8, 1936

DEAR MR. ROCKEFELLER:

Upon my return from a three months' visit and more in the Orient, I find your kind letter of January 25 upon the occasion of my retirement as a Trustee of the Rockefeller Foundation. Certainly I appreciated your kind words. I felt that I was not able to give the Foundation what it should have from me. My business experience has not been wide. I have conducted a small country-town industry employing only forty men, for forty years, but we have lived happily together and our average term of service now is something over sixteen years. Most of the men and women own their own homes and are happy in their work. I suppose that sort of a small paternal employer does not know much about things in the larger reaches of business, and I have always hesitated to give advice in the Board meetings. But when our deliberations skirted near the world of politics, there I felt competent to talk. I have survived in politics forty years and have known with some intimacy most of the leaders in our political life in that time. While I was in the Orient, I spent most of the time in the Philippines and China, a few days in Japan, and it seems to me you are entitled to my impressions. Here they are:

The Philippine job has been well done, a splendid piece of work in protecting public health. In China, I was happy at the whole pros-

[359]

pect. The only place where I was dubious was over the P.U.N.C. [Peking Union Medical College, a union of six missionary hospitals with Rockefeller Foundation support]. It is a splendid institution. Mrs. White had an attack of septic poisoning and went to the P.U.N.C. hospital and had marvelous care. No one can question the efficiency of the hospital and the intelligence of its general direction. The hospital furnishes a perfect clinic for the college. But there my doubt comes in the college. I fear it is equipping Chinese doctors who will not be able to practice their profession outside of the few great cities of China. They probably will have to teach other doctors, and I suppose there is a real need for young doctors in the interior of China. The graduates of the P.U.N.C. will not go to the country. They cannot. They would not know how to begin practice without elaborate equipment.

I saw in a little Presbyterian mission school in Peking what seemed to me a most valuable work. It was a vocational school in which the boys made all their own tools and made no tool more elaborate than they could make in a Chinese village. They were being taught to be good blacksmiths, good carpenters, good cement workers, good school teachers, good local engineers. And it seemed to me that if someway medicine in China could be stimulated by turning out young doctors who could practice in the environment which they most needed to enter, it would be more helpful.

I have no idea whether there is any sense in this or not, but it was the way I saw things. There can be no question about the efficiency of the Foundation's representatives in China. . . . And in Peking they are doing the work laid out for them by the Foundation. But I am not sure that, for all the magnificence of the college buildings, the perfection of the equipment, and the skill with which the organization is manipulated, the direction of the job may be headed in the wrong way. I don't know, but I have a sense of doubt when I think of the money that it costs.

I hope our paths may cross again. You cannot know how much I value the association with you, and with the other Trustees. It marked an epoch in my life, a happy and I hope a useful one. At least it broadened me and gave me something I needed even though I could not give to the Foundation as much as I might have done. If you are ever in this part of the world, won't you please come, with Mrs. Rockefeller, to visit Mrs. White and me in Emporia. A few days in a typical midwestern, old-fashioned country town, prosperous and democratic, still might renew your faith in the America that we all love.

[360]

Remember me most kindly to Mrs. Rockefeller. I recall sitting at a dinner table with her and our gorgeous talk. I knew her father [Nelson W. Aldrich] before her and what a man!

Carl Sandburg wrote White: "It is good you are back in the country again. Not that one man can do anything. But you help the atmosphere. My guess is that your prophecy will stand, unless the Republicans have a program and if they should win on mere opposition, the party will be washed up in 1940."

To CARL SANDBURG, Harbert, Mich., February 20, 1936

DEAR MR. SANDBURG:

It was good to see your handwriting in the note of February 16th that plunked down on my desk today. Come and see us.

I still believe in fairies, and I still hope that the Republican party will have enough sense to know that it can't go back to McKinley. If it tries to go back to McKinley, it will keep on going past Lincoln and Fremont to Franklin Pierce to the end.

With affectionate regards, I am—

To EMIL HURJA, Democratic National Committee, Washington, D. C., March 24, 1936

DEAR MR. HURJA:

I have your letter of March 17th in which you offer to tell me just how bad Landon is going to be licked. The answer is, I know. But on the other hand that answer is of even date. What will happen in seven months and a half is another matter. He may not even be nominated. Roosevelt might join the Ku-Klux or elope with Lydia Pinkham, or make Du Pont secretary of war, or otherwise blow up on your hands. Barring which I know the truth. . . .

While the Whites were in the Orient, William Randolph Hearst visited Landon in Kansas. The resulting Hearst support of Landon's candidacy alienated many liberal-minded people. White did his best to remove the "taint" of Hearst and, as this letter indicates, worked quite hard to sell Landon in the East.

New York City, to ALF M. LANDON, April 21, 1936

DEAR ALFRED:

I have been ten days in the East now, and I believe I can begin to report progress. When I got here I found exactly what I thought I would find and perhaps subconsciously what I was looking for, a deep distrust of you among responsible Republicans because of Hearst. This I found went as high as Hilles [C. D. Hilles, former chairman of the Republican National Committee] and extended throughout the financial crowd who, of course, will put up money but keep their fingers crossed, and it affected the rank and file of young Republicans.

So to talk to these people I deliberately produced my own alibi against Hearst in that interview in the Tribune which the Associated Press carried. After that I found I could talk fairly with these people, who did not think I was touched with the Hearst taint, and who felt I was your sincere friend. In this tone I talked to different groups. For instance, I squared up before a dozen people at Tom Lamont's [Thomas Lamont, New York banker] house. The other day, I talked for a quarter of an hour about you, your background, the kind of man you are and what you have done. I have had several luncheon groups of liberals and Republicans and have praised you highly. I am going down tomorrow to a luncheon at the Chase National Bank for a similar purpose. I am talking to young Republicans at a big meeting at the National Republican Club, Friday. In these talks I talk as honestly as God will let me about you, paint your warts and all, with no attempt to picture a messiah or a superman and yet, I think this method is the most effective that I can use. I am not so good when I grow lyrical.

Now about Washington—Clifford Hope [Clifford Hope, Kansas Republican Congressman] and the Kansas Congressmen assembled a dozen or twenty northwest congressmen right after luncheon Friday, and I talked for an hour the same as I talked before the crowd at

[362]

Lamont's. They asked questions and I answered them. The Kansas congressmen were nice enough to say that I made a good impression. At least, I tried. I talked before two or three groups of young New Deal radicals, newspapermen, Bill's friends, who think Bill and Katherine* are rich because they wash occasionally and I think I have made an impression on them. They are men mostly like Raymond Swing [news analyst], and all of them asked me to explain what Swing saw in you so interesting and attractive. I have done you a lot of good in this group. I saw Villard of The Nation and talked to Vandenberg [Senator Arthur Vandenberg]. I think I was able to tell him some things that he had not realized. I assume you want friends everywhere and you want men to know why they are your friends, on the basis of what you are and not on the basis of the Kansas-Coolidge myth. Anyway, that is my story and I am going to stick to it.

Capper [Senator Arthur Capper] took me over to Borah, who had been sending word that he wanted to see me, and I spent an hour with him talking platforms. I did not go into your candidacy at all. Borah wants everything his way, which is natural. You are the dog that has the bone and the other dogs never like the dog that has the bone. They see faults that are associated with the position of the bone and do not inhere in the dog that has it, so it was no use trying to convince him that you were a superior bred dog with noble instincts, but I think he will take my suggestion and come to the convention himself and go on the Committee on Resolutions.

Capper said to me, "Now, Will, don't talk Landon to Borah. You will merely get into a fuss and won't be able to do the thing you want," which was also my own feeling about the situation. As it was, I think we left upon very good terms with the door open for me to come in at the proper time and talk directly about you, and what is most important if you get the nomination, Borah will be of much more use to you in the campaign than I can possibly be at the convention.

I think the Republicans in Congress lean toward Vandenberg, chiefly because they know him. They do not know you. I think the Republicans in New York lean toward you because they think you can win and because they think you are in a general way decent and intelligent. I gather that New England will let us write the platform and let you take the nomination. I am sure that they should like to have the vice-presidential end of the ticket. I talked an hour or two

* Mr. and Mrs. W. L. White were now living in the East, where Mr. White was doing journalistic work.

to Ogden Mills [New York Republican leader], and I think he has a fine idea for the set-up of the convention which I must explain to you when I see you, because it is rather long and not in my mind entirely practical in its turn, but the idea has something in it. It entirely concerns the platform. Mills was not interested at all in the vice-presidency end of the ticket, and I have not talked vice-presidential politics nor did anyone talk to me about it. First place, I have no feeling or desire in the matter. Second place, it is dynamite and nobody knows it better than I.

It seems to be assumed here that you will win and everyone is eager to learn the truth about you. The Associated Press and the eastern papers have been carrying stories about Borah which have put you more definitely in the liberal group than anything else since your name came out. I shall have an opportunity today and tomorrow and the next day to find out how the down-town crowd in New York receives this picture of your liberal attitude, but it seems to me that whether they like it or not, it is the only attitude upon which you can win. In the meantime, at least for the next two weeks or so, I think your attitude should be one of impassioned silence, the less you say the less you will have to regret. It seems that looking back over the months since the pot began to boil you have handled yourself beautifully. You have nothing to regret and little to repair.

I shall probably be home Sunday or Monday, the 26th or 27th, but I can't get to Topeka until the middle of next week and really there is nothing to tell you more than I have set down here except what I shall accomplish in the next three or four days. I think the chief things I have done are to talk with Vandenberg and Borah, both of whom I know well enough to be fairly frank. Vandenberg seemed anxious to have the platform out of the way before the convention assembles and to have it as liberal as you would want to make it, and I think Borah would like to have a say in the platform unless he changes his mind and is afraid of the steel trap catching a foot and holding him regular. He will go into the platform convention. Fletcher [chairman of the Republican National Committee], with whom I talked for an hour, feels that it would be a fine thing for Borah to go in and strut his stuff and carry the convention so far to the "left" as he can. The further he carries it the better for you. If failing to carry it as far as he thinks he should go he walks out, then things will be different and not as we can predict them, but I feel fairly sure that even the threat of Borah's walkout will construct for us a platform that you could run on faster and further than you could run if

[364]

Borah did not help us liberalize the platform, even assuming his walk-out.

And so deponent saith nothing more.

White attended the Republican convention as a delegate and sat on the Resolutions Committee at the request of Landon. He then attended the Democratic convention as a reporter for the North American Newspaper Alliance. The Pearson story mentioned in this letter refers to a statement in the "Washington Merry-Go-Round" that Hoover was anti-Landon because of Landon's tie with Hearst.

To HERBERT HOOVER, July 1, 1936

DEAR MR. HOOVER:

Your letter of June 22 was on my desk when I returned from Philadelphia where I have been reporting the Democratic convention. It was pretty terrible. They took five days to do what should have been done snappily and with mounting interest in two days. Apparently the President didn't see ahead to realize how the ginger would go out of the party. He expected it to be a five-day mounting climax and to shoot the fireworks Saturday night. I saw the fireworks. They were wet. He had, from his point of view, an eloquent, if sophomoric speech, but still eloquent. It read much better than he sounded it. I am sending you, herewith, what I wrote about it, also my résumé of the whole thing.

Now about the Pearson story: I never for a minute was fooled by it or any other rumor that you were in the anti-Landon campaign, though I might as well tell you frankly that I would not blame you if you were, considering the California situation, which had my cordial disapproval from the beginning. But I was powerless to stop it.

But as it is, I know how you feel. I have never questioned what your position would be.

Landon is better than he seemed last May. He is, as I told you, a decent, square, kindly, courageous young man. Whether he will crumble or crystallize under the tremendous heat and pressure of the White House, God knows. He and I talking it over on the front porch of the house a few hours before I left for Cleveland, used exactly that figure of speech, crumble or crystallize under heat and pressure. I was frank and said: "I don't know." He said candidly: "Mr. White, I don't know." And I think he is frightened, which is a good attitude. The fear of the Lord is the beginning of wisdom. But he is not a coward and will go to it like a gentleman. Help him all you can. He is the best bet today. He is at least not vain, and I have never seen a man grow intellectually as he has grown in the last ten months.

If you come by this way, do drop in and see us.

White wrote "Landon: I Knew Him When" for the Saturday Evening Post, *July 18, 1936. After reading the article, Harold Ickes wrote White: "I could not for the life of me see, even on the basis of your deft portrayal of him, why anyone should vote for him for President." Later, White wrote another article on Landon for* the New York Times, *August 9, 1936. These two articles, with some additional material, were published in book form in September under the title,* What It's All About; Being a Reporter's Story of the Early Campaign *of 1936.*

To Harold Ickes, July 24, 1936

Dear Harold:

I have your letter about my piece in the Post. As far as I am concerned you can go ahead and slap me around all you please, not particularly for that but I fancy for most anything or everything else that comes into your head. And when you are done, you will not be saying anything about me that I haven't thought seriously.

It is so hard to know what a man ought to do. Landon, as I see him, is exactly the man I draw in the Post, no more and no less. I wasn't trying in the slightest to makes votes for him. I was trying to tell the God's truth about him, and there it is.

Fundamentally, he has nothing bad. He doesn't lie. He is more intelligent than the average. He is money honest and when he makes up his mind he has all the courage in the world and will go any distance without flinching. He has made a decent governor as governors go in a state where the millrun of governors, so far as decency and courage and honesty and intelligence, runs fairly high. We have no serious tradition of money using in our state politics in either party. The Democrats being the "outs" always have a fine line of high-minded silk-stocking statesmen who are used for window dressing for the rank and file of the party; generally haven't sense to pick their candidate out of their best men but take their noisiest, which I suppose is another way of saying that the Democrats are not used to following leadership. The Republicans have two scrapping factions. The division goes clear back to the break in 1902 or '03 when the progressives and insurgents began to roar. The bridge has never been built between the two. I have always been one of the leaders of the progressive crowd. It has generally run the state. Two or three times, we have lost to the Democrats. Once we lost to the conservative Republicans and kidnapped their candidate as soon as he was elected.

I have to tell you these things to explain the strings that held me. All these years we have been building up a very decent crowd of young fellows who are now in their forties and fifties and some of them in their early sixties; some of them along with me who can tiptoe and look into the sunset. It isn't so easy to step out and leave this crowd as it looks. Landon has always been one of my boys. His bad qualities are a mulish stubbornness and a Napoleonic selfishness. But he knows what he is doing, and I have noticed as his power grows he is more and more candid about his progressive qualities. I think as he feels his hold stronger he will reveal more and more of what I am sure is his progressive reactions. This is pure hunch. I have seen it operate many times in him. But I have been fooled on men before and may be fooled again. He has always done everything I asked. . . .

To JUSTICE LOUIS D. BRANDEIS, Washington, D. C., October 12, 1936

DEAR JUSTICE BRANDEIS:

This letter is timed to reach you on your birthday. It is just a word to tell you how much you have meant to me and to millions of your fellow Americans. You have built your life into the structure of our government. You have built your ideals into the hearts of your countrymen, and your work will live for a long time, in years, in decades, and I hope in generations, an inspiration to youth and a comfort to all who love freedom institutionalized into law.

Mrs. White joins me in most cordial remembrances to both you and Mrs. Brandeis.

*The best description of White's role in the Landon campaign is con-
tained in this letter. After Landon's nomination, he refused to play
a dominant role because of the reactionary elements that centered
around John Hamilton, Republican national chairman. While White
was supporting Landon, he also aided George Norris's campaign for
re-election in Nebraska. During the campaign, Senator Norris was
the head of a national liberal committee supporting President Roosevelt. In all his writings about Landon, White was careful to ask only
Kansans to vote for him as a gesture to their native son. Landon did
not even carry his own state. Roosevelt swept to victory, losing the
electoral votes of only Maine and Vermont.*

To Marion Ellet, *Concordia* (Kansas) *Blade*, November 9, 1936

Dear Marion:

You are dead right. I never booked passage. Before I left for the
Orient a year ago, I wrote three or four articles that were widely
distributed for Dave Lawrence's syndicate, the North American
Newspaper Alliance, and for the Associated Press.

When I came home the boom was looming out of obscurity. Hearst
was aboard. I wrote several articles indicating that I couldn't go along
with Hearst. At the Wichita convention, I begged Lacy Haynes
[a leading figure on the Kansas City *Star* and White's brother-in-law]
and the boys to take my name off the list of delegates at large. They
called attention to the fact that if I didn't go along, my absence would
hurt. I had no desire to hurt Alf. They wanted to make me chairman
of the resolutions committee. There I yelled loud enough to stop it.
They put me on the resolutions committee.

Before it was decided that I was to go on, I wrote two strong editorials which I thought would disqualify me. One was headed "Nix
on Coalition." The other demanded a constitutional amendment to
provide for the control of wages, hours of service, and working conditions for women and children in industry. I showed them to Alf.
He insisted that I go on. Like the man he is, he stood by me when
John Hamilton tried to put me off the resolutions committee because
of the two editorials. John's attitude convinced me that I had no
business in this campaign.

I have always been a free man. (I knew that when the time came
I was going to support George Norris, and that I was going to stand

[368]

by Jim Couzens [Senator James Couzens of Michigan]. And I knew that I couldn't swallow the Du Ponts and the Liberty League, the whole kit and boodle of expedient reactionary stuff.) So, in the convention at Cleveland, three minutes after John's gavel had fallen on his announcement of Alf's nomination, I sent Alf a telegram in which I congratulated him, gave him my love, and declared "from now on you walk alone."

My alternatives after the convention were these: I could elbow in at Topeka and, because I am bull-strong, probably I could have horned away some of the conservative and reactionary influences, and I might have given the campaign a slightly more liberal cast. But at what a cost! And I knew it was hopeless, and that if I won my point, I would be held somewhat responsible for the inevitable defeat which was looming ahead. But, if I had stayed under the kleig lights that beat about a throne, if I had won a point now and then, I should have had to make compromises which I could not make and be happy. (You know, Marion, I have written these last three or four sentences so many times in the last four months to so many friends that I could sing them backwards. I began in July.) My other alternative was to stay at home, do all I could and have done, a tremendous lot which also was futile. But I have had three stenographers part of the time and two all the time and have kept them busy. I didn't consult Alfred about what I was doing. Where I could put in a word I did. This is a tremendous country and literally thousands of people who knew my name, who realized that I would be in the Landon convention campaign, wrote me asking questions. Was Landon a drunkard? Did he balance the budget at the expense of the schools? . . . Did he say that $1.00 a day was enough relief for any family? Was he a rich man's son and did his father buy the governorship? Did he marry for money? Lord, gal, you never heard such a lot of funny questions as I have had to answer. And I have put a letter about the schools in every large regional daily in the United States and in the leading county daily in every county in Pennsylvania, Ohio, Michigan, Indiana, and Iowa. This, I hope, cleared the good name of Kansas. Apparently it didn't do Alfred any good—just whistling in the wind.

But to get back to the convention: when I got home I wrote him a friendly letter and told him that I would be a liability. My temperamental desire to say what I pleased when I pleased would rise up to damn him if I was anywhere next to him under the kleig lights. I told him I would not appear often in Topeka, and I didn't see him at his inauguration, though I should rather like to have been near him then.

For I am sincerely fond of him and Theo [Mrs. Alfred M. Landon], whose father was my boyhood playmate in El Dorado sixty years ago. He has been down to see me a couple of times. He sent me some of his speeches to revise. He has invited me on three of his train trips. Whenever he has asked for advice, I have given it to him. Sometimes he has taken it; sometimes he hasn't. But I have offered no unsolicited advice.

After all, it was his show and I have no feeling that I should butt in. Now I know precious well that nothing that he could have done or said, no advice of mine that he could have taken or rejected would have made the slightest difference in the outcome. This is a ground swell. The water of liberalism has been dammed up for forty years by the two major parties. The dam is out. Landon went down the creek in the torrent.

I have hardly known what to write him since election. I have known for two months that it would be terrible. I have known for a year what was coming. I tried to tell him the week before election what to expect as he sat on our front porch. He thought I was mad. So we haven't discussed matters of strategy, and I was glad to be relieved from any responsibility. I have had a beautiful summer, sweat through it all and am well and happy. As far as I can see, I have no feeling of loss, no feeling of pride or wounded pride in the whole thing.

I have intended to write you for a year and tell you how proud I am of the way you are using your talent. You have justified every good hope that I ever had for you. And I hope you will permit me to sign myself—

The overwhelming re-election of Franklin D. Roosevelt was a clear mandate to continue the policies of the New Deal. But never before had the Supreme Court worked such havoc with a president's program as it did during 1935 and 1936. The NRA, the AAA, the Bituminous Coal Act, and the Municipal Bankruptcy Act were some of the laws declared unconstitutional by the court. Six of the judges were over seventy years of age. President Roosevelt said that the Constitution was not to blame, and the court as an institution was not to

blame, just the human beings on it. On February 5, 1937, he pro-
posed the addition of younger blood by appointing one new judge,
up to a maximum of six, for every judge, who having reached seventy,
failed to retire. A great hue and cry was raised immediately over this
proposal. Congress debated it through the summer of 1937. In the
end the bill was defeated, but by that time the court had handed down
decisions favorable to the National Labor Relations Act, the Social Se-
curity Law, and the Railway Labor Act. Even though Roosevelt lost
the battle, he won the war. Shortly after the defeat of the bill the most
reactionary members of the court retired to private life. White was
opposed to the President's plan to add justices, and he attacked it in an
article for The New York Times, *April 25, 1937.*

To E. H. REES, Congressman from Emporia, Kan., January 19, 1937

DEAR ED:

. . . Now about the Supreme Court: You, who have read the Gazette all your life, know that in ninety-nine cases out of a hundred I
have backed the Supreme Court; indeed the two Supreme Courts, the
Kansas and the Federal Supreme Court. Sometimes I am fussy with
the district judiciary, but I notice that the Supreme Court by and
large, considered in terms not of years, not perhaps even of decades
but of a generation, marches pretty steadily in line with the popular
thought of the American people. I should hesitate to vote for any
drastic change in our judicial procedure. When I am chafed a bit at
the four to five, or six to three decisions that occasionally, though
not often, go against my ideas of public policy, I try to throw my
imagination into reverse and to realize what might happen to American liberties if a Fascist Congress should begin passing laws restrict-
ing those liberties. Then I should be most thankful for even a narrow
majority in the Court which would save those liberties. I feel that it is,
on the whole, much better to let things stand in the Court as they
are even though the status quo does sometimes halt the march of
American ideals of justice, even though among the nine old men four
or five are reactionary. I feel, to repeat, that it is better to let things
stand than to crowd the mourners, hurry the process of justice and
speed up the jump between popular opinion and realized institutions.
For after all, if popular opinion is sound, it is better to wait than to
be sorry.

[371]

As you know, Ed, I am supposed to be one of those impulsive scatterbrain radical liberals. But I hope you know that in serious matters I am as conservative as wisdom need be. You ask my advice about this court matter. I have no advice. I give you my opinion. It is up to you.

Strikers, disdaining traditional methods, employed the new technique of the "sit-down" strike, seizing possession of General Motors plants in Michigan and refusing to withdraw until their demands had been gained. Property-minded people advocated the use of state troops to drive the strikers from the plants. Governor Frank Murphy resisted such demands and used the troops to maintain order. White praised Murphy's actions in his editorial columns.

To GOVERNOR FRANK MURPHY, Lansing, Mich., March 15, 1937

DEAR GOVERNOR MURPHY:

I was glad to have your letter. The day the article appeared in the midst of the sit-down strike I sent you a copy of the editorial and merely initialed it W.A.W. which probably didn't mean anything to your executive force. I wrote on the margin of the paper "Give this to your sister."

You are doing a good job. I have been asked by the North American Newspaper Alliance, which represents the leading paper in every American city of over 100,000, to write a series of articles trying to explain in terms of popular philosophy what this turmoil means between labor and capital. I am trying to get hold of Lewis [John L. Lewis, head of the newly launched C.I.O.] and Green [William Green, head of the A.F. of L.] and possibly Sloan [Alfred P. Sloan, Jr., of General Motors] or some other top-notch industrialist to present their particular points of view not as propaganda but as representing the angles from which this disturbance comes. If I wire you, I wish you could talk with me for half an hour some day about the political angle, that is to say, the state's part in the industrial struggle representing the noncombatants and particularly the cause of industrial peace.

Mrs. White asks to be remembered to you and your sister most kindly.

White wanted a constitutional amendment, limiting the power of the Supreme Court to declare laws unconstitutional, submitted to the people in place of the President's bill to add justices to the court. He and Senator George Norris had considerable correspondence on this point. Actually, when the President's bill was defeated, there was no further attempt to revise the power of the court.

To Harold Ickes, March 19, 1937

Dear Harold:

There is no question at all between us about two things: First, the need of reform in the Supreme Court. Second, the fact that President Roosevelt is the ideal of the American people. Of course, Lincoln did not come into his power and glory until after he died. Washington was probably some such an ideal during his first term. There may have been a moment when Jackson reached the high point, which the President holds today, but Jackson could not hold it. Theodore Roosevelt, of course, was blessed by his enemies who were a considerable minority of the people and were entirely to his credit as indeed are all the instinctive foes of the President today. But he has developed in this court proposal a genuinely sincere, intelligent, unselfish, high-minded minority who, if they are forced to accept with compromise the President's proposal, will make a break in his otherwise shining armor.

On these two propositions, (a) the need for reform, (b) the President's popularity, there shall be no question between friends. But I do hope that he will be able to bring himself to accept some compromise which will take this proposition to the people. As I told you right after the election, George Norris and I began corresponding about the court thing, and I told him in December that I had a feeling of anxiety which arises from a fear that the reactionary swing which is bound to come will leave some president the power to so control the courts that our Bill of Rights will be curtailed.

Norris, I think, has that in view also. That consideration was the nubbin of our correspondence. I have since had letters from other senators very much of Norris' social and economic views who are deeply and honestly disturbed on that very phase of the question. Most of these senators have been devoted enough to the President— some of them have taken their political lives in their hands in his cause—to warrant him considering their viewpoint.

I have been waiting for your speech and haven't seen it. It will doubtless turn up tomorrow, and I'll read it through if it's the last act of an ill-spent life.

White played a dominant role in securing the ratification of the federal child labor amendment by the Kansas legislature. He had realized from his long experience that the only way to accomplish his objective in a democracy was to be more powerfully organized than the opposition.

To GIFFORD PINCHOT, Washington, D. C., March 30, 1937

DEAR GIFFORD:

The thing that happened in Nebraska would have happened in Kansas if I hadn't taken hold of it.* Four or five hundred dollars, which Arthur Capper and I and two or three others put into a jackpot, kept the wires hot with phone calls and phone messages to legislators and did the trick. You can't get anywhere by just making a speech for the Legislature. Incidentally, I rounded up the newspapers and that helped a little but not a great deal. The women's clubs, the labor organizations, and the churches, as centers to send out phone calls, telegrams and special delivery letters did the business. And then

* The amendment was defeated in Nebraska.

we had enough legislators pledged before the primary, and in the election pledged to these same outfits, and all we did was make them stand by the pledges. But you have to do that.

After a long and rather useless life in American politics, I have discovered that sentiment counts 25 per cent, organization 60 per cent, inertia of the other fellow 20 per cent, and if you succeed the rest of it is his blundering.

The Catholic Church put the trimmings to the amendment wherever it was defeated this year. But I think the church was inspired by the National Manufacturers and particularly textiles.

Thus endeth the reading of the first lesson.

To Mayor Fiorello LaGuardia, New York City, April 2, 1937

Dear Mr. LaGuardia:

I am a member of the jury of awards of the American Hebrew medal for the promotion of better understanding between Christians and Jews in America, and I have just been notified that you have been awarded the medal for the year 1936. I hope to heaven I had the good sense to vote for you, and I have a better than sneaking idea that I did as a member of the jury. But a man mustn't be too cocksure of what he did six months ago. Anyway, I am proud and happy to be a part of the machinery which presents you this award, and I want to take this opportunity to tell you how deeply I have rejoiced at your growing power for usefulness. If we had nominated you for president last year, the result might have been the same but the Republican position would be entirely different. Maine and Vermont would not be so lonesome.

You are a young man yet. I am tiptoeing toward the end of my three score years and ten, but I hope to live long enough to see you in the White House. Your vision, your intelligence, your courage and your kind heart are needed there.

With kindest personal regards, I am—

Harold Ickes published an interesting article on the Bull Moose party in the American Historical Review *for January, 1941. White read the article in manuscript form and made some suggestions and changes.*

To GIFFORD PINCHOT, Milford, Pa., May 17, 1937

DEAR GIFFORD:

I had a letter from Harold Ickes, the other day, who has written an account of the Progressive party from 1912 to 1917 as he remembers it. It is a stirring and tragic story, and it brought back to mind those splendid days when you and he and I and Jim and Victor [James Garfield of Ohio and Victor Murdock of Kansas] and Hiram Johnson, Myer Lissner, Chester Rowell [Hiram Johnson, Myer Lissner, and Chester Rowell were the three leaders of the California Progressive party] and a dozen or so men who really believed in the progressive vision were really trying to save the party from the strangulation which it suffered at George Perkins' hand. Harold's story brought it all back most vividly and brought back the other years from 1916 to the middle of the last decade when we were all working together. I remember the time when Harold was trying to interest the Republicans in your candidacy for president. He made a valiant effort, but I suppose the party had small use for men like us.

The other day Mrs. White saw something in a New York paper which indicated you were taking a crack at Harold for something or other. I was hurt a little. For I know whatever comes, Harold will be honest and imbued with a high and noble purpose. He has not changed, no more than you have changed, and we who were once so near and dear should not let anything come into our lives to lessen the bond of respect and affection which held us together so happily in another day. For it was a good day, and the fighting was worth while. God knows I didn't do much except stand around and cheer, but you boys who were fighting pushed the line forward or we could not be where we are now except for the ground you gave, all of you, in that splendid fight from 1904 on until the battleground changed and the new campaign began.

Pardon these sentimental admonitions and believe me always—

[376]

White not only wrote a letter to Mayor LaGuardia praising his attributes for the presidency, but he released a statement to the press that LaGuardia would make an excellent Republican candidate in 1940. Immediately, superpatriots of the type that had joined the Klan or supported native fascist movements like William Dudley Pelley's Silver Shirts, wrote indignant letters to White attacking both White and LaGuardia. Louis Adamic, publicist of the contribution of immigrant groups to American life, wrote White praising his stand for LaGuardia.

To Louis Adamic, Milford, N. J., July 27, 1937

Dear Louis Adamic:

It was good to see your signature at the end of a letter. I read your piece about Roper [D. C. Roper, secretary of commerce] in The Nation the other day and sat down and wrote him a letter telling him I thought it was a grand piece.

Now about LaGuardia. You should see the shower of brick bats, dead cats, and miscellaneous junk that is falling in my direction from the Nazis. I didn't know there were so many in the United States..It's been worth the trouble to get a sample of them.

It seems to me it's a pious act for any citizen, Republican, Democrat, Communist, Mormon, or whatnot, to say anything that will help LaGuardia lick Tammany.

Of all the evils which threatens this country, a corrupt and controlled vote is the greatest and hardest to combat.

Mrs. White joins me in kindest regards to you and Mrs. Adamic. Why don't you tune up the old flivver and come out and see us?

Drew Pearson and Robert S. Allen, authors of the widely circulated newspaper column, "Washington Merry-Go-Round," were particular favorites of White's. He frequently wrote them suggestions for their daily column.

Dear Drew and Bob:

Here's an assignment for you. You are about the only boys that can handle it. It's a book about this court battle. The one item that has intrigued me more than any other of the columns and pages and folios and news about this court show that I have read was an item in your column which declared that the President prepared his court message after a dinner with the Supreme Court last winter.

Follow up on that dinner. Find what happened. Relate it to the N.R.A. and A.A.A. decisions and trace the history of the battle from that evening until Garner* went over to Wheeler's† room and signed the armistice.

This battle will be known a hundred years from now. It is one of the notable constitutional contests in our government, easily comparable with the Dred Scott decision, which, by the way, you will find beautifully annotated in Burton's new book [T. E. Burton, *The Constitution of the United States*] about the Constitution. It will pay you to read that before you go into your book.

One of the dangers of your writing is your difficulty in taking a detached view. Very little has been written intelligently or said intelligently in favor of the court in the debate on the floor of the Senate. It has been fiery but it has been heat without light.

I wish as a penance for your sins you would look up the New York Sunday Times magazine for, I think, the first week in April and read something I wrote about the court there. Sparing my blushes, I think the real issue is found in the difference between the President's theory of political mandate and the theory as it was laid down in the Constitution by the founding fathers.

But that shouldn't bother you except that you ought to know that there was an intelligent side to this court contest, even if it was kept fairly secret and undefined. The story is a story that you two can unfold and no one else. The inside story of the White House. What happened at the dinner; what happened after his "now speech" that made him trim a little in his next speech; what happened to give him the notion that the country was with him. I think he had an easy majority on a nose count. But nose counts are only valuable at an election. The day after election the middle class moves in and runs

* Vice-President John N. Garner did liaison work between the rival camps in the Supreme Court bill fight.

† Burton K. Wheeler was an opponent of the President in this fight.

the show through its various organizations of public expression, the newspapers, the churches, the lodges, the clubs, the public corridors (from the Pullman's observation car on down to the filling station). The middle class for one hundred fifty years has organized itself to rule by public expression in these various outlets. The only way the proletariat makes its will public is in the mob and riot which are soon suppressed and generally remain echoes. That essential silence of his support in the proletariat, and the conspicuous thunder of middle-class opinion, swung Congress away from the President. Any president is powerless before middle-class opinion. And the sad ironic thing about the proletariat is that as wages rise, the boys in the proletariat join the middle class, become vocal through the middle class and so until we have one long catastrophic depression which will materially cut down the power of the middle class, no president can rely on mere majorities to back him up in any serious fight.

This is thrown in obiter dicta. But the book that you boys can write of this great battle, in the first place, should be part of the historical record. In the second place, if you do it as well as you can, it will make a pocket full of money, which, as I understand, having been in our noble profession now for fifty-two years, is the chief end of man with certain qualifications, amendments, restrictions, and hedging.

Here's another thing. I notice in your esteemed article last night that you took a crack at a lady. Not long ago you took another at the wife of the Brazilian Minister or something like that. Watch out. People resent it. Moreover, there lies the road to libel and a pretty woman looking at a jury doesn't have to have much material evidence to sting your clients. Take it from me and keep your column a "Gents Only."

Dr. B. C. Brown was a close personal friend who had met White in Europe during World War I. White's Coolidge book was published in 1938 under the title A Puritan in Babylon. *It offers a stimulating insight into the America of the "Roaring Twenties."*

DEAR BLANCHE:

It was good to hear from you. But I know you have something to do besides write letters. And I felt like a dog when I neglected answering yours so long.

Let me begin back where I left off. First, I'll tell you how I am, physically. The answer is, swell. I go in and let the doctor boys upstairs prod me and plug me like a watermelon and analyze my blood and everything, and I am as near normal as a man sixty-nine years and seven months may be expected to be. My sugar quota is less than that of either Puerto Rico or Cuba, about where it was four or five years ago. My heart's good and my digestion clicks like a corn sheller. If, for your sins, you read the Gazette, you will see what kind of work I am turning out. I am sandpapering that Coolidge book, and it ought to go to the printer in a week or two for publication next spring. The thing that delayed it was the discovery that I could use the letters of the late William Howard Taft to his wife and sons and daughter. He was more or less a White House familiar during the Coolidge regime and had a lot of good gossip about him. Without that, I could not get the local color of the White House in those days so well as I have it. And I had to mortise it into the book after the book was finished, and it took a lot of time.

I think I have written you at different times about our beloved President. I seem to have a recollection of telling you about seeing him in the White House, and of the distrust I felt in him and my fear that when he was thwarted he would blow up. That has been with me for the last four years since I saw him the first time as president. That sense of the unconscious arrogance of conscious class. He is in no sense democratic. Neither is he a free spirit. He is a bound and chained patrician who must give benevolences and issue commands— and not work with those who are trying to achieve a better social order. I think he has a God complex. Once in ancient Egypt a ruler hired his parrot to cry, "Hano is a God!" all day long. It seems to me that Roosevelt with his court and his astrologers and jesters is making Hano's mistake. Which is too bad, too terribly bad. For he has done so much that is good. His whole first year's performance was to my notion splendid, though he made a mistake, and so did all of us, in the conception of the N.R.A. and the A.A.A. which was not to be wondered at. It was hastily thrown together, and if the court had not wrecked it, it would have wrecked itself and maybe him with it and us more or less, if anything can wreck a hundred million people a going concern—which I doubt. The momentum is too great.

Anyway, I fear that he is in real danger of thinking with his bile rather than with his cortex, which also again is dangerous. And physically, if he does let his engine get hot, he will shoot a bearing for he is running on only half his cylinders. Physically, he cannot afford wrath and vengeance. And if he goes, there will be the devil to pay. For the Republicans have no leaders and the Democrats have no leaders. We are little better off than Germany, Russia, or Italy, in the matter of leaders. So I approach threescore years and ten without much regret. So far as I am concerned, I am willing to leave the show and catch the 5:15 for the shut-eye world. . . .

Over a hundred of White's fellow townsmen sent him flowers on his seventieth birthday. Birthday letters poured in from the entire country. Just before his birthday, Collier's *carried an autobiographical article by White entitled "It's Been a Grand Show."* Life *and* Look *magazines carried pictures, John Finley of* The New York Times *wrote an editorial, and Fox Movietone News filmed the occasion. White mentions in this letter the large number of letters he was receiving from people. All during this troubled decade, White received a huge volume of mail from people he did not know. They wrote to him asking advice on all types of problems. This inflow of letters reveals that he was becoming something of a folk hero to America. A rock of seeming stability and sound advice amid all the turmoil and trouble of the decade.*

To W. L. Chenery, *Collier's*, February 28, 1938

Dear Bill Chenery:

You certainly played the devil with me there in the Century Club last December when you suggested that article on "It's Been a Grand Show."

I have received more letters about that than anything since "What's

[381]

the Matter With Kansas?" appeared, when I was swamped for three months. Today, I have got a great stack of stuff that has mounted up to a size beyond belief. And here is a funny thing that happened: the Look people, last December, sent for some biographical photographs. And by some chance, which I had nothing to do with, published them, as you may know, early in February. Then John Finley, late in January, wrote a little editorial about my coming birthday. Those two things were not highly dynamic. But when the article in Collier's multiplied by Look, multiplied by the Times editorial began to explode, the little birthday party that I had planned, inviting the fifty or seventy-five country editors of this Congressional District to dinner, bloomed into national importance. Fox Movietone had a man here. The Associated Press had two picture photographers and a reporter, and along came Life with one of its crack staff candid cameraists. I am sending you an account of that party herewith. Also I am sending you one letter. I could send you half a dozen almost as good. But this letter is rather dramatic. It is about the boy from the Stone Age whom I mentioned in my Collier's piece. The man who writes this letter was a big boy when I was a little fellow in El Dorado. He left when I was six or seven years old, and I have no recollection of him. But he remembered me and Temple Friend.*

In the letter you will notice that he said that Temple Friend was a baby, six months, when he was stolen by the Indians, who left his mother scalped for dead. He was older than that, I think a little better than a year. But it is none the less a marvelous story and I thought you would like to read it.

I should be so happy if you would stop over here in Emporia sometime when you are passing through. Give me two or three days' notice, so that we can have the fatted calf. Then, in the meantime, permit me to sign myself—

Gerald B. Winrod, Kansas fascist, ran for the United States Senate in the Republican primary of 1938. White used his newspaper and his journalistic connections to tell the people of Kansas just what Winrod

* In the *Collier's* article White described a boyhood playmate, Temple Friend, who had been reared by Indians.

represented. After Pearl Harbor, Winrod was one of the individuals indicted for sedition, and his newspaper, the Defender, *was barred from the mails. One of the many anti-Semitic actions of Winrod was to print articles in his magazine, the* Revealer, *which in banner headlines "proved" "Roosevelt's Jewish Ancestry" from authentic Nazi sources. The recipient of the following letter was an old friend of White's who once had lived in Kansas City.*

To Jacob Billikopf, Philadelphia, Pa., February 28, 1938

Dear Mr. Billikopf:

. . . But from all that I know about the political situation in Kansas, I deeply fear that the Fascist, raw and unashamed, stands a fairly good chance to go to the United States Senate from this state, and while I shall expose him with all my heart and with all my strength, I am afraid, deeply afraid.

The situation is ripe for it. The idle mind of distressed people is turning, even if futilely and vainly, to any noise in the periphery, I mean any political noise, thinking it is a call of succor.

A distinct slump has come in the power of the President, if not in his popularity. He himself survives but his power to help his friends and punish his enemies is gone. Therefore, I fear that our nondescript Democratic senator will not be hard to beat. In the Republican primary, Winrod will be opposed by my friend whom I shall support heartily and with all the power I have—Clyde Reed, a rather advanced liberal, who has bad political manners and who has in two decades of public life accumulated a lot of enemies among the more reactionary conservatives. They do not like Winrod but the leaders will accept him as their candidate. And he will attract exactly the same kinds that flocked to the Klan and that gathered about Dr. Brinkley [Dr. John R. Brinkley, "the goat-gland specialist," who ran for governor of Kansas in 1930 and 1932] and that backed Huey Long. . . . This group is a minority group in Kansas, probably in all states. But when, in the Republican party, it votes as a man with the conservative faction, also a minority, it is likely to make a primary majority and to give Winrod the nomination.

If I knew what to do about it, I would do it. And I shall do what I can. But don't let anyone mislead you. The situation is terribly serious.

It was foredoomed that a Fascist should come from Kansas, which

[383]

has no Jews and no Catholics to speak of. So that we can ring no bells or blow no horns to rally those whom the Fascists would assail. It is a serious situation. It may be the first crack in our ancient liberty.

Or maybe I am just plain goofy. I am always glad to hear from you, and I hope you are well and happy.

Although White differed with the President on the Supreme Court bill, he never broke his friendly relations with Mr. Roosevelt. While White was at the Mayo Clinic in December, 1937, and January, 1938, undergoing an operation, the President wrote him a letter hoping that he would get back to writing soon "for we all need to jog people into speeding up their 'evolutionary processes of thinking.' "

To FRANKLIN D. ROOSEVELT, February, 1938

DEAR MR. PRESIDENT:

I have been waiting three or four weeks to answer your letter, to think of exactly what I wanted to say. At different times in the last five years I have had a hundred hunches to write to you telling you how to run the show. Mrs. White always says of me that when I get on a ship the first thing I do is to run into the captain's quarters and tell him how to steer the boat. So it has been quite a chore for me to keep hands off.

And now that you have given me a letter to answer, and that I know that I must make it brief, I am going to take what seems to me the most important thing I can say to you. It is this: Watch out for your health. Politics will take care of itself, if you keep your dauber up. Specifically—you are coming into the prostate zone. Don't dally with it. It whittles you down and gets your everlasting spiritual goat without you realizing it. I have been through it. The operation used to take six months or a year out of a man's life in his fifties, sixties and seventies and increased the death rate of old men scandalously. But last December I went to Mayos, where they have a bloodless operation done by an electrical gadget and without a general anesthetic. I talked

[384]

to the nurse while they did it, and when it was done they showed me a saucer full of tripe, and I was feeling frisky enough to tell them, for Heaven's sake not to put the pants on the wrong pile for that tripe looked like a Democrat. Which was regarded as a festive bit of humor in the hospital. I was in the hospital but four days and in Rochester ten days convalescing. After which I went back to work.

But I am dead serious about this warning as you walk into the danger zone of the years.

Here is another thing: A nice young press photographer, named Martin Black, took a picture of you that I fancied particularly. I am not enamored of your smile. I like you better when you bark than when you wag your tail and this is a barking picture. And I am sending it to you hoping you will autograph it, hoping I may frame it and put it in my office beside Margaret Bourke White's portraits of Ickes, Borah and Norris. I shall be very glad if you can decorate the white coat of this picture with your signature.

And further deponent saith not except to add most cordial greetings and best wishes for your health and happiness.

On April 22, 1938, the American Society of Newpaper Editors spent an hour in the White House with President Roosevelt. The President complained about the press being hostile to him, although he praised one of White's editorials in the Gazette *called "Not Fear of One Man." At that point White spoke up and said, "Mr. President, another president whose name need not be mentioned but whose initials are H.H. complained to me of the same thing in this room." The next day the editors elected White president of their society for the coming year.*

To WALT MASON, La Jolla, Calif., April 25, 1938

DEAR WALT:

. . . You ask me what I think about Roosevelt. He still remains a puzzle to me. It can't be all luck. There is no such thing. Yet his qualities never came out, never were revealed. He is surrounded by a lot of wise young men in their forties. I am almost persuaded that wise young men are smarter than wise old men; at least they have more courage in their wisdom. But also they are more liable to hit the bumps. And when this baby does hit the bumps, the air is going to be full of baby carriage wheels and didies and eiderdown quilts, "and the subsequent proceedings may interest him no more." I give it all up. It's too much for me. "So far so good" as the man said who jumped out of the twentieth story window and passed the tenth story.

When White started after Winrod's candidacy, the Winrod forces replied by trying to smear White with the taint of communism. They circulated a pamphlet entitled "How Red Is White?" A few years before, Elizabeth Dilling had characterized White as a dangerous Red, along with Sinclair Lewis, Harry Emerson Fosdick, and John Dewey, in her book The Red Network. *Winrod's revivalistic, preacher background worried White in view of the success that fanatics like John Brown and Carry Nation had had in Kansas in the past.*

To FRANKLIN D. ROOSEVELT, June 10, 1938

DEAR MR. PRESIDENT:

Here is the Kansas Senatorial situation: I have been afraid of Winrod for several years. He has all the elements of danger. He was a tent evangelist and knows the tricks of Father Coughlin,* Huey Long and Billy Sunday [a popular Protestant revival preacher]. He is a nice blend of the three, temperamentally, intellectually, morally. Until six or eight months ago, he was selling Jew-baiting literature in a little Seventh-Day millennial paper which he circulates. He sold, for instance, the "Protocols of Zion." I have made it my business to read his Weekly for several years. And when I saw the advertisement of

* Father Coughlin was a Catholic priest from Michigan who built a large radio following on anti-British, anti-Communist, and anti-New Deal appeals.

[386]

the Jew-baiting literature out, I was scared. It was about the time that he loomed into some slight national prominence in the fight on your Court Bill. The political hookup was obvious. He has all the money he needs for the radio, which is expensive, and he has been sending out, for more than a year, about sixty thousand weekly letters well stuffed with printing—circulars, mimeographed addresses, etc.—indicating that he has support, and lots of it. I heard the other day that he dropped a one hundred dollar bill in the plate at a Negro church meeting after one of his own rabble-rousing addresses. He speaks well, either on the radio or to an audience, and is a strapping, handsome, smooth-talking man much like a medicine vendor or a soap peddler. His religious angle is interesting. He is four degrees sub-Baptist, more fundamentalist than Bryan, believes in all the prophecies of Revelations. The Methodists in Kansas are uneasy about him for he is violently anti-Methodist. They are too liberal for him. It is important to know this in any estimate you may make of his political strength. For one cannot assume that he is dishonest. He really believes it.

His political appeal is deeply reactionary. In the primary he is gaining headway. Unless we can change the Republican situation, he will win.

Now for the Republican Senatorial situation in this state which you have a right to know: I am supporting Clyde Reed, but Reed is a sick man and cannot make a campaign. Reed's strength is his platform appearance. Now he has got to depend on a hand-shaking campaign. As a hand-shaker, he is worse than old Henry Cabot Lodge. He can pile up the votes in a Court House meeting and lose them when he marches down Main Street trying to be amiable. He has a tough-fibered brain. He knows what it means. He is courageous and he is fundamentally honest. Given his normal energy, he could lick Winrod, for this is after all a liberal state. Running against Reed and Winrod in the Republican primaries is an amiable, hand-shaking Cheshire cat named Dallas Knapp, who still thinks in terms of Blaine and Logan [Republican candidates for the presidency and vice-presidency in 1884]. He will garner a few votes from Winrod but he is comparatively unknown.

Reed's friends, and I am one, are trying to get him out of the race and get another more competent liberal in the race, or a good middle-of-the-roader, like Congressman Clifford Hope, or Homer Hoch, former congressman, or [Congressman] Frank Carlson. But Reed is sick and stubborn, and we are up against a terribly hard proposition. And the time is short.

Now about the Democratic situation: So far, McGill [incumbent Democratic senator from Kansas] is unopposed for renomination, as you know. But a strong group of Democrats, who more or less control the Democratic political machine, do not like McGill. They are not entirely reactionary, nor conservative. They are offended Democrats. They wanted Harry Woodring [Governor Harry Woodring of Kansas] and then they wanted Dudley Doolittle [former Democratic congressman from Kansas] to run, but they feel cheated and impotent. They are not strong numerically, but they are powerful politically. What they would do if the race lined up between a clever rabble-rousing conservative like Winrod and a rather colorless Democratic nominee like McGill is almost unpredictable. It is not as simple as you think, and I am scared stiff. My present feeling is that I shall support McGill against Winrod with vigor and enthusiasm, which, considering that I am on the Red Network along with our First Lady, may not help McGill. It may chase off his conservative Democratic support. But I don't know. I am puzzled and, of course, the weather is the X of our political equation. A good wheat crop at a good price, though you may not believe it, means Republican votes. This is normally a Republican state. The minor state officers survived your landslide. So did both Houses of the Legislature, and so did the Court House. And when the Republicans are feeling fat and sassy with a crib full of corn and a corral full of cattle, they revert to type and *you* cannot make them grateful. So they might vote for Winrod in spite of my screams.

I am satisfied that Dudley Doolittle can beat Winrod. It is a question whether McGill can do it because he has no personal strength, no charm, no pulling power. You can carry Kansas (but hardly for a third term). Your personal popularity is strong, unblemished. But in a hot political fight, with all the money that Winrod can command, with good crops, good prices and a normal Republican swingback, McGill is in doubt.

Homer Hoch could beat him under those circumstances easily, and you couldn't do much about it. You might even hurt him by a personal appeal if the tide happened to be running against you. By tide, I mean crops, prices, business conditions and the thousand little things that magnify themselves in the last sixty days of a campaign.

It is hardly more necessary for me to mark this letter confidential than it is for you to mark yours. If John Hamilton puts me up against the wall, and Jim Farley [the respective chairmen of the Republican and Democratic national committees] stands you up beside me, each of us for trafficking with the enemy, I hope someone will lend us a flag so that we can hold it up and tell the world that we died for our country and to hell with the party. A swell bunch of last words.

In the meantime, permit me to repeat the only message I would give you on your present job at your present age: watch out for your prostate, the fate of a nation hangs on it. Just to give you an idea of how I am thinking, I am sending you today's editorial about Iowa.

Shortly after this letter was written, White wired President Roosevelt urging the appointment of Felix Frankfurter to the United States Supreme Court. On January 5, 1939, he received a wire from the President saying "I have done it." Gerald Winrod was defeated in his Senatorial attempt although he gained over fifty thousand votes. The Republican candidate for governor, Payne Ratner, mentioned in this letter, was elected in November.

To Paul Kellogg, Survey Associates, Inc., September 16, 1938

Dear Paul Kellogg:

I am delighted to have your letter about Felix Frankfurter. I had a letter from the President a couple or three months ago which left the door open to me to write to him about Felix Frankfurter. When Cardozo died I composed this short letter to President Roosevelt:

I was able to round up two United States Senators who voted for Justice Brandeis' confirmation. President Hoover indicated that the seven dollar night letter that I sent him a day or two before Cardozo was named had weighed somewhat in the balance. If I could have the word to say to you now, it would be to urge the appointment of Felix Frankfurter to succeed Cardozo.

I did not send the letter. I have not been sure of myself since then. I am dead sure that I should be happier to see Felix Frankfurter

[389]

on the Court bench than to see any other man whom I can imagine there.

Here is the but—will not his appointment to succeed Cardozo give the Jew baiters a chance to say that the Jews have pre-empted a seat in the Court? Also the big rich reactionaries, both Jew and Gentile, have made Felix Frankfurter their head devil. The rich Gentiles are glad to fan the racial question. Would not their instinctive and entirely proper dislike for Frankfurter leave them free to encourage, more or less secretly, anti-Semitic propaganda? I have not answered either of those questions in my mind. I don't know. They rise and they have kept me from writing the letter which came out of my heart when Cardozo went. Still I do not know. I have been thinking of checking this up to Felix Frankfurter himself, but I have not done it fearing he might misunderstand.

I have fought against racial and religious prejudice for years. I am probably oversensitive. We Republicans nominated for governor of Kansas a young man, my dear friend and a consistent, courageous liberal, named Ratner, whose father was a Jew, whose mother was an Irish Murphy. We have just defeated a man named Winrod for senator who took the Nazi position—ignorantly I think, but by some strange intuition in his heart he is as good a Nazi as Hitler.

We will win the fight for Ratner in Kansas—I think. Maybe being in the midst of it and just having come out of the Winrod fight, some subconscious inhibition keeps me from stirring up another fight. I don't know. But I do know this. If I were sure Felix Frankfurter would take the job, I should go in.

Think this over and write to me.

To HENRY WALLACE, Secretary of Agriculture, November 15, 1938

DEAR HENRY WALLACE:

I am glad you found the note of affection in my letter. I knew your father, and I can understand a father's pride in all that you have done, in all that you have aspired, in the fundamental change of national thinking about the farm problem which your efforts and your outgivings have produced.

I think I have told you before that I only suspect two kinds of men who discuss the farm problem: first, the man who says there isn't any; second, the man who says he knows the formula or panacea that will solve it. The world changes so fast, I fear, and conditions here, because of the changing world, move so rapidly that it will be almost impossible, short of national isolation, to find anything that will work from six to nine months ahead of its adoption. And the six to nine months future leeway are necessary if one makes any attempt to solve the farm problem.

Which does not mean I think it hopeless, but which does mean we have a long road of trial and error ahead of us. And as you travel the road I have such faith in your sincerity, such belief in your essential wisdom, and have seen such conspicuous examples of your good courage that I can only wish you well and earnestly hope that you will find the thing that will click at the end of your quest. . . .

White's work as judge of the Book-of-the Month Club occupied a good deal of his time. In his later years he did not always make a trip to New York to attend the monthly editorial meetings. Instead he sent telegrams. Harry Scherman observed in the memorial pamphlet issued by the Book-of-the-Month Club following White's death: "When it was known he would not be present, almost the first thing the other judges would say upon their arrival was: 'What's Bill got to say?' They knew there would be some hilarious critical slant on the long yellow sheet, and he seldom failed them." O. G. Villard's book was Fighting Years; Memoirs of a Liberal Editor; *Ida M. Tarbell's was* All in the Day's Work. Machines Over Men *was written by R. F. Yates. A. Scheinfeld wrote* You and Heredity. Grapes of Wrath *was by John Steinbeck, and* Bitter Creek *was by J. Boyd.* Wind, Sand and Stars *was by A. de Saint Exupéry, and Charles and Mary Beard wrote* America in Midpassage.

To HARRY SCHERMAN, Book-of-the-Month Club (Telegram),
March 1, 1939

The three biographies, Villard, Tarbell, Jane Carlyle are tops. Villard and Tarbell to my notion much more important and salable than Carlyle which seems to be pretty sugary. Villard is controversial but a powerful job. Often I disagree with him but his craftmanship and his integrity of purpose give his book force and compelling interest. Miss Tarbell has wide public and her book would certainly sell to our clients. "Machines Over Men" is splendid but if we buy it we should pickle it until fall well after we had disposed of "Heredity and You." [It was a dual selection.] Now for the novels. Far and away the best novel is "The Grapes of Wrath" but it would be a mistake to buy it. Thousands of our readers would be offended by its necessary but to me quite inoffensive indecency. "Bitter Creek" is pure synthetic ersatz with dime novel characters, movie psychology and altogether pretty terrible. "Wind, Sand and Stars" would make a swell supplemental choice. [It was selected.] I like "America in Midpassage" and would rejoice in its selection but fear to recommend it because it is a little heavy for our buyers. [It was selected.] Too much like Walter Lippmann's swell book that flopped a few years ago. Will be in town National Arts Club next Monday. Hope see you.

White enjoyed the fraternity of the small town. For years he was in in charge of selecting the menus for the weekly Rotary Club luncheons. He considered himself quite a gourmet and took pride in the meals he ordered for the club. Fellow Rotarians frequently wrote to White asking for copies of his menus.

To W. F. SHUETTE, March 4, 1939

DEAR MR. SHUETTE:

I have your letter about the Rotary menu. I note that you suggest that I send you some menus that we have used. Generally speaking, I made them up out of my head and have no record. I find the boys like, for instance, rare broiled steak with shoestring potatoes. Also, they like corned beef and cabbage preceded by grapefruit and followed by apple pie à la mode. They take to chicken pie—not individual chicken pie but a big chicken pie set on the table for one of the members to carve. I find this carving stunt is always good. We serve a lot of our food in casseroles, and the boys will eat braised beef with potatoes, carrots, onions, and green peppers. They also like rare roast beef—not too rare—and once a year I serve them a sea food New-burg, lobster, crab, shrimp, scallops, pretty well spiced up with sherry and garnished with toast. I usually do that at Easter. In cold weather boiled spare ribs and kraut with boiled potatoes preceded by tomato juice and followed by ice cream goes pretty well. So does New England boiled dinner, boiled beef, pig's feet, fat frankfurters and boiled tongue together with cabbage, carrots, onions, and boiled potatoes with plenty of horse radish, mustard and tomato sauce on the side.

I always have a bowl of fresh green salad on the table to which they can help themselves, those who like it can take it, but I don't have little tippy dishes of salad served. I always try to have some cheap introduction to the meal—soup, fruit juice, melons in season—that sort of thing. The boys like to have individual apple dumplings with hard sauce or cream for dessert and shortcake in June when the straw-berries are cheap. Cheapness should be the key to the menus—have nothing out of season. I hope these will give you pointers enough. Thank you for your kind words.

Americans were stirred to a fever pitch in September, 1938, when British Prime Minister Chamberlain and French Premier Daladier met with Adolf Hitler and Benito Mussolini at Munich. To avert war with Hitler, the French and the British agreed to the dismemberment of Czechoslovakia. This step was supposed to satisfy Hitler. The next year, however, the European democracies finally realized that Hitler was out to dominate the world. Appeasement ended with war in September, 1939. As White indicates in his letter, the American people were beginning to fear for their security. Throughout the nineteenth century the British fleet had protected the Western Hem-isphere from invasion. By 1938, however, the British fleet alone was not enough to check Hitler's American ambitions.

I was sorry that I could not go to Kansas City when our mutual friend, Henry Haskell, invited me. But the bars were up, and I could not get away.

I have read your articles in the Sunday Observer, and it seems to me you have sized up American opinion accurately. There is, as you say, a certain amount of anti-Semitism in the United States, but it is badly organized and the forces of tolerance are doing what they can in an organized way to combat this anti-Semitism. But sooner or later in the United States we shall probably have to meet the challenge of the bigots rather definitely.

In informed circles here, by which I mean in American liberal leadership and somewhat in conservative leadership also, no one seriously blames Chamberlain for Munich. Munich became inevitable when England refused to join Stimson [Henry L. Stimson, Secretary of State in 1931 when the Japanese attacked Manchuria] in the protest against the Japanese invasion of continental Asia. The clock was tolling the golden hour from then until the conquest of Ethiopia. After that the habit of yielding to blackmail had become fixed. I believe that opinion in the United States, particularly in the western United States, is reasonably sure that nothing can be done about it now. It is a race between the aggression of the dictators and the economic forces inside their realms, on the one hand, and, on the other hand, the indomitable spirit of man in his yearning for freedom.

Perhaps it was wise to wait. No one can say until we find how much we have to pay in liberty and blood and treasure. We must watch the flood mount around our feet until the waters subside.

In the matter of relations with Great Britain, it seems to me we have come into a new sense of insecurity since Munich. Probably the insecurity has been there for several years, but the sense of it has not been made plain until now. Now we know that for the first time in a hundred years the United States is out on its own. We no longer lie under the protection of the British fleet. That protection has been "a very present help in trouble." I believe it has been the keynote of our foreign policy. Now we know that we must walk alone. And we are going in fear and trembling. We hesitate about arming. We are squeamish about Guam. Many of us want to scuttle and run from the Philippines. We have no national "rule Britannia" complex. And we are ripe for demagogues.

You have presented this feeling admirably in your first article, and

[394]

I thank you most kindly for sending it to me. I hope our paths will cross soon.

I am most sorry that I could not come to see you when you were in Kansas City.

The following letter about World War I was written as another world war was about to break out in Europe and the Far East. The world was being dominated by aggression. Japan had invaded North China in 1937 and was continuing her aggressions against the nation. Mussolini had seized Ethiopia, and Hitler had refortified the Rhineland, conquered Austria, and destroyed the independence of Czechoslovakia.

To Don Wharton, *Scribner's Magazine*, April 8, 1939

Dear Mr. Wharton:

I have your letter asking where I was between June 28, the day the Archduke Ferdinand was assassinated, and the beginning of the World War in August of that year. I was in Estes Park, Colorado, which is located in the heart of the Rocky Mountains. I had gone there to write a novel which four years afterwards appeared under the title "In the Heart of a Fool."

We were in a summer cottage on the mountain side and around us was a neighborhood of college professors and professonal men. We had half a dozen daily papers, two from Denver, two from Kansas City, the Emporia Gazette and a New York paper, I think the World. Mail came up from the railhead by coach and then by buckboard to our mail box. Because we had many papers, soon after the assassination of the Austrian Crown Prince, I can remember definitely that Carruth, professor of English literature at Stanford University, Charles F. Scott, a country editor and former congressman from Kansas, and F. H. Hodder, a professor of history from the Kansas University, and sometimes Chancellor Strong of the Kansas University used to gather on our porch at mail time to share the papers.

[395]

Sometimes their families came. We had a wide veranda, fourteen feet by fifty, and there was a fine powwow there every afternoon as the news began to get hot. None of us believed that hostilities would start. All of us were sure that something would stop the catastrophe, and I can remember the protests of Hodder, the history professor, who would pound on the table and declare vehemently, "I tell you, they can't go through Belgium, they can't, they can't, there's a treaty!" And he would give the date of the treaty, and when the headlines indicated that Liége was attacked, the professor thought the newspapers were lying and that the whole thing was made up and again reiterated, "They can't do that, there's a treaty." So deeply was civilization in those far days impressed with the fact that a treaty put up a barrier to the will of a conqueror! It indicated at least superficially a fairly decent world.

I can remember before the Germans entered Belgium and before England got in, we were all a typical midwestern middle-class group, dead sure that England would manage to stop the war. None of us thought that England would get in, and when the papers came up from the post office carrying the news of England's entrance, we were all sad and solemn for a few moments there on the porch looking over the quiet mountains and meadows with the brook stream gurgling through it. Little boys were fishing down there, our sons who went into khaki and were soldiers four years later. We did not dream that this could be as we sat there that day shocked by the news that Great Britain's entrance had made it a World War.

After the entrance of England, our middle-class board of strategy, sitting there on the front porch on the mountain side, began skirmishing for maps. We pinned up a map and made colored lines on it to indicate the daily advance of the troops. All that summer, until we broke up and left for our homes, that map showed the cancer of war slowly gnawing into Western civilization. Looking back at that day and time there in the heart of the Rockies, it is hard to conceive that such a world as ours was then could be on this planet, a world of faith in kings and rulers, a world of hope for the common man. Pippa no longer passes through that lush Mountain Valley singing her happy song.

Richard Wright wrote a powerful novel, Native Son, *depicting the problems of the Negro in Chicago's slum area. The book was selected by the Book-of-the-Month Club.*

To MEREDITH WOOD, the Book-of-the-Month Club, August 19, 1939

MY DEAR MEREDITH:

I have just finished "Native Son." It is a powerful book. It is an important book, but I think we would make a sad, tragic and excessive mistake if we took it. It is dealing frankly and with some artistic skill with a phase of American life that has not been touched, the slum Negro, the dirt, and it is ungodly vile dirt, is probably necessary to portray that life and make the point which the author makes so powerfully even though in the last third of the book he is just a little more interested in the moral of his fable than in the onrush of his story. But let that pass.

It is not for the mechanical faults that I feel the book should be rejected, but I am sure that important as it is and in places as beautiful as it is our crowd would refuse it and refuse it in great numbers if we took it. The twenty per cent of sophisticates would say three cheers. The sixty per cent of middle-class occasional book readers, who like to adorn their center table with "good literature," would be not only shocked but mad. It is a book that can't be put on their center tables and the twenty per cent of purely center table book patrons, who read little and talk much about books, would just jump off our list pronto. Unless you have got twenty per cent more than you need, don't touch it. I can't put all those things in a telegram. I shall express my opinion briefly, but I wish on the day of the meeting you would read this letter to the others assembled around the table. I should like to have a dozen of these books to distribute to readers who would appreciate the book, but I shouldn't like to buy seventy-five or a hundred thousand and dump them into our public.

On September 21, three weeks after Germany launched her invasion of Poland, President Roosevelt sent a message to Congress urging the repeal of the embargo forbidding the sale of arms and ammunition to nations at war and the substitution of a plan whereby the Allies could buy war goods with cash and transport them in their own ships. The embargo aided the aggressor and hurt the victims, since Germany was prepared for war and the Allies were not. The Allies needed equipment of war which the embargo prevented them from acquiring from the United States. White editorially supported the President's proposal.

To Bruce Bliven, *New Republic*, September 23, 1939

Dear Bruce Bliven:

Again, I have seen your release for next Saturday and I like it. I am afraid that a bad peace is possible no matter what Europe does if Europe defines its terms. One of the reasons—academic, of course—why I hope we can keep out is that we may be able to influence the terms of peace when peace comes. And I hope to all the gods at once that Franklin Roosevelt, when his great hour comes, will not fumble the ball and try to carry alone without teamwork as Woodrow Wilson did. If at that time he would call about him a strong, nonpartisan group—even Hoover should be in—and turn the job over to them, we might make a peace that would hold, a peace without malice, a peace without greed. How I have no idea, but it could be done.

I am glad always to see your story. The Gazette is supporting the President in the hope that he will not be too stiff-necked to make the reasonable compromises that his genuine friends in Congress suggest.

Late in September, 1939, White helped organize and chairmaned the Non-Partisan Committee for Peace through the Revision of the Neutrality Law, which stirred public sentiment for support of the President's plan to substitute the cash-and-carry plan for the embargo.

Congressional opposition to the change centered in the Republican members. White exerted every effort to make this issue nonpartisan, but, in the final vote when the President's bill passed, the majority of Republican congressmen voted against it.

New York City, to CONGRESSMAN JOSEPH W. MARTIN, Oct. 23, 1939

MY DEAR JOE:

Paul Leach [Washington correspondent of the Chicago *Daily News*] sent me a story from Washington the other day which seemed to indicate that an overwhelming majority of the Republican members of the House were planning to vote against repeal. I am very much concerned over this because I do not think the repeal of the embargo should be treated in any way as a partisan issue, and second, in case our failure to repeal the embargo should chance to have disastrous effects and might even possibly lead us into war, then the Democrats could properly charge us with responsibility for not repealing the embargo.

It seems to me only good strategy to see that a sufficient number of Republican votes are cast for repeal so that we could not be charged with the entire responsibility for preventing repeal. Of course, I am writing exclusively about the political angles of the matter. Personally, I think there is a moral consideration involved as well, and I would hate to have my party put itself in a posture where it can be charged that we played Mr. Hitler's game in the matter of the embargo.

We have no reason to fear the effects upon us of a French-British victory. We have a whole lot to fear in the case of a Hitler victory. If we fail to repeal the embargo and Hitler should win, we, as a party, will be vulnerable, or if we refuse to repeal the embargo and then later we are dragged into the war, again, we would be, as a party, in a very vulnerable position.

It seems to me that every possible consideration argues in favor of a sufficient number of Republican votes in favor of repeal to prevent the charge ever being successfully made that the Republicans were responsible for the failure of the repeal measure.

I wish you would give this angle of the matter a little thought and let me have your views.

[399]

On November 3, the bill to revise the Neutrality Law passed Congress. Secretary of State Cordell Hull wrote White thanking him for his patriotic efforts and observed: "Nobody knows better than I do how great a contribution that was; and everybody here is warmly appreciative of your valuable help." President Roosevelt wrote: "Dear Bill: You did a grand job. It was effective and most helpful! I am writing this note just to say: 'Thank you, Bill.' "

To Cordell Hull, Secretary of State, November 6, 1939

Dear Secretary Hull:

I was in Washington last Monday working on the Cash and Carry Bill. Every minute crowded me. Mrs. White and I expected to be back the following Thursday but the fight against the Cash and Carry Bill collapsed, I was no longer needed, Mrs. White had a bad cold, we both got homesick and pulled out for Emporia Wednesday night.

We will be back probably some time during the winter when I hope to see you and have a good visit. In this hurrying modern world I suppose good visits are not possible.

When I came home I had your letter and, of course, it made me most happy. I devoted three or four weeks of my time to this Cash and Carry Bill. I didn't work directly on any senator or representative. I was making the medicine of propaganda, filling the radio full of speakers like Al Smith, Monsignor Ryan, General O'Ryan, Mayor LaGuardia, and I had transcriptions of their speeches made and sent them out to the stations that carried the Coughlin poison.* Also, we assembled the names of several score of American clergymen and American college presidents who signed statements that we scattered by the thousands and tens of thousands across the land. I do not know that it did any good whatever. I have worked in Kansas on a homogeneous population with some efficacy for nearly fifty years. It is the first time I ever tried the national scene. I could not feel it respond as I do in Kansas, and I doubt if I had much to do with the result, but it made me happy anyway to get your letter.

Will you remember me most kindly to Mr. Berle and to Herbert

* Father Coughlin was arguing for isolationism in his weekly radio broadcasts. To counteract Coughlin, the White Committee sponsored talks by ex-Governor Alfred E. Smith; Monsignor John Ryan, Catholic theologian; General John F. O'Ryan of New York City; and Mayor Fiorello LaGuardia.

Feis [Adolf Berle and Herbert Feis were State Department officials]?
With warm personal regards, I am—

Carl Sandburg had just published his magnificent four-volume work
Abraham Lincoln—The War Years. *Earlier he had published a two-volume study* Abraham Lincoln—The Prairie Years. *Sandburg replied to this letter of White's by saying: "It is good to have your note about the Lincoln book. I like to think of it being out there in your house where the Lincoln tradition has had such rare loyalty. By a number of signs (Lloyd Lewis [Midwestern journalist and author] and I were talking about it) some of us know that you are lately doing some of the best work of your life. Often you have a Lincoln manner of saying terrible things so gently that the reader goes back to make sure."*

To CARL SANDBURG, November 23, 1939

DEAR CARL:
Here enclosed are half a dozen blank sheets which I should be happy if you would autograph. Four of them are for the four volumes of your Lincoln. Two of them are for the extra copy of "The Prairie Years" which I intend to give to a friend.

The fourth volume came today. I have been wandering through the others with great delight. What a job you have done. How inextricably your name will be linked to Lincoln's in the years to come. No one else has dug so deeply into the Lincoln lore nor has anyone arranged with such an understanding hand the wealth of material you have dug up. What a story!

Although the war, after the rapid defeat of Poland, was in a quiet stage, it was apparent to farsighted observers that this was only the lull before the storm. America stood in grave danger if Germany succeeded in dominating Europe and defeating England and France. The United States would, then, be faced with a triumphant Germany in the Atlantic and a triumphant Japan in the Pacific. On December 14, White received a letter from President Roosevelt asking him to spend a night at the White House. "I need a few helpful thoughts from the philosopher of Emporia," said the President. "Things move with such terrific speed, these days, that it really is essential to us to think in broader terms and, in effect, to warn the American people that they, too, should think of possible ultimate results in Europe and the Far East.... Therefore, my sage old friend, my problem is to get the American people to think of conceivable consequences without scaring the American people into thinking that they are going to be dragged into this war." By this time, W. L. White was in Europe as a war correspondent.

To FRANKLIN D. ROOSEVELT, December 22, 1939

DEAR MR. PRESIDENT:

Your letter, of course, pleased me greatly. But I am not as smart as you have been told. I do not know so much as I would like to know. In that endeavor to repeal the embargo law, I was pretty much of a stuffed shirt, fronting for a capable organization that had been set up by Clark Eichelberger* for many years and financed by our good friends, directed and led more or less by Shotwell.† I was glad to do what I could.

I am not sure that I can come to Washington in mid-January. I shall come if I can. Mrs. White is not well and we always travel together, and in the winter the Washington climate gets her down, and it doesn't do me any good. But you may be assured I appreciate the distinction and courtesy of your invitation.

I fear our involvement before the peace, and yet I fear to remain

* Clark Eichelberger had been executive director of the League of Nations Association for many years. He also served as executive director of the Non-Partisan Committee for Peace through the Revision of the Neutrality Law.

† Professor James T. Shotwell of Columbia University, a leading spirit behind a number of committees devoted to international problems.

uninvolved letting the danger of a peace of tyranny approach too near. Finland seems to need us.

By the way, did you know that Bill is over there representing a string of papers from Washington to Los Angeles—some thirty-five in all—and also talking every evening from Helsinki? He was out watching a battle yesterday, and last week while he was flying around some Russian bombers got on his tail, and he had to scoot into Stockholm. All of which makes me happy. It's the life he wants to live and God knows age should not put its bony hand upon him in any warning.

For years I have thought that this nation needed another Constitutional office, a man who was a dear friend of every president, who should be appointed the day he goes into office and not subject to any discharge while the President is in office. He should sit in the Cabinet at the other end of the table looking at the President, but having no authority to speak. He should sit on the other side of the room in the presidential office ten feet in front of the President, looking at him every day. And once a month the two should go into a room and talk for an hour and then shut up. The things that dear friend—constitutionally near the President all the time—the things he would think and say would help a lot, I think, a kind of an audible conscience, a kind of a reminder of what he hoped to do and be, a kind of a Father Confessor somewhere between a priest and a psychoanalyst. I would not give the man an official title, but I am sure that at the end of the first year the politicians and the star-eyed young reformers, and the chairman of the Judiciary Committee of the Senate would have a name for him. And whenever the President quoted his friend to anyone, the third person would look around nervously and cry: "Oh, that old bastard!" And that would be his title. It is the only job that I ever coveted. But I don't seem to be able to get any Constitutional amendments through. Yet, if I have any wisdom, it tells me that there is a swell reform. . . .

I know you are busy, but would you mind doing me this favor: Convey to Mrs. Roosevelt my warm admiration and three cheers! If you will agree to let her serve your third term, I shall be for you against all comers. Every time she does anything, she reminds me of T.R. She is his reincarnation, I think.

So, hoping for the best in January, but not too sure of it, I am proud to subscribe myself with the Season's most cordial greetings—

[403]

A Christmas card from Carl Ackerman, dean of Columbia University's School of Journalism, addressed to W. A. White, the Emporia Gazette, *Kansas City, Kansas, elicited the following letter from White.*

To CARL ACKERMAN, Columbia University, January 3, 1940

DEAR CARL:

I have your Christmas card, and it was good to see even a facsimile of your signature thereon.

I am enclosing you the envelope in which it came. Will you kindly call in your stenographer, cup her dimpled chin in the hollow of your hand, look into her eyes, which seem to have almost human intelligence, and tell her, if you think you can get it across from Homo sapiens to our lower cousins in the Kingdom, that the Emporia Gazette would be printed in Emporia and that Kansas City for the most part is in Missouri. In the process of imparting this information, you may have to use simple words, maybe signs, but I hope you can get it to her.

W. L. White was attracting wide attention by his radio broadcasts from Europe. One of his talks, "The Last Christmas Tree," inspired Robert E. Sherwood to write the Pulitzer prize play There Shall Be No Night. *Jonathan Daniels was editing the Raleigh (North Carolina)* Observer *and assuming a position of leadership among southern liberals. His book,* A Southerner Looks at the South, *won wide acclaim.*

To JOSEPHUS DANIELS, Ambassador to Mexico, February 3, 1940

DEAR JOSEPHUS:

That was a nice letter. How proud we are, you of Jonathan and I of Bill! I would rather be known only as Bill White's father than for any other fame or service that might come to me.

[404]

You speak of the Bible. It's such a beautiful book! So full of poetry; so full of wisdom; so full of comfort and of a deep knowledge of human nature! I am sorry when the young colts in the pasture dash away and refuse to put the bridle on. It will lead them through such lovely land into such joy, such satisfaction, such rich and wonderful treasures of lore and philosophy.

Mrs. White joins me in affectionate regards to Mrs. Daniels.

Countless thousands of individuals wrote White for copies of editorials like What's the Matter With Kansas? *and* Mary White *and for autobiographical material. He answered all these letters because as he once observed, "If anyone takes the time to write me, they deserve a reply." Generally, during the decade of the thirties and while he was chairman of the Committee to defend America by Aiding the Allies, it took two or three hours of daily dictation to reply to all his correspondents.*

To MR. HAROLD KLOOS, Akron, Ohio, April 16, 1940

DEAR MR. KLOOS:

I thank you most kindly for your interest in my work. I am sending you some material herewith. You ask me to what I attribute my success. The answer is I haven't had a success. I have lived happily because I have been busy and never have been bored a minute or out of a job. And for the same reason, I don't have any hobbies. I touch life at many points: in business, in editing, in writing books, on the political side, on music, and a happy family. You ask in what sports I am most interested. I never saw a basketball game. I haven't seen a baseball game for forty years. I don't like football. I am but a poor and fumbling pallbearer. I don't know how to play bridge. I don't know how to bowl. But I am the rocking chair champion of the Emporia Country Club. And that's all.

You ask how I spend my leisure time. The answer, I have none to spend. It is mortgaged to many activities as hereinbefore noted.

All during the winter of 1939-40, White was worried about the com-
placency of the American people toward the European war. As a
result, he and Clark Eichelberger decided to launch an organization
which would awaken the American people to the significance of the
Nazi movement. The German invasion of Norway and Denmark in
April, 1940, wrote White, "gave the people of the United States a
sickening sense of the reality of Hitler's purpose. . . . America began
to see what kind of a war it was, the fanatical conquest of a pagan
ideology which justified slavery, which exalted cruelty, which ban-
ished chivalry, scoffed at the equality of men, and was aimed straight
at the dignity of the human spirit." Shortly after May 10, 1940, when
Hitler invaded Holland and Belgium, White and Eichelberger
launched the Committee to Defend America by Aiding the Allies.

To NELSON JOHNSON, Ambassador to China, May 31, 1940

MY DEAR NELSON JOHNSON:

Mrs. White and I were glad indeed to have your letter. We have been wondering how things went with you and your letter was most illuminating. I am sending you some clippings from the Gazette which better than anything else can tell you what is in my mind. I am working hard on an organization to make public sentiment that will justify Congress and the President in giving immediate economic and material aid to the Allies, and I am sending you a little stuff about that. Our idea is to fill the radio and the newspapers and the Congressional mail with the voice of prominent citizens urging America to become the non-belligerent ally of France and England. I am afraid it is too late, and I stand aghast at what will happen if the English either scuttle their ships or turn them over to Germany.

The weather conditions in the Mississippi Valley point to fairly good June crops which means mostly wheat. You never can tell about corn, as you know, so early. Pastures are good, the stock ponds are full, the rivers are running for the first time in two or three years at this season. But all America is under a great cloud of sadness. I get a good deal of comfort out of being seventy-two years old. I used to hate to live in the middle of the second act. Now I hate the third act, but I suppose I have to live through it.

Mrs. White joins me in affectionate regards.

To Mr. W. A. Montgomery, University of Virginia, June 17, 1940

DEAR MR. MONTGOMERY:

I have your letter asking me when and where I said: "I have taken no exercises for years beyond acting as pallbearer for friends who have taken exercise." It was at a meeting of the Rockefeller Foundation. They were all men in their fifties and sixties talking about their golf and tennis. They asked what I did for exercise, and I said: "Chiefly acting as pallbearer for old boys who have taken exercise all their lives."

It may have been original or may not. When one passes seventy he should not be too sure of anything.

The Committee to Defend America by Aiding the Allies grew with remarkable rapidity to be a powerful organ for arousing public opinion. In June, France was conquered and Hitler prepared to launch his all-out attack on England. White and his committee urged the President to release to the manufacturers all the planes, guns, and ammunition that could be spared for sale to England. In spite of the danger that threatened American security, there were those who claimed that the United States could follow an isolationist policy. The Chicago Tribune, Charles A. Lindbergh, the Communist party, and the Socialist party clamored that this was not our war. White received many letters attacking him as a "warmonger" for his views that aid to England was essential to America's well-being. To all such attackers, he wrote a letter in the following vein.

To Mr. M. K. Craig, Banning, Calif., June 21, 1940

DEAR MR. CRAIG:

I am in this Committee to Defend America by Aiding the Allies because I think it is the only way to keep us out of war. And here is my reasoning:

If we have the good will of the Allies when they are defeated, which

[407]

seems likely, we can make arrangements to get their fleets. If we have their fleets, we can defy Hitler with our fleet in the Atlantic Ocean and theirs in the Pacific Ocean. If we do not help the Allies, if we turn our backs on them, they will see no reason for helping us by giving us their fleets. In which case, if these fleets go to Hitler, he will have the power to take the British possessions in the West Indies. These islands control the Panama Canal. In a few months he could build air and naval bases there and make much trouble for us. If we let him move in after defeating the British, he would be violating the Monroe Doctrine. He will not move in without the British or French fleets. But he will move in then and war will be certain.

There are, of course, two opinions held honestly by intelligent people in the United States. One is that to help the Allies keeps the war away from America by letting them fight the war in Europe rather than to wait until the Germans conquer Europe and turn their greedy eyes westward. The other opinion is your opinion and many fine, wise people hold it. There being two sides, perhaps the best thing each of us could do is to respect the honesty and integrity of each other's opinions and realize that there must be differences if there is progress in the world.

I am sending you a list of the members of our committee—business men, college presidents, teachers, preachers, farmers, labor leaders, bishops, a cross section of American life. I am also enclosing two editorials which express my views.

To Miss Ellen McLaughlin, The Grolier Society,
New York City, July 6, 1940

Dear Miss McLaughlin:

I have your letter asking for a short message for American children. Here it is:

The child in a democracy is a happy child because only in assured freedom is there happiness. Childhood and youth in this country should have the same passion for liberty as the German children have for race arrogance and the love of conquest. For however much sorrow and injustice surrounds one's life, with freedom the way out is open. Without freedom unhappiness is the doom of children wherever they are.

[408]

The European war was changing so rapidly that White organized a small committee to help him draw up the policy of the Committee to Defend America by Aiding the Allies. During July and August, 1940, German airplanes and submarines raised havoc with the British merchant marine and navy. In order to aid the British, stop a threatened invasion, and protect her supply line in the Atlantic Ocean, the White Committee urged the President to release fifty or sixty World War I destroyers to the British. The President carried this out by executive agreement in late August by which England in return allowed the United States to have bases in the British possessions in the Western Hemisphere.

To ROBERT E. SHERWOOD, New York City, July 26, 1940

DEAR MR. SHERWOOD:

I wrote you from New York rather formally thanking you for accepting a place on our policy committee. This is more personal. I want you to know how much I appreciate your advice.

Just now we are trying to get the United States, possibly under an executive order, to give priority rights to planes ordered by Great Britain. They have been getting in the last few months from 450 to 600 planes. I believe that they are now ready to order many more. We could have delivered more than that in the last three months but for some reason the British did not order them. Now that the orders are coming, it seems to me wise to get behind a move to ask the President to grant this priority, so long as we ourselves are well equipped and therefore the priority will represent to a considerable degree our surpluses.

We are also trying to get the President to trade in to the manufacturers some of our aged and obsolescent destroyers, a few of which have been reconditioned. The need for them is great in Britain and might be vital. If the President really wants to do it—it can be done. But we must show him that the country will follow him in this matter.

The third job before us is to find some way to get ships to bring British refugee children out of Great Britain into Canada or the United States. I feel that if the President would ask Hitler to allow us to send our ships, he would have to say either yes or no. If Hitler said no, he would give to the world the impression that the slaughter of children is as much of a military objective for Nazi armed forces as is any other kind of physical plant; I mean munitions factories, airplane plants, railroads and other physical things. Let him admit to the world that children's bodies will help him to produce a peace by force, and I am sure he will surrender much of the value of his physical equipment through the indignation of the world. At least I feel that we should urge upon the President to ask Herr Hitler this privilege for the British children. Do you know of any way that we might get the Pope to join the President in this? This would be a mighty arm of righteousness.

I should like to have your views and any suggestions you might make about these matters.

White was constantly irritated at the New York City Chapter of the Committee to Defend America by Aiding the Allies. He felt that this group failed to realize the different temper of other areas in the country, and that they were demanding too much power in committee affairs. Frederic R. Coudert, New York lawyer, was an important figure in committee affairs.

To FREDERIC R. COUDERT, New York City, October 22, 1940

DEAR MR. COUDERT:

... On my last visit to New York the grievances and complaints of the New York Committee occupied a good two-thirds of my time. I don't know what to do about it. I don't think it is the Committee. Maybe it is. Maybe it is the leadership of the Committee, or maybe it is just the New York complex that is full of the delusion that New York is the United States and that they have rights above other chapters. ... Why these people in New York ... run hog wild on side issues when the big job is so difficult, is too much for me. ... Once a year I break down and weep on somebody's collar and here are my tears and I'll shut up. But if you know of any way short of assassination to shut up that New York Committee and make them get in step with the national organization, I'll be deeply and eternally grateful to you. And as Blaine said to the Little Rock Railway President:

"Burn this letter.

"But don't do it until you have burned it in your heart."

White's belief that liberty was indivisible and worth protecting accounts for his antagonism to the Nazi way of life. Over the Columbia Broadcasting System on August 22, 1940, he told his fellow countrymen: "If Great Britain falls, a new phase of civilization will dominate Europe and will menace the United States and the Western Hemisphere. It is not a question of form of government between Great Britain and the European dictators. It is a way of thinking, a way of life, a social order, a slave economy that menaces the world, and the world cannot live half slave and half free."

To HENRY L. MENCKEN, October 23, 1940

DEAR HENRY:

I have your note saying you want to use a sentence of mine: "Liberty is the only thing you cannot have unless you are willing to give it to others."

And you ask me when and where I said it. It is one of my favorite wisecracks. I have used it a dozen times, though if you ask me where, I would have to tell you to dig into the files of the Gazette. I will promise to use it sometime today and then you can say, "From the Emporia Gazette of October 25, 1940."

I am proud that you liked it. I thought it was smart myself or I wouldn't have used it so often.

During the 1940 presidential campaign White was an enthusiastic supporter of Wendell L. Willkie. Since both Roosevelt and Willkie

[411]

favored aid to the Allies, White's opposition to Roosevelt centered around the third term. On the issue of foreign affairs, White, however, praised Roosevelt's stand throughout the campaign. This irritated enthusiastic Republicans. The results of the election did not find the Kansas editor bitter or disillusioned with American democracy. He advocated great mass meetings to "unite now on a national program for safeguarding American democracy and keeping war away from America by all possible aid to Britain and other nations resisting aggression." White lists Roosevelt's vote in this letter as twenty-five million when it actually was twenty-seven million.

To H. L. BAGGERLY, Los Gatos (California) *Mail-News,*
November 18, 1940

DEAR MR. BAGGERLY:

I have been on the wing for the last week and your letter finally caught up with me. I am sorry for the delay in answering it.

I note what you say about the Roosevelt victory. It was indeed a famous victory. I should say, however, the honors are about even. Where Roosevelt had the W.P.A., Willkie had the advertising propaganda. Apparently the politicians in the W.P.A. were stronger than the advertising propagandists.

I am in no way excited about the election of Mr. Roosevelt. I voted for Mr. Willkie with enthusiasm. The dirty cracks on one side were as bad as the dirty cracks on the other, and twenty-two million against twenty-five million levels it up so we are in no danger of a dictator. I never thought we were. The old ship is going to keep right on sailing along.

With kind personal regards, I am—

On November 27, 1940, White received the annual award of the National Association of Accredited Publicity Directors for "the most distinguished service in the whole field of public opinion formation." By this time, the Committee to Defend America by Aiding the Allies had 750 local chapters, in which about ten thousand people were doing active work. The committee had sponsored innumerable rallies, speeches, and radio talks as well as stimulating telegram and letter writing campaigns on Congress.

To J. EDGAR HOOVER, Federal Bureau of Investigation,
November 28, 1940

DEAR MR. HOOVER:

Last night I received an award from the National Association of Accredited Publicity Directors, Incorporated, for public service in connection with the Committee to Defend America by Aiding the Allies. Sitting next to me, the toastmaster told me that your name was considered in place of mine, and I wish most sincerely that you had taken the award, for you have done in the last year a tremendous, necessary job in a competent way, and I could wait, for the American public might realize by the dramatization of the bestowal of the award now the full extent of your public service.

Another thing: this week the Book of the Month judges, of whom I am one, chose a book called "Out of the Night" by a German who signs his name Jan Valtin. It is a marvelous story of a communist agitator of international scope who fell into the hands of the Nazi Gestapo, was taken to a concentration camp, and, of course, treated rough, turned Nazi spy, went into Russia and Norway, and escaped and came to America.

I am sending you the book. It's a most remarkable document—remarkable psychologically, remarkable as a revelation of a kind of work in continental Europe that will interest you. I wish you would read it.

And another reason why you will be interested in the book is that the author, under what name I do not know, was in the United States a dozen or twenty years ago, was sentenced to the penitentiary in California, and served his term. He is now an unregistered alien. After we bought the book—which means that we will buy 150,000 or 175,000 copies and pay a good many thousand dollars—we sent for him and his publisher brought him here. I have never seen so strange and tragic a face—never have seen a figure that interested me more from many viewpoints. Undoubtedly, when he registers you will run across him. His unpardoned service at San Quentin in California will probably mean his deportation. He knows it, and he's scared to death. I told him to file the book when he went to register. It doesn't contain the whole truth, but it does contain as much of his career as you can digest in a day, but the fact that he has this remarkable capacity for telling a story, and that he has a real literary quality makes him, it seems to me, an interesting person—an especially unique figure in the mill run of unregistered aliens.

I hope you will read the book and then I hope you will meet the man. I know that you will be just to him. I am calling your attention to him because he came through our mill, and it seemed to me was so exceptional that when he goes through your mill, he is worthy of your special attention.

P.S. Mr. Adolf Berle of the State Department has read this book, and I understand is fully acquainted with this case. It might be interesting to you to talk to him about it.

The December, 1940, issue of the Survey Graphic *carried White's review of Nicholas Murray Butler's autobiography,* Across the Busy Years. *President Butler wrote White thanking him for the kind review, which elicited the following reply from White.*

To Nicholas Murray Butler, Columbia University,
December 10, 1940

Dear Dr. Butler:

I am glad you liked my piece in the Survey Graphic. I hope there will be another volume of reminiscences and that your letters and papers will be preserved and published. They are bound to be great authentic sources for the men who will write the story of American life from 1890 to 1940. I wonder if in any fifty years on this planet the human spirit has produced such changes in man's environment and brought humanity to such a level of literacy and information about the universe and in wisdom about his conduct as that decade in which you and I have lived as young men, as citizens, and now as puzzled, somewhat saddened but I believe unshaken disciples of a great faith in man's essential long-run intelligence, integrity, purpose and courage. I hate to go out here at the end of the second act of this fast drama of the changing spirit of man for I know that the third act will have a happy ending. God knows how!

The Chicago Tribune was a vitriolic critic of the Committee to Defend America by Aiding the Allies. Its editorials denied that Hitler was a threat to America, and denounced William Allen White for asserting that the British fleet was America's chief weapon of defense against Nazi Germany. To one person who sent him a Tribune attack on his committee, he replied: "Thank you for your clipping. I would be surprised and deeply shocked if the Chicago Tribune would ever agree with me."

To FREDERICK C. HARBOUR, Chicago, Ill., December 20, 1940

DEAR MR. HARBOUR:

Thank you for your heartening letter. I don't worry about anything the Chicago Tribune does or says. I fancy it has lost all influence in this country, and we are going ahead about our job to help Great Britain arm while we get prepared for any eventualities. But letters like yours are most cheering and comforting.

On November 26, 1940, the William Allen White Committee adopted a policy which, without saying so, actually called for the repeal of the Neutrality Law and the convoying of ships. Back in Emporia by December, White was no longer as conscious of the gravity of England's danger as he had been while in New York. He was, also,

[415]

extremely tired from his arduous activities as chairman of the committee. Furthermore, he was worried by the activities of a group of distinguished citizens known as the Century Club group. This group believed that the United States should declare war and some of its members were in the White Committee. By December, the committee was facing a real dilemma. Aid to England was necessary for the security of the United States. Yet, this aid was being sunk on the high seas. The East and West coasts were more willing to support convoys than the Middle West. When White heard that the Scripps-Howard papers were about to attack the committee, he wrote the following letter. With his permission the letter was published as an "interview" on December 24.

To Roy Howard, Scripps-Howard Newspapers, December 20, 1940

DEAR ROY:

Look now, Roy, you and I have been buddies more or less, and I hope I have deserved the honor of your friendship these twenty years and more, and why I am sending this is on account that a friend in Washington says you are preparing to strafe our outfit and particularly me because we are heading HB for war. All right, only this:

The only reason in God's world I am in this organization is to keep this country out of war. I don't go an inch further or faster than Wendell Willkie or the American Legion or the American Federation or the National Grange; nor an inch further or faster than you went this month in the Filipino magazine on the Eastern question. I am abreast of you and no further, and I haven't changed since we talked in Chicago last July. The story is floating around that I and our outfit are in favor of sending convoys with British ships or our own ships, a silly thing, for convoys, unless you shoot, are confetti and it's not time to shoot now or ever. Another thing: The America First crowd keeps insisting that we are in favor of repealing the Johnson Act [law forbidding the United States to lend money to nations that defaulted on their war debts], a stupid thing to do because it would not help Great Britain and there are half a dozen other good legal ways to get aid to Great Britain. The President is following his own way. But the Johnson Act should not be repealed and we are not for it. Still one more charge: it is not true even remotely that we favor repealing [the Neutrality Law] to carry contraband of war into the

[416]

war zone. That would be leading us to war and our organization and I personally are deeply opposed to it. If I was making a motto for the Committee to Defend America by Aiding the Allies, it would be "The Yanks Are Not Coming." We could not equip them and feed them if they went. We have less than two hundred thousand ready, and we need them worse at home on the assembly belt than we need them in Europe. War would defeat the end for which our committee is organized to defend America by aiding Great Britain and would bring on a thirty-year conflict. The Yanks are not going because if they went to war they would lose our cause. That is my firm unshakable belief. And to strafe me because some members of our organization, who are not officially representing us, are martial-minded is as foolish and unfair as it would be to call the Knights of Columbus appeasers because Joe Kennedy [Joseph Kennedy, who resigned as ambassador to England] gave Roosevelt the Judas kiss. Not one official utterance of our organization has anything remotely suggestive that we feel the only alternative for American defense through aid to Great Britain is war. Moreover, I have sat in all executive councils, all policy-making committees, and I have never heard war seriously discussed in any official group of our organization at any time. I hope you know that I am not a liar, and I hope you feel I am not a sucker, and I trust you will believe what I am writing.

In spite of the tempest breaking about his head as a result of the Howard "interview," White had time to write the following Christmas letter to Harry Scherman, founder and president of the Book-of-the-Month Club. There is no doubt that the Book-of-the-Month Club through its selections over the past decade had very definitely influenced the literary tastes of America.

To HARRY SCHERMAN, Book-of-the-Month Club, December 26, 1940

DEAR HARRY:

We had a lovely Christmas yesterday, Sallie and I alone. We had our dinner with candles, and you will not know the sense of security and happiness your Christmas check brought us. All these years our relations with the Book of the Month have been stimulating intellectually and in the last ten years have brought us a sense of affection for you and Bernardine [Mrs. Scherman]. Talking that over yesterday, it made the candles glow. This letter is just to tell you that we are happy and want you to be as happy as you deserve for all the happiness you are bringing to so many others.

I know no other business in this broad land of the free that is bringing so much wisdom, joy and inner light to the United States as yours. How proud you must be of such a noble enterprise.

With affectionate greetings and all good wishes from Sallie and me to you and Bernardine, we are—

The publication of the Howard "interview" aroused vigorous comment. Isolationists like C. A. Lindbergh and the America First Committee claimed that White agreed with them. He, actually, did not and wrote them that he did not. Some members of the White Committee felt that his "interview" repudiated the policy statement of November 26. Some thought he had become an appeaser. Others disliked his use of the Communist slogan "The Yanks Are Not Coming." A number of people threatened to resign if White's interview was not changed. The Executive Committee was frantic. They telephoned and wired White continually for two or three days, but he refused to change his statements. The real trouble was the different temper of opinion in the Middle West and the East and West coasts. White represented the Middle West's slowness and reluctance to face the inevitable steps necessary to end the menace of Hitler and the Japanese. The East was more realistic. The following letter, to Lewis Douglas of the Executive Committee, explained his position.

Dear Lew Douglas:

This is a brief for the defense, and I wish you to read it to the Policy Committee. Two weeks ago Mr. Eichelberger [executive director of the White Committee] told me that Roy Howard had told Mr. Coudert [Frederic R. Coudert, prominent New York lawyer] that he intended to go after our committee. Mr. Coudert sent me a copy of a letter from Mr. Howard saying the same thing and regretting that Mr. Coudert was in the committee. For the Scripps-Howard newspapers across the country to go after our committee seemed to me a sinister sign of some strong influence at work either upon public opinion or behind the scenes. I don't know which. I don't know yet. But I felt that such an attack would hurt us, and because I have known Roy Howard for twenty-five years and his wife came from this part of the country, and I knew her as a child, I sat down and wrote him a personal letter. In that letter I felt it proper to deny the common charges of our opponents that we were in favor of four dangerous proposals: first, deliberately aiming at war; second, espousing proposals that would immediately lead to war, the three proposals being, convoys, sending American ships with contraband of war into belligerent waters, and the repeal of the Johnson Act. I denied that we were in favor of either of these four things. I cannot see now how by any stretch of imagination the denial of those four things in any way controverts our policy of November 26.

It seemed to me then, and it seems now, wise to make that denial as the price of an attack by the Howard newspapers. I did not consult the Executive Committee or the Policy Committee because I supposed, and still think, I was entirely inside of the intentions of the committee as expressed by the policy of November 26. I have always said that when we seemed headed for war my usefulness to the committee is over, for I do not believe we should get into the war, not so much from philosophical reasons as for practical reasons at the present time. And so far as I can see present events clearly, to get into the war would hurt Great Britain more than help her. And after all our committee is organized to defend America and to do so by aiding the Allies. And I don't see how our entrance into the war would defend America, and certainly it would not aid Great Britain.

It may interest you to know that I have received just as many telegrams from our committee in the Middle West applauding my action as have been received in New York questioning my action.

This, of course, is beside the point except that I have no desire to be considered either inconsistent or inconsiderate. I debated two days after Mr. Coudert's letter came before I tackled Roy Howard. And I debated another day after he asked me to make the letter public before I did so. It is the sort of thing that I would do again under similar circumstances.

My resignation seems inevitable if even a minority of the committee feel that this policy is unwise. My one earnest wish is that in giving out the news of my resignation we save our committee from embarrassment and from harm. I have asked Mr. Eichelberger to let the matter ride until I come to New York in late January when the *Churchman* will honor our committee by giving me an award for the work the committee has done. That will be a good springboard from which to announce that a younger man is needed in this place; that a year's strain has taken its toll upon my mind and body, and that I want to be relieved from the work. Which is the God's truth, and which I have told many friends, including some of our closest friends in this group.

I shall be happier than you can know to be relieved from the dreadful responsibility that has been a shadow on my heart since I began this work. I have been happy in it. I am proud of it. The associations I have made have been more than friendships. But I desire to close this chapter pleasantly and with the least possible shock to the work of the committee. I earnestly hope that no statement or commitment will be made which will force this issue at this time.

With warm personal regards, and the Season's very best wishes, I am—

P.S. Footnote: For the last six weeks I have been receiving letters from intelligent people, who were members of our committee, or its supporters, deploring the fact that we were going too far and too fast toward war. These came from men whose judgment I respect. They were not appeasers. They just didn't see the new phase of our activity. And I must confess that when Mr. Conant [James B. Conant, president of Harvard University] said to me that we needed new faces in this movement, I agreed with him deeply. And the winter would have seen me in a formal withdrawal, hoping that a younger man would take my place. This feeling probably is somewhat the result of my environment in the Middle West which has not caught up with the faster step of opinion on the Eastern Coast; which is

[420]

what it is even if it is not what it should be; something that I understand in hindsight but did not realize in foresight.

White's resignation as chairman of the Committee to Defend America by Aiding the Allies was sent to Lewis Douglas, Hugh Moore, and Clark Eichelberger of the committee's Executive Committee on January 1, 1941. A few hours before he sent the following telegram, he had received a wire from the Executive Committee urging him to come to New York City to quiet the rebellion in the committee's ranks over the Howard "interview," and to direct the campaign to support President Roosevelt's proposal to lend or lease equipment to the Allies. This ultimatum White could not carry out. He was tired and Mrs. White had been ordered to spend the winter in Arizona to counteract a sinus infection.

To LEWIS DOUGLAS, HUGH MOORE, AND CLARK EICHELBERGER,
(Telegram), January 1, 1941

The urgency of events has created a new tempo in our work and hence the need for quick decisions and close consultations. This I cannot give unless I come to New York for the winter. Mrs. White and I must leave for Arizona next week. At least for a month in a critical period I shall be unable to give as much time to the Committee as I have been giving. The Committee needs a full-time chairman. Obviously, I can serve the committee best by asking the Executive Committee to accept my resignation. I reach this decision with regret, yet I know it is wise. To every member of the Executive Committee I send my warm personal regards and the season's best wishes.

This letter demonstrates that White realized that war was inevitable for the United States. The steps we took from September, 1939, to December, 1941, to place ourselves unequivocally on the side of the opponents of the Axis had little to do with the involvement of the United States in a military way. What happened to us depended upon what Germany and her allies did, not what the United States did. Arousing America to an awareness of the danger of an Axis victory and fighting to send aid to those countries fighting the Axis, while America launched her own defense program, were the major contributions of the William Allen White Committee.

To The Rev. Allen Keedy, Shenandoah, Iowa, January 3, 1941

Dear Mr. Keedy:

I have your letter but I suppose you and I look at life from different angles. Of course, I don't think that Hitler will come sailing into New York harbor, but I do think that the totalitarian idea is on the march. The dictators are greedy for our wealth and have scorn for our liberty. Sooner or later we shall have to meet them with arms, how and when I don't know. Have you read "Mein Kampf?" Have you read the whole literature of totalitarianism—its aim and idea?

I should not be surprised any day to see Japan declare war on the United States and then the fat would be in the fire. Of course, Hitler will not declare war until he thinks it is profitable to declare war, that is until he can win a war. Nothing we have done or will do will bring him into the war until he feels it advantageous to come in. And, of course, we should never declare war on Hitler or anyone else until war has been declared on us. The sad part of it is that if Hitler knew how little we could do in war to aid Great Britain, and how much we can do outside of war, he would be smart enough to declare war on us. I am bitterly opposed to our entrance in the war as matters stand now and until we are attacked. Moreover, I am against sending American convoys for any ships, and I am not in favor of sending American ships with contraband of war into belligerent waters. Neither do I favor repealing the Johnson Act. I hope this answers your question.

A projected full-length motion picture of his life White found to be very disconcerting. He wrote this letter to Czar Will Hays of the movie industry asking his help in preventing the film from being produced and distributed. He was successful in his request, and no such picture was produced during his lifetime.

To WILL H. HAYS, Motion Picture Producers-Distributors of
America, January 3, 1941

DEAR WILL HAYS:

I am up against it and I need your help. This is a double SOS. Here is my trouble: about a year ago a man named William Rankin wrote to me to know if I would talk to him about a movie that he wanted to get up about me and the Gazette. I presumed he wanted one of those four- or five-minute news shorts that chink in once in a while in a program, and I said yes.

After some delay he appeared. I was out of town when he came. He had been here two or three weeks when I found that he was writing a full-length biography. I was surprised and the more I talked with him about it the more I was shocked. And when he left I told him that I didn't think there was much chance that I should approve any scenario he would write. But he was anxious to go to it, and I told him all right. And I signed an agreement to let him go ahead with the understanding that I should finally approve his scenario.

I see by the papers that MGM has bought his script. They are going ahead with the picture. I haven't seen his scenario. I wrote him two months ago on such a matter telling him that there was little hope that I could approve any scenario that was built upon my life. I am now pretty sure of it. I have not written to MGM. I don't know whom to write to. But can you tell them for me, please, that there isn't one chance in a thousand that if I do not approve it that I wouldn't do everything possible to prevent its production and later to prevent its distribution. I just don't want it.

Will, please head this thing off for me! Please stop it and save me the trouble that I am sure I am going to have if the thing comes to anything. A man in his lifetime just can't stand by and see a full-length picture of himself on the film. It would be too much.

[423]

A few days after his resignation from the committee, White attended a meeting of the midwestern chapters of the committee in Chicago. At this meeting, it was agreed that the committee's headquarters should be in Chicago, where isolationism was so virulent and where opposition to aid to Britain centered in the Chicago Tribune *and the America First Committee. In this letter, White expresses his gratitude to Hugh Moore, Frederick McKee, and Clark Eichelberger for their aid in conducting committee affairs. Although White did not want to be honorary chairman, Moore, speaking for the Executive Committee, insisted by observing that to refuse "would be a calamity to the cause to which I feel you have dedicated your life." The Executive Committee well realized that White's name, prestige, and guidance had helped make the committee a success.*

To Hugh Moore, January 6, 1941

Dear Mr. Moore:

In retiring as Chairman of the Committee to Defend America by Aiding the Allies, I wish to address this formal letter to you to let you know how deeply I have appreciated the way you and Mr. McKee and Mr. Eichelberger, who have been closely associated with me since the beginning of this enterprise and even before, have shielded my name in every way you could and, more than that, have given me the most loyal support that any executive could ask. I hope that you will convey specifically in terms to the new Chairman, whoever he may be, my feeling that you three are indispensable as advisers and executive directors of this organization. I especially commend Mr. Clark Eichelberger to the new Chairman. Mr. Eichelberger is indefatigable. He has boundless energy. He has keen vision and he is as honest as daylight and is loyal to the core. Our relations have been more than casually pleasant. A son could not have been more helpful and kind in cherishing my interests than Mr. Eichelberger. Probably my slowing blood, my instinctive caution that comes partly from the fact that I am from the Middle West and partly from the fact that I am nearly seventy-three years old sometimes made me feel that the tempo of my endeavors was being accelerated. But probably in the long run, it was for the good and I hope that he can forgive my caution and look back upon our relations with the respect and affection which I shall always cherish for him.

I hope you will convey to the new Chairman my definite feeling that this Committee cannot function in New York. It should move west to Pittsburgh, Cleveland, to Cincinnati or to Chicago. The influences in New York City, and to a certain extent in the middle eastern seaboard, are not conducive to national unity. I have felt for months that the New York Committee and certain influences in Washington were trying to create an atmosphere in which war sentiment would thrive. That irked me. And there was nothing to do, as you know, except to let it irk and then resign. I felt, and still feel, that this Committee should not get ahead of the President. Until he asks Congress for the right to send convoys, we should not be talking about convoys. Until he recommends the repeal of that phase of the neutrality law for which we fought so proudly ourselves, forbidding sending contraband of war in American bottoms in belligerent waters, we should not hint at the repeal of that law. I have all along felt that to urge the repeal of the Johnson Act was unnecessary, to court opposition and rile up the people in opposition to aid to Great Britain. And I hope that the new Chairman will bear these things in mind. And, if he is not on the job day and night, he will find the seaboard influence of impatient men hampering the work of the Committee in the West.

I am enclosing a clipping from the Kansas City Star for your consideration. I do not particularly care for the way your Mr. Donald Blaisdell [of the Washington Office of the White Committee] handles the incident of my resignation, as you will see by the clipping. It doesn't make it easier to become Honorary Chairman.

Of course, I shall be glad if you think it will help the work of the Committee, to lend my name as its Honorary Chairman. But also consider seriously, before you accept this offer that I may some time have to disagree with the position which the Committee takes. And while I shall not look for points of disagreement, if they come and if they are serious, I cannot blink them. I do not believe now, and I have never believed, that this Committee is organized for any purpose other than to Defend America by Aiding the Allies. I do not believe that we should prepare this country for war until the President and Congress itself feel that war is inevitable. Our job, as I see it, is to keep going a continual barrage upon Congress that will implement the sentiment of our Committee members that we should keep giving aid to Great Britain to the fullest possible extent which the law will allow and which safety will permit. It seems to me that the President has stated our function perfectly when he said "America must be the arsenal of world democracy." It is an honorable part to play in any war. It is the only part we can play in this war for at least a year until we are better prepared to enter the war than we are today. Feeling this way I must say so and I wish the Committee to know how I feel. I shall try hard to accept the wisdom of the new Chairman knowing that his wisdom will be guided by yours which I profoundly respect. But after all, I cannot promise in advance a support which I may have to withhold.

It seems to me only fair to tell you this and to make it a part of our record.

Don't you think honestly that perhaps when Mr. Gibson [Ernest W. Gibson of Vermont, the new chairman] comes in he would have a better chance if I were not an Honorary Chairman. If I am entirely disassociated with the Committee, when I feel like it I can say my say. All my life I have tried to rid myself of burdens and obligations like parties and churches and associations that might hamper me in speaking the truth as I see it. I know my truth is often cloudy and my hindsight is better than my foresight, and that I am a liability to my friends, and because you are my friends and because I must be what I am, I suggest in all earnestness that when the new man comes in that my name be quietly dropped. I am proud indeed to have worked with you. I am proud of all we have achieved. But don't you really think, under the circumstances, I can serve the Committee best by going my way? It is with regret and not a little pain that I say that I feel that for you and for the work of the Committee it will be for the best.

And now in closing, again let me say how much I have enjoyed your friendship; with what deep respect I have considered your advice and how grateful I look back upon the wisdom of your counsel. Let me count you as friends even though sometimes we may disagree.

White was correct that the position he had assumed in the Howard "interview" was the same path that the administration was following. President Roosevelt on December 29, 1940, had pledged the United States to be "the great arsenal of democracy." The President, further, stated: "If Great Britain goes down, the Axis powers will control the

[426]

continents of Europe, Asia, Africa, Australia, and the high seas—and they will be in a position to bring enormous military and naval resources against this hemisphere. It is no exaggeration to say that all of us in the Americas would be living at the point of a gun. . . ." Nowhere in the speech did the President advocate convoys or the repeal of the Neutrality Law. White, in this letter, however, underestimates the opposition in committee ranks to the Howard "interview." Actually protests had come from people all over the country and not just from the East Coast.

Tucson, Ariz., to JUDGE HUGO T. WEDELL, Kansas Supreme Court,
February 7, 1941

DEAR JUDGE WEDELL:

Thank you for your kind letter. Mrs. White and I have been away from home for nearly four weeks, and she is slowly recovering. I had an attack of the flu, which has left me a little wobbly, but I am all right.

You asked me for the story of my resignation from the Committee to Defend America by Aiding the Allies. Here it is:

After election, it seemed to me that the top was spinning; that the work was all marked out for the Committee. It was organized and there were seven hundred branch chapters in nearly every city of the United States. I talked with several members of the Executive Committee about resigning in November and got no cooperation there. Then I found a few high placed members of the eastern branches were ghost-dancing for war. Mrs. White had to come to the desert for her health. To stop the revolt, I would have had to go to New York permanently. I could not do it. I gave out a statement indicating wherein I thought the warmongers were going beyond the limits of our policy. They got mad, raised a little row in New York. Less than three of the seven hundred chapters were affected, but they were noisy, and I resigned, because I could not go east to ride herd on them.

My resignation apparently slowed them down. Events proved that I was right in my statement that there would be no convoys, that there would be no American ships sent with contraband of war into belligerent waters, and that we would not send men, but that we would become the arsenal of democracy. That has been my position all along. It is the position of the Administration. It is the position that Willkie will take, and it is the position that will become national policy.

Kindly remember me to all of my friends in the court. With warm personal regards to you, I am, as ever—

Captain Paul was by Edward Ellsberg. It was just such comments about books as the following that led Harry Scherman to write that "the telegrams were just ebullient blowings-off; they were deliberately exaggerated, and he knew that his confreres knew it." Chris is Christopher Morley, a fellow Book-of-the-Month Club judge.

Tucson, Ariz., to THE BOOK-OF-THE-MONTH CLUB (Telegram)
February 21, 1941

Still think "Captain Paul" is a waste of time even if the last chapter is the best tale of a sea battle I ever read, but not worth wading through two hundred thousand words of brackish dish water. However if Chris likes dish water because it's briny let's take it. [It was not selected.] See you Monday.

During March, 1941, the course of the war turned disastrously against the Allies. The sinking of Allied supply ships threatened to bring England to its knees. At this juncture, the Committee to Defend America by Aiding the Allies advocated that the United States convoy merchant ships to England. This new committee position naturally aroused the isolationists, who were unable to realize that war was inevitable for the United States.

[428]

DEAR CLARK:

I don't know whether I have told you that Mrs. White's trouble was high blood pressure. They are solving it but they cautioned me against any kind of excitement that may irritate her or involve us in any unnecessary worry.

Of late I have been getting many letters which do worry me, and because I feel it is not wise to keep them from her, they bother her too and are not good for either of us. I have been unable to come to the office except in the mornings since I returned home. A cold which grabbed me when you saw me has been hanging on. I have had to cancel two or three speaking engagements and am trying to keep down most activity. I shall come to New York soon for two or three board meetings, but I must have no worries on my hands.

All this is a preface to a sincere, earnest and irrevocable decision that my name should come off the stationery of the Committee. It is provoking discussion that I cannot meet, and I beg of you to explain to the Board and to Senator Gibson that they must give me my way in this matter. I quit with all manner of pleasant memories, with all pride in our achievement, and with the memory of the joy I had in working with you all. But I must disassociate myself with the Committee because of the controversial correspondence that is arising now at this crisis. If I am off the Committee, I can tell them to write to you people.

I should much prefer to have no publicity unless you think it is wise, in the removal of my name. Just let it disappear. The publicity itself might involve discussion and controversy which would be unfortunate, as you may understand from reading this letter, for both myself and Mrs. White. So again and finally, I beg of you to grant me this one request.

With warm regards to all of you, I am—

DEAR CLARK:

I have your letter about my resignation as Honorary Chairman. The convoy business didn't enter into it. I shall support the President when he orders convoys with all the enthusiasm possible, because I shall know then that it is the inevitable consequence of a rising tide of world war. But, as you know, I didn't want to needle the President specifically into the convoys. There is a point of difference between us there that I think is real, and particularly when you are an old man and cannot go to the war yourself you feel it.

And then, of course, as I think I wrote you last December, I prize my freedom more than anything else. And for the last month or two I have felt that I must not write anything in the Gazette, which could be quoted against the Committee, because my name was on the stationery. My points of divergence have not been important, but even unimportant I felt hampered just that much. This has been a great fight for a noble cause, and I am proud of my part in it, little as it was. And you and I, being honest souls, know how little!

To CLARK EICHELBERGER, July 29, 1941

DEAR CLARK:

Some time pretty soon I should like to write a piece about the President but I need data. So I am turning to you and hope that you and the boys can get it for me. I should like to spring it on the second anniversary of the war and the theme song would be that every move the President has made in foreign affairs for four years the isolationists have croaked that he was leading us into war. And yet for two years in the thick of the biggest war that the world has ever seen, he has kept us out; and his policy alone has kept us out because the isolationists would have let Great Britain go down, and we would be now up to our necks in a war with Hitler and unprepared. South America would be blowing up all over the lot. Mexico would be in danger. Martinique would be occupied by Nazi troops, and we should be in war for fair.

What I want to show is that from the time the President said that our frontier is on the Rhine—and I want the date of that—clear down the line, every move he has made has been toward keeping us out of war and his hypothesis has worked. . . .

My point is that at each step the President took, the isolationists declared that war was just ahead and that the President knew it and that the President was trying to provoke war. My contention is that he was trying to prevent war. As you know, the last time I saw him, after the election, he and Knox and Hull [Secretary of the Navy

[430]

Frank Knox and Secretary of State Cordell Hull], all three, protested that they did not want us to agitate for convoys at that time, and that they were not ready to send troops, largely because they didn't have any trained, nor equipped, and that at the very time when he was being abused as a hothead he was trying to put on the brakes and slow us all down until we could catch up with ourselves by a trained and equipped army of a million men.

I have been having some fun all by myself hammering away at the western congressmen trying to get them to vote for the President's pending bill. Enclosed find an editorial* that has made quite a splash out here.

There is no rush about this stuff. Ask some of the boys to get onto it and send me the details and I shall hammer out a story that could be printed on the second anniversary of the war. I think if we ever had an American statesman who has been firm and foresighted in his conduct of the foreign policy to keep us out of war, Roosevelt has been the man and that statesman. And I firmly believe now that Stalin has got his bear's claws in Hitler's face that Roosevelt is going to have his way and we will keep out of a shooting war and yet deliver the goods to Great Britain, which I have always favored even if I didn't think it should be done with convoys.

I wish to Heaven that the President and his Cabinet would let Wheeler and Lindbergh† alone. They are getting nowhere and one of the greatest blunders that a man can make in politics is to make a martyr out of a fool. And that's about what may be done if they keep hammering away at these two fellows.

With warm personal regards, I am, as ever—

On July 21, 1941, White declared in a Gazette *editorial that Republican congressmen had gone as far as they could "on the Quisling route."*

* This *Gazette* editorial of July 21, 1941, warned the Republican Congressmen to stop playing politics with national defense.
† Senator Burton K. Wheeler and Colonel Charles A. Lindbergh, both denounced by the President for their isolationist statements.

DEAR MR. WILLKIE:

"The time has come, the walrus said," when we have got to decide what we are going to do about it. The record made by the Republicans on the recent vote to retain the selectees begins to pile up a record that we cannot defend in the Congressional campaign of 1942.* Along about 1910, when the party in Washington was building up a reactionary record under Taft and Cannon and Aldrich, a group of Republicans, of whom I was a humble member, started out to put up liberal, progressive Republicans in the various states as candidates for senator and for Congress. In 1910 we made the first dent on the conservatives that had been made in the history of the Republican party. We turned up with a strong liberal progressive balance of power.

I have had some letters from various Kansas Republicans, suggesting that we go into the districts here with Republican primary candidates. It will do no particular good to do it here unless we are doing it as a part of a movement all over the United States.

There must be, in every Republican state, some group of Republican leaders who are willing to risk their hides for their country.

This is no time to make a statement—nothing like it. But it seems to me that a meeting should be held somewhere in the Middle West, unadvertised and fairly discreetly considered, at which Republicans of your views and mine should take counsel on what to do next year. The time is short.

I have no desire to jump in and get my seventy-three-year old feet wet and lead a crusade unless it has the backing of a pretty fair minority in the party. I am writing this to you in utmost confidence, to know what you think about the idea.

We just can't let Landon and Hoover and Taft and Lindbergh [Alf Landon, Herbert Hoover, Robert A. Taft, and Charles A. Lindbergh] carry the Republican banner without a fight for it.

---

* The Republican congressmen had just cast the bulk of their votes against the extension of the Selective Service Bill.

To F. J. HALL, August 25, 1941

DEAR MR. HALL:

I have your questionnaire about national defense and note you wish to know whether I think the American public has a correct estimate of the extent of the Nazi threat to our country.

The answer is: No, not by a long shot. In the first place, two-fifths of our people are more interested in the baseball scores than they are in foreign news. In the fall it will be football. In the second place, one-fifth of our people are intensely pro-German, for racial reasons, perhaps; somewhat for political reasons, as partisan Republicans or as Roosevelt-baiters; for family reasons, having young relatives of war age, and as being fat and contented and hating miserably the broomstick which prods the old fat sheep off the cool place in the green pasture beside the still waters. The other two-fifths see the truth and understand it. But they are some way like a train dispatcher, sitting powerlessly when he knows two trains are soon to meet head-on in the middle of a block. They are making nightmare outcries, but they cannot stop the trains.

This telegram again illustrates Harry Scherman's belief that the telegrams were "ebullient blowings-off," "deliberately exaggerated." The telegrams do illustrate, however, as Mr. Scherman has also pointed out, that they afford a glimpse of White's "unconventional mental operations." Joseph Davies's diary was entitled Diplomatic Papers *while* First Papers *was written by Martin Gumpert.* Ivory Mischief *was by Arthur Meeker. Only* Ivory Mischief, *of these three books, was selected.*

To HARRY SCHERMAN, Book-of-the-Month Club (Telegram)
October 15, 1941

My best bet is "First Papers." Fine view of America in the perspective of an intelligent European mind. It would make good dual or single choice. I liked Ambassador Davies' diary and State papers tremendously. It is an important and distinguished book, but standing alone as a single choice would not satisfy forty per cent of our clients. If it is used, should be used as dual choice. I don't like "Ivory Mischief." The adulteries become too monotonous after the first half dozen. They are repetitious and one longs someway for good vigorous assault and battery. The fact that this story is as long as Anthony Adverse does not signify that it will be as popular. I should say speaking broadly when a writer multiplies his dirty love affairs until they become mere biological case records he has lost the rabbit's foot of his art. Has become a mere chronicler of pathological incidents. Columbus book never arrived.

To STEPHEN EARLY, Presidential Secretary, White House, November 8, 1941

DEAR STEVE EARLY:

I am sending a package to you containing two copies of my son Bill's book about England [*Journey for Margaret*] under fire. It is a short book, and I wish you would hand one of these copies to the President with the affectionate greetings of Bill's proud parents. The second book is for you, being fifty per cent commission for handling this business, which is more than Fall got, or any of the boys who handled the little black bag!* But in these dangerous days when inflation is just around the corner, it seems to me this transaction should be properly financed.

Tell the President that if, owing to his Democratic ancestry, he can't read, to give the book to Mrs. Roosevelt, who comes from a good Republican family and probably will know most of the words in Bill's book.

Hoping this will find you the same, I am, my dear Steve, proud to subscribe myself—

* Refers to the Teapot Dome Scandal in the Harding administration.

[434]

During the last two years of his life, White devoted a considerable share of his efforts to aiding the Willkie Republicans secure control of the party. Politically, White was on intimate terms with the Kansas City Star's *managing editor, Roy Roberts.*

To Roy Roberts, Kansas City *Star*, January 30, 1942

Dear Roy:

You have been back at your desk now a week and I am happy about it. As we came through Kansas City January 1st, we saw in the Star the news of your operation and we were worried and anxious about you. I didn't bother you with a letter because I knew it wouldn't help you. But now that you are out, we want you to know that all your friends are rejoicing.

And oh, my dear boy, for God's sake take care of yourself! You are too valuable to leave in these times when we need men like you. You are affected with public use, like a public utility.

I was in Topeka for a few hours Kansas Day and the Republican gubernatorial offerings grade rather low. The best we can hope out of the lot is to pick a Grade B candidate. One of the reasons is that a first-class Republican realizes with terrible clarity that he will have to carry the isolationist record of the Kansas Congressional delegation in the fall campaign. So, instinctively, the first-class men are side-stepping the call to serve.

Our friend Willkie seems to be holding his own. I saw him in New York, had a good visit with him. I advised him, with all the earnestness of an ardent nature, not to get into the administration under any circumstances, and he said he wouldn't. If he goes in, his leadership will be handicapped because it will be said when he tries to rally people to the President, that he is merely ringing bells under Roosevelt's coattails, or if he criticizes the administration, being a part of it, he will be called an ingrate.

Sallie is particularly anxious to be included in this letter of affectionate congratulations.

[435]

Josephus Daniels had just relinquished his ambassadorship to Mexico when this letter was written. Daniels reprinted in his paper a White editorial attacking the Kansas Republicans for being against everything and for nothing.

To JOSEPHUS DANIELS, the Raleigh (North Carolina) *News and Observer*, February 20, 1942

DEAR JOSEPHUS:

I read the salutatory that you wrote when you came back from afar. It was a beautiful piece and I enjoyed it. I am glad you reprinted my "Blah, Blah" editorial about the Republican powwow at Topeka. It is the same everywhere. What I feared is that the Republican leadership outside of Willkie and Jim Wadsworth [Congressman James Wadsworth of New York] and perhaps Tom Dewey (they come with say fifteen to forty per cent discount for cash) are all sitting around waiting for some reverse in the American armed forces to break out with an isolationist itch and begin yelling, "Why are we fighting England's battles?" They are forever saying that we must support the armed forces of our country. They are forever clamoring about patriotic unity and then ending with a note beginning "but." It is but, but, but! Revealing, it seems to me, a very small, mean mind. In fact I am forced to the conclusion that their "butts are bigger than their brains."

We are glad you are back. You have done a grand job. Sallie and I want to see you and Mrs. Daniels. There are so many things in this world that are beautiful and fine even in this anguish, turmoil and dread that it would be good to sit down and talk it all over with you two.

Although the Christian Century *had been a caustic critic of White when he was chairman of the Committee to Defend America by Aiding the Allies, White never broke his friendship with Paul Hutchinson, the managing editor of the magazine. White reveals in this letter*

*to Hutchinson his belief that war was inevitable for the United
States regardless of what policy the country pursued.*

To PAUL HUTCHINSON, *Christian Century*, March 5, 1942

DEAR PAUL HUTCHINSON:

Thank you for your good letter. I read it with interest and, I hope,
profit. As I told you in my last letter, I read the C.C. from cover to
cover, and I particularly value two things: your secular editorials,
which are informative and bring me a lot of news which I don't get
anywhere else, and the letters from all over Christendom which are
packed with information that every citizen ought to have.

There is no use in pining about the events leading up to the tragedy.
I cannot see how any intellectually honest citizen, no matter which
side he was on in the preliminary stages of the war—America First or
the Committee to Defend America by Aiding the Allies (an ungodly
awkward name)—could view with anything like pride or compla-
cency his course. Millions of honest men and women on either side
doubtless felt that from their premises they were acting honestly and
wisely and with some courage. But the course of neither group could
have stopped the war. It was in the stars.

I honestly hoped, while I was at the head of the internationalist
group, that we could hold on and keep Britain afloat until Hitler
went down. But by the end of 1940, when I withdrew from the Committee because Mrs. White was ill and the doctor said we had to go to
Tucson, I felt that my job was done as far as it could be done. A few
intransigents in key places in the chapters in New York, Baltimore,
Boston and Washington were going too fast for me. I could have
dropped everything, moved to New York for the season, and licked
them on the ground they stood on, which would have left Mrs. White
alone in Arizona and I didn't think it was worth the while. And I
would do the same thing again. For, as I say, I had done all that could
be done along the line I started to do. Even if I had held them back, as
I tried to by a letter to Roy Howard protesting against convoys and
declaring that the Yanks were not coming and protesting against
other offenses of the ghost dancers for war, even then the inevitable
was fairly obvious.

But on the other hand, granting that we turned our backs to England after Dunkerque, then we would have had another inevitability.

[437]

We should have had to surrender and surrender and surrender to Hitler and Tojo—and finally fight.

I am pretty well satisfied that this whole show, from Sarajevo to Pearl Harbor, is some kind of a deep struggle in man's heart with his destiny. Man seems to be trying to pass from a civilization which for four thousand years man has been erecting on the basis of family, town and national self-sufficiency, to the vast interdependence made necessary by the coming of a machine age, where not only raw materials must move freely but the finished products thereof must not be bound or hampered. In that evolutionary struggle has risen a deep fear of the man of one talent that he will not survive. So he has turned for fifty years, in the politics of the world, slowly to collectivism, and at the same time, the world tendency was too largely, too narrowly nationalistic, and the clash has just blown the whole world clear plumb to hell and gone, speaking not profanely but with all the piety of my ardent nature.

So, my dear Paul, don't feel uneasy if you don't know where the world is going. Nobody does. God knows—He who planted deeply in the heart of man the pattern of his ultimate destiny which has been unfolding since man's first conscious hour when he knew good from evil—I repeat, God knows! And if you want any comfort, go to Job rather than to Roosevelt or Churchill.

In the meantime, give my dearest love to all the Hutchinsons. Mrs. White, who has read your letter, joins me in affectionate greetings.

The American State Department was under severe criticism for supporting Dictator Franco in Spain and for not breaking relations with Marshal Pétain and Vichy France. White's views on the State Department are pungently expressed in this letter.

[438]

Dear Bruce:

The Hoover book [*The Problems of Lasting Peace*, by Herbert Hoover and Hugh Gibson] is to be published by Doran and Company in mid-June.

Now about the stinkers in the State Department. Of course I think they rise out of the career system. The system should not be smashed. The idea is good. But what happens is that the career man who gets furthest has the most money. And, generally speaking, young men who have the most money, and therefore, the most conspicuous careers, are sons-in-law.

Fifty years ago we had a Kansas statesman who was eighteen years old when he helped found the town of Emporia and was a colonel in the army in the Civil War in his late twenties, a printer who later became a lawyer and a banker, a two-fisted politician who, as chairman of the Public Lands Committee of the United States Senate in the eighties, when the railroads were girdling the continent, accumulated a lot of money, maybe a million, which was a lot for that time; maybe two million—no one ever knew. He was a hard-headed, two-gallused aristocrat. He loved patronage, used it decently for his friends. But he couldn't abide the State Department and the career men. They were always thwarting him. They spotted him as the vulgarian that he was and his voice rose in a barbaric, impotent yawp which has echoed through Kansas all these fifty years while the grass has been growing on old Plumb's [Senator Preston Plumb] tomb: "The State Department has just two breeds of horned cattle—full-blooded sons-in-law and high-grade sons-of-bitches!"

Whereupon he would have none of it and roamed the Interior and the War Department and the Post Office Department where his kind had their will and their way in the days of Hayes and Arthur, Garfield and Harrison.

But I think there is something in his theory and we must do something looking toward improving the system rather than wrecking it. Probably it is going to be hard to do either. But any president could do it who wanted to. And we should try to make Roosevelt want to. It is one of the curses that has come upon us in this war—the property mind of the "full-blood son-in-law."

I don't know just exactly how much good it does to write to the President these days about matters as remote as the reorganization of the State Department. I am willing to join. I am willing to go where our friends want me to go. But I have no light or leading except that I know it is a mess and that it has got to be cleaned up if we take leadership in the peace. . . .

White was always devastatingly frank in the advice that he gave his old friend and former presidential candidate, Alf M. Landon.

To ALF M. LANDON, Topeka, Kan., July 15, 1942

DEAR ALF:

I had read your Elks speech clear through and my objection to it—the reason why I thought it was fundamentally wrong—that you emphasized the difficulties rather than the needs for some kind of a world organization to save the peace. I have no plan. I don't string along with Clarence Streit [proponent of a federal union for the world's democracies and author of *Union Now*]. I follow Hoover closer than any other one man as he has set forth the case in his book [*The Problems of Lasting Peace*]. But world organization of some kind must be necessary. It is wiser, it seems to me, to prepare the popular mind to accept as inevitable some kind of organization rather than to raise the obstacles—and they are genuine obstacles—which are cropping out all the time in your speech.

A lot of fellows after the American Revolutionary War were tremendously impressed with the obstacles to national unity under the Constitution. They were more afraid of the obstacles than they were desirous of the constitutional unity, and they were wrong. Probably they were right in that real obstacles did exist. But the Constitution and the unity that came therefrom were of more importance than the obstacles.

And that is why I said and I think your speech stinks.

Who does not know all that you say about the different kinds of civilization? Our object is to get some kind of a scheme or some set of regional plans that will organize those different civilizations in some kind of a workable world order. It not only can be done—it

[440]

must be done. And the problem will be solved more easily, not by ignoring the tremendous difficulties but by trying to find some way to overcome those difficulties. Certainly, the way of peace will not be found by stressing the difficulties and making them seem insuperable. That is why I didn't like your speech and still don't like your speech. That is why I like Hoover's book better than your attitude.

I think it will be a lot easier to get along with China, for instance, than it will be to get along with Great Britain. But this is no time to stress our distrust and dislike of Great Britain. We have got to live with the old hag—a sort of emeritus mother-in-law of the world, a decayed dowager, and while we should not blink the facts about her, I don't think it is wise at this time to emphasize these facts. We can take care of England all right, Alfred, but our trouble is going to be with Russia and the radical revolutions which are inevitable in Central Europe when the war stops, no matter who wins the war. I liked your speech before the last much better than this one.

All of which leads up to this: I think it is time for you and Hoover and Willkie and Joe Martin and half a dozen senators and public men to get together on a public statement of foreign policy after the war. There are no vital differences between you and the so-called internationalists, if you would just swallow about a dime's worth of pride and try to team together, not to formulate the terms of the peace—that would be silly—but to set forth the broad, fundamental foundations of peace which would guide the Republican party not into isolation but into some kind of a workable, practical, common-sense policy of peace upon which we can stand in 1944. We will get nowhere in this Congressional election this year because we don't stand any place in particular, this year!

This is said in all affection, Alf, but with great seriousness. When I look into the future, even two or three years, I am shocked, indeed horrified, at the spectacle, the inevitable spectacle which rises before me no matter who wins the war. The duties of a decent victor will be burdens and not tokens of triumph.

With warm regards, I am—

Bernard De Voto's The Year of Decision *dealt with the year 1846 while Margaret Leech's* Reveille in Washington *portrayed Washington, D. C., during the hectic Civil War days.* The Year of Decision *was selected and* Reveille in Washington *had been a selection in 1941.* Seed Beneath the Snow *was by Ignazio Silone and Brainard Cheney wrote* River Rogue. *Neither of these books was selected.*

To HARRY SCHERMAN, Book-of-the-Month Club (Telegram),
July 15, 1942

Seems to me by all odds the best buy is De Voto's "The Year of Decision" it will stand up with "Washington Reveille" although not so interesting a period and of course with no great figure in it but still it is dignified job of which we can all be proud. The Italian book "Seed Beneath the Snow" I found tedious. The dialogue is carved in basswood and the characters are pure theater for me at least the interest does not rise. "River Rogue" is the dirtiest book I ever read. Not that I was shocked by it. The fences, barns, and outhouse walls of childhood's golden hour gave me great familiarity with general idea of book. I feel that it would outrage at least a third of our readers, and don't feel we should risk that when we have reasonably acceptable book like "The Year of Decision." If you don't take it and there is any support for it why can't we hold it over. With our start it may easily attain the centertable championship for nineteen forty-two.

The primary victories of Republican Hamilton Fish in New York, of Democrat Lee O'Daniel in Texas, and of Republican C. Wayland Brooks in Illinois—all isolationists—provoked the following letter to White's former colleague in the Committee to Defend America by Aiding the Allies.

Dear Mr. Eichelberger:

This is written in Colorado. In rummaging through my desk here I found an envelope addressed to you. It was reminiscent of the summer of 1940 when I was talking to Willkie from this cabin and the President, Stimson, Knox, and you. We were cooking up harmony on the destroyer deal and a pretty good edible batch came out of the skillet.*

Since I have been here the primary results in New York and Texas have come in—Ham Fish of Dutchess County and "Pass the biscuits, Pappy" O'Daniel of Texas. Just before we came out Curley Brooks won in Illinois. I have been trying to figure it all out.

The first and most obvious thing is that in the primary, and the partisans voted within their parties their former factional conviction, isolationism as an issue did not work. Whether it will work in the election is still a fairly open question.

I doubt if it will. Very likely if a man yells loud enough to his partisan supporters that he is a hundred per cent for the conduct of the war and a complete victory of the United Nations, he has proved to them at least that he is a true and loyal American which is all that can be asked in war time. When the peace comes he will of course revert to type and become a cantankerous isolationist. Sisyphus will have to roll the stone up the hill again. It is the penalty or the price of liberty, I suppose.

But you who are in the thick of it, who never take off your armor, who always have the smoke of battle in your eyes, probably would like to know what an old codger thinks up in these snow-capped peaks. It seems to me that Dutchess County and rural Texas where O'Daniel got most of his strength typically represent a greedy plutocratic reaction, on the one hand, and a moron mind of ignorance and underprivileged, on the other hand. The thing that shocks me in fear is that Illinois, a fairly typical middle-class midwestern community, where Curley Brooks had his strength, should react just as the plutocrats and the morons react. "Hic fabula docet!!" We didn't begin our job early enough, and we didn't have time to go deep enough before the calamity was on us. We should have organized our first committee in '36. Perhaps the response would have been slow, but we ought

* A discussion of the relation of the Committee to Defend America by Aiding the Allies to the release of fifty overage destroyers to England can be found in Walter Johnson, *The Battle Against Isolation* (1944).

to have had the neutrality defeated instead of repealed. There was our first battleground.

I am fairly sure that we stand now as a nation in dreadful danger. I cannot figure today a majority of the American people who would support our ideals of peace, and I am scared stiff that they will fall for a peace of appeasement when Hitler is ready for it in November. If Russia goes out of the war, and Hitler offers England and the United Nations a peace that will save us whole and let the Atlantic coastal countries, Scandanavia, and France form a buffer between Germany and Great Britain, under those circumstances we have not a sound understanding majority in the United States to head off appeasement in the peace! The movement here will be backed by Dutchess County and the hillbilly section of the South. It will strongly appeal to the bewildered middle class. Only those who knew in 1939, '40 and '41 definitely what the war was about will be opposing this peace. We are in terrible danger. Our menace is not military defeat, but a fundamental lack of understanding in the American heart in the middle class. Hatred of Roosevelt and fear of a fourth term if the war goes on—and particularly if it goes on after a series of tragic losses and defeats for the United Nations—we are "standing in the need of prayer!"

Lifting the electoral rock of Texas, Dutchess County, and Illinois shows an awful lot of scorpions and spider eggs—potential poison in the United States.

Of course, I have no lack of faith for the ultimate victory. I fear however I shall not live to see it, perhaps you and your generation will have to hold it as a hope. Perhaps this world war and another and another will be required to get the truth to Dutchess County and rural Texas.

This is hardly a cheerful letter, but I wanted to write to you when I found this old envelope unused, so take it for what it is worth.

When Republican reactionaries and isolationists began to rally around the presidential candidacy of Governor John Bricker of Ohio, White began to sizzle. On March 17, 1943, he wrote an editorial filled with fighting language, and he denounced Bricker as "an honest Harding—

[444]

To HARRY HANSEN, April 8, 1943

DEAR MR. HANSEN:

Thank you for your letter which I have read with great interest and, I hope, profit.

Now about our friend, Rotarian John Bricker. All that you said of him could have been said with equal truth about Warren Harding. But the trouble with Rotarian Bricker is that he is not forthright. It may be the timidity of ignorance. That was one of the things that was the matter with Harding. He just didn't know the significance of things. Or Governor Bricker's cautious foxiness may arise because he has learned the politician's trick, not to declare forthrightly for anything because he may run into a minority against it which might become a majority.

His statement to the New York Times about our foreign policy after the war was a perfect masterpiece of blah. It just didn't mean anything and could be interpreted both ways. It was exactly the sort of statement that Harding issued twenty-four years ago on the same issue when he was in Bricker's place.

I have no doubt that he has made a good governor. I have no doubt that he is an honest man. But I do think that in the presidency he would be a menace to the peace of the world.

While in New York in April, 1943, the Whites were taken sick. From this time, until his death on January 29, 1944, Mr. White's health became increasingly precarious. The following letter was written to two old Bull Moose friends.

[445]

Dear Margaret and Raymond:

Your letter written on our fiftieth wedding anniversary finally caught up with us. We were two weeks in the hospital. Sallie had a bad attack of flu and I had double pneumonia. The sulfa drug relieves pain and danger in pneumonia very quickly but it leaves the period of convalescence nearly as long as the old treatment left it. We have been home two weeks but are still housebound. There is nothing wrong with us except that I have no gimp and don't care whether school keeps or not.

Being seventy-five, I am forgetful. I don't know whether I sent you a speech I delivered month before last and another I delivered last month, so I am going to take a chance and risk it. I want you to read them.

As we approach the peace—and we are certainly, like sinners, standing in slippery places—I get more and more frightened at the limitations of our political institutions and the size, the tremendous, unbelievable size of the political job before us, and the economic commitment we must make in the next two or three years if the peace shall become really a victory and not the prelude to a debacle.

You catch some of those things in the Gazette and perhaps know how I am feeling, though I haven't written anything for a month. But I am just scared stiff.

And the fourth term bothers me—not that I would be so afraid of Roosevelt if it was the second term, but every year he is in the White House now he deteriorates, deteriorates physically and sloughs off power in his leadership due to the natural distrust of the country for a man who has such faith in himself and so little in God that he thinks he is indispensable. People know, I think, deeply and instinctively, that when a man becomes indispensable to a democracy, it is no longer a democracy and that weakens the President for the greatest task that ever has faced any man on this planet.

It may take another false peace and another war to develop the spiritual qualities in the people that will make them worthy of the great leader who is necessary to do the work ahead of us. I suppose we should not be silly and expect it to be done overnight, in a day or in a decade, and should be thankful if it can be done in a century.

How I should like to see you and sit and talk with you!

[446]

To George Field, Freedom House, New York City, May 25, 1943

Dear Mr. Field:

... We cannot, of course, win the peace until we win the war. But after unconditional surrender, if we win the peace, the United States must continue the same effort that has made victory in war. Nothing less on our part than the same unconditional sacrifice for the peace that we have demanded in unconditional surrender will hold the peace longer than it takes to rearm and re-form the next line of battle.

We are in for a ten years' struggle, ten years in which we must put in our American energies, our American production, the full strength of American credit and unstinted consecration of American sacrifice—not into a grand do-good adventure, *not* into making the world beautiful and Utopian, but in a cold-blooded, hard-boiled try-out to put world civilization back on its feet so that in the rehabili-tated world we may find American markets. The capitalist system must not break down. But unless capitalism is willing to organize to sacrifice, to envision its own self-interest in the renewal and revival of civilization, the war will be a failure.

In isolation, we are only prepared for another Armageddon until finally faith in democracy fails. Then a weary disheartened world may turn to some totalitarian tyranny and we shall regiment mankind in inevitable economic slavery.

Just before this letter was written, Congress passed the Connally-Smith antistrike bill over President Roosevelt's veto. It was the first wartime overriding of a presidential veto. Wendell Willkie, in White's eyes, was the great hope of the country.

Dear Wendell Willkie:

Here is your opportunity! The country is without a leader. Events which you had nothing to do with have broken Roosevelt. No other voice but yours in this whole country can reach all the people.

I beg of you to grasp the opportunity. Now is the time to talk seriously, plain and with the eloquence that is fired in your own brave, honest heart to the American people. It is a solemn duty, a golden opportunity.

Attack the fundamental domestic policy of the New Deal and not the President. Handle him with tongs. Explain why deficiency spending will bring us to the brink of ruin. Tell the people that the extension of governmental powers into planned economy in time of peace is the denial of liberty inevitably. For the very theory of planning requires that man shall be a wooden figure without will, without individuality, that he shall be in short that powerless human sheep, the economic man, a political and social eunuch.

The people are ready to hear this. They are yearning for new leadership. We are entering an interregnum. Either Hitler and the storm troopers, the boys in the pool hall under the leadership of Ham Fish, Martin Dies, Gerald Nye and Colonel McCormick will come out and take leadership and bash the heads of liberals everywhere, or you will take leadership, and the time is short.

Mrs. White and I are leaving for Colorado tomorrow, Estes Park. I had to write this letter. I couldn't go away without doing so. And I earnestly beg of you to call your friends together, take counsel with them, and step out boldly into the position you must fill, and which if you do not fill will be filled by someone else who will lead this country into revolution and bloody revolt. I feel this deeply and seriously or I should not be writing it.

Estes Park, Col., to Wendell L. Willkie, July 20, 1943

My Dear Wendell Willkie:

... What I was driving at in my last letter was the fact that sometime soon, this fall, you should make a deliberate attempt to state the case of intelligent, patriotic Americans on the various domestic issues: (a) labor, (b) finance, (c) social security, (d) postwar em-

[448]

ployment. Also, you should tackle the foreign relations—first, as of today; second, after the surrender; and third, so far as possible the just and permanent peace.

If you could get a series of speeches set two or three weeks apart, and make a series of speeches along these lines which could be put into a little book to be issued next winter or early spring, you could take the leadership which now is going begging. Roosevelt has lost the ball; I doubt if he can ever get it again. Bricker will only fumble it. Dewey doesn't dare try to grab it at this time. Stassen is handicapped by his job; so is MacArthur. You are the only American of either party who can step out and take the moral, intellectual and political leadership of this country. It must be done with dignity, but at the same time without a mealy-mouthed humility. You are quite right in saying, "Don't take yourself too seriously." But after all, you are what you are, and the situation is what it is and not something else, and if you could make a series of speeches along the lines just suggested in various parts of the country, New York, New England, the South, the Lake States, the Missouri Valley, California, Denver or Salt Lake City, and the Northwest—I think you would be doing yourself and your country a great service. My only caution in these speeches would be not to mix up the subjects—don't try to cover too much territory in one speech. Avoid the President when you possibly can. Don't wisecrack at him, but when you have something to say, don't pull your punches or slap his wrist. Sock him with all you've got but with a dignity that becomes a patriot and a great cause.

This letter is dictated entirely by a desire to further your cause.

With warm regards in which Mrs. White joins me to you and Mrs. Willkie, I am, as ever—

While in Colorado, White received a letter from George Fort Milton, who was writing a book on the presidency called The Use of Presidential Power 1789–1943. *The questions that he asked White elicited the following letter:*

[449]

DEAR GEORGE FORT MILTON:

Now about Wilson. I have been thinking ever since your letter came about the questions you raise. Of course, the presidency began to change its quality when Theodore Roosevelt came to the White House. And as Wilson afterwards wrote, without the people the President is nothing, which is just another way of saying that the Executive is something more than an administrator, although that job must be well done; he is a leader, the voice of the people, and if the people are dumb or sluggish about the issues which the President is pressing, he will get nowhere as a leader. Wilson, until October, 1918, was a competent leader of the people. During the latter part of 1918 and the first two months of 1919, Wilson was a leader of the world. He was speaking a language that they understood about issues that were deeply important and universal. But I am inclined to think that although the office grew tremendously in power, and although Wilson for seven of his eight years was a competent leader, he failed where he did fail because of his personal qualities—his aptitude to distrust his friends, his incapacity to do business with his enemies, and his fatal, deadly faith in his own judgment. This country was in vastly more danger of following a dictator under Wilson than it is under F.D.R.

F.D.R. is, if you ask me—which you don't—an old bull who is losing his cud. He is not the man that he was in 1936 and the job has multiplied by ten. I don't fear that he will lead us into Fascism. What I fear is that he cannot lead us at all. I feel that his political impotence is the great danger that we face as a nation, because there is no other leader in sight with the tremendous world prestige which Roosevelt enjoys, who once could have guided us into and through the turmoil that lies ahead of us after the surrender.

Houghton Mifflin asked me not long ago to take my Wilson book and revise it in the light of the great volume of correspondence that has been published since Wilson's death. The Wilson book went on the press less than six months after his death. This correspondence will reveal a lot about the environment in which he worked. But I doubt if it changes my opinion about the man. I wish you all manner of luck in your endeavor, and if I can help you in any way let me know. By the way, the first thing you ought to do is read Laski's

[450]

book on the American presidency. I think it is published by the Viking Press.*

The Republican Postwar Advisory Council met at Mackinac Island early in September, 1943, and issued a statement calling for "Responsible participation by the United States in postwar co-operative organization among sovereign nations. . . ." Governor Dewey of New York issued a statement, about the same time, advocating an Anglo-American military alliance. The Chicago Tribune immediately accused Dewey of being "anti-American."

To WILL AND MABEL BECK, Holton (Kansas) *Recorder*,
September 13, 1943

DEARLY BELOVED:

. . . We got home a week ago and I am much better and Sallie is all right.

If you have got around the office a Chicago Tribune with the editorial comment on the Mackinac Island conference, I should like to have it. I'd like to see what kind of a conniption fit the old colonel throws, and I'll bet he turned flip-flops when Tom Dewey advocated an alliance with Great Britain.

The old colonel ought to read the answer in the stars. The world is moving toward understanding and a deep realization that unless we create some sort of a world tribunal to keep the peace, the boys in the pool hall are going to take the show and run the earth.

I hope you are well. . . .

* Harold Laski, *The American Presidency* (Harper & Brothers).

Late in October, 1943, the Emporia editor underwent a major operation at the Mayo Clinic. A month after the operation, he returned to Emporia but his health failed rapidly. The following letter is one of the last that he wrote before his death on January 29, 1944.

To FRANK MOTZ, the Hays (Kansas) *News*, November 23, 1943

DEAR FRANK:

Thanks for your good letter. As you indicate, I have tried to keep my friendships through the years with the Kansas newspapermen and a few politicians, most of whom think I am crazy. And as I see life in the perspective of a gas mask at the hospital, maybe I am. Here is something that will give you a giggle:

As I went under for the last time, the surgeon said I chuckled and said: "Well, here's goodby to time and space!" and faintly tittered myself into unconsciousness. I woke up two hours later in the hospital bed and heard Mrs. White repeat over and over: "Will, you're all right. Your pulse is normal, your breathing regular." And she said I smiled and said: "Sallie, I'm riding the rim of the utmost star," and sighed sweetly back into the Elysium of my dream. A little later, perhaps fifteen minutes, I called her saying: "Sallie, I'm sinking."

They had given me some kind of a morphine derivative which produced that sinking effect. She repeated over and over what she had been saying, that I was all right, not to be scared. And I heard Bill say with his funny, throaty chuckle: "Father's scaring himself to death thinking he is going to die." And I thought that was so funny that I giggled back to sleep! And the strange part about this is that both Bill and Sallie said that Bill said no such thing. Anyway, it was funny whether it happened or not.

Mrs. White joins me in affectionate regards.

INDEX

Quay, Matthew: 39, 41, 43

Railroads, influence of, in politics: 68–70

Reactionary forces: and return to "normalcy," 199; under Harding, 205; of the twenties, 206, 272, 273; White's opposition to, 349, 350

Real Issue, The: 6, 23, 25, 188

Reciprocal trade treaties: 340

Reed, Clyde: 241–243, 292

Rees, E. H.: 371

Regeneration of Colonel Hucks, The: 5

Republican El Dorado (Kansas): 4, 5; Emporia, 23

Republican Party: analysis of main problem of, 150–154; bosses in, 70–72, 74; conservatism in, 192, 193, 203, 204; convention of, 284, 288–290; and Kansas Day Club, 51; Long-Bristow Contest and, 85, 92; and old-liners' attack, 37; postwar council of, 451; progressivism in, 76, 128; White's reform plans for, 349, 350; White's support of, 10–14, 53, 54

Rhymes by Two Friends: 154

Riley, James Whitcomb: 140, 154

Roberts, Elizabeth: 143

Roberts, Roy: 435

Robins, Mr. and Mrs. Raymond: 446

Robinson, Mrs. Douglas: 89

Rockefeller, John D., Jr.: 359

Rockefeller Foundation: 248, 251, 359, 360

Roosevelt: A Force for Righteousness: 72, 75

Roosevelt, Franklin D.: fourth term of, 446; letters to, 282, 342, 384, 386, 402; re-election of (1936), 368, 370; White's early analysis of, as president-elect (1932), 329; White's changed opinion of, 334, 335, 339; White's opposition to, 380, 381

Roosevelt, Theodore: administrations of, 97; and Bull Moose Party, 132, 133, 138; death of, 194; denunciation of Middle West by, 172–174; as editor, 130, 131; as governor, 149;

letters to, 31, 34, 39, 41, 56, 64, 72, 75, 79, 82, 90, 91, 94, 96, 97, 110, 113, 124, 130, 138, 144, 157, 168, 172, 182, 191; and loss of leadership, 178; message of, to Congress, 94; nomination of, as vice-president, 34; philosophy of, 93; as president, 39–44, 58; presidential boom for (1911), 128, 129; refusal of, to run (1916), 168; speech of, at Osawatomie, 113; White's meeting with, and support of, 6, 7, 10

Roosevelt, Theodore, Jr.: 261, 329

Root, Elihu: 19, 73

Rowell, Chester: 312, 349

Russia: White's impressions of (1933), 337, 338; White's views on recognition of, 19, 20

Sacco-Vanzetti case: 271, 272

Sandburg, Carl: 361, 401

Saturday Evening Post, The: 29, 58, 329

Scherman, Harry: 391, 418, 433, 442

Scott, Charles F.: 86, 108, 202

Scribner, Arthur: 48

Scribner's: 35

Seabury, Samuel: 347

Shatzer, Grace L.: 328

Sherwood, Robert E.: 409

Shuette, W. F.: 392

Simonds, Frank: 271

Sinclair, Upton: 78, 174

Smith, Alfred E.: 240, 282, 284–288, 290

Smith, Charles W.: 142

Smith, F. Dumont: 204

Some Cycles of Cathay: 252, 260

Spooner, Senator: 134

Staff, *Gazette,* The: 98

Star, Kansas City: 5

Start, C. T.: 221

Steffens, Lincoln J.: 33, 55, 78, 166

Stevens, Guy: 268

Stewart, J. H.: 161

Story of a Country Town, The: 210

Stout, Ralph: 74

Stout, Ruth: 283

Stratagems and Spoils: 35, 47

Strong, F. H.: 109

347, New York City, 162, State Department, 439, world peace plan, 440; in world affairs, 15–21; writing methods of, 116, 117

White, William L.: 16, 34, 124, 194, 208, 236, 302, 363, 403, 404, 434

Whitlock, Brand: 148, 260

Who Killed Cock Robin: 172

Wilkins, Ernest H.: 319

Williams, Chauncey L.: 28, 188

Willkie, Wendell L.: 411, 412, 432, 435, 447, 448

Wilson, Woodrow: as exponent of progressivism, 146–148, 155; denounced by Theodore Roosevelt, 166, 167; elected president (1912), 138; illness, 201, 204; motion picture on, 256–260; telegram to, 161; war message, 179; White's opinion of, 10, 17, 18, 204; White's biography of, 240, 241, 252; in world politics, 197, 198

Winrod, Gerald B.: defeat of, 389; White's protests against, 382–384, 386–389

Wood, Leonard: 192

Wood, Meredith: 397

Woodhouse, Edward J.: 284

World War I: entrance of United States in, 179, 180, 181, farmer and, 184; governmental control during, 185; outbreak of, 155; and peace terms to Germany, 163; and peace policy of White and mid-west, 161; signing of Armistice in, 194; sinking of *Lusitania* in, 160; U. S. preparedness program in, 164; western attitude toward, 176, 179; White's denunciation of, 180

World War II: beginnings of, 393, 394; and Committee to Defend America by Aiding Allies, 406–411, 415–422, 424–430; embargo in, 398

Young Men's Christian Association of Emporia: 233